Clinical Work with Children

by Judith Marks Mishne

THE FREE PRESS

NEW YORK LONDON TORONTO SYDNEY TOKYO SINGAPORE

THE FREE PRESS
A Division of Simon & Schuster, Inc.
1230 Avenue of the Americas
New York, NY 10020

Manufactured in the United States of America

10 9 8 7 6 5 4 3 2 1

Library of Congress Cataloging-In-Publication Data

Mishne, Judith.
  Clinical work with children.

  Bibliography: p.
  Includes index.
    1.   Child psychotherapy. I. Title. [DNLM: 1. Psycho-
Therapy—In infancy and childhood. 2. Psychopathology—
In infancy and childhood. W8 350.2 M678c]
RJ504.M57   1982   618.92'8914   82-70990
                                            AACR2

ISBN 0-7432-1185-5

To my parents
Dr. & Mrs. Moses Isaac Marks

You must know that there is nothing higher and stronger and more wholesome and good for life in the future than some good memory, especially a memory of childhood, of home. People talk to you a great deal about your education, but some good, sacred memory, preserved from childhood, is perhaps the best education. If a man carries many such memories with him into life, he is safe to the end of his days, and if one has only one good memory left in one's heart, even that may sometime be the means of saving us.

Epilogue,
The Brothers Karamazov,
Fyodor Dostoyevsky

Contents

Acknowledgments

With deep appreciation and regard I would like to thank a number of people and institutions for their help and support. I am grateful to Gladys Topkis, now at Yale University Press, for helping me begin this book. Her early efforts have been sustained by the aid and counsel of Joyce Seltzer of Free Press who made valuable editorial suggestions and patiently helped me organize and reorganize this manuscript. Copy editor Debbie Weiss and typist Donna Ritter proved invaluable in providing moral support and prompt and skilled technical assistance.

I have been priviledged to have had the opportunity to teach Treatment of Children at a number of graduate school programs, namely, the University of Chicago School of Social Work, Columbia University School of Social Work, Smith College School of Social Work, and New York University School of Social Work. I am most indebted to my students who, over the years, have stimulated questions and ideas and taught me much about their struggles and pleasures in work with children and parents.

I am especially grateful to the faculty of the Child Therapy Program of the Chicago Institute of Psychoanalysis, for the rich training I received. I thank Doctors Weiss, Gelman and Rocha and Mr. Jos. Polombo, my control case supervisors, who provided support, wise counsel and inspiration, and, despite the passage of time, remain mentors.

PART I

Introductory Considerations

CHAPTER 1

Child Therapy: An Overview

This book aims to provide a clear and comprehensive presentation of the fundamentals of child psychotherapy for use primarily by graduate students and beginning practitioners of social work, child psychiatry, and clinical psychology. Ackerman (1947) suggests certain broad correlations regarding the respective areas of responsibility for caseworker and psychiatrist. In his view, the dynamic level at which the two professions meet is the so-called ego level. Ego represents the organizing, adaptively patterned functions of the total personality, which are oriented toward both the outer real world and the inner conflicts between impulse and conscience. Since the ego serves as the dynamic link between social reality and unconscious, as well as the link between individual and group motivation, it is also the common ground where the special interests of psychiatrist and caseworker meet. Hamilton (1947) notes that by bringing psychoanalytic psychiatry into the practice of social work, the child guidance movement sheds light on the oldest concern of social work, namely, family interrelationships and interactions.

The literature on child psychopathology and therapy is dominated by the writings of child analysts, which requires students or beginning clinicians to translate this material for use in their own nonanalytic tionships between children and their foster parents fail to develop. Finally, multiple placements for a single child keep the child family-less for the duration of childhood.

Currently, slogans and panaceas frequently guide practice. Treatment programs show little respect for individualism, denying diagnosis and molding professional perceptions of clients' needs to fit the modality of the agency. Blind adherence to "either/or" approaches has emerged. In the child welfare field, we note the foster-family/institution controversy, the recent push for indiscriminate deinstitutionalization of all children, and the current belief that adoption will insure "permanence." Suggested is that not all children are adoptable; some, due to early damage and losses, with resultant ego deficits, can neither respond to nor tolerate the intimacy of family life. Though stated fifty years ago, Thurston's caution (1930) seems more appropriate than ever. Rather than providing any one type of care for children, he felt the community should provide "an all-inclusive approach" involving an "orchestration of community facilities. Kadushin (1974) noted that recent research has softened the negative attitude toward the institution, with a resultant greater readiness to use it when it meets the needs of the child.

What can we learn from history? Perhaps the most important lesson is that although progress has been made in children's services and innovations have improved various practice approaches, there is no panacea. Mayer et al. (1977) have noted the failure of both indiscriminate institutionalization and indiscriminate deinstitutionalization. Neither exclusion nor inclusion of the parents seemed to solve the problem. The emphasis on the permanent responsibility and total involvement of the substitute parent gave way to the division of the care of the child between parents and substitute caretakers. The rigidity of permanent care was followed by the flexibility of a series of transitional arrangements, which, in time, may give way to another kind of child placement. We can predict that inflexible adherence to adoption will also give way, as it is recognized as being unsuitable for sizable numbers of children.

The overriding goal of this text is to underscore the need for flexible, discriminate, individualized planning for children. It is hoped that this presentation will in some measure increase the clinician's tolerance of anxiety and thereby avoid the creation of the defensive, demoralized professional who is drained of both empathy and a sense of individualism.

CHAPTER 2

Child Therapy: A Historical Perspective

Psychoanalysis

The development of child psychoanalysis may be dated to the first published report (Freud, 1909) of the psychoanalytic treatment of a child, Little Hans, who was treated for a phobia by his father, with the guidance of Sigmund Freud. Following this publication, it was some time before children were treated directly. In the late 1920s, Anna Freud was trying to convert a psychoanalytic interest in childhood as it is recalled by adults into a concern with childhood itself. Under her leadership, the new profession of child analysis was born.

In 1926 and 1927, Anna Freud gave a course of lectures at the Vienna Institute of Psychoanalysis on the technique and theory of child analysis. In these lectures, she contrasted her point of view with that of Melanie Klein. Melanie Klein and her followers, who are sometimes referred to as the English School, follow the original Freudian principles, but with several critical differences. First, they disregard the effect of environment almost entirely, and operate exclusively with innate biological factors. Second, complicated psychological conflicts are attributed to the infant; the Oedipus complex is considered to exist in the first year of life. The timing of the formation of the superego is an issue of controversy even among orthodox child analysts. In her paper, "On the Development of Mental Functioning" (1958), Melanie Klein places the beginning of the superego in the second quarter of the first year of life. Her account of its formation has to do with the projection of the death instinct into the outside world for the sake of self-preservation. In her view, a full superego of the utmost harshness and cruelty exists in the child before the resolution of the Oedipus complex. Anna Freud and most other child analysts hold a very different view.

Klein's assumption of an intricate psychic system elaborated soon after birth and capable of highly sophisticated fantasies is at variance with current theories about the infant's mental and emotional capabilities. Klein held that every infant undergoes phases of grave abnormality, and that emotional health can be safeguarded best by early and universal child analysis. According to this view, the individual experience of the child is not crucial to the production of a neurosis; nor is speech essential to the treatment. The technique is based on the interpretation of the child's play, which is considered to be the equivalent of free associations in adult patients. The analyst tells the child what his play means. In contrast, Anna Freud and the Viennese School analyze only exceptional, troubled children. They also stress work with the family, be it parent guidance, environmental manipulation, or direct therapy with the parents, much more than does the English School. Kessler (1966) describes the approach of the Viennese School as follows: "Interpretation of play and unconscious conflicts is much more conservative, more attention is given to the ego defenses, and the child's participation is much greater" (p. 371). Although the view of Anna Freud and the Viennese School is more generally accepted, in very recent years, Melanie Klein's play therapy techniques have received considerable attention and her notions about inborn psychosis (autism) have been considered more seriously.

Child analysis parallels adult analytic treatment in terms of frequenty of sessions—four or five times a week—in order to promote an intense relationship and maintain a continuous flow of material. To be accepted for analysis, adults and children have to have substantial ego strengths to be able to tolerate the anxiety aroused in this intensive uncovering therapy and, at the same time, to be able effectively to handle most aspects of daily living (e.g., work, family responsibilities, school). Dreams and free association are vehicles for uncovering unconscious conflicts. Children use play, drawings, and the like as their form of free association. The therapist handles the material evoked by interpreting and making connections that the patient cannot see independently. "Sometimes these connections are between the past and the present, sometimes between a defense and a feeling, sometimes between a fantasy and a feeling. The process of interpretation is to enable the patient to recognize his feelings, his defenses, and thus to make the unconscious, conscious" (Kessler, 1966, p. 371). Anna Freud compares child analytic goals to those of adult psychoanalysis, i.e., to "undo the various repressions, distortions, displacements, condensations, etc., which had been brought about by the neurotic defense mechanisms until, with the active help of the child, the unconscious content of the material was laid bare" (1946, p. 71).

Psychoanalysis, as a specific mode of therapy, is extremely demanding, long-term, and expensive. A very small proportion of people with emotional disturbances seek this kind of treatment. "The investments of time, effort and money are too great, and the number of qualified psychoanalysts is too small for this method of treatment to be applied on a mass scale. Furthermore, for a variety of reasons, . . . formal psychoanalysis would not be the treatment of choice for the majority of psychiatric patients, even if an analyst and the necessary time and money were available" (Dewald, 1964, p. xv). The method of psychoanalysis was devised for neurotic patients. It is not the treatment of choice for adults or children who act out their problems, who are living under intolerable conditions, or who suffer from weak or defective egos. Though psychoanalysis is the treatment of choice for only a relatively small number of individuals, as a general theory of behavior, personality development, symptom formation, and structure of the mind, it is the most inclusive.

Psychotherapy

Child analysts and child therapists use their understanding of child development and psychopathology in many ways other than classical psychoanalytic treatment. Psychotherapy is a mode of treatment focused less on unconscious conflicts and more on treatment goals, to try to relieve children of the symptoms that place them at odds with their environment. Children are seen less intensively than in the analytic situation, usually once or twice a week. There are similarities of technique, but differences of objectives, based on a diagnosis that reveals the complexity, structure, and genetic roots of the illness, as well as patients' ego strengths. It is obvious from the previous material that psychotherapy is the more frequently employed therapeutic intervention with adults and children. Psychotherapy may be long- or short-term and may involve individuals, groups, or families.

Psychotherapy implies a patient-therapist relationship in which there is an interchange of verbal and nonverbal expression that furthers the treatment aim of freeing the patient of disturbing symptoms and incapacitating internal conflicts. Often the term "psychotherapy" is limited to treatment by a physician (psychiatrist) or psychologist. The treatment relationship between other professional therapists and their clients may be called child analysis (by a medical or lay analyst), casework, or counseling. But

> in terms of what transpires in the treatment situation, these designations are sometimes artificial. Many feel that the type of therapy differs among the professional groups, that the social worker practices chiefly superficial and supportive therapy, while the psychiatrist, and to an even greater extent, the psychologist, engages in "deep, uncovering" therapy. . . . But in the majority of treatment cases, the methods of all skilled workers in the field are the same. Good therapy has much in common, regardless of the label [Shaw, 1966, p. 364].

Definition of Child Psychotherapy

At present, child psychotherapy is often defined as one or more of the following: relationship therapy, activity therapy, release therapy, play therapy, counseling, guidance, diverse group therapies, interpretive therapy, and remedial education. In this text, child psychotherapy means psychoanalytically oriented psychotherapy. In this author's view, such a theoretical base is the only practical one: "if therapy is to be rational, one theory of personality development and of symptom formation must obtain for all methods" (Brody, 1964, p. 387). In psychotherapy, the therapist does not attempt the goals of analysis, i.e., "the unconscious conflicts underpinning a neurosis are interpreted systematically, in which transference manifestations develop and may mature to a full transference neurosis, and in which the Oedipus complex is reached, worked through, and resolved, according to the psychosexual maturity of the child at termination of treatment" (Brody, 1964, p. 386).

In psychotherapy, less regression is encouraged than in analytic treatment, and the focus is more on the interpersonal child-therapist relationship and the here-and-now, rather than on early infantile conflicts. The therapist assumes a more active supportive stance than the nondirective analyst, to aid children (1) to increase their capacity for reality testing, (2) to strengthen their object relations, and (3) to loosen their fixations. One would not attempt to analyze a child who lived in a traumatizing, problematic, chaotic home situation, in that parents living under such stress could not support, tolerate, and sustain their child's intense and demanding treatment. Child therapy, on the other hand, very often involves work with children who do live amid considerable chaos, and the therapist must often take an active role with the family, in terms of parent guidance, educational intervention, and environmental manipulation. Depending on the parental strengths and weaknesses, it is generally beneficial for them to see someone who is not simultaneously treating their child (especially if work with them must be intense and ongoing), due to the issues of confidentiality, privacy, and the child's need (in most cases) for exclusive possession of the therapist.

In conclusion, child therapy (group or individual treatment) can encompass a wide range of modalities, including expressive insight, support, guidance, clarification, play therapy, and release therapy. Repressed material may or may not be touched. The therapist may or may not offer advice, guidance, or clarification about reality. The relationship with the child may or may not contain transference elements. In comparison to the analyst, the therapist is more of a real object, who may or may not be actively involved in environmental manipulations, e.g., at the school or residential facility. Caution must be taken lest the therapist take on too powerful a position, thereby contaminating the therapy. This is a common dilemma in residential settings where the therapist has the power to bestow privileges, set restrictions, permit home visits, and the like. A child welfare worker involved in placing a child outside the home cannot be both the administrative authority figure and the therapist. A child cannot express feelings such as hostility in the therapy hour without fear of retaliation as long as there is the reality of reprisal. Children cannot both comply and hide feelings and be involved in a psychotherapy relationship. Thus, the less power and authority the child therapist has in the child's daily life, the better.

Personal and Professional Requirements of a Child Psychotherapist

The selection of applicants for specialized study in child psychotherapy raises questions about who wishes to do this kind of work and who is best suited for it. All therapists, whether they work with children or adults, must be able to build an interpersonal relationship in which a special experience can take place. Prospective therapists should already demonstrate a capacity for this kind of communication if they are to use themselves as instruments in facilitating such a relationship. In Kris's paper (1956) on the vicissitudes of insight, he lists the following three integrative functions of the ego which are essential for a therapist, for the treatment process, and for the achievement of insight in both patient and therapist: (1) self-observation, in which the ego is split into observing and experiencing parts; (2) control of the discharge affect, which is related to therapists' tolerance of need tension in themselves and patients; and (3) control over regression, which permits therapists to empathize with patient's regressions, manifested by their transferences, without loss of their own reality testing functions or identity.

In the course of treatment, therapists must work with patients and themselves, and, in a sense, live in two worlds—the past and present, the real and unreal, of themselves and someone else simultaneously. Therapists must be able to live another person's life by *empathic* understanding. This empathy comprises a feeling that emerges spontaneously and enables therapists instantaneously to sense patients' apparent emotions and to penetrate their screens of defenses, which often hide their real feelings (Olden, 1953). In Olden's opinion (1953), adults can empathize more readily with other adults than with children, due to age differences and differences of ego structure. Since children's egos are in flux, progressing and regressing without following any reliable pattern, they repeatedly bewilder adults. Finally, therapists must come to terms with their own childhood and their own infantile needs, and gain some perspective toward those needs, so that they will not feel seduced or endangered by being confronted with the child's manifestations of primary processes. In this way, therapists can permit themselves guardedly to live in the strange fantasy world of children, to be their guide, and to enjoy their growth (Olden, 1953).

In addition to empathy and communication skills, Littner (1969) stresses the need for therapists' self-observation. He notes that child therapists rarely feel neutral toward their child patients. The novice child therapist's inner feelings may range all the way from warm friendliness to actual dislike. The trained child therapist, because of greater experience, self-knowledge, and understanding of the therapeutic interaction usually does not react so strongly. Littner discusses the range of responses: being proud of a child; being disgusted by a child's failures; feeling angry in the face of a child's provocativeness, lateness, or missed appointments; feeling rejected by a child's depreciation of the help offered; feeling bored; fearing an aggressive adolescent; feeling ashamed when one is sexually stimulated by a patient; feeling rage toward the patient's parents; feeling fiercely overprotective of the child, etc. Often therapists have unrealistic responses to a child because their own unresolved conflicts are triggered by the child. Problems in treatment arise when children successfully draw therapists into their interpersonal defenses, provoking therapists to enact the role "assigned" to them. Only through self-observation and an increasing awareness of understanding of their own feelings, thoughts, and behavior toward the child can therapists learn about the specific conflicts currently experienced by the child (Littner, 1969).

Child therapy as a profession can only begin during one's formal professional education in medicine, social work, or psychology. Because of the special dimensions, the unclear communications from children, and the special drains on the therapist, child therapy is seen as a specialty, requiring lengthy, ongoing training, experience, and supervision. Ultimately, to be able to do intensive psychotherapy with adults or children, any aspiring therapist will need some personal treatment. This is necessary in order to acquire a therapeutic objective empathic response that embodies the necessary self-awareness and self-observation, and that controls against regression and acting out through and/or with patients. A personal therapy experience aids the child therapist in the necessary tolerance for primary process, fantasy, and ambiguity, all of which are encountered in clinical work with children. As clinicians, we may or may not have encountered, struggled with, or lived through the pain and stresses that our adult clients experience. But as children, we were all engaged in the same struggles for autonomy, separation and individuation, and identification; we all suffered the same fears of separation and failure that our child patients are currently experiencing. Thus child therapy strikes continuous responsive cords in all therapists in a unique, stressful, and universal manner.

PART II

Assessment

CHAPTER 3

Process and Form of the Diagnostic Evaluation

The writings and research of Hartmann, Kris and Loewenstein, Jacobson, Spitz, Mahler, and, more recently, Kohut and Kernberg, examine populations with defective or faulty ego structures. These populations are referred to as "less than neurotic," and include "borderline" and "character-disordered" individuals. These labels are not meant as a pejorative depreciation, but rather, are shorthand descriptions of severely damaged child and adult clients, signifying that severe traumas, deprivation, disorganization, and frequently, inconsistent mothering have occurred in their first five years of life. The psychopathology of this sizable population has required new conceptualizations of classic psychoanalytic treatment, and the new approaches have become known as psychoanalytically oriented psychotherapy. They are offered here with an ego psychological perspective to provide a conceptual framework of assessment and treatment that offers support for those patients with less than adequate, less than intact, ego structure. Such children constitute the majority of clients seen currently at child guidance and mental health clinics, and in the vast array of child welfare programs.

The need to maintain a sharp division between psychoanalysis, as a treatment modality, and psychotherapy—for children or adults—must be stressed. The commonly held belief is that psychotherapy differs from psychoanalysis in a quantitative direction only whereas, in fact, there is a difference in treatment technique and goals, based on the different structures of the neurotic and the "less than neurotic" ego states. The neurotic child or adult has a strong sense of identity and can differentiate self and others; thus the therapist can be regarded as a separate person. The more intact ego structure of the neurotic child suggests more ego strengths, such as the ability to tolerate frustration and delay, to modulate and moderate drive expression (i.e., sexual and aggressive actions and feelings), and to present thought and verbalization before actions and drive discharge. These latter examples of neutralization permit this relatively more intact child success in maintaining therapy, minus immediate rewards and gratification. Such children present the capacity to form a therapeutic alliance with a separate individual, the therapist, rather than a symbiotic merger and symbiotic alliance based on faulty self/other distinctions. With the neurotic child, regression is safe, and thus is permitted and encouraged via treatment techniques such as free assocation, very frequent sessions, and the use of dreams, play, and drawings.

The less than neurotic child cannot tolerate an anxiety-inducing, regression-promoting therapy that deals extensively in the uncovering of unconscious material. One of the severest problems of the psychotic or borderline child is the failure of repression, along with the propensity toward regression. Thus the treatment focus is to avoid overwhelming anxiety and regression and to strengthen the ego—even frequently putting the "lid on the id," in the hopes of taming the drives to make them less formidable to the ego. Using clarification and suppression, not using a couch, and making appointments less frequent all are ego-building approaches that promote more effective neutralization, better defensive capacities, and better differentiation of self and object. In the following chapters, the above distinctions will be clarified via presentation of the continuum of childhood disorders, ranging from the least intact ego state (severest disorder) to the most intact ego state (mildest disorder).

The seminal work of Réné Spitz (1965) and the confirming research of many others (Provence and Lipton, 1962) have shown us the damaging effects and implications of infants in institutions. These researchers' findings show us infants and toddlers with stunted and/or twisted ego development, namely: impaired relationships with people; weak emotional attachments; no discrimination, trust, or emotional bonds; impaired capacity to anticipate and defer immediate gratification; retarded speech and meager interpersonal communications of all forms; play that is impoverished and repetitive; impaired sense of self; low investment in toys, people, and self; and excessive rocking, head banging, and other self-injurious activities. The importance of what Spitz calls "good enough mothering" is crucial for the child's development of a belief in the consistency and constancy of the inanimate object, i.e., the world of things, which is dependent on consistency and constancy of the human object.

Toddlers with an optimal start who are transferred to group communal care often evidence gradual but serious regression. A well-adjusted child whose feelings are object-directed, who shows interest in the world, and who achieves phase-adequate accomplishments can change, reflecting all the characteristics of an autistic child, by withdrawing and becoming uncommunicative, out of reach of parental affection, apathetic, and listless or wildly aggressive, with screaming and struggling, and by turning from the search for human objects who are unavailable to the available inanimate ones (Anna Freud, 1969). Anna Freud comments on a most disturbing scene in a documentary film on separation, in which a child is "cuddling the oversized teddy as if it were the mother, like the Harlow monkey" (1969, p. 142). Anna Freud concludes that perhaps all autistic children were normal once, though this awesome and overwhelming disorder of uncertain origin is one which many of us are reluctant to ascribe to purely psychological factors. There are many conflicting views on the etiology of autism, and the differences regarding etiology are further reflected in the various treatment techniques prescribed.[1]

A Developmental Diagnostic Approach

The diagnostic schema prescribed here is based on an appraisal of the structure and development of the ego. "Ego" is best defined as a group of functions. In the structural sense of the word, the ego gradually evolves in the newborn infant from an undifferentiated state. This ego-id matrix has a potentiality based on constitutional factors (the genetically determined growth pattern of the central nervous system, the special senses, and the body in general) and experiences in the surrounding world in relation to objects. The ego therefore occupies a position between the primal instincts, based on the physiological needs of the body and the demands of the outer world, and, as the internalized psychic representative of both, it serves to mediate between the individual and external reality. In so doing, it performs the important functions of perceiving the physical and psychic needs of the self, and the qualities and attitudes of the environment; it then evaluates, coordi-

---

[1]An overview of autism and treatment approaches for it are included in the review of childhood psychosis presented in Chapter 6.

nates, and integrates these perceptions so that internal demands can be adjusted to external requirements; and finally, in an executive way, the ego brings about relief from drive tensions and wishes through a discharge made possible either by a reduction in the intensity of the drives (taming) or by a feasible modification of the external situation. The important task of the ego, therefore, is to achieve optimum gratification of instinctual strivings while maintaining good relations with the external world and the superego, which is the internal representative of the standards of behavior and moral demands imposed from without, and threats that result from failure to meet them. For this task, protective devices must be available to reduce excessively strong internal and external stimuli. Physiologically, the sense organs are equipped to select only certain stimuli and to reduce the intensity of others. This is especially important in infancy, when other defenses have not yet developed adequately. (At that time, the physiological mechanisms serving this purpose are referred to collectively as a "protective shield" or "stimulus barrier.") Psychically, certain defensive functions are also developed and maintained to protect against conscious awareness of those demands of the id (primitive urges, impulses, biological needs, etc.) and the superego that would give rise to conflict and intolerable anxiety.

Defenses are struggles of the ego to protect itself against danger—i.e., the threat of eruption into consciousness of a repressed wish—associated with some real or imagined punishment that would cause anxiety or guilt. Defenses always operate unconsciously so that the person is unaware of what is taking place; they may result in a deletion or distortion of some aspect of reality. Examples of defenses are repression, displacement, reaction formation, projection, isolation, undoing, introjection, identification, denial, and turning against the self, as in depression and masochism. Defenses rarely operate singly—they occur together in clusters. Denial is a primitive defense that serves to avoid awareness of some painful aspect of reality—e.g., a fantasy formed to erase a disagreeable and unwelcome fact. In adults, denial results in severe pathology. An example of a more sophisticated adaptive defense is sublimation. Ego functions such as perception, motor capacity, intention, purposeful planning, intelligence, thinking, speech, and language mature relatively free of such conflict. These are autonomous or conflict-free spheres of the ego.

As a part of its adaptation to reality, the ego must also develop the capacity for relatively stable relationships with objects. This involves the ability to form and maintain affectionate, close ties to others, with minimum expression of hostile feelings. Object constancy thus is established. In the progressive development of ego functioning, differentiation of the self from the object world is succeeded by object constancy, and finally, in adolescence, by the capacity for object love. For object love to develop, infantile objects and an extreme degree of self-love—narcissism—must be relinquished.

If the environment is suitably benign, reality is gradually mastered—objective thought occurs, autonomous activities increase in extent and power, and a reasonably efficient regulation of the drives is achieved. However, maturation of specific ego functions continues well into adult life, as the individual develops a steadily increasing capacity to love, to work, and to adapt to the surrounding world. Ego-alien behaviors are those which are not in consonance with the ego—in relation to drives, affects, ideas, or behavior. These ego-alien behaviors are seen in the neurotic but not in the ego-syntonic character-disordered individual. Ego distortion is characterized by: (1) a developmental incapacity or impairment in the ego that adversely affects the whole development of ego functions—most specifically, those concerned with psychic defense and adaptation; and (2) a developmental impairment of certain major ego functions, which is characteristic of infant and child psychosis, and is also found in borderline and psychotic adults.

Ego modification and ego supportive treatment are often misunderstood because the terms associated with them are used interchangeably in the literature, with a consequent blurring of meaning. Thus, clarification is offered here. *Ego deficits* refer to constitutional impairments in the ego that are contained within the apparatus of primary autonomy. *Ego deviations* result from aspects of development that occur too early to be considered normal, i.e., premature precocious ego development. *Ego distortions* are impairments of the ego which result from internalization of faulty perceptions of self- and object-representations. An *ego regression* is the result of a backward movement of an ego function from a higher level of development to a lower one, manifested by loss or diminution of function, e.g., loss of speech, locomotion, or sphincter control. Therefore, diagnosis includes the following considerations: degree of modification of the ego; highest level of ego development reached; and where ego regression exists at the time of the diagnostic evaluation (Blanck and Blanck, 1974).

The application of this developmental diagnostic approach in work with children is clearly stated by Anna Freud:

> When diagnosing the mental disturbances of children, the child analyst is confronted with difficulties which are due to the shifting internal scene in a developing individual, and which are not met with in adult psychiatry. One of these difficulties concerns the fact that, during development, symptoms, inhibitions and anxieties do not necessarily carry the same significance which they assume at a later date. Although in some cases they may be lasting, and the first signs of permanent pathology, in other cases, they need

be no more than transient appearances of stress which emerge whenever a particular phase of development makes specially high demands on a child's personality. . . . Another difficulty for the diagnostician is bound up with the well-known fact that there are no childhood alternatives to the adults' efficiency or failure in sex and work, vital factors which are used in adult psychiatry as indications of intactness or disturbance. . . . Since, thus, neither symptomatology nor life tasks can be taken as reliable guides to the assessment of mental health or illness in childhood, we are left with the alternative idea that the capacity to develop progressively, or respectively, the damage to that capacity, are the most significant factors in determining a child's mental health. Accordingly, it becomes the diagnostician's task to ascertain where a given child stands on the developmental scale, whether his position is age-adequate, retarded or precocious, and in what respect; and to what extent the observable internal and external circumstances and existent symptoms are interfering with the possibilities of future growth [1962, pp. 149–150].

Anna Freud (1962) believes that the diagnostic appraisal of the child serves both practical aims—the decision for or against treatment, and the choice of therapeutic method—and theoretical aims—the attempt to formulate clear pictures of the initial phases of those mental disorders that are known now principally in their latter stages, the attempt to distinguish transitory from permanent pathology, and the general aim to increase insight into the developmental processes themselves.

Fixation

In considering fixation, which holds the child back on the developmental scale, we note the tendency in psychic development for residuals of earlier phases to acquire and retain strong "charges" of psychic energy and to play a significant role in later development of mental functioning. Arrests of development occur in instinctual, superego, and ego organization, permitting in various degrees the persistence of primitive ways of gaining satisfaction, of relating to people, and of reacting defensively to old, even outmoded, dangers. In addition to insufficiently understood constitutional reasons for fixation, e.g., inherent differences in the functioning of the various erogenous zones and in ego givens, there are inevitable experiences in which the developing immature ego is overwhelmed by too much stress. These traumatic experiences usually involve an unfortunate combination of excessive gratification and excessive frustration. With disturbances of development and conflict over current functioning, regression to remnants of earlier functioning that are "fixed" in the psyche is possible. In their unconscious functioning, at least, neurotic patients are pinned or fixated to the past.

Regression

We see two types of regression: libidinal and ego regression. Libidinal regression is a retreat to an earlier phase of instinctual organization, especially of the infantile period. Such a falling back occurs when a predetermined maturational step presents patients with difficulties which they are unable to master. Often this is determined by earlier unresolved conflicts and anxieties which leave areas of weakness in the preceding developmental phases (i.e., fixations), to which patients are more likely to regress. A simple example of libidinal regression may be observed when—at times of emotional stress—a 5-year-old child resumes thumbsucking, a habit previously abandoned. Aggression and aggressive modes are grouped under the category of libidinal drive expression. Some important questions at the time of the diagnostic evaluation are: What is the aggressive expression at the disposal of the child? Does it correspond to the level of libidinal development? Is the direction toward the object world or the self?

In childhood, the development of sexual drives is still fluid and libidinal regressions are common when the child is under stress, e.g., at times of illness or fatigue; they do not necessarily indicate pathology. This is also the case during adolescence. Regression serves as a defense, protecting the individual against the intolerable anxiety that genital sexuality arouses. For example, when adults are overwhelmed with anxiety and guilt that cannot be mastered in the face of heterosexual genital sexuality, they may fall back to infantile sexuality, repressing genital sexuality with some prephallic form, and thus developing a perversion.

In ego regression, the mind may revert to modes of functioning typical of an earlier period. Such reacquisition of old patterns is a frequent accompaniment of libidinal regression and occurs in response to a variety of needs that arise from internal and external pressures. The many causes of ego regression include unpleasurable feelings, such as anxiety or guilt; mental pathology, such as neurotic and psychotic processes; bodily pathology, especially of the central nervous system; and disorganization of functioning caused by drugs. The most common cause of ego regression in the neuroses probably is the unresolved Oedipus complex with its associated castration anxiety, penis envy, and guilt, which evoke unconscious sexual and aggressive impulses.

The concept of regression is intimately related to the hypothesis that in the course of attaining adulthood, an individual passes through a series of maturational phases or psychosexual phases—each with a phase-appropriate mental organization. The make-up of each such organization is inferred from the way instinctual drives discharge, ego functions operate, and conscience and ideals guide. When a phase-appropriate organization is substantially disrupted, regression occurs.

The term "instinctual drives" refers to libidinal and aggressive drives and their discharge. In doing a diagnostic assessment, one attempts to assess libido with regard to phase development. In the sequence of phases (oral, anal, phallic, latency, preadolescence, adolescence), one attempts to assess whether the child ever proceeded to the age-adequate stage—especially beyond the anal to the phallic level. Some important questions at the time of the diagnostic evaluation are: Is the current level the highest level maintained, or has a higher level been abandoned regressively for an earlier one? In terms of libido distribution, is the self cathected as well as the object world? With regard to object libido, what are the level and quality of object relationships (e.g., narcissistic, anaclitic, object constancy, pre-Oedipal, Oedipal, post-Oedipal, adolescent)?

Nagera (1964, p. 222) notes that it is "frequently possible at the diagnostic stage to ascertain how much, in certain neurotic developments or disorders of children, is the result of regression and how much can be ascribed to fixation." This crucial observation is in line with Anna Freud's comments on prognosticating a child's future mental health. Nagera continues, "Fixation points indicate a certain degree of arrest in drive development. In regressive phenomena, on the other hand, the drives have at one point or another reached a higher level of development but were, as a result of conflicts at these higher levels, forced back to earlier development points" (p. 224). The higher the level of development originally attained, the better the prognosis. Nagera suggests that fixations and regressions can be diagnosed by observing children's behavior, games, play, attitudes, interests, fantasies, and symptoms. In addition, the background material presented by parents serves to clarify, confirm, or correct our observations.

Evaluation Criteria

There are specific criteria suggested as guidelines for consideration at the time of referral or the first contact with a child and the child's parents. In beginning the assessment or evaluation, Kessler (1966) suggests scrutiny of (1) the age discrepancy, i.e., the difference between the child's chronological age and behavioral age level; (2) the frequency and duration of the symptom(s); (3) the number of symptoms; (4) the degree of social disadvantage; (5) the intractability of the behavior; (6)

the child's personality, or general adjustment; (7) and last, and often overlooked, the degree of the child's inner suffering. These criteria are aids in determining the child's progression, fixation, or regression in age-appropriate tasks. The objectives in an assessment are to determine how, and in what areas, the child differs from others of the same age; to assess the chronicity of the child's problems; to appraise areas of strength in the child and the child's family; and to aid in conceptualizing some hypothesis about possible contaminating factors—be they past, present, constitutional, or family induced. One obviously needs to know how the family handled the child presymptomatically and how they are currently handling him or her. One makes a simultaneous assessment of the child's parents to determine subsequent recommendations and future work. One should ascertain to what extent parents contribute to the maintenance of the child's problems, and in contrast, to what extent they support healthy aspects of the child's personality.

The initial assessment may well be tentative, since diagnosis is an ongoing process throughout the course of treatment; in addition, it is subject to change as new material is gathered. Kessler (1966) recommends that a diagnostic formulation include symptomatology, etiology, prognosis, and treatment plan. McDonald (1965) adds "the child's conflict, child's personality and developmental progress, constitutional and organic impairments and major psychological traumas, and the child's and parents' external world" (p. 601).

The parents and the external world require additional discussion. A clinician wants to have a very clear grasp of family life, which includes the interpersonal relationships and structure in the family and extended family; the employment situation and financial reality; the childcare arrangements; and the additional support systems or lack thereof, via social ties, neighborhood and social mores, religious affiliations, life style, values, and any other services or systems that have aided the family.

Psychological testing is rarely routinely done, nor is it recommended that it should be done with each and every case.

Whether to make use of intelligence and projective tests is a matter to be decided individually about each child. Consultation with the psychologist can help in the decision. Results of IQ tests sometimes can be obtained from the child's school. If tests are used, they should be carried out for a specific purpose rather than as an ill-defined bit of routine. The child must be prepared for the test, preferably with a reason for the testing which will have specific meaning in relation to his own problems. . . . If tests are used, it is important that the child as well as his parents be informed of the results. The reports often include evidences of the child's emotional conflict. Evidences of ego strengths, which every child demonstrates in some form during the testing procedure, also should be included in the report

Then the test report can serve as a stimulus to the child's healthy ego functioning, rather than as a sentence pronouncing him a failure because of his problems [McDonald, 1965, p. 599].

An appraisal of a child's physical condition is essential during the assessment process, and may well require a physical and/or neurological exam. Organic pathology must be considered and attention must be given to chronic physical diseases and disabilities that exact some emotional stress and adjustment.

It is crucial to note how and what the parents share in giving material. The importance is far beyond factual data such as the child's developmental history (e.g., the precise timing of walking, talking, toilet training). The parents' emotional attitudes, past and present, are more telling than hard data. For example: Does the mother guiltily recount depression in her child's first years? Does she therefore have amnesia about the conventional developmental milestones? Is the father aloof and indifferent to the assessment process, complying with clinic policy that both parents be seen? Too often fathers are not included in work with or on behalf of their children, and the total burden, blame, and responsibility falls on the mother. Fathers may spend less time with their young children, but they are crucial agents in a child's development, separation-individuation, identifications, etc., and should be actively and routinely involved on behalf of their children. Do parents present apathy, anger, helplessness, enthusiasm, or empathy in relation to their child? Parental affect, the nature of parenting provided, and parental motivation are probably the key prognostic issues that serve as guidelines for the ongoing planning for therapy.

Process of the Diagnostic Evaluation

In contrast to the current mental health trend toward dispensing with diagnostic evaluation, the view advanced here is that such evaluation is crucial; thus, a thorough discussion of the process of assessment is offered. Because of the dearth of psychiatric and social work literature on the subject, this discussion will integrate the more abundant psychoanalytic literature on diagnostic evaluation. Many writers note that treatment begins with the first contact, and clinicians in agreement with this view plunge into treatment in the first session. The recent preoccupation with treating large populations of child and adult patients has led to ever briefer treatment in the effort to treat more patients in less time. While this goal may be socially valid, it has little to do with the needs of a given patient. The thrust of this discussion is that time is never saved, but in fact is lost, by the omission of the assessment process.

The distinction between evaluation and treatment is not merely a semantic one. McDonald (1965) suggests that a basic confusion is introduced when the initial contacts with a child and his or her parents are regarded as "treatment" before any insight is gained into the structure of the problems and before a recommendation can be formulated. Often a feeling of relief may accompany the first visits. But this introductory experience cannot provide specific therapeutic measures aimed at altering the causative factors contributing to the emotional disturbance in question. Such specific treatment cannot be undertaken until a diagnostic evaluation or assessment has been done. Furthermore, between evaluation and treatment must come the important step of a conscious decision upon the part of the parents, and often of the child, to undertake the treatment.

Some clinicians speak of contracting and mutual goal setting in the opening phase of treatment. But how can clients engage in such endeavors before they understand the reasons for choosing a given treatment modality and the nature of that treatment, including an estimate of the time and cost involved? Beginning treatment before formulating a diagnosis is analogous to prescribing antibiotics indiscriminately for any undiagnosed physical disease. There are various modalities of ongoing intervention, but few agencies and clinics provide the full range. Without a diagnostic assessment, clients may simply be forced into whatever modality a given agency offers, with no differentiation of case need. The reality that an agency cannot be all things to all people, but indeed should often refer clients elsewhere, underscores the need for assessment as a separate and distinct phase. As Buxbaum (1954) states: "diagnostic and dynamic considerations, rather than philosophies, should be introduced in order to select the best therapeutic procedure for specific cases" (pp. 299–300).

Even though treatment does not begin with the first contact, a therapeutic atmosphere can indeed be created with the first phone call. Respect is offered the parents who call and attention is paid to their assessment of the severity of the situation. Receiving information and understanding from the clinician can provide the parents with considerable initial relief; they are no longer alone, but are receiving intelligent caring, listening, and empathy, and have begun an attempt to unravel what often has been an anxiety-inducing or anger-producing situation for both parents and child. Listening and exploration are crucial during the assessment process. However, clinicians do not maintain an objective distance, they may overidentify with the parents (and possibly respond to their guilt) by minimizing the child's problem before they know much about it—to attempt to provide the parents with some quick relief. Clinicians must guard against becoming infected by parents' anxiety and giving premature opinions and recommendations.

Instant advice should not be offered, as parents may find it exceedingly presumptive that their long-standing, bewildering difficulties are so obvious to another.

The Child's Parents

The assessment process sets the stage and, one hopes, serves as the beginning of an ongoing alliance between the parents and the clinician. Parents' observations and feelings are legitimatized and their concerns are given entitlement and respect. They are responded to as the most important persons in their child's life—which indeed they are, as treatment will flounder or terminate without their ongoing help, support, and collaboration. The process of assessment stresses the importance of observation and verbal communication in therapeutic work, diminishes any aura of mystery or magic about such procedures, enables the parents to feel actively involved and to focus their attention and interest on specific observations about their child, and affords relief for parents' guilt and anxiety as they join in an effort to help their child. Finally, parents have a chance to form an impression of the clinician during the assessment phase (McDonald, 1965).

This latter point needs elaboration and expansion. Too frequently omitted in the literature is client or patient response to the clinician. In a private practice situation, if there is some negative interchange, or bad fit, the client is free to leave and locate another therapist. In social agencies, clinics, and the like, the parents are expected to like and accept whoever is assigned the case. In many clinics, parents may never even meet their child's diagnostician or subsequent therapist. If they object, raise questions, or wish to have some contact with the person seeing their child, too frequently they are labeled as intrusive or resistive. Comfort regarding the professional seeing one's child should not be the privilege of the financially independent family alone. This degree of respect offered parents should become more widely standardized as part of the routine assessment process; if the parents and child are not interviewed by the same clinician, the parents should have the opportunity to get to know the professional who is interviewing their child.

In collecting data for the diagnostic assessment, the diagnostician must recognize and respect parental resistance. For example, parents may object to a necessary school inquiry. Instead of ignoring this resistance, its underlying fears and sources should be identified and worked through with the parents, thereby allowing the contact with the school. If there is not a working through of the parents' conflicts before proceeding further, the resistance frequently increases and becomes attached to endless ongoing issues, such as fees, the time of appointments, and even the parents' willingness to engage in ongoing contact. Frequently, parental cooperation is not attained, and the case begins to flounder, ending with a gradual disengagement or sudden termination. If parents' resistance and ambivalence are very high, as if often the case when parents feel forced to comply with the school's edict to secure help for their child, little can be gained by sidestepping the parents' attitudes and seeing the child alone. Latency-age children almost universally cannot benefit from therapy efforts that do not include contact with their parents.

In many situations, strong parental resistance offers a clear diagnostic message of where treatment intervention should begin—namely, with them. In such cases, work with the child is held off until an alliance with the parents has been established. Too frequently, this option of beginning a case via work with the parents alone is not even considered. Too often, the result is the child seen in isolation, with little accomplished, since an hour or two a week hardly constitutes magic or a bulwark against the child's ongoing situation at home.

Thus far, all discussion has focused on the natural parents when, in fact, a sizable child population in foster care is seen at child treatment agencies. Very frequently, foster parents transport the child for treatment under the orders and direction of the child welfare placement agency responsible for their foster child, but refuse to have any contact themselves. They choose not to invest their time and emotional energy in a situation which they did not originally create. While many foster parents are cooperative and invested in their foster charges, they may do no more than supply whatever history they can plus transport the child. Foster parents, as well as natural parents, may feel threatened by what they perceive as the scrutiny and judgment of the outside professionals.

Finally, a not uncommon dilemma in child therapy with youngsters in foster care, is the lack of genuine collaboration and sharing between the child guidance clinic and the child welfare agency, with the former frequently reporting that its recommendations are ignored, that there is an ever-changing procession of welfare workers, and that there is no continuity to case planning and management. Too frequently, there are abrupt upheavals and changes of foster homes. Such interferences to meaningful, fruitful child therapy can be anticipated during the assessment process, when some issues of collaboration and ongoing communication may be worked through prior to beginning contact with a child. Such working through is essential given the injurious effects—and sense of loss—when the case disintegrates, or is prematurely terminated, and the child loses yet another person.

Outside Sources of Information

The assessment phase is the time to secure information from outside sources, e.g. schools, pediatricians, hospitals, and agencies who have previously known and worked with the family. Confidentiality, securing parental permission for inquiry, plus completing written release of information forms are standard procedures. A word of caution: sharing confidential information with a school system or other source must be carefully considered, as the latter probably does not observe the same code of record-keeping and privacy as is customary in treatment settings. Labels and dynamic formulations frequently are casually entered into a child's school record, which follows the child throughout his or her school days. Thus, it is obvious that various forms and editions of information will be shared, depending on the setting receiving the report from the child therapy agency. It is usually wisest to express no opinion or conclusions about child or parents until after the follow-up interpretative interview with the parents. During this interview, clinician and parents can jointly determine what and how much should be shared.

Preparing the Child

The initial assessment phase of contact is the logical time to help parents prepare the child for his or her initial interview. The goal of such preparation is not to avoid anxiety, but rather, to help the child cope with a normal realistic anxiety about the interview by providing realistic information about it. An unprepared child may become overwhelmed by a surprise visit to an agency. If parents have resisted preparation of the child, almost the only observation the interviewer can make is of the child's panic; other aspects of the child's functioning remain obscured. Hence, preparation helps the child and also helps the therapist to make more meaningful observations.

Parents often are uncertain about what to tell their child, and need support to present the facts to the child. A visit to a therapist is not without reason, nor is it a meaningless play session. Children who are worried often find great relief in the knowledge that help is being sought. A frank series of statements by the child's parents and teacher regarding their concerns about the child's school problems can relieve the child of what was felt to be a private painful burden. The forthcoming visit should be presented with openness, forthrightness, and a desire to be supportive of the child. Not infrequently, parents cannot prepare the child in this supportive context, but rather, indicate anger, inconvenience, and frustration that the child creates trouble at home.

Such a variation becomes another diagnostic indicator of the direction of future work with parents. Some parents become anxious about what the child may reveal about them and family life. The clinician may be able to allay such fears via assurances that there is no competition for the child's affection, that there is no surreptitious attempt to learn secrets about the parents, and that a child's ability to develop his or her own private mental life is a healthy sign of growth. Despite such reassurances, some parents remain frightened and anxious, which provides additional diagnostic data about areas that will require future ongoing work and support.

The age of the child determines how far in advance he or she should be told about the assessment. The very young child with an undeveloped concept of time can generally be told a few days in advance, simply and briefly. The older child may need more time to digest the event. The adolescent, ideally, has had considerable independent input in the decision to seek help. (This is obviously not the case when the adolescent is a nonvoluntary client, e.g., referred by the juvenile court, or some such agency of power). Ideally, parental preparation should also include some attempt to assist the child to articulate fantasies, concerns, apprehensions, and feelings about the pending contact. When parents prove incapable of this empathic task, the clinician must provide the child with the opportunity to raise questions and share fears. Often the mother must accompany the child into the initial session; she may continue to do so for an extended period once treatment has begun. This is to be expected with very young children and with cases such as symbiotic psychosis, where neither child nor mother can separate and let go.

Normally, the latency-age child will be able to go alone into the office for the assessment session. However, there are special extenuating circumstances which may preclude this, even with the well-prepared latency age child. The following vignette illustrates one such case.

A boy, age 6, came for his first session and would not be separated from his mother. Mother had anticipated this, and she and the therapist had decided that her role would be one of sympathetic nonparticipation. The boy had lost his father about six months previously in an automobile accident. The therapist stood at the door and discussed the boy's refusal with him.

T: I think you're afraid of being shut up in this room. You're afraid of what might happen to you. Perhaps you are afraid that I might give you shots or something.

P: I don't like it in there. I want to stay with Mommy.

T: I expect you're afraid that something might happen to Mommy if you leave her. You're afraid that Mommy might not be there when you come back. You want to watch her in case she goes away.

p: My mommy is sick. (She had a cold.)

t: I can watch your mommy through this open door, and your mommy can watch me, too. I can see that she is there and that she is looking well.

p: Why can't you see me in here?

t: Because you might want to tell me things you don't want other people to hear. (Patient buries his head in his mother's lap.) Besides, I can help you better in this special room. (Therapist retreats a little into the room.) I am going to be in here just in case you want to come.

p: I don't want to come. (Whispers to his mother, who smiles at him but makes no response.)

t: I know you are worried about coming in, because you are afraid something bad will happen to you.

p: I'm not afraid of anything. (Buries head in mother's lap.)

t: You're afraid that Mommy might leave without you.

p: I'm not afraid of anything. (Pauses.) My daddy is dead.

t: I know just how sad that must have made you feel.

p: He was killed in an auto.

t: I can see just why you must watch over Mommy all the time.

p: It looks dark in that room.

t: Things always look darker when you're afraid.

p: I'm not afraid of that room. We've got a room like that at home.

t: I expect it's the same sort of room, but new places are always a little frightening. You always expect that something bad's going to happen in them.

p: Nothing's bad in that room.

t: That's right, only what we imagine.

p: Why don't you go into the room?

t: That's just what I am going to do, and I hope you will come with me, so we can both see what it's like. (The boy comes in slowly.)

p: This is your room.

t: Yes, this is my room.

p: I can watch Mommy from here. Hi, Mommy. (His mother smiles at him and waves.)

t: She'll always be waiting for you just there.

p: It's not a bad room.

t: It's a good room for helping boys when they have worries.

p: I'm going out now.

t: Thank you for coming in. Perhaps you will stay longer next time. (The next time he stayed the whole session, and reiterated the story of how his father was killed, explaining that "it was no one's fault") [Anthony, 1964, pp. 116–117].

By contrast, the adolescent will much more easily understand the role of the clinician and the purpose of the assessment interview. The teenager may vehemently deny any problems, which in itself reflects anxiety. The parents need to emphasize that they wish to help their adolescent son or daughter, that there is a rational basis for his or her current problems, and that the child's privacy will be respected. Teenagers must understand that they can share or withhold as they wish, that they will not be seduced or forced into exposure. Special considerations for children of all ages are required if there's been a traumatic experience with a prior therapist or physician, or if there have been many family separations. The young child may need extensive reassurance of the obvious, that the parent or foster parent will wait and take him home.

Reference to the not uncommon phenomena of the adolescent's opposition to treatment contact and the assessment process raises the overriding question of children's resistance and fear, and whether they should have a say in the decision to see a therapist, even initially. Many parents report their child's opposition, rage, and temper tantrums at the prospect of being taken to see the therapist. When parents question the wisdom of an assessment based on their child's resistance, they are unsure, ambivalent, or resistive to clinic contact and possibly, consciously or unconsciously, have communicated this to the child. Further, we can hypothesize that opposition and tantrums are generalized responses, over and beyond the proposed contact at a mental health or child guidance clinic. Young and latency-age children obviously are lacking sufficient ego development (i.e., judgment, perception, etc.) to be entrusted with major life decisions. They should not be allowed autonomy regarding attendance at school, the necessity of medical and dental appointments, or the approval of medical or dental procedures. Nor should they be allowed freedom of choice regarding therapeutic procedures. Because parents' own resistances are frequently profound, considerable work with them often needs to be done first, before they will support their child's coming to the clinic. The dilemma of the overwhelmed parents who plead that they can't get their child to the session is a diagnostic sign that requires further scrutiny of possible parental resistances, ineffectualness, and ambivalence, as well as overriding problems in the home regarding limits and controls. In such cases, the clinician is wise to remain firm and patient, clarifying the situation, rather than allying with the regressive, infantile stance of the parents.

Conclusion

The process of assessment is a separate and distinct phase of child therapy that precedes treatment. The assessment will provide guidelines for ongoing treatment planning, via applications of diagnostic and dynamic considerations that are applied in a differentiated individualized fashion, case by case. The assessment sets the stage for the beginning of an alliance between the parents and the clinician, and the child and the clinician. Problems regarding parental ambivalence and resistance become apparent during this period, serving as indicators of the best approach to beginning ongoing work. During the assessment process, the diagnostician helps parents prepare their child for the work ahead.

Form of the Diagnostic Evaluation: A Developmental Profile

There are many ways to approach assessment. It is common procedure for agencies and clinics to have their own form or outline for the diagnostic evaluation. Some practitioners attempt to formulate a systems analysis of a child's interrelationships and functioning, and others employ various outlines and tools in an ego assessment. There are a number of developmental outlines and profiles that try to take in as many variables and areas as can be observed and then integrate the findings in order to arrive at an assessment of a child. A development approach that looks at many developmental lines at the same time has been developed by Anna Freud and her colleagues (see Eissler et al., 1977), who have devised a format to assess the child, adolescent, and adult client. Their approach emphasizes an assessment of the total personality, rather than one isolated aspect. Flapan and Neubauer (1975) have used this developmental approach to create a short assessment outline for nonclinical professionals and paraprofessionals. They cite two separate but major considerations in assessing the child: (1) whether there is pathology and (2) whether any existing pathology has interfered or is interfering with development in significant areas.

The Anna Freud Profile (or Diagnostic Profile) is a most useful tool for teaching and improving diagnostic and treatment skills; it increases the precision of clinicians' thinking about child development and gives them a better grasp of what they actually know and don't know about a given child. Free-floating empathy, intuition, and personalized and possibly erroneous responses to the child and/or the parents give way to a greater clarity of observations. The Diagnostic Profile for the assessment of childhood disturbances is based on a psychoanalytic theory of childhood development. This profile, which is now used for all diagnostic work at the Hampstead Child Therapy Clinic, enables the clinician to assess behavior in structural, dynamic, economic, genetic, and adaptive terms. The original profile was devised to facilitate the organization of clinical material under psychoanalytically meaningful headings before, during, and after therapy. The profile begins with the usual data: reason for referral, description of child, family and personal history, and possible significant environmental influences. The assessment of development follows, and information is sought regarding drive development, ego and superego development, lines of development and mastery of age-appropriate tasks, genetic assessments (i.e., regression and fixation points), dynamics and structural assessments (i.e., conflicts), and the interplay of internal and external forces. Assessment of general characteristics (i.e., frustration tolerance, sublimation potential, overall attitude to anxiety, and progressive versus regressive tendencies) is the last item prior to the final diagnosis.

Anna Freud and her colleagues (1965) have cautioned that the Diagnostic Profile must not be treated as a questionnaire, must not dominate the interviewer's attitude during the diagnostic examination, and must not be shared with the patient. Rather, it should serve as a framework for the clinician's thinking and a method to organize findings after they have been elicited, assimilated, and digested by the clinician.

General systems theory is the study of interactions within an organization. Its basic thesis is that all complex interrelationships follow similar rules and processes, the study of which allows one to grasp the organization of subsystems into larger wholes, at times according to hierarchical arrangements. According to von Bertalanffy (1968), the most effective psychoanalytic application of the principles of general systems theory is Anna Freud's use of the concept of lines of development (1965). Gedo and Goldberg (1973) cite the unique organization of psychoanalytic data in this concept. Anna Freud has demonstrated that many areas of functioning, or lines of growth, can be traced through a person's life history. Some of the most important lines of development outlined, such as object relations, include libidinal phases, defenses, and various adaptive patterns. Any area of individual personality that represents interaction among maturation, adaptation, and structuralization may be followed in this novel manner. Anna Freud notes that in normality there is a general correspondence among the various developmental lines in their overall progress; imbalance among points of progression along various lines, on the other hand, is an indication of developmental difficulty or psychopathology.

Similarly, Gedo and Goldberg (1973) state: "A valid assessment of individual personality requires consideration of all relevant lines and their complicated interactions in a total configuration. It is therefore necessary to develop criteria about which lines of development will be relevant for the identification of the various psychopathological entities" (p. 8). This schema may be compared to that of Piaget's regarding cognitive development. Piaget (1952) presents a most effective application of systems theory. He has outlined and elaborated stages of cognitive development which can be further differentiated into substages and which, in their overall organization, form an epigenetic system. The epigenetic concept of development, which has relevance for the present discussion, views the formation of structure as the result of successive transactions between the organism and its environment; that is, the outcome of each phase is understood to depend on the outcomes of all previous phases.

CHAPTER 4

Objectives, Findings, and Follow-Up Interview

Some agencies have a routine order of procedures for collecting evaluative data (e.g., parents are seen, schools are called or visited, and pediatricians are consulted before the child is seen). Parents often are seen together initially if the family is an intact one, then separately for several sessions, and ultimately together again for the follow-up interview. Three to five appointments with parents is often sufficient, though they should be seen as many times as is reasonably necessary to obtain the history, as they or parent substitutes are usually the major sources of historical material.

Interviewing the Parents

It is important initially to inquire how the parents happened to seek help, and why now. Though critical emergency situations do arise in regard to child assessment and child therapy, one rarely, if ever, is confronted with something out of the blue. Rather, issues and problems that have been festering and brewing for some time may reach a climax. Initially one would also want to know what appears to be the precipitant for the consultation, what symptoms exist, and how the family and school have responded and are responding to symptoms. The history and development of the present complaint, including the child's awareness of it, are important. It is important to ascertain whether the child's intrapsychic disability has motivated the parents, or whether the child, as patient, is communicating about the intrapsychic problems of one parent, or the interpersonal marital problems of the parents. Obviously, it is important to know whether parents are self-referred, or come at the urging of a teacher or an edict from the school, given the indicators here regarding motivation and/or resistance.

The facts and feelings about the child, the child's problems, and the parents' reactions and attempts till now to handle it themselves might well be all the actual data collected in the first session, though parents will begin to form some impression of the therapist, who is also forming impressions of them, their feelings about their child, and their feelings and modes of communicating together as a couple. One hopes that some mutual initial rapport will be generated between clinician and parents in this first meeting. The clinic procedures and dilemmas (e.g., waiting lists) and administrative routines for scheduling appointments, paying fees, contacting school, etc., should be presented during the first session to allow for questions, clarification, and airing of possible potential resistance.

The second session with one or both parents should focus on obtaining as complete a developmental history as possible. Fathers are more active in early caretaking than they used to be and not infrequently have joint or sole custody after a divorce, so father may well provide some of the early developmental material. The subsequent appointments routinely focus on history of the courtship, marriage, and, if necessary, divorce. The purpose is not to pry into the parents' own private lives. Most parents have some anxiety about an investigation of their lives and are relieved when the clinician reminds them that they are asked about themselves only for the sake of evaluating their child. For example, instead of asking parents bluntly about their sexual relationship, the clinician may ask whether the child has ever shown sexual curiosity about them, observed them undressed, or observed their sexual relations; phrased in this way, the inquiry is solidly grounded in the task of the evaluation of the child (McDonald, 1965). Parents have not come as patients, and their launching into their own sexual difficulties, for example, often reflects a weakening of defenses in the face of anxiety. While such revelations are of diagnostic significance and will affect recommendations, the clinician should try not to let the assessment process become a study of parents as if they were the patients.

The subsequent appointments with parents explore their own personal histories and family-of-origin relationships. Too often this is omitted or glossed over—despite the well-known phenomenon of the repetition compulsion, and the frequency with which parents repeat their own painful pasts, be it divorce, child abuse, alcoholism, or family violence. Having a clear picture of the parents' own past is the best insurance that the therapist will develop empathy for the parents. Child therapists, especially beginning practitioners, must struggle with the almost universal phenomena of rescue fantasies, child advocacy, and difficulty in relating to and working with parents. Parents do not cause physical or emotional injury to their child willfully, with deliberate, premediated malice. Rather, parents who act out on their spouses and children must be viewed as ill, disturbed, out of control, and not in contact with reality if they are to be engaged on behalf of their child, as well as themselves.

As noted earlier, the therapist wants to have a very clear grasp of family life, including the interpersonal relationships and structures in the immediate and extended family, and the employment, health, educational, and financial realities of the family. Also important are child-care arrangements, and additional support systems or lack thereof, via social ties, neighborhood and social relationships, and religious affiliations of the family. Life style and values, and past or present aid to the family from other services and systems are also significant. Highlighted for attention in a history are the often omitted areas of medical illness, hospitalizations, accidents, separations, deaths, births of sibs, and housing and sleeping arrangements. The facts themselves are less crucial than the parents' and child's emotional attitudes toward them. The special foci and emphases of further exploration will be based on parents' emotional tone regarding certain topics, plus the nature of the presenting symptoms. As a history unfolds, clinical sense and practice wisdom generally inform the therapist where to explore further, as well as where not to explore, given potential enormous resistance. The child's age also directs where focus and emphasis need to be placed with regard to developmental stages. Parents may reveal the child's major areas of difficulty by their own emphasis on a phase of the child's development, which may be expressed via excessive anxiety or criticism about the child's difficulties. On the other hand, an unrecalled phase of development may indicate repression about a highly charged and painful period.

Interviewing the Child

The purpose of the interview with the child is to observe and evaluate, not to treat. The child should be seen as many times as necessary in order to gain sufficient observations to formulate a diagnostic assessment and eventual recommendations. However, if a child is seen too many times, the child may develop enough of a relationship with the diagnostician to suffer when their relationship is ended. It is important that the clinician review with the child why he or she has come, and what they will be doing in their meeting together. If the purpose of the interview is not brought out, the child feels passive and helpless in the face of a mysterious stiuation. (McDonald, 1965) If the child shows obvious feelings of anxiety, it is important that they be identified to assure the child that these feelings are understood, accepted, and appropriate for such a situation.

When seeing the child for an assessment, the following questions are important to keep in mind. What does the child focus on? What does the child avoid? When does the child become uncomfortable or anxious, and how is it manifested? What does the child do when he or she becomes anxious? What does the child communicate, directly and indirectly, about significant people (parents, siblings, peers, and teachers), significant areas of function (school, play, body, etc.), sexuality, and sexual identity? The therapist should attempt to identify and help the child deal with anxiety. If defensive measures are used to avoid conscious recognition of painful feelings, the failure itself becomes an important observation of the child (McDonald, 1965).

Latency-age children are the most frequently treated child population in clinics and agencies. The following questions are pertinent in assessing latency development: Are there indications of an emerging set of personal initiatives directed toward figures and experiences outside of the home and separate from family activities: Are there progressively "self" centered motivations toward schoolwork, especially reading? Is there an ability to make friends, or have a circle of friends? Is there some capacity for empathy? Has the child developed hobbies and appropriate peer play? Does the child have the capacity for "objective" observations and judgments in regard to each member of the family? Can the child plan for himself or herself? Are there indications of the types of ideal selves that motivate the child's behavior?

Diagnostic Impressions

Thus, with the aid of the Diagnostic Profile to organize material, diagnostic impressions, and preliminary formulations regarding the child can be made. They will be based on clinical observation of the child; and information from parents, teachers, and any additional sources such as pediatrician or psychologist. Clinical judgment, practice wisdom, inference, interpretation, and integration should reveal a total description of the child today (and the presenting complaint), including (1) the child's social context, comprising the family's socioeconomic-educational status and life style, and a description and general impression of parents; and (2) a descriptive cross-section of the child's current functioning, according to parents and others(e.g., peer relations, school functioning, relationships with parents and other adults, play, work, sexual identity, self-concept). All of this material should point to the nature and etiology of the child's major conflicts and anxieties; the child's way of dealing with frustration, delay, anger, guilt, etc.; and the nature of the child's object relations.

Conclusion of the Evaluation: The Follow-up Interview

There are various ways clinics describe the interview with child and parent where the assessment findings and subsequent recommendations are shared. The "follow-up interview," the "informing interview," or the "interpretive interview" is the most crucial point of contact thus far, and will· determine the worth of the entire evaluation. A poorly conducted session can undo all of the preceding work, while a successfully conducted session will consolidate observational findings, communicate the diagnosis and recommendations and cope with any anxiety and resistance aroused by the latter, and motivate the family to act on the recommendations (McDonald, 1965).

Parents and child are frequently anxious and eager to learn the results; even if they already know the findings and recommendations—which is often the case—they still need consolidation and integration. These tasks require the greatest skill of the clinician plus the parents' continued active participation. The purpose of the sharing is to make the total evaluation and assessment process a meaningful and effective experience for the parents and the child. If parents and child can integrate the findings and commit themselves to ongoing work, it can be a turning point in improving the well-being of both. It is not an end point, but a new beginning.

Anxiety and resistances generated by the diagnosis and recommendations may interfere with the family's ability to accept and integrate the evaluation experience, and they must be recognized and dealt with. Ordinarily, family members will have established a relationship with the clinician through the assessment process. This relationship should be monitored and differentiated in accord with the likelihood of the case remaining in the clinic, and the probability of the evaluator becoming the ongoing therapist. Too close a relationship can interfere with referral out or case transfer. Obviously, a negative experience during the evaluation will also interfere with ongoing work and recommended interventions. In many settings, clients and patients pass through a large number of staff members' offices, seeing one person for intake, another for the assessment process, and yet another for the ongoing treatment process. This reality is not presented as a blanket criticism. For some families, this shift is hard to tolerate, and for others it is handled with relative ease and comfort. This staffing and assignment pattern is routine in settings teaching trainees of various disciplines, all of whom must have varied practicum experiences and thereby cannot absorb every case with which they have had initial contact. Difficulties in the relationship between family and clinician during the assessment can interfere with the efficacy of the follow-up contact and can complicate the transfer of the child and parents to the new ongoing therapist. Usually, parents and child are seen separately for the follow-up interview.

The significance of the presenting symptoms must be ascertained, and important developmental, family, and environmental factors that have a bearing on the child's problematic current functioning must be reviewed. The parents should receive the clinician's explanation of the conflicts that seem to be confronting the child, and where and why the child seems "stuck" developmentally. The significance of the child's conflict and its potential effect on the child's long-range personality development and future adjustment often must be estimated. The clinician's sharing of this material can greatly increase the parents' insight into their child's problems.

Recommendations need to be presented simply and in clear language, minus the jargon of the profession. They are not always quickly accepted. Parents, child, and clinician frequently need to consider the emotional significance of recommendations, plus the practical matters, such as other needs in a household; other children; the time involved in treatment; and the scheduling of appointments, fees, and transportation for therapy.

The emotional impact of becoming a patient must not be underestimated. Latency-age children might very much desire therapy and cherish their relationship with their therapist, yet feel shame and stigma if their peers should find out they are in treatment. For example, Ann, a 10-year-old girl in treatment for two years, who is motivated for and invested in her therapy, and who has made steady and substantial improvements in her familial relationships, peer relationships, and academic work, still tells her inquiring friends that she can never play after school on specific days because of "dental" appointments. Ann is punctual for sessions and strongly cathected to her therapy and therapist. Her sophisticated, urban parents are in treatment themselves. Ann has sharply chastized them for ever revealing to close friends and relatives that she is in treatment: "If they want to air family business, they should blab about their treatment, not mine." Ann has only confided her secret to one peer, another adopted child who has also been in therapy.

Professionals often lose sight of the impact of therapy on a child and/or parents, minimizing the investment of time and energy, and the effect on a family's schedule of several appointments a week. Over-enthused beginner clinicians may swamp a family with expectations for a myriad of appointments and modalities of treatment, and erroneously see resistance when a family simply sets limits to their participation. Recommendations can also involve intensive therapy or serious changes in a family (e.g. when residential placement or special education is recommended for a child). Recommendations regarding ongoing parental contact frequently are less clearly formulated and will be covered in more detail later.[1]

McDonald (1965) notes that in follow-up interviews, parents often will respond to the clinician's recommendation of direct therapy for the child by pressing the clinician for management suggestions. If the therapist fails to recognize the parents' denial and resistance, and gives the requested suggestions,

> he is in effect saying that he himself does not believe it really will take a direct treatment of the child to help him. Instead of responding with details about management, the therapist must recognize and cope with the parents' anxiety. . . . Of course, it may at times be appropriate to give some immediate management advice during the follow-up, but it should be done when the parents can really hear and use it, rather than at a point where it acts only as a tranquilizer for their own anxiety [p. 607].

Parents generally will accept the reality that a long-standing problem cannot be "advised away" easily; and that, despite everyone's deeper understanding now, considerable work will be necessary to promote change and gain.

There are a number of situations where a therapist surmises that though a child presents some problems, the child has been brought to the agency as the parents' "ticket for admission." That is, they are unconsciously seeking help for themselves or for their marriage. A recommendation for individual or marital treatment may indeed be the recommendation, minus any offering of therapy to the child. There are instances where a child not engaged in direct treatment can benefit greatly by improvement of the family milieu or by improvements in parenting, via parent guidance.

McDonald's practical suggestions about the follow-up interview with the parents (1965) are useful to bear in mind. It is helpful to begin the follow-up interview by asking the parents how their child has been

[1]See Chapter 12.

since he or she was last seen. This question reaffirms the clinician's interest in the child and provides a logical entrance into the material of the follow-up proper. In presenting the diagnostic formulation to the parents, it is important to stress the child's assets as well as his or her problems. Not only is this approach reassuring but it is also relevant to the eventual resolution of the child's conflicts, which must be achieved via the ego strengths of the child.

The interview with the latency-age and older child usually should be done with the child alone, and after the interview with the parents. In general, the approach used with the parents is also appropriate for the child. The clinician should share with the child the assessment observations, impressions, and recommendations, and should help the child deal with anxiety and resistance. The recommendation should be presented as logically fitting into the understanding of the child's problems. A child might wish to know parental reactions, which frequently can be shared openly. However, if the parents have been very resistive to the recommendation, the clinician may withhold their full reaction from the child. It is not useful to create dissension between child and parents, since this only increases resistance to the recommendation and involvement in ongoing work. Obviously, honesty is important and honest impressions can be given to a child. When the clinician and parents differ, this fact can be recognized with the child while giving parental opinions and authority due respect.

Adolescents should always be seen for a follow-up interview, given the need for their understanding and cooperation. Some adolescents may accept and follow a recommendation in the face of parental opposition. Latency-age children sometimes may be seen for follow-up, but are often dependent on their parents for an adequate report about the evaluations. The nature of the latency-age child's problem and recommendation also may determine the necessity of seeing the child for follow-up. With preschool children, a follow-up with the child is rarely indicated. The closeness of parent and child at this time suggests the advantages of parents' handling the results with the clinician's help.

CHAPTER 5

Case Example of a Diagnostic Study—Fred

Introduction

The case of Fred is offered to acquaint the reader with the assessment process, the data gathered, the contact with parents, and the diagnostician's observations of the child. The organization of the material or diagnostic evaluation is in accord with the Developmental Profile, an application of Anna Freud's Diagnostic Profile (1965).

Diagnostic Evaluation

REFERRAL

Four months before his referral, Fred G., a 3-year-old white boy, developed a consonant stutter, which has worsened over time. The family pediatrician referred Fred to the clinic for a psychiatric evaluation because of the clinic's reputation for child diagnosis and treatment, and also because of the family's financial eligibility.

The family was scheduled by the intake worker for a "three-way" diagnostic evaluation, in which all three family members were interviewed simultaneously by different staff members, after which the case was staffed in a case conference. No other sources of information were probed at the time of the evaluation.

HISTORY OF COMPLAINT

Fred's stuttering was acutely precipitated. Mother even remembered the hour when the stuttering began. Father had been away from the family for thirteen months. He returned at noon one day, and by 6:00 p.m., Fred had begun stuttering. Prior to this, Fred's speech had developed normally and was very clear. In fact, mother said Fred was quite verbal. The stuttering has since increased, and when the family moved three months ago, Fred began to be teased about his stuttering by the other children on the Navy base where his father was stationed. This teasing angered both parents, who seemed empathic with Fred's shame. As mother said, "He doesn't know why he's stuttering, and it [the teasing] isn't fair."

The diagnosticians who interviewed the parents found each to be genuinely interested in and concerned about their child, whom they seem to be quite invested in. At the time of the original evaluation and staffing, therefore, it seemed clear that the parents were primarily motivated to bring the child to the clinic because of his interpsychic disability. However, at the time of the completion, or follow-up, interview, when both parents were seen and treatment was recommended for Fred, the parents requested contacts for themselves. Information obtained in subsequent child guidance contacts revealed that while the mother was empathic with Fred's difficulties, she also was using them to ask for help for herself. Subsequently, another clinician was assigned to the mother. It must be noted that at the time of the evaluation, it seemed as though Mr. and Mrs. G. were motivated solely by their child's problem.

THE CHILD TODAY

Apart from his stuttering, Fred seems to function fairly well for a child his age. There are no sleeping or eating difficulties, and toilet training had been accomplished with no subsequent regressions. Father did complain that Fred often attempts to sleep with parents, but he (father) has been taking a strong stand on the issue lately. A very strong-willed child, Fred sometimes attempts to boss around his mother. He plays with other children well but feels ashamed when they tease him about his stuttering. Neither father nor mother expressed any concern about other areas of Fred's functioning at the time of the evaluation. They both get along well with Fred, and father spoke with considerable pleasure about how his son had grown during his absence and how much he enjoys spending time with him now.

DEVELOPMENTAL HISTORY

Fred, a full-term baby, was born by Caesarean section because the umbilical cord had become positioned over his skull. Mother related that there was grave concern for their safety, but "we managed to pull through it." She was not aware of any problems that had been created by the Caesarean delivery and she was able to leave the hospital with her infant after five days. She noted proudly that Fred could almost stand up and braced himself when held, which she felt was somewhat unusual. Fred was considered by all to be a very active child. In describing him, mother said, "He's been such a good baby," and then, "I suppose I shouldn't still call him a baby, but he is a good baby." This was said with a great deal of warmth and feeling for the child.

Fred's early eating and sleeping patterns were good. He would wake once during the night for a feeding (he was bottle-fed) and then go back to sleep. There have been no sleep disturbances. Mother indicated that Fred had a pacifier until he was about 18 months old, at which time she rather abruptly took it away from him. She told the diagnostician Fred didn't need it anymore and also that it didn't look good hanging out of his mouth. However, after Mr. G. went overseas (when Fred was about 18 months old), he sent the boy a Superman pillow, which Fred still takes to bed with him every night. In terms of a transitional object, the diagnostician felt that the pacifier and the pillow were linked, inasmuch as the pacifier was lost at about the same time the father sent the pillow.

Mother remembered Fred's developmental milestones very well. He began sitting up at five months, standing at seven months, and walking at eight and a half months. He was readily toilet trained at age two and a half.

Mrs. G. became pregnant with Fred shortly after her marriage to Mr. G. Mr. G., who was having difficulty finding employment, joined the Navy toward the end of the pregnancy. Within two or three weeks of Fred's birth, father was transferred to a distant base for three months' schooling in mechanics, after which time he returned to the family. Then, when Fred was three months old, Mr. G. was restationed in California. The G.'s lived in California for fifteen months, but they moved several times in quick succession because of financial difficulties. They finally were placed in base housing when Fred was just under a year old. Then, when Fred was 18 months old, father was sent to Okinawa, where he remained for 13 months. At this point, mother and baby moved into a small, one-bedroom trailer in the maternal grandparents' (mother's mother and stepfather) backyard, and Mrs. G. and Fred shared a bed.

When Fred was about two, mother went with her stepfather to work on a construction job for about six weeks. Every weekend she saw Fred, who was being cared for by the maternal grandmother. When the job was finished, Mrs. G. returned to the trailer, where they lived until Fred was two and a half. At that time, she went to Detroit to care for her aged, dying grandfather. During this month-long separation, Mrs. G did not see Fred at all, and when she returned to him, she was saddened because he greeted her with initial indifference. There were no further separations or difficulties until her husband's return three months later, at which time Fred's stuttering began. The family was restationed a month later at their present base.

Father and son have gotten along well since father's return. Father is greatly pleased by Fred's growth and enjoys playing with him. Fred is interested in airplanes and boats, and father likes to take him to the hangers where he works. Mother and son are also close, and Mrs. G. enjoys staying home with Fred.

POSSIBLE SIGNIFICANT ENVIRONMENTAL INFLUENCES

The G.'s are decidedly lower-middle-class in terms of values and life styles. Father is a low-ranking technician in the Navy and formerly was a truck driver. Neither parent is college educated. Their speech evidences their lack of complete education, and their clothes, the financial difficulties encountered in the service. The diagnostician who saw the mother felt that cultural factors needed to be considered in this case. He felt her to be sincere but uneducated, and suggested that her empathic breaks with the child (for instance, sleeping in the same bed with Fred while her husband was away and leaving him at age two) were egosyntonic to her social class and value system.

Mrs. G.'s father was physically abusive toward her mother, and her parents were finally divorced when she was about eight. Her mother remarried when she was ten, and Mrs. G. is very fond of her stepfather. However, his work (heavy construction) necessitated frequent moves when she was growing up. In fact, in one year she attended nine schools. She failed two different grades, but did much better in high school, with the exception of history and science, which she failed. High school was a positive experience for Mrs. G. and she formed a number of close friendships there. Her parents were settled, creating a stable residential situation for the first time in years. After high school, she attended a school for veterinary technicians, but flunked out of this program. She subsequently enrolled in bookkeeping and accounting courses, at which time she met her husband. They began living together and eventually got married.

Mr. G. had some difficulty giving background information about his family of origin. His parents separated when he was nine, and even though his father remained in the same area, he saw very little of him thereafter. Mr. G.'s father was an alcoholic who was not physically or emotionally available to him. According to Mr. G., his two older brothers did not provide support or guidance, either. After he graduated from high school, Mr. G. got special automative training, at which time he met Mrs. G. He did have some contact with his father during his adult life and was attempting to establish a closer relationship at the time he left for Okinawa. Mr. G.'s father, who had been ill, died a few days after Mr. G. departed for Okinawa. This was extremely difficult and painful for Mr. G., who had been keenly disappointed and frustrated in his relationship with his father. He expressed a strong wish to have a very different kind of relationship with his own son.

While mother was away from Fred (and while father was in Okinawa), the child was cared for by the maternal grandmother. Although little was mentioned about the grandmother in the diagnostic interviews, father did state that Fred had some difficulty separating from the grandparents when the family moved to their present base, as Fred had established a very close relationship with them.

INTERVIEWS

Fred was seen for two diagnostic interviews, once with his mother and once by himself. In the first interview, when Fred refused to leave his mother, the diagnostician suggested that they both come in for a while and later, if Fred felt comfortable, mother would leave. As it happened, mother stayed for only twenty minutes. Initially, Fred sat on his mother's lap and resisted her taking his coat off. The diagnostician reiterated that mother would stay until Fred felt relaxed and comfortable about being alone with the diagnostician. Some play materials (crayons, paper, a teddy bear, a toy telephone, play dough, a water gun, a ball, and a cigar box full of small cars) were offered, but Fred expressed no interest in them. Instead, he showed the diagnostician some small toys (two cars and two people) he had brought with him from home, and she expressed interest and appreciation. Then Fred looked up at the office window (it was a basement office) and expressed curiosity about the cars being "up high." The diagnostician explained that the cars just seemed high because she and Fred were downstairs, but he didn't seem to understand. Then the diagnostician took the cigar box full of cars and one of Fred's little people and showed him how, when the person was up, the cars were on the same level, but when the person went downstairs, the cars were higher. This made Fred laugh and he took his coat off and asked the clinician to do this again, which she did.

Fred then jumped off mother's lap and said he wanted to play with the play dough. He played with it for about fifteen minutes, which showed a good attention span for a child his age. He used the lids of the cans to press down on small balls of dough, making thin cakes, which he offered to his mother (still needing to involve her in his sphere of action). Mother acted appreciative of these gifts. The clinician commented on how much fun it was to squish the play dough and give mother gifts. A few minutes later, Fred tentatively offered the clinician a play dough cake, but he took it back a moment later. He continued to play with the play dough, using all the different colors and eventually making one big cake. On his own initiative, he then began to put the play dough away. He then noticed that there were a few pieces of play dough left on the rug and he asked the clinician to put them in the trash, which she did. It seemed that after his free play, Fred needed to be supercontrolled.

Fred then began to experiment with the toys, trying them all before settling on one. He picked up the toy telephone, yelled "no one home," and slammed it down. He ran the cars across the floor. He picked up the gun and said, "water, water," and then put it down. Finally, he went over to the toy cabinet and got a box of toy soldiers. He took delight in taking the pieces out, one by one, and asking the clinician what they were—a soldier, a tank, a rifle, etc. At this point, Fred's mother, who was no longer directly involved in Fred's play, stood up and told Fred she was going for her interview now. Fred looked sad, which the clinician commented on; then she asked Fred if it would be all right if just the two of them played for a while, after which she promised to take him out to his mother. He reluctantly agreed. He kept playing with the soldiers, placing some of them on the chair his mother had just vacated. The clinician commented that he seemed to want to be near mother. About five minutes later, he asked where his mother was, and the clinician told him that she was seeing Mr. S. and that she would take him out to his mother when their time was up. This appeared to reassure him.

Fred spent the rest of the hour having the diagnostician set up soldiers, which he then shot down ("pow pow") with the water gun. He seemed delighted when the gun made each soldier fall. Five minutes before their time was up, the clinician told Fred they had just a few minutes left. He was also told that he would be coming back to see her one more time. He responded with a loud "no!" which turned out to be a reaction to the hour coming to a close, rather than to the idea of coming back. He was extremely cooperative about cleaning up, however, and apparently happy to be reunited with his mother in the waiting room. A rather severe stutter was apparent throughout the interview ("m-m-mommy," "c-c-car," etc.).

At the beginning of the second diagnostic interview, Fred protested (with a whining vowel stutter, "m-o-o-o-ommy!") when his mother explained that he would be seeing the clinician alone today; yet, he came rather agreeably when the clinician stretched out her hand to him. He seemed to relax when he saw the toys and asked if he could again take out the play dough. Fred's play with the play dough paralleled the play in the first hour (he made balls or hunks of it, then squashed each piece with a lid, made a cake, and said it was "breakfast time"). The clinician introduced a family of puppets to eat the "breakfast," hoping that Fred would show her what breakfast was like at home. The puppets in the box included mother, father, big brother, sister, toddler/baby, and various animals. Fred served breakfast to the mother, the father, and then the baby. He then said, "Daddy go to work," and marched the father away under the desk. Then he harshly commanded the mother, "Go to bed!" Empathizing with how Fred must feel when mother dictates his bedtime, the clinician took the mother puppet's part and said, "Do I have to go to bed? I don' wanna go to bed." Fred replied, "Go to bed!" and he threw the mother in the empty box. He then took the big brother puppet from another pile of puppets, fed him breakfast, and commanded him to go to bed. This figure was then thrown in the box on top of the mother puppet. The baby puppet then went through the same routine, so that all three figures ended up in bed together. Fred made the father puppet come home from work, took the other puppets out of the box/bed, and served them all more play dough. He also brought each figure a drink of milk, using the empty play dough cans for glasses.

Fred asked for the box of soldiers and played "shoot-the-soldiers-with-the-water-gun," a game he had enjoyed during the first hour. He also took delight in shooting down the family puppets as well as the animal puppets. Fred responded to the clinician's comments that he seemed to enjoy shooting the soldiers and puppets by turning and shooting her. He seemed delighted when she slumped her head and said, "Ya got me," and ordered this reenacted several times. However, he then appeared to become anxious and hid behind the side of her desk. She asked, "Where's Fred? Where's Fred?" and they played a game of hide-and-seek, which ended with the clinician being shot with the water gun when she found Fred. Fred seemed beside himself with joy and had this reenacted about eight times. He asked if they could go back to the play dough and served the clinician "breakfast" (a play dough cake) at the play table. The clinician indicated that they had five minutes left and suggested that they put the toys away together. Fred seemed to enjoy clean-up time, especially as he was able to incorporate a good deal of aggressiveness into the activity. With great vindictiveness, he threw the family of puppets and the soldiers back into their respective boxes. The clinician told Fred that it had been nice to meet him and that perhaps they would meet again. Would he like that? Fred nodded "yes" and left cheerfully. During this second interview, Fred stuttered only about half as much as he had during the first one and, on the whole, his speech seemed clearer.

DIAGNOSTIC FORMULATIONS

Fred, a well-developed, bright 3-year-old, initially related to the diagnostician with appropriate shyness, but then relaxed as he sensed her acceptance of his feelings and behavior. He related to the clinician in a friendly way, but more as a self-object than as a person in her own right (ordering her around in the play situation to fulfill his inner needs). The circumspection with which he examined the toys (and the clinician) indicates that he is not an impulsive child and that he is eager to please. He was able to bring closure to free play by helping clean up. While he was initially unable to separate from mother, he was gradually able to play without involving her directly and handled the separation (when mother did leave) quite well, turning the chair she vacated into a transitional object and verbalizing his concern about her whereabouts. On the other hand, it is significant that he had to ask where she was even though he had already been told, and also that he cried when she wouldn't join him for the second interview, even though he had been told about this previously. In sum, although separation is definitely an issue for Fred, the way in which he handled separation from his mother in both diagnostic interviews points toward a positive prognosis.

Fred showed continuity from hour to hour (resuming play with the play dough, an activity of the first hour, in the second session) and, at the same time, the ability to expand on this play through increased experimentation with new play materials and games. In both hours, Fred's play was aggressive. Indeed, the decreased stuttering may have been the result of his expression of aggression in the first hour (shooting the soldiers). In the second hour, Fred seemed to zero in on the source of the aggression.

Looking back, the scene with the puppet family seemed to be a microcosm of this diagnostic statement, in play form. It showed Fred's psychic dilemma: daddy going away, mother and child being in bed together, and then a stranger joining them. The stranger, of course, was Mr. G. returning from Okinawa (to Fred he was indeed a stranger), coming between Fred and his mother, who had shared an extremely close, overstimulating relationship in his absence. In the play, father was a split object. Although all the figures eventually ended up in the bed together and eating together, it was not a pleasant play reunion. In fact, Fred's next play association was to shooting soldiers with a gun. The clinician's reconstruction of Fred's conflict, then, on the basis of the interview material and the information provided by mother and father, pointed toward Fred's stuttering (speech inhibition) as a defense against hostile aggressiveness, the hostility having been triggered by father's return from Okinawa (experienced by Fred as separation from mother) and, more importantly, by mother's separations from Fred during father's absence (particularly the month-long separation when he was two and a half).

In general, Fred's development seemed to have moved along at a fairly age-appropriate pace. His oral development seemed good, and there were no eating or sleeping disturbances or medical problems. His toilet training seemed adequate with no regressions, and there did not seem to be any strong fixations at a drive level. Rather, his stuttering problem was related to the painful separations from his mother during his second year, a time when much of the normal separation-individuation process normally takes place. The first separation when mother worked on the construction job was probably somewhat repaired by her weekend visits with Fred. Fred's indifference toward mother after her return from her month-long visit to her grandfather most likely signified intense anger over her having left him, which he had to act out behaviorally rather than express verbally. There was some recovery from this trauma when Mrs. G. returned and she and Fred resumed their overstimulating living arrangements, but when Mr. G. was due to return (an event which Mrs. G. anticipated eagerly), her cathexis again flowed away from Fred. To Fred, his father's return probably was experienced not as a reunion but as another separation from mother. It was now father, not Fred, who shared mother's bed. Again, Fred could not verbalize his feelings, but defended against his aggression by inhibiting his speech. At the age of 2, Fred's most recently acquired skill was speech and, as it developed during the period of the separations, speech development became attached to the loss of his mother.

That Fred's aggressiveness is linked to pain over separation is well illustrated by interview material, particularly in the second hour, when the hide-and-seek game ended not with a "peak-a-boo, I see you," but with a shot between the clinician's eyes. The question arises: Why was Fred unable to express his aggression directly with mother as he did with the clinician? The answer can be found in the second diagnostic interview: immediately after the aggressive hide-and-seek game, Fred served the clinician breakfast at the play table, offering her a "gift" of play dough. He was clearly afraid of losing his mother's love if he expressed his aggression too openly, so he had to placate mother by disguising it (stuttering bears no overt resemblance to hostility). Mother had to be pleased at all costs, for if she found out about Fred's anger, she might be lost to him—or so Fred feared.

An interesting observation in hindsight was Fred's angry display toward the toy telephone in the first interview ("No one home!"). In the early weeks of treatment, Fred continued to disdain the telephone.

Eventually, it came out that during his mother's absence, she had tried to call Fred on the phone, but for him this had been a painful reminder of her absence rather than a reassurance that she still existed and would return.

In sum, Fred seems to be suffering from a developmental interference that took place during the separation-individuation phase of development. His stuttering may be seen as a defense against rage over his mother's repeated absences and also signifies the giving up of his most recently acquired ego achievement, speech.

His mother is full of good intentions but has not always been empathic with Fred's emotional needs, having no understanding of the effect of their separations. Thus, at an age when his ego was weak and immature, Fred had to deal with the two maternal extremes of overstimulation and prolonged absence. As a result of the separations that occurred between the third and fourth subphases of Fred's separation-individuation (and transition periods are always times of marked vulnerability for the child), Fred suffered from "true separation anxiety," with consequent rage defended against through stuttering.

Fred is too young to be considered neurotic, categorically. His character structure is still very much in the making, and his symptom is a direct response to external factors in his life. He therefore falls into the diagnostic category of "developmental interferences," which concern external conflicts between the child's drive and his environment. In contrast, the older neurotic child, adolescent, or adult suffers from internalized conflicts between the different structures (i.e., id, ego, and superego) of the personality.

PART III

Psychopathology of Childhood

CHAPTER 6

Autism and Psychosis

Autism

Definition

Of all developmental disabilities, autism is one of the most difficult to understand.

> Wide differences in severity, periodic changes of the symptoms, confusing and inconsistent nosology and the lack of specific physical signs make diagnosis a difficult procedure. The behavior of autistic children is bewildering to parents, and thus it is often difficult to obtain an adequate developmental history. Unless the physician suspects autism and knows which symptoms and signs to elicit, the diagnostic process may be thwarted from the outset. Too often parents are told, "Let's wait, he is just slow in developing and will probably catch up soon." Initial parental concern arises at different ages [Ornitz and Ritvo, 1976, p. 609].

One mother may note oddness and strangeness at birth and in the first few months—while others seek no attention or evaluation until the child is school age. Ornitz and Ritvo (1976) note that the most frequent initial complaint is that of a delay in speech development, while earlier, subtler symptoms are often overlooked or denied. Thus, they recommend always including autism in the differential diagnosis when evaluating any child with a developmental disability.

The syndrome of autism was first identified by Kanner in 1943, when he noted "autistic disturbances of affective contact." In 1944, he employed the term "early infantile autism," stressing that the symptoms occurred in early infancy. In the 1950s, in the study of severe disorders in young children, the concept of "atypical development" was elaborated on and came to include Heller's disease, childhood psychosis, childhood schizophrenia, and autism or mental defect. Rank and her colleagues noted the following outstanding clinical symptoms:

> withdrawal from people, retreat into a world of fantasy, mutism or the use of language for autistic purposes, bizarre posturing, seeming meaningless stereotyped gestures, impassivity or violent outbursts of anxiety and rage, identification with inanimate objects or animals, and excessively inhibited or excessively uninhibited expressions of impulses. While the specific clinical picture varies from child to child, the features common to all are lack of contact with reality, little or no communication with others, and a lack of integration and uniformity in ego development [Rank, 1955, pp. 491–92].

Mahler has used the term "symbiotic psychosis" to describe children who present symptoms similar to those of the above group along with a tenacious clinging to their parents. Ornitz and Ritvo (1968) suggest that since such clinging behavior may alternate with emotional unresponsiveness, the term "symbiotic psychosis" does not necessarily describe an independent disorder. In her studies of schizophrenia in childhood, Bender (1956) has employed labels such as "pseudoretarded" and "pseudodefective" to underscore the difference between typical mental retardation and autism. "Childhood schizophrenia," as well as the more general and less clearly defined terms "infantile psychosis" and "childhood psychosis," are also used for such child patients. Obviously, there is semantic confusion and controversy regarding these labels. Some researchers stress that autism and childhood schizophrenia are two distinct syndromes. Rutter (1972) emphasizes the following differences: (1) familial factors (absent in autism but present in schizophrenia), (2) age of onset, (3) symptoms, and (4) history and course of the disease. Another view holds that there is a continuum of one disease process that includes autism and childhood schizophrenia.

Bettelheim has linked parental pathology to the child's autistic behavior. He views the autistic behavior as the result of the child's paranoid reaction to the mother made chronic by the mother's unconscious behavior during the child's early development. He conceives of the nursing infant as passionate rather than passive, and emphasizes body language and mutuality between mother and infant. He notes the importance of how the infant is held (gently or rigidly) and believes that tensions create nursing struggles, with resultant maternal reactions to being rejected. His view suggests that autistic children fail to become active in their own behalf and suffer from once having had a vague image of a more satisfying world. He views infantile autism as a state of mind that develops in reaction to feeling oneself in an extreme situation "entirely without hope" (Bettelheim, 1950). He states that autistic children do indeed relate to persons, though not in a positive way. He notes a manner of "passionate indifference" which defends the child against the parents' conscious or unconscious wish that the child not exist.

Mahler conceptualizes early infantile autism as a fixation at, or regression to, the most primitive normal phase of extrauterine life— namely, the normal autistic stage. She notes that the most conspicuous symptom is that the mother, the representative of the outside world, seems not to be perceived at all by the child. Like Bettelheim's notion of autism as a defense, Mahler's (1968) view is that the child's self, the bodily self, seems not to be distinguished from the inanimate objects in the environment, so that there is a "primary lack or a loss of differentiation between living and lifeless matter, which as an acquired somato-psychic archaic defense develops soon or immediately after birth." Mahler notes that the Spitz studies revealed no anticipatory posture at nursing, no reaching-out gestures, and no specific smiling response. Autistic children characteristically become attached to a highchair, a toy, or some other lifeless object. They turn a deaf ear toward mother and the entire world; there is a specific and active warding off of the mother. Mothers frequently complain that "I could never reach my baby; he never smiled, cuddled or made any appeal for help." It is Mahler's thesis that the symptomatology and behavior patterns of infantile autism are due to infants' inability to utilize the ego functions of the symbiotic partner, the mother, to orient themselves in the outer and inner world. Thus, in Mahler's view, these babies enclose themselves in a small world of their own.

Descriptive Characteristics

There are conspicuous characteristic behavior patterns of infantile autism, such as an obsessive desire for preservation of sameness and a stereotyped preoccupation with a few inanimate objects and actions towards which the infant shows the only sign of emotional attachments. These preoccupations and intolerance of change are what, in Mahler's view, distinguishes autism from an organic syndrome. Another difference between the autistic child and the organically damaged or psychotic child is the former's seeming self-sufficient contentedness when left alone. Many autistic children are described as presenting an intelligent and pensive facial expression but "looking through" people. Some are mute while others talk to their inanimate fetish companion or imaginary objects with gestures; if they do speak, their language is not used for functional communication—rather, it is like the signals seen in earliest infancy. Mahler notes that autistic children command the adult to serve as a semianimate or inanimate mechanical device. All of these behaviors are attempts to "de-differentiate and de-animate, as they try to shut out, to hallucinate away the potential source of sensory perception of the living world which demands emotional social responses" (Mahler, 1968). There is a lack of hearing response and frequently no startle reaction to the mother's voice, but there is fixed attention to language *not* used for communication. Most frequently, this language is echolalic, repeating phrases heard on a mechanical device such as a phonograph or TV. Noted is a grossly deficient pain sensitivity, as well as little sense of bladder and bowel urgency or satiation following a meal. There is generally a paucity of autoerotic activities and a prevalence of rather aggressive behaviors such as head banging, self biting, and rocking. The latter activities seem to indicate a pathological sense of body boundaries; they are repeated to enable the child to feel alive.

Mahler distinguishes between the autistic child and the symbiotically psychotic child as follows: the autistic child has never libidinally cathected the mother whereas the symbiotic psychotic child has done so, but either is fixated at, or has regressed to, the stage of preobject relationship where the mental representation of the mother is fused with that of the self. Overwhelming as are both pathologies, Mahler's developmental view suggests that autism is the most primitive childhood disorder, and that symbiotic psychosis, by virtue of some libidinal cathexis to mother, suggests more ego development, and thus a somewhat better prognosis. It must be noted that at the beginning of the symbiotic phase, the autistic shell that protected the infant against external stimuli begins to crack. Protection against excessive, stressful stimuli is now the responsibility of the mother—who becomes the protective shield. The symbiotic psychosis points to poorly differentiated self- and object-representations, but a definite human tie, whereas autism is a defensive armor resulting from total fear of human contact and the danger of annihilation. It is crucial to attempt to ascertain the highest level of ego development and object cathexis, in that frequently a child achieves some human tie and entry into symbiosis and some partial separation-individuation but then regresses to the autistic position, to "secondary autism" as a "secondary defense" (Mahler, 1968).

Mahler's conceptualization is based on her developmental perspective, namely, that under ordinary circumstances the infant emerges from the "normal autistic" phase of the first weeks of life (Freud's primary narcissistic stage and Spitz's objectless stage) to enter into a symbiotic bonding with mother. The normal symbiotic phase (Mahler's term borrowed from biology to note a close functional association of two organisms to their mutual advantage) coincides in time with what Anna Freud called "the need-satisfying object relationship." Anna Freud and Spitz speak of the preobject and part-object phase, when the object (mother) brings relief of tension, imprinting in the child's memory traces of good mothering that constitute confident expectations of forthcoming relief and that lead to the omnipotent mother-child fusion and undifferentiation.

In a review of research on infantile autism, Rutter (1969) disputes the psychogenic view of autism developed by Bettelheim and others, pointing first to the oft-noted and puzzling reality of an autistic child's normal siblings, who are difficult to account for if the family was indeed a pathogenic breeding ground. He also questions the concept of the so-called "critical period"—0–6 months—during which the child is supposed to experience mother's unconscious rejection, noting that developmental research has shown that an infant of 0–6 months simply does not have the perceptual equipment necessary to pick up subtle rejections from the mother. Waxler and Mishler (1972) explored the patterns of communication in families with a psychotic child; they suggested that any variations in parental behavior toward the psychotic child and the normal siblings were a *response* to the ill child rather than a causative factor. Controlled studies have shown that the extreme emotional stress of having an autistic child can induce or precipitate emotional disorder in susceptible parents (Creak, 1960). Hintgen and Bryson's review (1969) of recent developments in the study of severe childhood disorders rules out parental psychopathology as a causative factor in child psychosis. Research has centered on neurobiological explorations, biochemical research, and neurophysiological studies. Recently, there also have been metabolic and hematological research efforts. There have been attempts to link autism with premature birth, developmental aphasia, retardation, specific organic brain syndromes, maternal deprivation, and a brain stem disturbance involving the central connections of the vestibular system (Ornitz, 1974).

Despite the wildly divergent explanations for this syndrome, most clinicians concur on the major behavioral characteristics: disturbance of perception; disturbance of development; and disturbance of relating, as manifested by poor or deviant eye contact, delayed or absent social smile, delayed or absent anticipatory response to being picked up, aversion to physical contact, and a preference for the inanimate to the human object. There are disturbances of speech, and language, which may take the form of total delay, as in mutism, or may confine themselves to fixations along the normal course of development. Echolalia is a common feature and frequently is accompanied by misuse or reversal of pronouns. When functional speech is developed it is usually atonal, mechanistic, and lacking in inflection and emotion. There are frequent disturbances of motility, and noted commonly are bizarre movements and mannerisms, such as floating, toe-walking, and twirling, twiddling and/or flapping of the hands. Some children make lunging or darting movements of their bodies, rock, sway, roll or bang their head, or bite themselves.

Primary autism usually is clearly demonstrated by 36 months of age via "irregularities in development, and disturbances in the modulation of sensory input, relatedness, and language. The presence of these symptoms is necessary and sufficient to establish the diagnosis" (Ornitz and Ritvo, 1976, p. 612). There are specific diseases that are known to occur in association with autism. These include congenital rubella, specific organic brain syndrome, mental retardation, and seizure disorder. In addition, one must differentiate autism from diseases with overlapping symptoms, such as environmental deprivation (maternal deprivation and hospitalism), anaclitic depression, developmental aphasia, and sensory deficits. This last category includes syndromes that have been described in the research literature under the rubrics of disintegrative psychosis, late-onset psychosis, acquired autism, and childhood schizophrenia (nonorganic type).

Treatment Interventions

Given the dizzying array of approaches to and explanations of the etiology of autism, there is understandably a vast array of varying interventions proposed. In Whittaker's rejection of the family etiology hypothesis (1976), he criticizes Bettelheim's "parentectomy," or complete separation of the child from home and family so that the child undergoes a total therapeutic reliving experience in a residential treatment center. Ornitz and Ritvo (1976) emphasize that there is no rational or specific treatment for autism:

> In spite of strong claims by partisans of particular treatment approaches and much dedicated effort that has gone into their implementation, no treatment has been demonstrated to alter the natural history of the disease. Many different approaches have been attempted, including family therapy, psychotherapy and counseling for parents, psychotherapy for the autistic child, behavior therapy, speech therapy and special education. Therapeutic approaches also include day treatment, residential placement, psychiatric

hospitalization, medication with a number of different psychotropic drugs, hormones, megavitamins, sensory isolation and even LSD [pp. 617–618].

However, despite partial improvements such as decreased symptoms, autistic children definitely remain autistic. Ornitz and Ritvo (1976) advocate early recognition, continuous medical supervision, periodic reevaluations, and a flexible approach. "Parents should be viewed as paraprofessionals who frequently can best implement symptomatic treatments such as behavior therapy" (p. 618). They see behavior therapy as a universal ingredient in all good parenting, connoting the parents' approval and disapproval. Above all, these authors advocate patience: one must recognize that spontaneous improvements and regressions are likely to occur despite the influence of the most optimistically presented symptomatic treatment plans. They conclude that the prognosis is guarded; despite treatment, approximately two-thirds of all patients will continue to manifest intellectual and cognitive deficits severe enough that they remain classified as retarded throughout their lives.

This bleak picture is only mitigated when we consider the distinction between primary and secondary autism, the latter syndrome connoting more adequate initial development, followed by regression and atypical child development in response to the actual or emotional loss of the mother, late in the first year or early in the second year of life. Mahler notes that the peak of symbiosis occurs in the third quarter of the first year, at the onset of the separation-individuation phase, when the infant is just beginning to differentiate between self and object. Separation-individuation takes approximately two years (from about 6 to 30 months of age), depending on the child's developmental readiness, and pleasure and ability to function independently. Separation-individuation is an intrapsychic process in the context of physical and optimal emotional availability of the mother. If there is a disruption in this process, symbiotic psychosis can occur. If the symbiotic defensive regression fails, the child is forced into the autistic position; thus, secondary autism is seen as a secondary defense. Given the fact that the child originally had moved beyond autism, the prognosis for secondary autism, though guarded, is far less bleak than that for primary autism. The infant in the symbiotic phase has become aware that need-satisfaction cannot be provided by oneself but comes from somewhere or someone outside. During symbiosis, a state of undifferentiated psychic fusion between infant and mother, the infant's "I" and "not I" are not distinct from one another. This "delusional somatopsychic omnipotent fusion with the representation of the mother, and in particular with the delusion of a common boundary between two physically separate individuals" (Mahler et al., 1975, p. 45) is the bedrock and basis of all subsequent human ties and bonds. Given traumas and disruptions, it can also be the point to which a pathological ego may regress in cases of severe disturbances of individuation, such as the psychoses (Mahler, 1968).

Case of Jimmy

The case of Jimmy is offered to acquaint the reader with a latency-age child who presents a classic picture of secondary autism. Rarely is a syndrome observed in pure form; often both autistic and symbiotic symptoms are apparent. A provisional diagnosis frequently suggests a combination of all the childhood psychoses. A differential diagnosis is often difficult to obtain and should be more than a label. The goal of diagnosis is to ascertain the highest level of ego development achieved by a given child, which is of prognostic value and also offers guidelines for treatment planning. Thus, strengths as well as weaknesses are assessed. However, with autistic children the ego development is meager, given the massive arrests and/or regression.

Diagnostic Evaluation

REFERRAL

Jimmy S., a 6-year-old, black, handsome, normally developed, Catholic boy, was referred by the Dysfunctioning Child Center at R. Hospital with a diagnosis of childhood psychosis with autistic features. Jimmy's pediatrician had referred him to R. Hospital. There were no previous psychiatric hospitalizations or treatment. Jimmy was admitted to R. Hospital with a provisional diagnosis of childhood schizophrenia, symbiotic type. Presenting complaints upon admission were: increasing withdrawal, secondary autistic defenses, severe temper tantrums, minimal speech, echolalia, sleep disturbances, and rocking.

INFORMANTS

Mr. S., a 41-year-old, slightly obese but handsome black Catholic man, had exceptional difficulty in involving himself with Jimmy's hospital treatment. For the first five or six months of Jimmy's hospitalization, he failed to keep numerous appointments and was hospitalized himself on two occasions. The last hospitalization involved excision of a cyst from his back as well as a hemorrhoidectomy. Although he was basically a warm, sensitive, depressed individual, he was quite guarded, defensive, and distrustful initially. He felt tremendously guilty about his neglect of Jimmy throughout Jimmy's earlier years. He was fearful of his own emotional state and as a result was greatly threatened at the prospect of involving himself at the hospital. Initially, he also tended to be manipulative and distant. However, later Mr. S. became very much involved in the diagnostic process in the treatment of his son.

Mrs. S., a 43-year-old, obese but attractive and neatly dressed black woman, was extremely depressed, preoccupied, slightly agitated, and masochistic. She was very much involved all along in Jimmy's hospitalization. Frustration with her husband's noninvolvement made her threaten him with divorce action if he did not become more involved with Jimmy.

Both Mr. and Mrs. S. were needy, dependent, distrustful people who often tested the clinician's genuine interest in them as well as in their son. Although they became increasingly cooperative and motivated in the course of their weekly therapy sessions, both continued to wear sunglasses to each interview, symbolic of their continued attempts to maintain some distance. Both Mr. and Mrs. S. had a history of creating problematic explosive situations at work and elsewhere, which they then passively (almost seemingly inadvertently) triggered off, making themselves "victims of circumstances." Despite such manipulative measures, which gradually diminished over time, the couple elicited very warm and positive counterreactions from the clinician.

DEVELOPMENTAL HISTORY

During the time that Mrs. S. was pregnant with Jimmy, the family lived in a four-room apartment. Mr. and Mrs. S. slept in the bedroom and the three children slept in the dining room. Mr. and Mrs. S. were actively looking for a home.

During this time Mr. S., a policeman, was having considerable employment difficulty. He was accused of "loafing on the job." He stated that at the time he was, in fact, not aggressive in his police work and was not making any arrests. During the third trimester of Mrs. S.'s pregnancy, Mr. S. was transferred to another district where he was the only nonwhite police officer. He felt that his superiors were placing him in an uncomfortable district. However, Mr. S. found that he liked most of his new colleagues.

Mrs. S. experienced morning sickness during her pregnancy with Jimmy. She also had fibroid tumors of the uterus and moderate toxemia, which made her edematous and hypertensive. Mr. S. stated that his wife worried considerably about the varicosities on her legs.

Jimmy was born on March 19-- after a ten-hour labor. Mrs. S. and Jimmy remained hospitalized for eight days. Jimmy weighed 7 lbs., 8 oz. at birth and was considered a healthy baby. A maternal aunt went to live with Mrs. S. and Jimmy for a short time upon Mrs. S.'s return from the hospital. A paternal aunt cared for the S.'s other children in her own home. Jimmy cried a lot initially but then became "very good," always appearing content and moderately active.

Jimmy was breast-fed until he was six months old. He had a very difficult time being weaned from the breast and was stubborn and rejective of the bottle when it was offered. It was at this time that mother started school five evenings a week. Mrs. S. was pursuing a masters degree in music and had one more year to complete. During this time, Jimmy rejected everything any member of the family offered him.

Mr. and Mrs. S. reported that Jimmy was saying "Mama" and "Dada" at six months. He never crawled and began walking at eleven months of age.

At the age of one and a half, Jimmy would say "Leave me alone" and would not talk after that. At this time, Mrs. S. finished school and began teaching kindergarten half-time. Mrs. S.'s difficulties with the head teacher, whom she believed was jealous of her, made her extremely nervous; she cried a great deal but managed to finish out the academic year.

When Jimmy was about two years old, several significant events took place. First, Jimmy's maternal grandfather, with whom he had spent a great deal of time, died of a heart attack at the age of 76. Mrs. S. reacted to her father's death with shock, hysteria, and depression. She was unable to talk or become interested in anything. Second, the family purchased a new home and moved into it. Third, Jimmy's paternal grandmother and 17-year-old aunt moved in with the S.'s. The paternal grandmother took over Jimmy's care, becoming very involved and interested in him. Bowel and bladder training were instituted on the grandmother's arrival and completed when Jimmy was three. Jimmy liked to watch TV commercials but showed no interest in any of the programs until the age of five. Fourth, Mrs. S. began teaching first grade in another school, but again, difficulty with the other teachers, on account of their "jealousy," led to her dismissal.

When Jimmy was three years old, he would ask for milk, saying, "want milk." Mrs. S. noticed that he did not use any personal pronouns. At the age of three and a half, Jimmy began attending nursery school.

When Jimmy was four years old, his mother miscarried at five months due to uterine fibroids. At the same time, the paternal grandmother was also hospitalized. It was found that she had advanced cancer of the pancreas; she died four months later. Mr. S. reacted very strongly, crying frequently and becoming depressed, uninterested, and preoccupied. Once again, he began getting complaints about his work. Mr. S.'s. sister had several nervous breakdowns as a result of their mother's death.

At the age of five, Jimmy was advanced to the 5-year-old nursery group. However, he insisted upon returning to the 4-year-old nursery group and was permitted to stay there the following year. Supposedly, Jimmy was getting along fairly well in nursery school.

MEDICAL HISTORY

Jimmy received all the childhood immunizations. Although as an infant he was susceptible to colds, he never had any serious illnesses. The only common childhood disease that he had was the mumps, at age five.

PARENTS

Father's early childhood was characterized by numerous long separations from his parents, who were entertainers and traveled a great deal. His aunts took care of him when his parents were away. When he was two, his parents separated, and he was shifted around between his aunts and his mother's closest friend until the age of seven.

At the age of eight, Mr. S. was placed in a Catholic boarding school, where he remained for the next two years. He recalls feeling very lonely and depressed in this understaffed school. At the age of ten, when Mr. S.'s mother remarried, he left the boarding school and took up residence with his mother and his stepfather. Mr. S. refers to his stepfather as "father," condemning his biological father. Mr. S.'s mother traveled off and on with a band throughout his youth; Mr. S. attributes his lack of respect for, and frequent hatred of, women to his mother's constant desertions.

At 16, Mr. S. enlisted in the army, where he served for two years. After an honorable discharge from the army, he played pro football for a year. Subsequently, he enrolled in a musical college while working part-time at a post office. After three years of college he quit, stating "I never finish anything." When he was 21, Mr. S.'s youngest sister was born and he became her caretaker. He spoke of his mother having changed from a jovial, direct, strong-willed person into a very high-strung, nervous, moody person who felt that nobody loved her. At 22, Mr. S. secured a civilian job as a night security man for the army headquarters. During working hours, he drank heavily and wrote poetry. He became a professional gambler as a sideline. He maintained both of these jobs until he married his current wife some five years later.

Mother's parents married at age 14 and lived in South Carolina. Mrs. S., who was the sixth of nine children, grew up in the north, where her family had moved to get away from intense racial prejudice. When Mrs. S. was seven years old, a man in the apartment building where the S.'s lived attempted to molest her and one of her sisters. Mrs. S. matured early—she "had the body of a woman" at age 11. She says she turned into an introvert at this time, feeling shy and fearful around others. In high school, she tried to look "like an old maid." Although she was studious, she never made the honor role, a failing that she blamed on her teachers. She also recalls having a very difficult time because of racial prejudice.

In general, Mrs. S. felt very alone in high school, at home, and at church. She completely identified with her mother, with whom she had a strong symbiotic tie. With intense affective anger, Mrs. S. described her mother as "perfect," a good Christian who always helped others. However, on second thought, she also saw her mother as loud, talkative, and domineering. Her mother, who had been very active in church fund-raising, was once accused of stealing church money. Mrs. S. heatedly avoided that the church and its members were responsible for her mother's death.

At 19, Mrs. S. was the first "colored girl" to be accepted at A. Conservatory College. She recalls being subjected to intense racial prejudice at this school, where she was given a scholarship. At 24, Mrs. S. won a national singing contest. A year later, she won another singing contest and was offered the substitute lead in "Porgy and Bess." She turned down this offer and later blamed her sister for making her miss this opportunity for fame and success. Mrs. S. completed a masters degree in music.

At the time Mr. and Mrs. S. met, Mrs. S.'s mother was dying and Mrs. S. was terrified at the prospect of being left alone. For this reason, she pushed Mr. S. to marry her at once, even though she did not love him at the time of their courtship and marriage. From the beginning, the marriage was stormy and ungratifying for both spouses. Each had strong dependency needs for the other. Mr. S. reluctantly agreed to live with his in-laws so that Mrs. S. could continue giving 24-hour care to her mother. After two months, Mr. S.

caught chicken pox and went to live with his parents. After recovering from his illness, he moved into a rooming house. Mr. and Mrs. S. did not see each other for six months, at which time their oldest son was born. Father was never notified by mother or maternal grandparents of this child's birth. After Mrs. S. had been in the hospital for nineteen hours, the paternal grandparents learned of the forthcoming birth and notified Mr. S., who drove mother and child home to maternal grandparents. With intense anger and resentment, Mr. S. stated that Mrs. S. did not inquire if he would like to see their newborn child. After dropping Mrs. S. off, Mr. S. did not see her again until she brought the baby over a few months later. Upon Mrs. S.'s father's death, he agreed to rejoin his wife at her parents' house. Once again, they had no privacy.

Shortly after their reunion, Mrs. S.'s mother died and the couple moved in with one of Mrs. S.'s sisters. After this sister began "meddling with my affairs," as Mr. S. put it, the couple moved in with another sister. Moves and joint residencies with relatives have characterized their life style and marriage.

INTERVIEWS AND TEST DATA

Physical Examinations.   Jimmy, at age five and a half, was a cute little boy who weighed 42½ pounds and measured about 44" (both around the 50th percentile). Head circumference: 20½". Chest Circumference: 21". EENT: enlarged tonsils, clean. Ears: could not be examined due to the child's extreme fear of the otoscope. Eyes: normal. Chest, abdomen, and genitalia: all within normal limits as well as extremities. On neurological examination, DTR were present and symmetrical. There were no Baninskis. Coordination was good. When brought in the room, Jimmy was extremely restless and frightened of the examiner and of the various tools. When allowed free activity, he mostly rocked on the rocking horse and rolled cars back and forth on the floor, absorbed in his own activity and ignoring mother and examiner. When talked to, he mostly answered echolalicly, but spoke spontaneously when he was very anxious to convey something. For instance, he asked "where is the car?" when approached by the medical tool. Accomplished very little with a crayon which he handled with both hands. Tried but could only make a very gross copy of a circle. Could not light the otoscope after being shown repeatedly how to do it. Mother was irritated by her son's shortcomings and threatened to force him to comply. Child showed no affect towards either mother or examiner and eye contact was poor throughout.

Neurological and opthalmological examinations revealed no neurological or visual abnormalities.

Psychiatric Examination.   Jimmy, a beautiful child, was nearly unreachable in terms of human relatedness. At first, he seemed almost totally unrelated, but it became apparent that he was actually "negatively related." He was aware of the environment, but needed to work hard to keep others from impinging upon him in any way. He avoided eye contact except for occasional quick glances. He smiled inappropriately. He was constantly in motion, moving from one area to another, from one toy to another, without apparent plan or goal. He seemed to have had few experiences which could foster growth, even of the most essential character structures. To have gotten as far as he had with such extreme experiential deprivation suggested a superior genetic endowment. Strongly recommended was immediate, most intensive psychotherapeutic intervention in a residential treatment center.

Social Service Examination. Jimmy, a 5½-year-old boy, had a history of hyperactivity, lack of speech, sleep problems, and temper tantrums. His older brother and two sisters were doing well in school and presenting no behavior problems. At the time Jimmy was born, Mr. and Mrs. S. had too many other problems to be concerned with the new baby. They allowed themselves to ignore Jimmy's problems until recently. At this time, having solved many of the problems in their marriage, they were seeking help for Jimmy and for themselves regarding their handling of Jimmy.

Psychological Examinations. Jimmy was seen for psychological examination at the age of five years, six months. Though he was found to function within the range of moderate mental retardation on the Revised Stanford-Binet Scale, Form L, the tenuous quality of his adaptation to the testing situation convinced one that this estimate was minimal. Many apsects of Jimmy's behavior suggested psychosis, in spite of the fact that he had developed speech. It was quite apparent that therapeutic intervention should be brought about as quickly as possible.

At age seven years, eight months, Jimmy was given the following tests:

Wechsler Intelligence Scale for Children (WISC)
Test of Visual Motor-Integration
Draw-A-Person
Peabody Picture Vocabulary Test
Portrait of Stanford Binet Form L-M

As it was not possible to administer any of the standard projective tests, discussion of test results will be limited to the intellectual battery. Extensive behavioral observation was possible and will be presented and interpreted in lieu of projective data.

It was possible by use of candy rewards to get Jimmy to complete the Peabody Picture Vocabulary Test. His score was equivalent to that expected of a child of six years, ten months; ten months behind his age expectancy. This was equivalent to an IQ of 90, which would place Jimmy on about the 28th percentile of children his age. This estimate was probably fairly close to Jimmy's maximum ability, although at the end of the test he was perseverating on the upper left picture. This might have been due to emotional blockage or boredom and thus his optimal level might be a bit higher than indicated by his score. Another factor to be considered is that Jimmy's main motivation for completing the test was to receive bits of candy, offered after every few trials. Toward the end of testing Jimmy became distracted, or possibly satiated, and his attention decreased. A more intrinsic motivation also might have raised his score somewhat.

The Developmental Test of Visual Motor Integration was completed in crayon. Since it was designed to be done in pencil, and because Jimmy's

attention and concentration here were also minimal, the results are presented with caution and should not be interpreted as indicative in any way of
Jimmy's optimal performance. There were several items where it was quite
probable that Jimmy might have passed had he been working in pencil and
concentrating. His performance was equivalent to that of a child of five
years, ten months; one year, ten months, behind his age expectancy. Administration of the WISC and Binet tests was limited to a few items because
of Jimmy's limited attention span and his difficulty in giving verbal responses
to verbal questions.

When the examiner first walked up to Jimmy's desk to introduce himself,
Jimmy got up and walked to a closet, and then went to the far corner of the
room. Then the examiner sat near Jimmy's desk and waited until the child
returned. Jimmy seemed unaware of the examiner's presence. The examiner
began to make quiet comments about Jimmy's play, slowly moving closer to
the desk. Eventually Jimmy allowed the examiner to sit at his desk and they
rolled up clay snakes together. Jimmy talked rapidly to himself and showed
no reaction when the examiner explained that they would be going up to his
office the next day to play some games and do some puzzles.

The next morning the examiner returned to find Jimmy alone in the
schoolroom watching Sesame Street. Jimmy did not respond to the examiner's greeting and questions about the show, but began to masturbate. The
examiner commented, "Jimmy, is school the place to do that?" After a short
pause, Jimmy replied, "This is school." "Yes this is school," the examiner
said, "and school is not the place to do that. The other children will be
along shortly." Jimmy then said absently, "other children." After a pause,
he buttoned his pants and zipped his fly.

When the other children arrived along with the teacher, Jimmy expressed reluctance, and then a refusal, to leave, leaving in tears only on the
firm demand of the teacher. Once in the office, Jimmy's first words were "go
back to Ann's class?" to which the examiner replied, "after a while, Jimmy." This interchange was repeated at intervals of five to ten minutes
throughout the three examining sessions. Jimmy's first activity was to take
two small cars from the Binet Kit, crayon one to resemble a police car, and
play with them, causing many crashes in which the police car always took
the worst beating. He repeatedly asked, "What does the police car do?"
None of the examiner's responses had any effect on the subsequent repetition of the question. Jimmy did comment that "Daddy" was a policeman,
but the significance of the police car game could not be determined.

Jimmy often lapsed into a kind of perseverative game in which he would
write something and ask the examiner "What is this?" When the examiner
answered, Jimmy would laugh, write some more, and repeat the quetion.
The first instance of this activity involved four-digit numbers and the second
instance involved automobile names. Jimmy's command of auto names was
surprising: he was able to write "Buick LeSabre," "Pontiac," and "Buick
Electra 225," and could even draw the dagger-shaped insignia that is found
on Pontiac hoods. However, he also wrote down combinations such as
"Pontivan," "Vantruck," "Robo" (a name on a tow truck he drew), "Rvat"
(on a car), and, inexplicably amid all the cars, "midway." At times, he

would leave letters out of words—particularly "r" in trucks and "i" in Pontiac. Sometimes he would catch his mistakes; at other times, the examiner had to point them out. He drew several "people" at the examiner's request, all of them very primitive, not much more than stick figures, with very large round eyes and minimal legs. He could not seem to concentrate long enough to embellish the figures with any details. As the sessions progressed, it was more and more difficult to distract Jimmy from his repetitive play with the cars, clay, and blocks to engage him in test-related activity. He would begin fantasy play and have a running conversation with himself as he crashed cars into piles of blocks, ran over blobs of clay with them, and built towers of blocks, shattering them all over the floor. In order to give a flavor of Jimmy's behavior at these times, an excerpt of Jimmy's speech is presented below, with his play activities inserted in parenthesis. There was much animation in Jimmy's voice and he spoke at a slightly rapid pace. At times he sounded truly emotional, yet it was almost as if he were playing a part, or reading a script.

> Bobby, cut it out. . . . God don't attack me, go away ahh . . . (said with apparent fear) don't get in the way, boys. Got a car (running over clay with car), going to the city. . . . I'll kill em and cut 'em off, cut 'em off. . . . Mr. Sot, call me Mr. Sot, answer me! (spoken as if in desperation) Little boy (playing with clay), why you go to Quiet Room fa? 'Cause he's behaving himself. . . . My name Keith, I'm in the Quiet Room, dammit. . . . Don't say that, don't say that, don't say that, . . . coochie crunch (tore up clay and threw it on floor). Clean up, clean up the teeth, gonna stay here, clean, clean, clean, thank you (cleaned up clay from floor). Clean 'em off, jump 'em, junk teeth.

As might be concluded from the above, Jimmy appeared to be out of contact with reality much of the time, with little coherence or order in his thought processes. The fascination with numbers and words of a specific type, as well as the repetitiveness of his play and speech, indicated the presence of an ongoing psychotic process. There appeared to be some castration themes in the "don't attack me" and "cut 'em off" comments, and the fascination with police cars and crashing destruction was phallic and aggressive in nature. It was probable that Jimmy's father played an active role in the present situation, and that the Oedipal conflict had not been genuinely approached. It was impossible to judge from current test data whether there was an organic component, but with so low a score on the Developmental Test of Visual Motor Integration, organicity could not be ruled out.

However, Jimmy did demonstrate some surprising strengths. His Peabody Picture Vocabulary Test IQ of 90 was in marked contrast to an earlier Stanford Binet IQ of 50, even though the latter was an admittedly low measure. Initially, he was slow to relate to strangers, but later contacts showed surprising ease. In fact, as this report was being written, Jimmy walked by the examiner's open door on his way from school. He walked in, said, "Hi, Don," and asked if he could come back. The examiner said he didn't think so and Jimmy began to ramble about "doing work." He left shortly thereafter, still talking to no one in particular. Even though his speech was rather disjointed, it was apparent that Jimmy felt he had made a friend, or at least had enjoyed the "testing" experience and wanted more of it. The fact that Jimmy did use speech and seemed to play and talk about important themes in his life was another positive sign. It was difficult to assess any therapeutic progress in Jimmy since the examining psychologist had not known Jimmy previously. However, comparison of Jimmy's current behavior with that noted in an earlier psychological report indicated some improvement in concentration and emotional control.

DIAGNOSTIC IMPRESSIONS

As the above psychologicals after two years of residential placement indicated, despite some gains, Jimmy still was functionally retarded. He demonstrated all of his previous autistic and psychotic behavior. Dorm and school staff said he knew the names of adults and children, but remained aloof and withdrawn, self-contented when left alone. He liked to rock on his bed, masturbate, or gaze out the window, quietly chanting the names of cars to himself. He showed some animation regarding police cars, undoubtedly related to his policeman father. He related to female dorm staff and therapists in a part-object fashion, noting and responding to their attire. He would lean against the slacks or jeans of a female staff member, and become hysterical and agitated at a female leg in nylon stockings. This apparently recapitulated the frenzy he used to feel when his mother changed from pants (at-home garb) to stockings and a skirt to depart for work. As a tiny toddler at his mother's knee, the stockinged leg connoted separation and abandonment—thus, the still-frenzied response to the maternal part-object.

Jimmy had some visual recognition of words but no reading skill or academic development. His sense of self and other remained fragmented, and the world held meager safety for him. While he did respond to the environment as long as it remained absolutely clear and predictable, any change created overwhelming terror and bewilderment for him. His long-term placement was interrupted because of funding cutbacks. He was discharged to his parents, with arrangements made for placement in a community day treatment program for autistic children. The prognosis was bleak, and staff members of the residential facility questioned how long he could be contained at home.

DIAGNOSTIC FORMULATIONS

Both Mr. and Mrs. S. were bright, sensitive, and appealing, as well as extremely dependent, depressed, preoccupied, and immature. Both were fearful of becoming totally dependent upon a person who would fail them. Mr. S. had experienced the almost total loss of his mother throughout childhood and a series of losses and abandonments of mothering figures. One would suspect a fair degree of rage toward mother figures. Concurrently, there was a striving and longing for a mother interested in him.

Mrs. S. had experienced long separation from her mother at a very early age. There was the constant danger of mother (herself) becoming seriously ill and dying. One could imagine that Mrs. S. had some frightening fantasies concerning illness and death. As a result of the above factors, Mrs. S. had been an obedient, dependent, "good" child who succumbed to her mother's wishes and directions; she had readily accepted a symbioticlike relationship with her mother from the age of five until her mother's death. It was highly probable that mother would not have married and/or developed a second meaningful relationship if maternal grandmother had not become seriously ill and died.

Both Mr. and Mrs. S. complained that their spouse did not fulfill need gratifications or direct enough attention toward him/her. They were highly competitive with, as well as depreciating toward, each other. Succinctly, they were involved in an intensified sadomasochistic relationship. When feeling depleted and overwhelmed with adult and family responsibilities, Mr. S. somatized and isolated himself in the bedroom for long periods of time. Mrs. S. developed severe tics around the eyes and became markedly depressed and despondent. Both continued to sustain the attitude of "it's me against the world," and, periodically, "it's us [family] against the world." Both felt inadequate, especially regarding their marriage and the parenting of Jimmy. Mr. S. stated it as "I never finished anything," and Mrs. S. expressed it as "There was always one thing [obstacles] that stopped me from becoming a success in anything I did."

Upon the couple establishing their own home, Mrs. S. had remained a housewife for five years. Shortly after Jimmy's birth, Mrs. S. had resumed academic pursuits and obtained full-time employment as a teacher. Mr. S. strongly objected to and resisted his wife's efforts outside the home, although depending greatly on her income, on the basis of a "messy house," meals not served at a time suitable for himself, and the care of the children. Mr. and Mrs. S's anger and resentment toward each other—the feeling that the *other* spouse should assume the parenting for Jimmy—resulted in Jimmy being deprived and neglected. He had been confined to his crib with the door shut. It had been unpredictable as to when he would be fed and changed within a nonstimulating environment. The oldest sibling had attempted to care for some of Jimmy's needs when he was home. Jimmy had been used as a pawn or weapon in the parents' marital conflicts. Finally, Mr. S. was very competitive with Jimmy.

The diagnosis was childhood psychosis with autistic features; the prognosis was guarded. Treatment recommendations included continued long-term placement in a therapeutic setting; intensive individual psychotherapy for Jimmy; and marital psychotherapy. In addition, both parents could benefit from individual psychotherapy, but such treatment was highly impractical at the time of this writing.

Psychosis and Childhood Schizophrenia

Definition

Psychosis, another multilabeled gross syndrome that can be traced back to trauma in the first year of life, connotes profound personality disorganization marked by both ego and libidinal regression. Psychoses of childhood are generally divided into two groups: (1) symptomatic psychosis, the result of a physical illness (e.g., delerium following illness and fever), the injection of drugs, or a convulsive disorder; and (2) functional psychosis, such as childhood schizophrenia or manic-depressive psychosis (the latter rarely, if ever, appears in childhood). The psychotic state is marked by the following characteristics: bizarre behavior, delusional ideas, inappropriately labile and intense affective reactions, withdrawal, disturbances in sense of and contact with reality, hallucinatory experiences, difficulty in communication, loose associations and thought connections, and hypochondriacal concerns.

Symbiotic Infantile Psychosis

Symbiotic infantile psychosis was first described by Mahler. It is a functional psychosis of childhood which usually appears during the second, third, or fourth years of life. Its onset is more dramatic than that of early autism because there has been more ego development. Although both constitutional and environmental factors play a role in the development of this syndrome, constitutional factors are not as important here as in infantile autism.

ETIOLOGY

The roots of this psychosis lie in the symbiotic phase of development—the period of ego growth following the normal autistic phase. The symbiotic phase begins at about three months of age and is slowly replaced during the next two years by the separation-individuation phase. During the symbiotic phase, the normal mother and child have a close relationship on which the infant's ego relies heavily for support and emotional nurture. As the child begins to crawl, to walk, and to talk, this symbiotic relationship gradually diminishes and the child becomes more of a separate individual. The normal child is able to accomplish this emotional and physical separation successfully—the child with the symbiotic psychosis is not able to do so.

The symbiotic psychotic child is unable to separate from the mother. When the intense symbiotic union with her is disrupted by external factors, such as illness or the birth of a sibling, the child deteriorates quickly because the inadequate ego is overwhelmed. Prior to this deterioration, the child might have been developing adequate speech and motor skills. The onset of illness often is marked by regression, with increased dependency on the mother and anxiety or panic at her absence. Speech may become garbled; logic and coherency yield to primary-process thought. Posturing and grimacing may occur. Contact with reality diminishes and flights of fantasy take over. Sleeping and eating habits become disturbed; enuresis and/or encopresis may appear. This process of deterioration may occur very rapidly or may take months.

Children with symbiotic infantile psychosis cannot interact with peers. They lose interest in age-appropriate activities and are unable to maintain contact with reality. Thus, they cannot relate normally to anyone. Their overwhelming anxiety is manifested by clinging tearfully to mother or by "melting" into whoever holds them. While these children cannot learn uniformly, they may have isolated areas in which their knowledge is superior. Like autistic children, symbiotic psychotic children find change most stressful. They need reassurances of ritualistic routines with compulsive characteristics. Minus intervention, regression may continue, with the symbiotic psychotic child becoming more and more autistic.

Most psychotic preschool children present features of autism and symbiosis—so that the pure form of either is rarely seen. The prognosis depends on age of onset and highest level of ego development attained. With symbiotic psychotic children, the previously unrecognized pathological tie to mother is traumatized and psychotic symptoms appear. These children have leaned too heavily on the maternal ego and cannot emancipate themselves. (Treatment interventions are similar to those for autism and childhood schizophrenia.)

Childhood Schizophrenia

The most frequently seen childhood psychosis is childhood schizophrenia, which occurs before the age of 11 and reveals pathology at every level and in every area of central nervous system functioning (Bender, 1956). Whatever the descriptive label or areas of impairment, the "earmark of the diagnosis is a mammoth deficiency in the functions of adaptation and behavior required for adequate living-in-the-world. Every schizophrenic child is seriously lacking in fundamental tools for perceiving, ordering, and manipulating reality and he is dramatically devoid of a sharply delineated, well-differentiated, and confident awareness of himself in the course of his actions" (Goldfarb et al., 1969, p. 2).

Schizophrenic children most frequently present an unusual appearance—due to patterned grimacing of their facial muscles, and the inability to care for bodily secretions, bodily extensions, and personal belongings. The characteristic pathology is active and reactive anxiety, given their recognized inability to experience a clear-cut percept and to grasp the reality of identities, boundaries, and limits. These children merge diffusely with the objects in their environment, evidence distortions of thinking, and often are intensely attentive to particular aspects or details of objects, such as the color of a toy, or parts of a toy. The integrative grasp of the normal function and proper use of the object—including the integrative capacities to perceive, to remember, and to order perceptions and memories into an organized reality-sustaining environment—is missing due to the basic ego deficit. Schizophrenic children are perplexed and totally without stability. Shaw (1966) notes that they do not differentiate other people or themselves from inanimate objects in the environment; they frequently play with a part of their body as if it were a toy. They use incorrect pronouns, confusing self and others. Because they cannot distinguish their body and ego boundaries, these children suffer much confusion, misery, and anguish. At times, they experience complete disintegration and disorganization with attacks of panic and rage.

Bender (1956) notes that the significant problems of childhood schizophrenia concern identity, body image and function, object and interpersonal relationships, and orientation in time and space. The essential difficulty is the inability to differentiate one's self and one's thinking from the rest of the world. This inability produces severe anxiety, which leads to symptom formation such as open masturbation and/or preoccupation with elimination.

When childhood schizophrenia develops before language is well established, there is usually more retardation and inhibition. Any speech that has been acquired may deteriorate, resulting in mutism, garbled sounds, and/or echolalia. Language is not used as a means of communication but as a repetitive expression of anxiety about one's identity and orientation. For example, one child may believe he is an automobile tire; he will lie limp and wait for his counselor to pump him up before entering the lunchroom. Another child will insist he is a hissing radiator and only vocalize via hissing sounds. Yet another, who is sure his limbs are about to fall off, repeatedly voices, anxious, frantic questions that allow no time for adult reassurances and comfort. The language of such children often consists of distorted, shortened sentences and secret made-up words that are really signals.

Often one can make seemingly good contact with schizophrenic children. They may be engaging and show unusual aptitude in isolated areas (e.g., mathematical facility, knowledge of the planets or dinosaurs), but their knowledge is not transferable, coherent, or useful in normal thinking. Since these children have no stable points of reference, they experience catastrophic bewilderment and panic, followed by a vain search for sameness and constancy. This is exemplified by Matthew, age 12, who has been confined in an exceptional children's ward of a state hospital for the last 5 years. He is obsessed with time and wears several watches at once. When anxious, he calls out the hour in Tokyo, Moscow, Rome, New York City, etc. Although his mathematical calculations are nimble, quick, and accurate, they do not serve to secure him more adequately in time and space.

Beres (1956) describes the disturbances in the various ego functions of schizophrenic children, broken down into seven groups.

1. Disturbances in the child's relation to reality include the following: (a) adaptive difficulties, such as inappropriate behavior, the inability to cope with change, and failure to relate socially; (b) disturbances in reality testing, such as projection, rationalization, denial, and delusional or hallucinatory distortions; and (c) disturbances in the sense of reality, such as estrangement, excessive feelings of déjà vu, oneirophenia, cosmic delusions, and confused body and self concepts.
2. Disturbances in drive control include conduct and habit disorders, accident proneness, excessive impulsivity and tension states, catatonic and manic excitement, lack of excretory mastery, and psychomotor retardation.
3. Disturbances in object relations include infantile psychotoxic/psychic deficiency diseases, narcissism, autism, symbiotic and anaclitic relationships, and hypercathexis of the self.
4. Disturbances in thought processes include drive-organized thinking with loose associative links, preoccupation with instinctual aims, autistic logic, distortion of reality, magical thinking, and lack of time and place referents.
5. Disturbances in defensive functions include the emergence of primary-process thought, overreaction to stimuli, impaired drive and emotional control, déjà vu experiences, frightening sleep phenomena, and an increase in parapraxes.
6. All the autonomous functions show impairment.
7. Disturbances in synthetic function consist of dissociation, intolerance for change, and the inability to "bind" psychic energy.

In addition, Beres (1956) notes a lack of goal directedness in the schizophrenic child's aggressive outbursts, which reflect severe disturbances of the very early mother-child relationship. Superego functions are so impaired in the ego-deviant schizophrenic child that it may be difficult to find any evidence of conflict, guilt, or the capacity to postpone gratification. Thus, impulsivity, antisocial behavior, and narcissistic relationships are manifest.

Childhood schizophrenia obviously is not a unitary disease entity: it is merely a label indicating dramatic deviation, with impairment in virtually every aspect of adaptation to life. Goldfarb et al. (1969) sum up the prevailing view of its etiology: "While we recognize determinants such as heredity and brain damage in our theory of the etiology of childhood schizophrenia, we are impressed with the importance of situational factors. We view each of the child's responses as being a manifestation of a dynamic interplay between his particular capacities

and dispositions and the external social forces with which he is confronted" (pp. 3–4). Thus, the disease is caused by intrinsic disorders of
the child and/or pathology arising from distortions in the family
relationships.

TREATMENT INTERVENTIONS

Goldfarb et al. (1969) comment that

> when the schizophrenic child is physiologically intact, one frequently ob-
> serves a background of environmental failure entailing . . . a dramatic pa-
> ralysis of parental functioning characterized by extreme passivity marked
> uncertainty, lack of spontaneity, absence of empathy with the child (so that
> awareness of his needs is lacking), bewilderment and inactivity in the face
> of socially unacceptable or bizarre behavior, and a nearly total absence of
> control of the child. A therapeutic climate is characterized by adult re-
> sponses that are the polar opposite of those manifested by such parents. . . .
> It is our belief that notwithstanding theories of ultimate cause, such as
> heredity or brain damage, each schizophrenic child has somehow missed
> the social complement necessary for his development into a whole person
> [pp. 7–8].

Views regarding prognosis vary: the pessimists suggest that, at best,
one can expect only limited improvement in social conformity and
adaptability. A crucial prognostic factor is the age of onset; the earlier
the onset, the poorer the prognosis. A second crucial factor is the degree of disturbance in language function: the less severe the disturbance, the better the prognosis. Goldfarb et al. (1969) examine the gains
a schizophrenic child can make in a residential therapeutic milieu
based on what they call "corrective socialization." They note that studies have shown the range of individual responses to be very wide: some
children show no improvement while others show dramatic improvement. "Systematic studies of change indicate that among schizophrenic children free of neurological involvement, the great majority
improve, while among those with neurological impairment, there is
considerably less progress" (p. 145).

Goldfarb et al. (1969) emphasize that, while learning machines are
useful for improving specific functional responses such as language,
the primary therapuetic agent must be a human being. Further, they
state that the ultimate goal in treatment is the development and consolidation of normal patterns of human attachment and relatedness. Goldfarb et al. recommend achieving this goal via a benign, predictable,
structured residential environment that provides corrective socialization and individualization to meet the unique needs of each child.
Consistent contact with therapists, teachers, and counselors is crucial.
For some children, individual therapy is not of primary importance but
the constant surveillance of psychoanalytically oriented staff is invalu-

able. Chemotherapy may sometimes be useful, insofar as it alters the child's accessibility to stimulation and influence. However, Goldfarb et al. (1969) warn that "Drugs do not in themselves undo the complex skein of learned responses or create entirely new behavioral characteristics. Merely making a child manageable is not equivalent to cure, or genuine improvement" (p. 143). With sufficient therapeutic personnel, most children are manageable without drugs.

Goldfarb comments on the widespread pessimism regarding the possibility of change in the families of schizophrenic children, which results in exclusion of the family from therapeutic considerations. At the Ittelson Center that he directs, as well as in many other programs with the long-term goal of returning the children to their homes, work with the families is regarded as crucial and fruitful. The recent paucity of excellent residential treatment programs, funding cutbacks, and the antiplacement stance of many professionals and child welfare offices have led to the development of day treatment programs and theraputic day schools that attempt to serve these damaged children.

Case of James

The case of James presents a vivid picture of a schizophrenic latency-age child. As noted earlier, childhood psychosis often presents a mixed array of autistic and symbiotic characteristics and symptomatology. Because James possessed language skills, he was able to make considerable progress, as manifested by his cognitive and ego development. Nevertheless, questions must be raised about the appropriateness of discharging him to his parents' care after his two years in residential treatment. The decision to discharge James was based on community funding patterns rather than on the therapeutic conviction that the child's gains were sufficiently internalized to be maintained at home. Nor was there sufficient evidence that the family could and would support further psychotherapy once James was discharged. For these reasons, the prognosis at the time of termination was guarded.

Diagnostic Evaluation

REFERRAL

James B., a large, semiobese white 10-year-old boy from a lower-class family, had a curiously flat, unblinking stare that seemed to look through one. He spoke in a shrill, mechanistic voice, often referring to himself as "Snoopy" or "Peanuts." When agitated, he would wring or flap his hands, and grimace and contort his face and body. The year before his referral, when he was nine, James was placed in a primary classroom for children with learning disabilities. James was able to learn on a one-to-one basis but was unable to apply his acquired knowledge on a social and practical level. According to the school social worker, James remained in an elaborate fantasy world, did not learn from experience, and had a very low frustration tolerance. His teacher's active attempts to help James acquire some social and group living skills failed and James regressed considerably. His parents were unable to take James out. One parent always stayed home with him, as he was out of control. James was put on several kinds of medication—only thorazine proved to be at all helpful. Both parents were concerned about James and cooperated in efforts to help him.

At the age of ten, James was referred by his school psychologist and a consulting psychiatrist for a differential diagnosis to clarify his specific areas of dysfunctioning. He presented such a confused, mixed array of pathology that he was described as "an anomaly of nature." The original diagnosis of mental retardation was definitely ruled out. Although the initial opinion of staff members was that James was schizophrenic, later there were conflicting views as to whether James was psychotic. The assessment of his capacity for object relations—that is, whether he could relate to people as individuals—was seen as the main diagnostic task. In the formulation of a dynamic diagnosis, material from both the developmental history given by the parents and James's behavior in therapy sessions was organized along developmental lines.

DEVELOPMENTAL HISTORY

Object Relations. Parents' report about James' infantile responsiveness to others was contradictory. Apparently, he smiled, laughed when tickled, and cried when colicky or hurt. He showed none of the usual separation anxiety until he was above five or six years old. Then he would scream, wet and soil himself, and tear the house apart when the parents went out. As a result, the parents gave up going out altogether when James was about six. James was known as "Silent Sam" because, after the age of about one and one half, he stopped using the few words that he knew. He also stopped responding to parents and showed no awareness of his siblings until the birth of Ron when he was eight. Speech reappeared suddenly when James was six, during a two-week stay with his maternal grandmother, who fed him so much that he gained twelve pounds. He had a series of fetishes (or "false selves") similar to his current "Charlie Brown" fetish.

Eating. As an infant, James had a strong urge to suck. He was "a pacifier baby" but would not accept mother's attempt to substitute a pacifier for the bottle when he was colicky. Weaning from the bottle started when James was nine months old, at the birth of a sibling. James resisted and mother kept trying to make him give up the bottle until he was two and a half years old. At that time, she abruptly took it away forever after he bit off the nipple and sprayed milk all over the newly painted nursery.

Junior foods were no problem but James reacted to Mrs. B.'s cooking by refusing the food and vomiting. Mrs. B. saw his behavior as directly related to her. James did not try to feed himself until he was two and a half years old. He did not drink from a cup till age four. Despite this resistance to mother's push for James to be more independent, which was very frustrating for her, James liked to lick bowls and help himself to Mrs. B.'s baking. She complained, "James is always working at my food." Mrs. B. baked a lot for holidays. She tried to keep the children out of her cookies and cakes both to save what she had for guests and because she was continually worried about weight. Consequently a very frustrating situation was created around holidays, with mixed messages about whether one should or should not eat mother's food. Actually the message was that one was to eat only when mother said so. It was not too surprising that the parents complained that James was at his worst around holidays. (Christmas was also his birthday, which added additional problems.)

Toilet Training. James had long, drawn-out battles with mother over toilet training from age one and a half to six. James urinated in the toilet by age four or five. At age five and a half to six and a half, James wet and soiled himself when parents went out. James finally potty trained at age six.

Peer Relationships. James was indifferent toward his closest two siblings, but was delighted with the two babies, whom he liked to tickle and poke, However, he assumed no responsibility for them. His only "friends" were younger, more retarded children who looked up to him. At the time of his referral, James was still at a narcissistic stage in which other children were of no concern as rivals for mother's love.

Toys and Play. James never participated in shared activities. He had a series of fetishes and assumed different roles. When he did attempt to play games, it had to be by his rules, which disturbed his parents. His ongoing interest in books began at an early age. Searching behavior was prompted by reading the book, "A Child Is Waiting," which is about a woman who likes a retarded child. James always enjoyed water play. Baths and books were used to soothe him.

PARENTS

Since parents had realistic difficulties (transportation, babysitters, Mr. B.'s work hours) in keeping regular appointments, information about their backgrounds was very limited.

Mrs. B. was a plump, heavily made-up woman in her early thirties who thought of herself as the "giving mother," showering her family with food and gifts. Her gifts were conflictual for James; she baked a lot and then limited his intake, gave him toys and then cautioned him not to break them, which put a severe strain on his poor impulse control. She was very reserved with James and spent most of her sessions talking to the therapist. She seemed at a loss as to how to relate to James. At first, she was somewhat defensive, but she developed a positive transference in the effort to understand James. She tried to follow therapeutic suggestions about handling James.

Mrs. B. was an only child who identified completely with her own children. Her father was a policeman who specialized in work with juveniles. He injured his back and developed ulcers when Mrs. B. was in the eighth grade. During the first two years of the B.'s marriage, the couple lived with Mrs. B.'s parents. Mrs. B. always maintained very close contact with her mother, even after the B.'s moved out of her mother's neighborhood. When James was about two and a half, Mrs. B.'s father became bedridden with a heart condition. He died about six years later. Mrs. B. did not seem to have grown out of her very early need for a constant mothering figure. In fact, her mother was still her main support. Her father's illness must have contributed to Mrs. B.'s fear of injury, especially the damage her own impulses might cause.

Mr. B. was a fairly good-looking man of medium build. He was more reticent but also more relaxed than Mrs. B. He showed some warmth but, like Mrs. B., had not differentiated his children much. He expected James to take the initiative in their relationship, but this seemed to stem more from not knowing what to do than from any inner conflicts. Mr. B. was conscientious about following therapeutic suggestions regarding James.

Mr. B. had a sister five years younger and a half-sister fifteen years younger. His father, a "ne'er do well, ladies' man, and good talker," was married to his sixth wife. He had left the family when Mr. B. was five years old. Mr. B. thought he took after his "hard-headed and emotional" mother. When he was a sophomore in high school, he couldn't get along with his mother, so he went to live with his father for a couple of years. He still had trouble with his controlling, stubborn mother, as did Mrs. B.

Mr. B. had trouble finding and keeping jobs. According to him, he had been disappointed repeatedly by men who promised him a good opportunity. A year before James's referral, Mr. B. gave up driving his own cab as a financial loss. At the same time, Mrs. B.'s father died and she threatened to leave Mr. B. However, Mr. B. got his current job in an auto parts shop as well as working part-time on the side, and the crisis passed.

CURRENT LIVING SITUATION

The B.'s, a family of seven, lived in a two-bedroom bungalow. The parents slept on a hideaway bed in the living room while the children slept several to a room in bunk beds, cots, and even in a sleeping bag on the floor.

Summary of Treatment

Early in James's residential treatment, he seemed oblivious of the therapist's presence, even as a part object. He darted around a lot, moved in bizarre, disconnected ways, and made incomprehensible sounds. He also tried frantically to call his mother on the phone despite the fact that his parents did not have a phone at the time. This behavior, which appeared to be a desperate cry for help from the *idea* of a mother since the possibility of actual contact with her overwhelmed him with anxiety, gradually diminished over time. Except for a temporary setback at the time of the therapist's first vacation, James seemed to progress fairly steadily toward increasingly verbal communication and more interaction with the therapist. James moved from autistic involvement with Charlie Brown books to solitary activity with watercolors to hide-and-seek games with the therapist. Despite the fact that he always had to "win" at hide-and-seek, at least such game playing involved the therapist as a necessary participant. In addition, James began to play with clay, making and "eating" pretend pies, throwing the clay in anger, and making footprints in it with the father doll.

Thus, in early sessions, James showed potential for object relatedness and a beginning development of object constancy and a sense of self, but his contact with the therapist as a need-fulfilling object remained tenuous and was subject to rapid regression. James still showed primary-process thought and had some compulsive defenses; he could also be manipulative. Those sectors of his personality caught up in mastering overwhelming separation anxiety seemed to operate in a psychotic fashion, that is, according to a delusional system rather than reality.

After two years of inpatient treatment, three general interrelated themes were clear in James's sessions. First, he had a strong need to be close to or even merge with the therapist, to act as if he and the therapist were identical. When he was frustrated in his attempts to be one with the therapist, he seemed to lose contact and felt "dead" and "like an unattached planet." However, warm, positive affectual contact scared him because it stirred up sexual feelings. Even more troublesome than sexual feelings were angry feelings, which sometimes resulted in his breaking contact completely. This theme of merging was exemplified in the puppet play he often used to act out his conflicts. He made a girl be a boy and vice versa and acted out their being together or being apart and falling down. This play paralleled an oft-repeated interpretation about his feeling that he would fall apart if he and the therapist could not be together, sharing everything.

The second theme, which was connected to the first, was James's wish to be in charge and to be omnipotent. An example of this wish was his fantasy that he was a big, strong, angry "hairy man" who went "boom." Going "boom" was so frightening that he tried to run away from the therapist—and from his angry feelings which made him fall apart. In the past, he had used schedules to help put things back in order. Lately, he had less of a need for such an external organizer.

The third main theme was James's ambivalence and anxiety about growth. Every step forward brought with it the fear of being abandoned. James's anxiety about growth had been aggravated by his repeated experience of being pushed away every time a new sibling was born.

Physically, James had shed his excess weight and was a very appropriate-looking 12-year-old. His physical skills showed a corresponding improvement as he lost weight. He had much better control over his behavior and impulses than he had had when he entered residential treatment. The hand-clenching and bizarre contortions of his body and face had diminished. He was less easily frustrated, his speech was clearer and less mechanical, and he generally demonstrated more autonomy and a greater awareness and understanding of his environment. His dependency on schedules had decreased and lacked its former compulsiveness.

James had interacted with peers at the treatment center via his participation in a music group, although his peer relationships were still rather shallow. With the adults at the center, James had become more verbally expressive and communicative, although his ambivalence persisted. His home visits seemed to have gone smoothly and his parents were pleased with his progress.

Recommendations

During his residential treatment, James progressed from a defensive position of secondary autism (robot flapping, primary-process state), to a fairly extended period of symbiosis with his environment (with a need for totally external controls), to secondary-process verbalization, object relatedness, frustration tolerance, and some differentiation of self. He developed some degree of object and self constancy, but, as this was the latest psychological achievement, it was also the one most susceptible to regressive loss. It was difficult to assess termination at this point. James's history of premature ego development with subsequent breakdown would indicate the need for a gradual transition from residential treatment to a protective, therapeutic environment.

CHAPTER 7

Mental Retardation

Definition

Mental retardation under DSM III (American Psychiatric Association, 1980) is defined as a "significantly subaverage general intellectual functioning: an IQ of 70 or below on individually administered tests. . . . [with] concurrent deficits or impairments in adaptive behavior, the person's age being taken into consideration [when] onset [is] before the age of 18. [p. 25]" Kessler (1966) states that there is controversy over the criteria, meaning, and measurement of intellectual malfunctioning and social impairment, and over the relationship between the two concepts. She notes that dependence on IQ as the sole criterion of mental deficiency is largely an American practice, and cautions that IQ results alone are not sufficient to warrant a diagnosis of mental retardation—there must also be a concomitant behavior problem. Appreciation of the limitations of the IQ has led many authorities to advocate social criteria as the best means of separating the mentally retarded from the normal population.

Etiology

Work (1979) notes that

> many of the categories of severe retardation occur in relation to biologic syndromes that involve and disfigure the entire body. These range from hydrocephalics through necrocephalics, with a host of intermediate somatic conditions. On the other hand, as one goes up the intellectual ladder, the appearance of the individual is not necessarily distinguished from the population at large. Function then becomes of greater importance [p. 403].

Within the pathological group, there is a great variety of organic determinants. Kessler (1966) notes that retardation may result from deficiencies of, or damage to, the central nervous system from one of the following:

1. Chromosomal abnormalities (Mongolism or Down's syndrome)
2. Prenatal infections (rubella during pregnancy, maternal syphilis)
3. Iso-immunization (blood-type incompatibility resulting in kernicterus)
4. Premature birth (birth weight is the important factor)
5. Birth trauma
6. Cranial anomalies (e.g., microcephaly, hydrocephalus)
7. Defects of metabolism (phenylketonuria, cretinism, galactosemia)
8. Childhood accidents (head injuries)
9. Childhood diseases (e.g., postmeasles encephalitis, lead poisoning)
10. Heredo-degenerative cerebral diseases

When retardation is due to brain damage, Shaw (1966) notes that the "retardation is considered secondary to the brain damage" (p. 253). He also notes the high incidence of retardation associated with specific physical handicaps, especially sensory and perceptual defects. For example, undiagnosed deafness in children leads to social isolation and slowed intellectual development, and children with aphasia frequently evidence a lag in mental development.

In addition to organic causative factors, in approximately 75% of all cases, etiology is also ascribed to cultural-familial and environmental deprivations, especially in impoverished urban and rural children. These children of poverty are often born to undernourished mothers whose pregnancies are ill-cared for, with a resultant high prematurity rate. These mothers and children are often unprotected by customary public health measures and suffer from inadequate nutrition, perhaps even severe malnutrition. Many authors (e.g., Pavenstedt, 1965; Eisenberg and Earle, 1975) have described the environmental deprivation and chaotic homes of these children; language and speech are inadequate and the normal tactile sensations of life are missing. School failures in these children inevitably lead to emotional disabilities and behavioral problems.

Another group of children presents retardation of a psychogenic nature. Children with childhood psychosis, autism, and mild or minimal brain dysfunction fall into this category. This group is frequently described as pseudoretarded, and the mental retardation is a "concomitant of psychosis, severe emotional disturbance, neurotic disorder, or other types of major personality disorders during infancy and early childhood" (Work, 1979, p. 405).

Assessment is crucial in attempting to delineate the trainable and educable children, and thus to provide a better understanding of the mild and moderately retarded children and those who present secondary retardation. Tarjan (1972) notes the need for better methods of measuring intelligence and adaptation. The concept of IQ may very well give way to a profile schema of assessment that indicates assets and deficiencies.

Interventions, including educational and training programs, parent counseling, and psychotherapy, are also necessary. Kessler (1966) believes that the paucity of research on psychotherapy is due to the long-held assumption that the mental defective is incapable of profiting from psychotherapy. In addition, "the tremendous demand for psychotherapeutic time and the scarcity of trained personnel have forced clinicians to give what little time they have to those cases which promise maximum results for minimum time" (Kessler, 1966, p. 190). Kessler also notes that since social and cultural deprivation is a primary cause of the retardation of many educably retarded children, there is a vast unserved parent population in need of help.

Descriptive Characteristics

Learning disturbances or disorders have been discussed in the literature more than any other aspect of child psychopathology. Terms are often imprecise and overlap. The child with a myriad of academic and behavioral symptoms, who most commonly is referred as presenting psychiatric problems with learning disabilities, actually may be suffering from a minimal brain dysfunction syndrome. Giffin (1981) describes the following characteristics of a child with a neurophysiological handicap: a subtle uneasiness in gait; difficulty in alternating movements; and/or problems in the tracking of the eyes, all of which reflect a neuromuscular dysfunction. Most noticeable is a lack of inhibition, an overly rapid verbalization of personal thoughts, and impulse-driven neuromuscular behavior. These children classically show hyperactivity, thinking disorders, specific learning problems, disorders of speech, and equivocal neurological findings. Clearly, the emotional lability, the impulsivity, and the thinking disorders may make the determination of organic versus psychogenic etiology problematic. Silver (1979) stresses that children with a minimal brain dysfunction syndrome have a total life disability that affects not only their normal learning process but also their self-concept, self-image, self-esteem, peer and family relationships, and social interactions. Usually, secondary social and/or emotional problems develop. If these children are properly diagnosed and treated with a combination of psychotherapy, special educational programs, and appropriate medication, they have potential for a reasonably successful future.

Even with relatively minor defects, a marked disequilibrium in the relations between mother and child often occurs at the time the defect is recognized. The mother may become very depressed, anxious, over-solicitous, seductive, or otherwise defective in her nurturing functions. This change in the mother-child relationship further traumatizes the child (Niederland, 1965).

Anthony (1976) suggests that a major difficulty of any deformity or abnormality is the mutual parent-child problems in narcissistic development. There are disturbances first in the parents' narcissistic process, depending on their unique and specific vulnerabilities. Not uncommonly, the injury to parental selves as omnipotent creators of perfect offspring is quite severe and out of proportion to the defect as assessed by others. Inevitably the injury to the parental selves is transmitted to the child and becomes part of the child's self. In addition, grandiosity is inevitable for the child who can injure the parents simply by existing. Thus the child will be empowered to inspire and manipulate via guilt and shame, keeping the parents in a state of impotence and helplessness. Fortunately, the covertly grandiose self can be reached and constructively modified via the treatment in interventions described below.

Treatment Interventions

Anthony (1976) stresses the crucial role that educators and parents can play in the dawning intellectual life of young children. Anthony believs that by serving as an auxiliary to the child's incomplete mental apparatus, the parent or educator can even prevent the development of learning disabilities. He emphasizes the developmentally appropriate and necessary use of adults as part objects performing some aspects of the tasks being mastered. Thus, the importance of collaborative therapeutic work with the child, and the child's parents and teachers, can hardly be overemphasized.

Differential diagnosis is critical in delineating learning disabilities. For example, there are three types of reading disability alone—primary and secondary reading disability, and reading disability associated with brain damage (Shaw, 1966). In addition, there are disorders of writing, spelling, arithmetic, and speech, all of which may occur in association with reading disability. Most cases of primary reading disability will show some of the other disorders as well. Children with severe primary learning disabilities have a poorer prognosis when their disabilities are associated with brain damage as opposed to neurotic learning inhibitions. Tutoring and special education are essential concomitants to psychotherapy, as therapy alone, is ineffectual. Conversely, the secondary emotional problems can aggravate the primary disability and initially the child's limitations may appear more profound than they actually are. Kessler (1966) discusses underachievement and indicates that it is predominantly a male problem, related to the child's early experiential conflicts with parents. She highlights eating and toileting problems that are later displaced onto the learning situation: e.g., food and learning refusal; anal conflicts and the resultant refusal to produce for the teacher; family secrets and the danger of learning; sexual overstimulation and the not uncommon phenomena of enuresis and poor academic performance, which are due to the child's view of his or her genitals as defective. Some children appear to inhibit learning to avoid growing up, to avoid anxiety and competition, or to fulfill a need to fail based on an unconscious wish for punishment. Recommended are the combined interventions of tutoring, individual psychotherapy with the child, and family therapy with the parents and child.

Case of Martin

The case of Martin amply demonstrates differential diagnostic dilemmas that occur when several etiological factors are apparent. Martin evidenced primary deficiencies of an organic nature, as well as maternal mishandling. Clinical planning for a retarded, defective, nontypical personality such as Martin's requires education, therapy and work with the parents. The case is presented in accord with the Diagnostic (Anna Freud) Profile, which emphasizes developmental lines, points of arrest and regression, and ego functioning.

Diagnostic Evaluation

REFERRAL

Martin P., a 6½-year-old white Catholic boy, was referred to the hospital by a community mental health clinic, where he had been in speech therapy for some time. Martin had long-standing learning and behavioral problems, and the family had consulted a myriad of physical and mental health resources. The parents expressed confusion about the cause of Martin's difficulties and requested a comprehensive diagnostic work-up; the mother tended to see the problem as organic in nature. In school, Martin did not follow instructions, could not finish his work, and had a short attention span. He was hyperactive, swore and fought a lot, and lately had been pulling his pants down and exhibiting himself to neighborhood children, who call him "mental" or "retarded."

At home, he was calmer and more manageable with father, but totally out of control with mother. He continually swore at her and attacked and threatened to kill her and his 4-year-old brother. He called her "shit hole, face hole, fuco fanny" and exhibited himself to her, saying "touch my pinko." Sometimes he spoke to her about hurting it—e.g., "pierce my pinko," and he had actually hurt his brother's penis. When father was home, Martin never exhibited himself or had swearing and kicking outbursts. He had kissing and handshake rituals with the maternal grandfather after his daily visits; when he was not allowed to practice these rituals, he would bang his head on the living room window. Lately, he had developed compulsions involving endless hand washing. He was very difficult at bedtime and at meals, often making outrageous requests (e.g., spaghetti for breakfast), with which mother always complied.

HISTORY OF COMPLAINT

Parents stated that they first noted problems when Martin was two and a half. He had no speech and was not toilet trained. They consulted various doctors and, when Martin was three, they enrolled him in the Easter Seal program. There he received some speech therapy and supervised play hours. After three to four months without progress, the parents sent Martin to a nursery school for retarded children, which he attended for six months. The school psychologist found an IQ of 85, indicating that Martin was slow, but not retarded. At her recommendation, Martin was enrolled in a kindergarten readiness program for a full year; the year before his referral to the hospital, he attended a public school kindergarten. Neurological examinations showed a "slight organic abnormality" and/or the possibility of childhood epilepsy, but Martin didn't respond favorably to any of the drugs he was given to treat this condition. At the time of his referral, he was not on any medication. The following medications had been attempted: (1) Dilantin and phenobarb, (2) Dilantine and Nyciline or primodone, (3) Dilantine and Mesantain, (4) Redlyn (which made him wilder), and (5) hydrozide.

School settings consistently managed Martin more easily than mother did. She did not involve herself in any extended kind of counseling of therapy, claiming that all professionals blamed her completely for Martin's problems, told her she was not firm enough, and suggested that she lock Martin in his room, stop the grandparents' daily visits, etc. Mother was extremely anxious and her reaction was to be very controlling, presenting endless lists and a flat affect. Father was completely bewildered, denied the severity of the situation, and hoped that Martin would grow out of his difficulties. Martin was acutely anxious and spoke of becoming a good boy. The school wished to arrange a special placement and, according to mother, was awaiting the work-up.

THE CHILD TODAY

In addition to the above material, it is essential to note that mother perceived Martin as an overpowering tower of strength. The parents and Martin were diminutive in stature and the mother felt completely unable to stop Martin's physical attacks on her and the younger brother. At home with mother, Martin had a position of omnipotence, virtually controlling mother and brother every waking moment. At school, he was fearful, got teased, and was unable to fend for himself. He was aware of his inability to learn and handle schoolwork, and was defensively aggressive and hyperactive. His recent obsessive hand washing appeared to be another sign of his acute anxiety. His exhibiting himself to mother and peers seemingly indicated his castration fears and the need to reassure himself of his masculinity in the face of aggressivity from mother and neighborhood children. Thus Martin, a damaged child, inept in every area and aware of it, was powerless away from home and omnipotent at home, where he dominated mother, brother, and grandfather, and seemed to feel safest with father.

DEVELOPMENTAL HISTORY

Mr. and Mrs. P. had been married eight years. Mother became pregnant with Martin at the end of the first year of marriage. Martin was not planned and—although mother took no precautions—she said she would like to have worked longer. Martin was a full-term baby. No nursing was attempted and adjustment to the formula was difficult, with many changes. Mrs. P's parents, who lived nearby, visited every day, with grandmother helping in Martin's care. There was much excitement and happiness over the birth of the first son and grandson. Martin was a difficult baby from the beginning, suffering severe colic the first three months. He was fitful, constantly awakening and screaming, with violent tantrums for the first four or five months. Mother was frightened by Martin and frustrated in attempts to comfort him. Martin used a pacifier for ten months. Night rocking started at seven months and never abated; at the time of referral, Martin was able to rock a bed across a room. Head banging began at nine months and ended at the end of Martin's first year. Banging the walls at night lasted till age five.

Feeding was a profound problem, as mother was always concerned that Martin wouldn't get enough food. She was unable to wean him from the bottle until he was four and a half. Martin would not eat baby and junior jar food until age three and a half. At the instigation of his nursery school, Martin finally began to eat solids at about four years. He still ate erratically, with mother meeting all his demands.

Martin sat up at 7 months, said a few words at 10 months, and walked at 13 months. Toilet training was inconsistently handled and was not in fact accomplished until Martin started nursery school at age four. Martin regressed and became hostile and unruly at the birth of his brother. Father felt uncomfortable with his wife's requests that he punish or scold Martin. He said that "scolding does little good and when I'm home the children follow me about and things quiet down."

Martin never made a satisfactory school adjustment and could not handle the tasks of latency, i.e., school, learning, peers, and play. He appeared very much like a nursery-school-age child, which was probably due in large part to his low IQ and general immaturity. Disturbances of the phallic phase, such as castration anxiety and death wishes, seemed very prominent. In addition, the behavior disorders of the toddler, i.e., destructiveness, messiness, temper tantrums, and separation problems, were very prominent.

POSSIBLE SIGNIFICANT ENVIRONMENTAL FACTORS

Other than a T & A (tonsillectomy and adenoidectomy) at close to six years of age, Martin had not had any serious medical illnesses, but the repetitive medical examinations, EEGs, and medication attempts in two years prior to his referral had to have been traumatic for him. When Martin was five, his father was away from home on business for two weeks; this was described as a trauma for Martin. However, these events were relatively recent and Martin had exhibited profound developmental difficulties since birth. It would appear that mother's fear and anger toward Martin since his infancy had had the greatest influence on Martin's personality development, and had exacerbated his organic problems. Clearly, Martin was a most difficult child to live with and, from birth on, mother had been frustrated in all attempts to comfort him. However, she appeared to be a seriously disturbed person herself, with a peculiar, schizoidlike flat affect. She made almost no eye contact and talked nonstop, handling her anxiety with obsessive-compulsive intellectualization and the citation of endless lists. She was too controlling to share her emotional interaction with Martin. Father reported in a separate interview that she screamed and hollered constantly at the children. She totally dominated all interviews but was quite incapable of looking at her own involvement with Martin.

PARENTS

Mr. and Mrs. P. were both 28, Italian, and relatively uneducated. Mr. P. had immigrated to the U.S. as an adolescent and had always worked hard and saved his money; the P.'s owned their own home. They both appeared to be of average intelligence, shy, and without close friends. They remained close to relatives and the Italian community, depending on their Italian club for their social life.

Mrs. P., an only child, was adopted at age three weeks. Grammar school was stressful, as the other children teased her about her slowness. She did better in high school, went on to take a commercial course, and worked in an office until her pregnancy two years later. Although the content and vocabulary of Mrs. P.'s speech indicated that she was intelligent, her affect was very peculiar. She was brought up in a strict Catholic home that prohibited smoking and dating before age 17. Mrs. P. spoke of her parents as "saints." Mrs. P.'s mother, who was in poor health for fifteen years, died last year. Mrs. P. had not worked through her mother's death and had suppressed all expression of aggression toward her mother.

Mr. P., the fifth of seven children, was born in an Italian village near Venice. His father farmed and finances were always a problem. His father immigrated to the U.S. when Mr. P. was 13; after four or five years, he returned to Italy permanently because his wife refused to immigrate. When Mr. P. was six, his older brother immigrated to Australia for work and, though they corresponded, they had not seen each other since. Mr. P. immigrated to the U.S. at age 15 when an aunt sent for him. He wrote to his relatives in Italy, but had not seen them since his move to the U.S. He could give little information about his parents. Despite the fact that his father had a hot temper and threw things when drunk, Mr. P. remembered him as a good man. He was closer to his mother, a quiet, religious woman who was devoted to her family. In the U.S., Mr. P. attended school for eight months and graduated from grammar school. He then attended night school for two years while working in a brick yard. He worked at a factory for nine years and was promoted to foreman.

Both Mr. and Mrs. P. denied marital problems, citing Martin as their only problem and worry. Mr. P. stated he could "take" Martin more easily than his wife could and didn't think the situation was so serious. Doctors had told him that "childhood epilepsy" could be outgrown. His pain during this diagnostic study was striking, particularly in contrast to his wife's repressed anxiety and focus on lists, dates, and mechanics of arrangements. Mr. P. did suggest that his father-in-law's daily visits and unasked-for advice created problems. Mrs. P. denied any such problems, although referring material indicated considerable conflict around the father-in-law. Again, mother seemed frightened and controlling, wanting to focus solely on organic causation and behavioral problems while avoiding all emotional issues. The diagnostician suspected that there was considerable marital difficulty.

INTERVIEW

Because Martin was anxious and could not separate from his parents for very long (only tolerating twenty minutes the first interview), the diagnostician saw him a second time. Martin, a blond, well-scrubbed, sturdy-looking 6-year-old, was small for his age. He was immaculately attired, smiling, and friendly, sitting between his parents in the waiting room. He grinned at the clinician and kissed his parents repeatedly before separating. As he entered my office, he queried, "No shots, not shots?" After the clinician reassured Martin on that score, he sat down and looked at toys, crayons, and paper. In response to the clinician's questions, Martin said he had come to play and talk. He used the toy animals in sterile play—taking them out of the box, standing them up, and chattering about their colors. He took one hard candy for each member of his family and two for himself, focusing on their colors.

He then referred to the colors of the crayons and tried—not very successfully—to draw pumpkins and print his name. In immature but intelligible speech, he talked of school fights, falling into dirty puddles, and scary boys who hit him. He then associated to other scary things and, in toddlerlike fashion, spoke of his T & A. He next referred to his upper teeth and the fact that a front one had been knocked out by a baseball when he was playing catch with his dad. He looked out the office window at the traffic below and made random friendly comments; then he began to hoist himself up against the large windowpane, using the desk and a bar at the window for leverage. He stopped easily at the clinician's request. He wandered about and talked about being a bad boy at home—saying bad things and fighting. He only alluded to mother once and felt very threatened. He found it easier to talk about fights with his brother. The diagnostician did not push Martin at all and, as he became more relaxed, she asked him to play with her. He compulsively lined up each toy animal and doll. Whenever one fell on the floor, he would get anxious as if he expected to be scolded for being messy. He did respond to the clinician's reassurances, but soon thereafter he wanted to see his parents and go home. As though to reassure himself, he reiterated several times that his parents would wait for him. When the clinician reassured Martin that he could return to his parents, he began to clean up and put the toys back. He danced out to his parents all smiles— much like a very young child. He seemed pleased when told that a second appointment was scheduled.

Martin came to the second interview with his father. They went through even more prolonged separation kisses, and Martin could not separate easily. Before entering the office, he had to return to his father, use the toilet, and wash his hands. Upon entering the office, he touched some candy and wanted to leave again to wash his hands because they were sticky. This compulsivity continued and Martin began to wipe the rear office desk, noting drops of water from when plants had been watered. He responded to questions and spoke of much hand washing at home.

Martin then seemed to settle down a bit and wished to play with the same toys as in the first interview. He seemed to become too rapidly engrossed with the diagnostician in that he asked her if she liked to play baseball, and then asked her to come home with him to play and to be at his brother's birthday party that day. When told about the extent of their contact, he smiled, but insisted that she come home with him. He seemed upset at learning this was the last appointment and immediately turned to the candy, wanting dozens of pieces for himself and each member of his family, He played in the same rather repetitive fashion, making several random references to the T & A and lost tooth. He spoke next of being a bad boy who said bad words. He said he would become a good boy and "play better" at home and with children. He referred several times to big kids fighting with him. He spoke of his mother as follows: "The dark also scares him and he gets mommy to be with him at night. Mommy is better at night. Then she doesn't yell. But he'll now be a good good boy." Martin stayed in the office forty minutes and had great difficulty leaving, asking for more candy and pressing the clinician to come home with him. He tried to keep the clinician in sight as he left, calling repetitive goodbyes to her.

DIAGNOSTIC FORMULATIONS

Martin gave ample evidence of primary deficiencies in his ego functions. On recent psychologicals, "organic impairment of some magnitude" was noted. His full-scale IQ of 59 was at the retarded level. This IQ score was considerably lower than that of previous tests (he once had received an 88) and might well be explained by secondary interference with other ego functions. Immaturity and overwhelming anxiety were handled by hyperactivity and motoric drivenness. Martin could not sublimate his aggressive impulses and had a very limited attention span and low frustration tolerance. His learning was grossly impaired. Whenever Martin experienced any stress or anxiety, he had little control of motility; he could not tolerate delay. At home with his mother, where the stress was greatest, his ego vanished. In the interview with the diagnostician, in contrast to the stressful testing session with the psychologist, there appeared to be more ego intactness, as evidenced by more synthesis, more control over motility, and better reality testing. Thus, despite the serious primary deficiencies, the emotional overlay could not be ignored.

Although Martin was struggling with phallic issues, he had not genuinely entered the Oedipal phase (i.e., experienced any romantic feelings for mother). His wish to get mother into bed was based on infantile omnipotent needs, night fears, and separation anxieties, rather than on Oedipal needs. This appeared to be due to his generalized immaturity and manifest fixation at each earlier libidinal phase. There was marked sexualized energy invested in oral and anal issues. Mature eating had not been established, and eating itself was a power struggle. Further, Martin was orally sadistic and verbally attacking, especially of mother. The anal phase appeared to be Martin's true level of libidinal development. He was preoccupied with messing, cleaning up, tormenting, motor restlessness, tantrums, and all the other behavior disorders of the toddler at the height of anal sadism. Although Martin used some sexual words in outbursts at mother, they appeared to be imitative—and thus, tormenting, anal, and aggressive, rather than phallic. Martin did not have the ego development and rich fantasy life that accompany normal Oedipal development.

It seemed that Martin's cathexis of the self was mixed, in that, at home, where no limits were set, he was omnipotent though fearful, while at school and with peers, he was confronted with the difficulties resulting from his poor endowment. He was "a bad boy," an all-powerful giant, "a retard," and a most lonely, anxious child who was aware of his deficiencies. Martin had reached the state of part-object attachment, but had not achieved object constancy. The mutual ambivalence of Martin and his mother constantly interfered with the cathexis of the mother. Mother, who offered every infantile gratification, was a feared object due to her lack of limit setting as well as her constant barrage of unconscious murderous rage, which Martin seemed to act out for her to a degree. In short, Martin was fixed in the ambivalent relationship of the anal sadistic stage.

Martin had not achieved any control over his aggressive impulses. His aggression broke through constantly, especially with his mother. When he was frustrated in any way, he attacked, yelled, and had profound tantrums. His overwhelming anal aggression was turned outward against peers and family members. When he exhibited himself to peers, it was not sexual, but rather, the ragelike reaction of the toddler doing something "dirty."

Martin's superego was very primitive and immature. He completely denied responsibility for his actions, often blaming his brother for his own misbehavior. Denial and projection were the primitive defenses of the toddler. Similarly, Martin's "make-up" gift of candy or a kiss was the primitive restitution effort of a 2- or 3-year-old. No doubt this lack of adequate superego development stemmed from his intellectual limitations and lack of empathy for others' feelings. There seemed to be only meager introjection of parental authority into his superego. Martin's conflicts were not internalized or between drives, but rather, were external, in that he and his environment were at cross purposes with one another. His ego had sided with his id impulses and, overall, he presented an infantile picture.

Although Martin had attended nursery school and kindergarten, he had not attained emotional self-reliance. At home, there was no independent body hygiene and management or control of motility. Martin had temper tantrums in which he banged his head. Some degree of management was seen at school, though he was hyperactive and distractible. Martin had no friends and was narcissistic and egocentric in his social outlook. He was fearful and angry when teased, with little or no sense of his role in conflicts. He could not play with any purpose or creativity. In school, he had only learned to print his name and recognize some shapes and colors. However, his IQ did not appear as low in the diagnostic interviews. His poor test score and school performance reflected severe emotional pathology.

Because Martin was grossly mishandled at home, the treatment of choice would be a therapeutic day program, where he would receive special schooling and psychotherapy in a firm, predictable daily environment that offered proper social experiences and recreation as well. Mother would be threatened by any improvements he might make and would also require extensive psychotherapy.

Martin presented a retarded, defective, and nontypical personality resulting from primary organic deficiencies and maternal mishandling that distorted development and structuralization. The psychologist's diagnosis was "chronic brain syndrome, with retardation in intelligence, extreme emotional immaturity, depression, anxiety, and extreme immaturity in impulse control."

Treatment Plans and Prognosis

Treatment goals and prognosis were guarded. It was imperative that Martin and mother be involved in an extensive program before any greater disparity developed between his level of functioning and chronological age. A day program seemed to be the most viable possibility. It must be noted that Mrs. P. had assiduously avoided any therapy for herself. It might be helpful to involve her prior to enrolling Martin in a day care program. Finally, although the diagnostic focus was kept on Martin, an assessment of his brother was clearly needed as well.

Addendum

Martin was successfully referred to a therapeutic day school, which provided small classes, individualized instruction, and milieu, group, and individual treatment. As a consultant to the day school setting, the diagnostician was able to follow up on this successful referral. Both parents were seen in therapy and, after the first year, the younger brother was evaluated as well. After entering this school, Martin demonstrated substantial and consistent cognitive growth and ego development.

CHAPTER 8

Pre-Oedipal Disorders

Those of us engaged in child welfare services and child therapy are encountering increasing numbers of parents and children with profound psychiatric disorders. This increase is not simply a function of better clinical techniques; there has been an actual increase in the prevalence and severity of child pathologies. Societal conditions, notably increased family disorganization and breakdown, seem to be contributing to a higher proportion of families in crisis exhibiting violence and substance abuse, with resultant alienation and a need for services. Specifically, the instance of severe character pathology, psychosis, and borderline conditions has increased. The borderline syndrome is a bewildering diagnostic entity that causes havoc for parents and children, as well as for the professionals attempting to plan and provide services for such clients.

The theoretical underpinning offered here is an ego psychological perspective that embodies a developmental approach. Normal and pathological child development are seen on a continuum—with disorders caused by arrests or fixations in the course of normal chronological development. The earliest developmental stage is the "normal autistic" state of the newborn infant, who is self-enclosed and unaware of the outside world. The denial of the outside human world is due to the extensive proportion of time asleep, the infant's normal stimulus barrier that shuts out household noises, and the "good enough" mother who effectively modulates the environment. Gradually, this pattern shifts and the child no longer responds solely to inner sensations of hunger, distress, and discomfort. Rather, there is a slowly evolving awareness of self and others and gratification comes from the outside in the form of mother. Mother is slowly taken in, first in part-object fashion—the breast, the bottle, the voice, the face, and the comfort and solace provided. This is the crucial early bonding and attachment of mother and child. If a child remains fixated in a self-enclosed world—or regresses back to it—autism, the most profound pathology, results. Mother has not been responded to—or rather, has been shut out and responded to negatively. Of course, constitutional and neurological factors also play a part in autism.[1]

In normal development, the next step after bonding and attachment is symbiosis, most eloquently described by Margaret Mahler (1968). She borrowed the term from biology, noting the union of two organisms for their mutual advantage. In this case, the child totally and completely needs the mother and the mother needs to be needed. The child's fantasy is that mother and child are one. Over a two-year period, the child begins to separate and individuate, gradually becoming a distinct and complete person in his or her own right. Magical thinking and omnipotence permeate the thinking of the toddler. Mother, when gratifying and soothing, is all good; when she frustrates and limits, she is all bad. Maldevelopment at this early developmental stage causes an arrest—or what Mahler calls "symbiotic psychosis"—with the refusal to surrender the magical thinking and omnipotence of toddlerhood. Mother remains a split object—either all good or all bad—and self and other are not distinct. The child commands the parent and the total environment via the temper tantrums of toddlerhood, or the period known as "the terrible twos." This twisted and stunted development may come out of massive frustration, due to the sudden unavailability of the mother—be it due to illness, death, or the birth of a sib that causes mother to ignore her toddler. Some very infantile mothers, without such a percipitant, recoil from their 2-year-old who needs limits and protection. They were more comfortable with the tiny baby that they could hug and cuddle, and become alarmed at the child's growing self-assertion, exploration, and normal opposition. Massive overgratification is the other potential contributor to this condition—with no expectations of the child to accept limits and boundaries or to struggle for mastery, be it in the realm of speech, waiting, or tolerance for delay. Total indulgence prevents the gradual integration of the reality

[1]For further discussion of autism, see the case of Jimmy in Chapter 6.

principle. Again, pathology arises out of normal development—the stage of symbiosis—when the necessary ingredients of optimal frustration and consistency are lacking.

The third major developmental milestone for the young child is separation-individuation and the development of object constancy. Separating and individuating means becoming a separate person with clear self/other boundaries. No longer is there a fantasy of omnipotent control of, merger with, or engulfment by, mother. Mother is no longer the all good or all bad split object. The normally developing child can love irrespective of frustration and can tolerate ambivalence toward parents. The parent is permanently introjected by the child. Thus, normal 3-year-olds can comfortably attend nursery school, as they have a vivid memory of mother's face and ministrations, and are certain that mother will be home awaiting their return. This *evocative memory* soothes the child during absences from mother. Borderline children lack both an evocative memory and object constancy. They cannot recall persons and they continue to split objects into all-good/all-bad categories. This lack of evocative memory is exemplified by a borderline woman who terminated therapy after eight years when her therapist moved to another city. She needed a photograph of the therapist because she could not remember her in her mind's eye. This lack of evocative memory and object constancy is rooted in the lack of constancy and consistency of the primary object—the mother. Because of these basic ego deficits, borderline children and adults are subject to panic, anxiety, and impulsivity.

Borderline Syndrome

The term "borderline" has come into increasing use in the last twenty years as a description of a severe form of pathology. In clinical practice, it is still often misused and misunderstood. The borderline syndrome is often seen as a transitory state between psychosis and severe neurosis; thus, children who have fleeting periods of psychosis and intense ego disruption are quickly labeled "borderline." This syndrome has long been used as a catchall category for cases that are difficult to diagnose. However, in the last few years, the borderline syndrome has come to be described as a pathology in its own right. It must be noted that categorization, when properly used, is not pejorative toward clients, but rather, provides clarity about clients' ego strengths and deficits. Once the latter are understood, appropriate treatment interventions and environmental manipulations (e.g., contact with schools, camps, day care centers, and child welfare services) can be planned.

Definition

In the late 1940s, as we gained greater knowledge of the developmental childhood psychoses from the studies of autism (Kanner, 1943) and symbiosis (Mahler, 1952), another closely related childhood disturbance immediately began to be reported in the literature. This disturbance went beyond neurosis but did not meet the recently delineated criteria of childhood psychosis. Mahler (1948) described children who had "a certain kind of benign psychosis" that appeared neuroticlike. In 1958, Geleerd reviewed "borderline states" and carefully separated them from the childhood psychoses. It was clear that borderline pathology was linked to arrests and fixations at a "higher" or more advanced level than those of autism and symbiosis, but at a lower level than those of neurosis.

Since the mid-1950s, several major clinical studies have attempted to describe borderline disorders and to develop theoretical formulations within which the resulting observations could best be understood. In contrast to the chronic and rather fixed ego deviance that most authors described in borderline children, Ekstein (1966) noted markedly shifting levels of ego organization within the same child. His patients oscillated quickly between primitive ego states (e.g., temper tantrums) and age-appropriate ego functioning. Rosenfeld and Sprince (1963), in their work with Anna Freud, did a profile analysis on a series of borderline children. They noted that there was a typical lack of phase dominance in psychosexual development and thus one child could simultaneously evidence marked oral and anal features. They specifically explored the impact on the personality of the child's inability to use repression and neutralization. They also felt that the central issue in borderline children was their struggle between primary identification with objects and object cathexis. Much of the borderline child's anxiety, they noted, was due to fears of fusion with the mother.

The literature has slowly delineated the boundaries of borderline pathology, separating it out from the neuroses and psychoses. Many articles have clarified the differences between borderline pathology and prepsychotic or latent psychotic conditions, and between borderline pathology and regression from severe neurosis.

Etiology

Per Mahler's developmental schema, the borderline syndrome is the result of arrest or regression at the third crucial developmental milestone, i.e., a separation-individuation failure. As noted earlier, Mahler uses the term "symbiosis" for the bonding that unites mother and infant into one organism, creating a closed system or oneness between two separate individuals. The essential feature of symbiosis is the hallucinatory or delusional omnipotent fusion of child and mother—i.e., the delusion of a common boundary between mother and child, which starts at 3–4 months. The peak of symbiosis is at 4–5 months; at this time, differentiation, the first subphase of separation-individuation, begins. Stranger anxiety at 6–8 months, when the loved one is distinguished from all others, signifies optimal symbiosis. Practicing (second subphase)—crawling away from mother—and rapprochement (third subphase)—walking away but scurrying back to mother for emotional refueling, shadowing and darting away, wishing for reunion and fearing reengulfment—are highlighted by the 24-month turning point, when toddlers recognize that the world is not their oyster. At this point, under optimal conditions, there is a surrender of secondary narcissism. The final subphase of separation-individuation is the consolidation of individuality and the beginning of emotional object constancy, which should solidify by age three. This is the time that the good and gratifying mother and the bad and frustrating mother are fused into one beloved mother; i.e., the mother is loved, irrespective of gratification or frustration.

This crucial developmental process is perhaps more easily understood if we think of adolescence as the second round of separation-individuation. The adolescent wishes for independence and autonomy, but is in conflict over still present dependency needs. Thus, the teenager vacillates between infantile and adult behaviors, wanting the perogatives of the adult world while also wanting to be cared for. Rebellion and defiance, on the one hand, and dependency and the wish to be taken care of, on the other, cause the teenager's upheaval. The teenager finally moves into a more genuine emancipated state, culminating in the identity formation of young adulthood.

Thus the borderline syndrome is the result of a separation-individuation failure. Separation for the borderline patient does not evolve as a normal developmental experience, but, on the contrary, evokes such intense feelings of abandonment that it is experienced as death. To defend against these feelings, the borderline child clings to the maternal figure and fails to progress through the normal developmental stages of separation-individuation to autonomy. Often the mother is also borderline and has failed to separate from her own mother. She fosters the symbiotic union with her child, encouraging dependency to maintain her own emotional equilibrium. She is often threatened by and unable to deal with her child's emerging individuality. She depersonalizes the child and projects on the child the image of her own parents or siblings; or she envisions the child as a perpetual infant or object who can be used to defend against feelings of abandonment. She clings to the child to prevent separation, discouraging the child's moves towards individuation by withdrawing her support.

Borderline patients do not become psychotic and do not lose total touch with reality. Particular levels of developmental arrest and specific forms of aberrant development have shaped typical borderline ego development and sense of self. These arrests promote fixed patterns that we can ultimately identify as the borderline syndrome.

Deficiencies in crucial ego functions—such as the perceptual and executive abilities—and fixations leave borderline patients unable to deal effectively with the internal or external world. The narcissistic, magical, and omnipotent fantasies erected by these patients to contend with these deficits and to protect themselves from painful memory traces of a traumatic injury of childhood are of little help in coping with the realities of the real world.

Descriptive Characteristics

Between the ages of one and a half and three, conflict develops in the child between the developmental push for individuation and autonomy and the withdrawal of the mother's emotional supplies that this growth would entail. Growth equals loss. Thus, developmental arrest of the borderline child occurs either in the narcissistic or in the early oral phase. The earlier the arrest, the more the child will resemble the psychotic; the later the arrest, the more the child will appear neurotic. The developmental arrest produces severe defects in ego functioning, the persistence of the defenses of the ego and object splitting, a failure to achieve object constancy, and the simultaneous development of a negative self-image.

Characteristics of this ego structure include: failure of normal repression; persistence of primitive mechanisms of defense, with reliance on projection, introjection, regression, and denial; impairment of the ego's synthetic function; a lack of basic trust; a failure of sublimation of raw instinctual impulses; fluid ego boundaries; deficient differentiation between inner and outer stimuli; poor reality perception; poor frustration tolerance; poor impulse control; object splitting; and reacting to objects as parts rather than wholes, and as totally gratifying or totally frustrating. There is intense oral dependency and a need for affection and approval; rage and frustration result when this need isn't met. The child fears his or her feelings will destroy self and object. To deal with this fear, the child splits both self and object into two unrealistic parts—the all-good or all-bad mother and the all-good or all-bad self.

In the evaluation of the borderline child, it is the whole gestalt, rather than single symptoms, that determines the diagnosis. Chronic and conspicuous problems in ego development tend to indicate borderline problems, while neurotic children show a minor range of such developmental deviations. Fundamentally, borderline children maintain their capacity to test reality, and do not evidence the hallucinatory or delusional problems of childhood psychosis such as autism and symbiotic psychosis.

Borderline children commonly cannot manage their excessive anxiety. Their ego deficits and paucity of age-appropriate defenses cause them to feel frightened and overwhelmed. They are inept at appraising the outside world and its expectations. For the borderline child, danger induces fears of annihilation. These children fear separation from parental objects most.

In borderline patients, we frequently see neurotic symptoms of a hysterical, phobic, or obsessive-compulsive nature, which represent attempts to ward off more regressive and primitive states. Often the higher-level borderline child shows a superficial adaptation to the environment and a pseudoability to maintain object relations. As many autonomous ego functions are not impaired and intellectual endowment, cognition, memory, etc., may be adequate or even superior, intellectual functioning may be acceptable or even excellent. However, despite good academic functioning and an array of neurotic defensive symptomatology, the neurotic symptom formation is fragile, fleeting, and not fully structuralized.

Phobias can multiply and cause intense restrictions and inhibitions, as exemplified by Sally, age ten, who first manifested separation problems at age six. Help was sought, and the mother reported agency dictums that she be "firm" (how, she did not know) and that Sally and her 13-year-old brother not continue to share a bedroom. There were innumerable attempts to help Sally when she presented a full-blown school phobia, and fears of eating, at age nine. Psychiatrists attempted medication and hypnosis and recommended that the parents use physical force. Sally, who was most suggestible, was phobic about school, elevators, and swallowing; she avoided most foods and at times wouldn't go out at all for fear that falling leaves or other objects would get into her throat and cause strangulation. Of superior intelligence, Sally had always excelled at academics; once she was back at school, she again demonstrated excellent school achievement and age-adequate peer contacts. Though neuroticlike phobias and obsessions still preoccupied Sally, she had already demonstrated insight into her underlying fear of separation from mother. In her own words: "Lots of people, even adults, need to have their mothers always available and near. My mother's kind of like that with her mother."

Impulse and drive expression in borderline children frequently is excessive, out of keeping with precipitants in the environment. Temper tantrums, rage, frenzy, and weeping can often erupt with surprisingly little warning. One 12-year-old borderline girl in a residential placement was impulsive and constantly agitated; she would storm off in rages, or impulsively pierce her ears with an icepick. With borderline children, one never can predict what will occur next, though one can predict agitation, given these children's severe responses to changes in their environment. Masochistic trends (including self-mutilation), paranoid ideation, and dependency are common borderline character traits, especially in periods of regression. As noted earlier, borderline children have failed to achieve object constancy and lack an evocative memory; thus, they cannot mourn, and object losses and separations are disastrous.

Borderline children unconsciously introject their parents' negative attitudes toward them; these attitudes then become part of their own self-image, which lacks cohesion and well-modulated self-esteem. The guilt that these children feel for leaving or wishing to leave the mother erodes their capacity to move towards individuation and is intensified by the rage and desire for revenge provoked by the deprivation.

The consequences of the separation-individuation struggles are abandonment depression and oral narcissistic fixation. In discussing the borderline adolescent, Masterson (1972) highlights the abandonment depression and the resultant acting-out behaviors that are often used to ward off the depression. The adolescent initially may present mild boredom and difficulty in concentrating in school, followed by hypochondriacal concerns, and later, by excessive physical and sexual activity. More flagrant acting out is expressed via delinquent behaviors, drinking, drug use, sexual promiscuity, slovenly dress, defiance, and running away. Frequently, a sexual relationship is used by children of both sexes to substitute for, and avoid engulfment by, the maternal figure. Many adolescents diagnosed as borderline have presented what appeared to be solid and appropriate development through latency, with the borderline features not appearing until adolescence. We now understand that in fact the earlier "good" adjustment was fragile and the balance maintained was precarious. Under the onslaught of the pressures of adolescence, the initial separation-individuation crisis that was not mastered in toddlerhood resurfaces in florid and dramatic form. Clinical observation and careful history gathering provide evidence for this syndrome's earlier existence in *dormant* form; it is not until the second and final separation-individuation crisis during adolescence that the syndrome is activated. Parental divorce, illness, or unavailability frequently precipitate the adolescent's decline, which has been avoided prior to this constellation of stresses.

The self-other components of borderline children's relationships are often wearing and draining on those who are closest to these children, as they tend to disregard the real and human characteristics of these important people totally, investing the latter with projected need-fulfilling characteristics. That is, others must live out roles prescribed by the child. The interpersonal relations of borderline children are characterized by a lack of empathy in that these children are unable to perceive and react to the needs of others. The self-absorbed borderline child does not perceive others as separate and distinct individuals; rather, the child responds to them narcissistically, in terms of the child's own needs and wants.

Many of the difficulties encountered in the development of the ego of the borderline child also impede the development of the superego. For example, ego functions such as perception, reality testing, and synthesis participate in the development of the superego structure; when these building blocks are impaired, problems in superego development occur. While the borderline child has many problems with the process of internalization, some prohibitions are introjected. Because most of these introjects are endowed with intense aggression, the superego of the borderline child will often appear intolerant, primitive, and inconsistent, with frequent breakthroughs of aggressive impulses. This inconsistency is due less to the sanctioning of the behavior by the borderline child's superego, and more to the brittleness of the defensive structure and the power of the impulses themselves. Thus, the delinquent behavior of the borderline adolescent is bewilderingly inconsistent, with pockets of guilt amid large areas of guiltless affect.

Treatment Interventions

The most frequently referred to therapeutic intervention for borderline children is individual psychotherapy. Many clinicians and researchers also stress the management role in work with these children and the necessity for out-of-the-office structure (e.g., special programs). Since borderline children react intensely to frustration and change, it is essential that they live in a supportive, minimally stressful environment. Institutional placement (i.e., residential treatment centers, hospitals, or day treatment programs) is often necessary for borderline children with severe impulse problems. In these settings, one can best control the changes and frustrations of the child's daily world. Where impulse control is not a major problem, active work with parents, school faculty, and significant others is usually critical to the creation of an adequately benign and sympathetic surround.

In the course of ongoing therapy, one is struck with the paradoxical splits of borderline children. While they are in contact with reality, their sense of reality is distorted. They can be tenacious in holding on to irrational fears that create a sense of paralysis and distort their understanding of cause and effect. Some children retreat into a narcissistic fantasy world, denying age-appropriate expectations and perceptions. Ekstein (1966) stresses "interpretation within the metaphor" in work with borderline children. The therapist must not puncture the child's fantasy, play theme, or denial, but rather, must follow the child until the child relates in a part-object fashion. Gradually, the therapist will become a more distinct and trusted fused object in whom good and bad are united. Empathy, patience, and a long-term commitment go far in helping the child achieve some measure of separation-individuation, self and object constancy, and a more tolerant and flexible superego. Therapy with these children must include ego supportive work, with reflections and interpretations addressed to affects, feelings, and defenses, rather than id content. Individual long-term therapy, together with a supportive, well-organized living milieu, should lead to a diminution of the child's internal disorganization. In addition, ongoing work with the child's parents or caretakers is essential to the maintenance of an accepting, consistent, and nurturant surround. Frequently, mothers will not let go and permit the child a treatment relationship unless they too are receiving help.

Therapeutic interventions require "delineating borders 'within' the domain of borderline" (Pine, 1974, p. 341). It is erroneous to seek a unitary concept of the borderline child. The extent of ego deviance and of shifting levels of internal disorganization, and the nature of the aberration of object relationships, dictate therapeutic planning. In general, the less inner structure the child possesses, the more outer structure he or she will need. Placement facilities or day treatment programs may be used to supplement individual therapy, and frequency of therapy sessions may be adjusted, as needed, to stabilize the child.

Case of Donald

The case of Donald presents an early adolescent with borderline syndrome, depressive features. The unavailability of both parents during Donald's first year of life, his estrangement from his usually absent father, and the continual, profound marital anger and discord culminating in the parents' recent divorce all contributed to Donald's failure to achieve separation-individuation or impulse control (particularly regarding aggressive impulses) and created severe pre-Oedipal arrests and fixations. However, Donald's prognosis was better than his poor history (i.e., long-standing social and academic problems and more recent aggressive acting out) would indicate;

he was psychologically minded and seemed capable of, and eager for, long-term interpretive biweekly therapy.

Diagnostic Evaluation

REFERRAL

Donald S., a 12-year-old white Jewish boy, was referred to the clinic for financial reasons by a child psychiatrist who had been privately evaluating him. Donald had had many psychiatric evaluations; the precipitant for the present referral was that mother and father had been divorced for nine months and mother was now better able to act on her concern about Donald's long-standing severe academic and behavioral problems in school. He had no close friends and would not participate in any organized activities. He primarily talked on the phone and watched TV. Mother began actively seeking therapy for Donald six months before this referral. At that time, Donald was given psychologicals and was briefly seen by Dr. H. Mother and Donald both disliked Dr. H. and his recommendation for residential placement. Despite their negative reaction to this doctor, they did complete the evaluation there. There was a consultation with a neurologist, who referred the case to Dr. N. Father was described as refusing to see the need for therapy, and being oppositional and refusing to finance placement. He never paid the bills for the recent psychiatric contacts. Mother stated her intention to assume financial responsibility and had made regular payments. There had been and would be court litigation over past bills, as well as custody of Donald and his 16-year-old brother, Robert. Mother believed that the children were simply pawns and that the custody fight was more harassment than genuine. There had been a court investigation of the home and the children had been interviewed. The court date had been set and mother had no question that she would be allowed to retain custody of the children. Father recently transmitted to the court his nonsupport of her continued custody. Mother thus stated that once the court actions were over, Donald's treatment would no longer be a problem, in that she would be responsible for it financially and, since he would not have custody, father's opposition could only be verbal, with no actual consequences.

Mother said she had consulted Dr. F. when Donald manifested reading difficulties at age six. Dr. F. recommended more contact with father and time for maturation. Mother had brief contact at a family agency, where she received a recommendation for more extensive and intensive therapy. This led to a two-year contact with Mr. N., a social worker in private practice. He saw her and her husband, and she believed that this treatment gave her the courage to get a divorce. Last spring, Donald was referred to a nearby clinic for testing, but the divorce interrupted this plan.

HISTORY OF COMPLAINT

Mother described concerns about Donald since he was three, when his night fears made him constantly come into the parents' bed. Mother would put him back in his bed and he would continually return. He did not sleep soundly until age five. In nursery school, mother felt he had problems, was isolated, was unable to play with others, and would sit off by himself. She felt he was not ready for kindergarten, but the teacher was confident that he could handle it. Mother felt major school problems were manifest in the first grade. Donald's reading difficulties were very apparent and he had only short-lived friendships.

Currently, he appeared overactive, clowning around and fighting, and was hungry to be socially accepted. He was mainly alone or with disturbed, acting-out children. He had been failing in school recently. It was known that he had experimented with marijuana on one occasion; supposedly he was not acting out with drugs now. He had become frantic and explosive at home, and ran away once but was retrieved by his brother. He shouted threats of suicide on one occasion.

Mother had long been aware of and concerned about Donald's problems, and had sought professional help for some time. She was at a loss as to how to handle Donald; she set curfews, but did not wish to nag or supervise his schoolwork as she had been advised to do by the school. She requested treatment for herself as well as aid in more effective parenting of Donald. Mother had been preoccupied with marital problems until recently and, in the past, apparently was unable to deal with Donald directly or secure treatment for him. Donald had cooperated with the prior brief psychiatric contacts, but vacillated between concern and denial regarding his symptomatology. In the course of this diagnostic study, although he was somewhat ambivalent, he was very cooperative and open in his desire for help. He wanted to get started and requested one of mother's appointments for himself recently; he also inquired constantly when he would begin regular therapy appointments.

THE CHILD TODAY

Donald was a well-built boy of 12, but because of his mop of long blond curls, he looked quite effeminate. Basically he was handsome, but the hair made his face almost fragile. He tried to convey an air of bravado and street savvy. This air was evident when he tried to be funny telling about all his acting out, especially in the classroom. However, the underlying depression and anxiety were also available, and loneliness was a dominant theme, when not denied via projection onto parents, peers, and teachers.

During the course of this study, Donald's marginal grades became failing marks, and he appeared scared and helpless. His peer relationships were marginal. He had no close relationships with boys and talked endlessly on the phone to "girlfriends" who shared worries and concerns. He referred to one girl as his "lady psychiatrist." He was not involved in any ongoing sports or enjoyable recreation. He fooled around with his guitar, watched TV, and complied with Hebrew School in order to be Bar Mitzvahed in the spring. He complained about visits with his father, due to father's possessiveness of him as an object, their lack of communication and his being taken along on father's dates. He conveyed more warmth toward his mother and brother, but still felt alone, in that they were preoccupied with their own lives and worries. He spoke most warmly about this dog. His self-concept was that of a lonely and needy boy who did not know how to improve his situation. His feelings of helplessness seemed to overwhelm him. He could not compete with boys and involved himself primarily with girls. The helplessness and passivity that he attempted to defend against seemed due to an unconscious feminine identification. He attempted to defend with superficial masculine overcompensations in his acting-out behavior.

DEVELOPMENTAL HISTORY

Mr. and Mrs. S. had been married for sixteen years. Mrs. S. was 19 at the time of marriage, and Mr. S. was 29. There were problems early in this marriage, which worsened as she became more independent. Mr. S., a traveling salesman, was always gone during the week. Mrs. S., an attractive woman, described trying to raise her sons alone due to her husband's absence. Robert, age 16, was born immediately after the marriage. Mrs. S. had some artistic interests and had actively involved herself at the local Community Center in art classes. In recent years, she had friends and contacts in the peace movement, as well as in art circles. Mr. S. strongly opposed these friendships, due to his supposedly reactionary leanings. Conflicts about this and about discipline for the children were described as long-standing.

In the years immediately before the divorce, Mr. S. became increasingly depressed, stayed in bed on the weekends, and demanded Mrs. S.'s undivided attention. These problems coincided with his increasing sexual impotence and accusations that his wife was frigid. His sexual impotence and retreat to his bed from Friday night to Monday morning were described as coinciding with increased explosions and complaints about the children's schoolwork and long hair, and complaints about Mrs. S. in front of the children.

Money had been a chronic area of conflict. For several years, Mrs. S. had been working part-time doing freelance market research, something that she didn't especially like (interviewing about products). She continued it because of the flexible hours that enabled her to be home with her children after school and at lunch. Money was still a major area of dissension and acting out. Child support payments were late and Mrs. S.—supposedly on the advice of her lawyer—sought psychiatric consultation about Donald without giving Mr. S. advance notice. Mr. S. refused to pay since he didn't agree to it. Mrs. S. acknowledged a prior immature and uninvolved attitude about family finances. She stated that she was not materialistic and never overspent, but was inattentive to budgeting and planning. Mrs. S. had only one year of college and no real career training.

After the divorce, Mrs. S., Robert, and Donald continued to live in their old, spacious apartment. Mrs. S.'s preference was for comfortable casualness. It was not clear if housekeeping was substandard or if her accounts were guilt-ridden responses to her husband's frenzied rigidities. Music lessons, mild political activism, and art seemed to be family themes.

Treatment was also a major family theme. At the time of Donald's referral, mother hoped for treatment for Donald and herself; she described Robert as also eager to see a therapist. Father was described as the resistive and uncooperative one. Mrs. S. said that two or three years ago, she made an appointment for herself at a nearby clinic that had been recommended by her marriage counselor of two years. She cancelled that appointment because she was fearful of looking at herself and the marriage more deeply, in that, at the time, she didn't have the courage realistically to consider a divorce.

She felt that the divorce had only afforded a legal separation and that her own problems and her children still tied her to her ex-husband. She was concerned about the effects of these ties on her relationships with other men. She was concerned about her concurrent involvement with two men. Her affect was deceptively bland, in that she denied, repressed, and had difficulty being in close touch with her feelings. Recently, she experienced more overt anxiety, manifested by nausea, a harried feeling while driving, and the burning of dinner (with company over). She felt stirred up by the pending court hearing as well as her plans for a two-week Acapulco trip with the man she was most involved with. Her sons knew the men she dated and apparently were aware of the nature of the attachments. She said they hoped she would remarry. Mrs. S. said she was not really ready for any final commitments. It was implied that her handling of sexual needs stemmed from concerns about her own femininity arising from her ex-husband's impotence and accusations that she was frigid and homosexual. She presented these accusations with irony and humor, and as further evidence of her ex-husband's irrationality.

She continuously consciously struggled to understand her part in the marital problems, something she was helped to see via prior treatment. However, this seemed to be a rote catechism rather than something internalized. She consistently defended against inner feelings and subsequently was often bland. Affect seemed more accessible, when her rage and feelings of degradation and harassment were more openly discussed.

Donald was a planned child; Mr. S. had wanted a girl and Mrs. S. had had no preference. Mother suffered morning sickness all day with this pregnancy as she had with her older son. Medication (Compazine) for this nausea during the third month caused a severe reaction and she was hospitalized for spasms and epilepticlike seizures. She was traumatized by this 5-day hospitalization; the complete work-up with EEGs, etc., aroused much anxiety about the effects of her illness and the medication on her baby. She was vague about the rest of the pregnancy. Since she had no spontaneous labor, it had to be induced, as it had been with her older son. She had feared having a stillborn baby and, after delivery, fainted and had to be revived. Donald was a large baby—8 lbs., 10 oz. As mother came out of the delivery room, she fought with her husband about her length of hospital stay because he wished to save money and have her come home quickly.

No nursing was attempted because of inverted nipples. Mrs. S. described acute anxiety about handling Donald after birth. She kept her distance from him and had to be urged by her nurse to become involved. Her panic was very strong. She described the same panic and depression after the delivery of her first son. She described acute physical discomfort as well, due to a bout of hemorrhoids that appeared right before delivery and lasted six weeks or so. Mrs. S. was not sure how long she was depressed. She said her husband's anger about not having a girl or a formal bris (Jewish circumcision ceremony) for Donald further upset her. Supposedly his interest in a bris was never shared until after the appropriate time.

Mother was somewhat vague about Donald's early history, which might reflect the extent of her depression. She had no memory of cooing and thought words were discernible at a year, followed by no verbal communication until age two. Donald used the bottle and pacifier until age three and no earlier weaning was attempted. He walked at about one year. Mother was vague about toilet training and thought Donald was clean and dry with little trouble at age three. She lacked a clear memory of his earlier years. At age three, Donald manifested night fears, came into the parents' room constantly, was taken back, and always returned. Mother said she was perpetually tired till Donald was five and slept soundly. Mother's only explanation of the sleep disturbance was that maybe Donald, who shared a bedroom with his brother, was frightened by Robert's grinding of his teeth in his sleep.

Donald was enrolled at the Community Center nursery at age four. He was isolated and had consistent trouble with the other children because he could not interact, play, or share. On one occasion, he swung a baseball bat at another child (and missed). Mrs. S. was continuously concerned and baffled by the reassurances of her friend, the director of the nursery, that Donald was "so beautiful" and would come along. She felt he was not ready for kindergarten, but he "was cute and manipulated well." Problems were full blown in the first grade. The reading problem was very apparent. Socially, Donald felt rejected and experienced only short-lived friendships.

Now, too, mother felt Donald was lonely and isolated and expected too much from peers. Donald was failing in school; mother said he avoided reading and gave the same book report over and over. He resisted his brother's encouragement and suggestions. (Brother was an avid reader and was very involved with music, but was an uneven, undisciplined student.)

Mother described Donald as good with his hands (e.g., able in ceramics, art projects, and model building), but unable to follow written directions. His room was a disorganized clutter and he horded like a squirrel. Mother was uncertain whether Donald was stealing; in the past, some coins had been stolen.

Donald and his mother seemed to have more of a peer type interaction than a parent-child exchange. They discussed things and in the past had done art projects together; mother painted and was interested in creativity, politics, and individuality. She had always recoiled from limit setting. She had been depressed and greatly preoccupied with marital discord in Donald's early years. Her husband's dependency needs had surprised her (as her husband was ten years her senior) and drained her. Now she feared the apparent weakness of her son and was most apprehensive in daily interaction with him. She wanted to be permissive and not intrusive, but her confusion about appropriate limits might have come across as a lack of support. She wanted to counter what she described as the father's rages, rigidities, yelling, and threats.

Donald expressed resentment of father's possessiveness for the eight hours every Sunday, especially when he felt "forced" to visit father's girlfriend, whose children he disliked. He was jealous of Robert, who only had to spend four hours with father because of Sunday afternoon orchestra practice. Mother was concerned by the children's hateful, bitter comments about father to relatives: "He is their father and I worry about their guilt." Immediately before the parents' separation, father was physically abusive to Mrs. S. for a very brief period. Donald referred to this with contempt and fear, which seemed to characterize his current overt, conscious relationship with his father. Neither mother nor Donald remembered any closeness between father and son. Both boys recently said that they had no memory of father in the family; they were described as furious about the court custody hearing and Donald hysterically stated that he would kill himself or run away if placed with father.

Donald conveyed warmth and a feeling of realibility about his older brother. There did not appear to be very close contact because of the age difference and Robert's involvement in music. Until three years ago, Donald shared a room with Robert. He was enormously shy and self-conscious, dressing and undressing in the closet and possibly fearful of his genital development as compared to his brother's. He would wear bathing trunks under his clothes when he went for a doctor's appointment. In the ten months prior to his referral, he had been exhibitionistic, greeting mother en route to the bathroom in the morning with an erection and only underwear on. This dramatic change in ten months might have been realted to the parents' separation and/or to his increased genital development. Unquestionably, he was sexually aroused by mother's romantic relationships (no sex took place at the S. home, however), as well as Robert's current sexual exploration with a girlfriend in the S. home. At age four, Donald was described as "romantic" toward mother. For some years now, he had wanted little contact with her in public. At home, he was described as warm and physically demonstrative. His manner toward mother seemed to indicate genital differentiation and a traumatic triadic relationship with his parents.

Donald had never made a satisfactory school adjustment and did not handle the tasks of latency (i.e., school, learning, peer relationships, and play). The castration and death fears and wishes of the phallic Oedipal period, with the resultant inhibitions, masculine overcompensation, and passive feminine learnings, were being carried into preadolescence. Donald's adolescent development would seem to reflect his latency-age deficiencies. Oral overgratification (i.e., his prolonged dependence on the pacifier and bottle) seemed linked to his current dependent and helpless stance in the face of learning and mastery.

POSSIBLE SIGNIFICANT ENVIRONMENTAL INFLUENCES

Donald had the usual childhood illnesses, but no unusual hospitalization. He wore corrective shoes for a mild condition of weak arches. He had long-standing speech problems and in the year prior to his referral suffered head-aches, tentatively described as migraine. Following his birth, mother was depressed and afraid to handle him. He was exposed to severe marital conflict culminating in his parents' recent divorce. Their conflict over mon-ey and the children continued, with a custody hearing pending.

PARENTS

Mrs. S., the sole parent seen during this evaluation, was the oldest of four married, college-educated children. The most significant feature of her background was her stormy, eroticized relationship with her father, charac-terized by much fighting, chasing, and inciting of one another. Mrs. S. described kicking her father in the groin at age 15 and having sexual rela-tions with a boy at age 15½. She describes general closeness with her sibs and parents now. Her mother, "a martyr," originally had opposed the di-vorce. However, after she learned the facts, she was supportive and helpful, as was the father, who offered financial help as well.

Mrs. S. was an attractive and intelligent woman who evoked an in-creasingly positive response from the clinician. During the diagnostic study, she showed movement in terms of increasingly spontaneous affect, warmth, and empathy toward Donald. According to Mrs. S., both she and Donald were very anxious for him to begin long-term therapy as soon as possible. Mrs. S. recognized that Donald might become resistive (they both were resistive to Dr. H.'s recommendation for placement), but stated that she was committed to two or more years of therapy for him, possibly several times a week. Mr. S. was ordered by the court to finance Donald's treatment and mother stated that she'll pay directly for his treatment—and await reim-bursement from her ex-husband—so that treatment did not become yet another financial battleground.

INTERVIEWS WITH CHILD

It was prearranged that Donald would be seen twice. At his first interview, Donald left his mother in the crowded waiting room and came with the clinician easily; he looked somewhat anxious and smiled tensely. He was dressed very appropriately in casual school clothes, but his long blond curls made him look somewhat effeminate. When he took his jacket off, his very masculine body movements made him look like a miniature male college hippie. He appeared appropriately anxious and gradually relaxed about halfway through the hour.

The clinician began by referring to Donald's ideas about seeing a new person, in that he had had prior contacts with several doctors. He launched into an account of his contacts with Drs. G. and M., speaking clearly and intelligibly, with no evidence of his reported speech problem. He said he had had a lengthy evaluation with Dr. G., had never liked the man, and especially had abhorred his recommendation for placement. He had liked Dr. M. very much and felt he could talk easily with him, but their contact had ended because of money problems. He knew that Dr. M., the director of the clinic, had arranged treatment through the clinic, which would be "cheaper and easier" for his mother to manage. His mom felt he should have therapy, but he didn't see the point and didn't worry about school since he'd never be a "sissy goodie-goodie grind who studied all the time." When the clinician wondered about his grades, he was vague about his course of study and referred to marginal grades that he "could fix, to get by, at the end." He said he'd done that before.

He then launched into an excited account of behavioral acting out, denying both the seriousness of his actions and any underlying concerns. He spoke nonstop of inflicting tortures on substitutes, running about the classroom, flying paper airplanes, and fighting in the hall, lunchroom, etc. He emphasized toughness and a need to prove himself in the new school. He's in junior high, having barely missed placement in a "special" adjustment school that he had wished to attend. He and his friends feel they have to prove themselves in this new school.

In relation to friends, he spoke of more acting out (e.g., running through yards, stealing apples, fighting). He's not involved in sports because they get "boring." He's good at baseball, but "who wants to do that every Saturday?" He likes boy-girl parties and alluded to kissing parties via teasing and comments about "lights out and dancing." Currently, he's not invited to parties, which he blames on his mother's early curfew. Since he turned down one invitation because he would have to leave too early, he's received no further invitations. He generally has a girlfriend whom he talks to constantly on the phone. Girls make more loyal friends, keep secrets, and understand. He referred to endless phone calls and some phone games. He tells his current girlfriend all his troubles; only once was he betrayed and the confidence broken.

He said his troubles stemmed from his parents' divorce. "It was awful to remember them holding hands and then, in the end, seeing father hit mother." He doesn't like to see father every Sunday.

I'm not his property but he makes me be with him eight whole hours. Robert is lucky. He only has to be with him four hours 'cause he has orchestra practice Sunday afternoon. I wish I had some place to be. I hate his girlfriend and the bratty kids. We fight and I'm just there, never doing anything I like. Mom is better, but she works, dates a lot, or is on the phone. Robert has his music, but I have my dog.

Donald launched into a detailed account of his dog's loyalty. "He licked my face when I cried when I was told the divorce was for sure. Sometimes he sits in my bed and we watch the sun rise. I used to be scared of the dark and keep the drapes open, which would make me wake up early."

Donald eagerly looked forward to the second interview, and said the clinician was easy to talk to and maybe therapy would be a good idea, especially on Monday and Wednesday, so he could miss Hebrew. (He laughed about missing Hebrew.) He thought that it might be easier to see a male therapist after the evaluation, but was tentative and hesitant about this.

At the second interview, Donald initially seemed more comfortable and at ease. The clinician was struck by his pronounced eagerness to get into the office and his subtle reluctance to leave. (Mother reported the following week that Donald wanted her appointment times with the clinician and no longer talked about having a male therapist. She had thought he should be treated by a male therapist for "masculine identification" and was interested and surprised by his response to the two appointments.) Donald knew the clinician had to see his mother because of the pending court actions. He was told that, at the end of his interview, recommendations would be shared with him.

The clinician spoke of therapy as hard work; she said that it would probably last for several years and might require more than one session per week. Donald's response was clearly positive. He said maybe therapy was a good idea, though his father felt Hebrew School was more important.

> But I'll be Bar Mitzvahed this May and that will be over. I don't want to miss time with my friends, especially since I'm gone all day Sunday and stuck with my father. But I do have bad dreams, one especially over and over. Let me draw it. My mother, brother, and I are sitting in the living room around the coffee table. There's an awful rushing noise of water, 'cause there's a river in the living room. . . . There's a rush of wind and a black batman with wings is flying up the staircase.

Donald said he's been having this dream for a year or more and thought it had something to do with his family and the divorce.

He repeated verbatim his account of learning of the divorce, weeping, and being comforted by his dog. He spoke of having to spend time with his dad over the Christmas holidays and of his mother going out of town for the weekend and shipping him off to his grandmother's. He resented having no say about his time and always being subject to his parents' plans.

He then blamed his mother for his present school placement and indicated his worry about handling academic expectations. He had wanted to go to the special adjustment school that had helped a friend of his with similar school problems. In response to the clinician's questions, he indicated a desire to do better and thought that therapy might help him with that. He acknowledged not studying, but stated that sometimes when he did study, he got even lower grades than when he did next to nothing.

He went on to express his anger that father was making them all go to court.

> He says he wants me and Robert, and he really doesn't. I'd never live with him. He just screams and yells a lot and you never can talk to him. I know the court won't put us with him. Mom is better, you can talk to her at least. Robert is nice, but not home a lot. I like him and can talk to him. When I ran away once, so angry, he brought me back. I can't remember what I was so mad about. I get mad a lot.

At the conclusion of the interview, the evaluation procedure was again reviewed. The clinician acknowledged her awareness of all the painful changes in his family, and indicated the need to resolve the question of therapy soon. Donald left somewhat slowly, with no verbal reaction to the clinician's comments. However, he seemed to respond nonverbally to her empathic response. He was more overtly depressed than in the first interview and made no reference to acting out.

DIAGNOSTIC IMPRESSIONS

The clinician felt that Donald evidenced some positive movement in the course of the second interview. He moved away from an excited, defensive, and amused account of his acting-out behaviors in school. Further, after denying and dismissing concerns about his academic performance in the first interview, he was able to express concerns and a desire to improve his studies in the second session. He acknowledged his pain and underlying depression, and recognized that worries and nightmares are appropriately brought into therapy. His experiences with previous therapists made him somewhat defensive at first.

In both interviews, Donald demonstrated a capacity to relate and to express feelings. Although he evidenced many defenses, some of a primitive nature, they did not appear rigid or impenetrable. He gave an intelligent and articulate account of his current situation, as well as his own reactions to it. The clinician felt that he was motivated and capable of entering into a therapeutic alliance. Thus, all in all, Donald seemed to be more treatable than his history might indicate. He could consciously agree to the concept of long-term biweekly therapy and was described by mother as eager to get started.

Further, his life situation since his parents' divorce seemed to have improved, in that chronic, frenzied parental discord had greatly diminished. Donald's mother seemed committed to long-term therapy for Donald, had had some herself (for a two-year period), and was desirous of more for her own benefit, as well as to assist in her parenting of Donald. Mother and both sons were psychologically minded and were aware of their emotional reactions, fantasies, etc.

The major concern was the question of Donald's ego strengths, which currently seemed shaky. His overall social and school adjustment were very poor and had been weak for a considerable period. His learning problems dated back to the first grade. However, the aggressive acting out seemed relatively recent, in keeping with his preadolescent development.

In conclusion, Donald's presenting symptoms of confused sexual identity and learning disorders required long-term interpretive therapy. Because his dependency needs were great, treatment would be lengthy and arduous for both Donald and his therapist. However, Donald did seem able to use insight-oriented intensive therapy.

DIAGNOSTIC FORMULATIONS

Donald's basic ego apparatus was intact. His memory, reality perception, and control of bodily functions was appropriate. His ego functions, however, reflected weakness and shakiness beyond what was appropriate for a boy on the brink of adolescence. Their lack of synthesis resulted in poor impulse control, poor frustration tolerance, and questionable reality testing in regard to facing responsibilities regarding social problems, and learning and behavioral disorders in school. He was failing school and had a pronounced reading disability. His defense system appeared to be creating secondary interference of his ego functions. Defenses of repression, denial, projection, and reaction formation were evident. His passivity and helplessness were denied by his exaggerated masculinity (e.g., acting out aggressively in school). He was defending against his castration fears and anxieties about sexual identification.

Donald had not reached the phallic stage of development and had not resolved the pre-Oedipal conflicts due to separation-individuation failure; in addition, he reflected oral overstimulation. Latency was stormy due to the above unresolved conflicts and resultant learning disorders, which appeared to age six, when Donald was in the first grade. The long-standing marital difficulties of his parents and his fear of his father prevented any solid masculine identification. Thus, as a preadolescent, Donald was ill-equipped to handle the resurgence of drives and, in fact, was doing worse than ever socially and academically. At times, his low self-esteem and low cathexis of the self were denied and repressed; at other times, he felt extremely lonely and worthless, uncared for by himself or his parents. He had not reached the stage of object constancy, but appeared fixated at the level of oral dependence, quite possibly due to mother's depression and inability to be close to him during much of his first year of life. The feminine identification, which he struggled with, denied, and repressed, was the result of a negative self-representation; he preferred girls as friends to avoid competition and failure with male peers. Donald had not achieved adequate control of his aggressive impulses. He acted out profoundly in school, and also turned his aggressive drives inward, as manifested by his learning disorders and threats of suicide. Rage at home seemed to be at the oral helpless level while outbursts at school seemed more at the Oedipal level to cover his passive and feminine longings.

Superego development was also weak and shaky. His superego was probably a harsh and punitive one, which unsuccessfully tried to control aggressive feelings and wishes, as well as strong sexual feelings toward mother. Thus, breakthroughs of aggressive impulses (e.g., impulsive stealing) occurred, followed by much guilt.

There was significant external conflict with peers, the school, and parents. Because of lack of mastery and competence in the social and academic spheres, his chronological development was further impaired. Donald's internalized conflicts seemed most significant. Libidinal and aggressive drives fixated at the oral and anal periods created impulsive and immature behaviors that were punitively handled by his harsh superego. Internal conflicts between male/female and active/passive drives also seemed of major significance.

Mother's difficult pregnancy and delivery, and postpartum depression and anxiety created deprivations at once for Donald. His father's protracted absences, which probably stimulated and frightened Donald (his night fears and getting into the parents' bed for two years), made him ill-equipped to handle any genuine separation-individuation. Fears and fantasies interfered with learning, and no academic or social competence was ever acquired. The parents' extreme marital conflicts and absorption in their difficulties made little consistent parental attention available for Donald.

Donald had not progressed from dependence to self-reliance and could not function or learn with autonomy and consistency. He was totally dependent on mother due to alienation from father and peers. His social exchanges were primarily with girls as confidantes. He did not take adequate care of his room and belongings. He had never taken satisfaction or pride in his body (dressing in the closet and excessive shyness) or in academic achievements.

Ego and id development were immature and faced a punitive superego. Donald appeared to need intensive, long-term therapy. It was hoped that mother's treatment would make her less fearful of her own aggressive impulses and better able to limit and discipline Donald with more reason and consistency, till his ego could internalize controls and frustration tolerance. As it did not appear possible to work with the father, Donald would have to work out a less conflicted and fearful masculine identification independent of the father.

Donald showed severe arrest and fixation at pre-Oedipal levels. His lack of early sufficient gratifying symbiotic bonding with mother was seen as due to her severe depression and unavailability during his first year of life. Then and since, she had been preoccupied with profound marital problems, and had remained cathected to her older son for any and all emotional gratifications. Donald received far less from both angry and emotionally unavailable parents—notably in the toddler years—and thus had developed far less substantially than his brother. In Anna Freud's words (1965),

> . . . there is permanent drive regression to previously established fixation points, plus simultaneous ego and superego regression which leads to infantilism, borderline delinquent, or psychotic disturbances. [p. 147]

Narcissistic Personality Disorder

Definition

"Self-esteem" is defined by Webster as "a high opinion of oneself, respect for oneself." The positive evaluation of the self obviously is a precondition for one's well being. Rothstein notes (1979, p. 893) that recently there has been considerable controversy concerning patients with "narcissistic disturbances," which is reflected in the many descriptive and diagnostic labels used to refer to these patients: narcissistic character, phallic-narcissistic character, narcissistic character disorder, narcissistic personality, and narcissistic personality disorder. Despite the variety of labels and the lack of formal application of narcissistic theory to children, clinicians have noted frequent narcissistic disturbances in schizophrenic, borderline, and manic-depressive patients of all ages.

Freud used the term "narcissistic neurosis" exclusively for psychotic illness, to differentiate it from transference neurosis. Reich (1960) uses the term in a much wider sense. She indicates that narcissim denotes a libidinal cathexis of the self, which only becomes pathological under certain conditions: "(1) in states of quantitative imbalance; e.g., when the balance between object cathexis and self-cathesis has become disturbed and objects are cathected insufficiently or not at all; (2) in infantile forms of narcissism which are frequently—but not always—present in states of quantitiative imbalance" (1960, pp. 215–216). In discussing narcissistic disturbance, Edith Jacobson (1964) noted that self-esteem is the expression of harmony—or lack of harmony—between the self-representation and the wishful concept of the self. Self-esteem has been seen as an expression of infantile feeling of omnipotence, an evaluation of potentialities, and an acceptance of limitations. Reich (1960) notes that a person's inner image is very much influenced by the superego—and that satisfying the demands of one's superego is a mature form of self-esteem regulation.

Etiology

Van der Waals (1965) describes pathological narcissism as more than a fixation at early narcissistic stages of development and a lack of normal object love; it is also characterized by the simultaneous development of pathological forms of self-love and object love. He further states that normal narcissism and normal object relationships develop simultaneously, as do pathological narcissism and pathological object relationships.

Kernberg (1970) believes that a re-fusion of the internal self and object images occurs in the narcissistic personality at a level of development at which ego boundaries have already become stable. Thus, such patients are not subject to psychotic regression. Kernberg postulates a fusion of ideal self, ideal object, and actual self images as a defense against an intolerable reality in the interpersonal realm, with a concomitant devaluation and destruction of object images as well as external objects. In their fantasies, these patients identify with their own ideal self images in order to deny normal dependency on external objects and their internalized representations. The normal tension between the actual self on the one hand, and the ideal self and ideal object on the other, is eliminated by the building of an inflated self-concept in which the actual self, the ideal self, and the ideal object are confused. Sometimes a cold, hostile mother's narcissistic use of a child makes the child "special" and sets the child off on a search for compensatory admiration and greatness. The child develops the characterological defense of devaluating others. Many such patients occupy a pivotal family position, such as being the only and/or brilliant child, or the one to fulfill the family aspirations.

Kohut (1971) puts forth a different view of the etiology of the narcissistic personality. He describes two separate lines of development—an object line and a narcissistic line. The object line of development is the accepted ego psychology view, encompassing stranger anxiety, symbiosis, separation-individuation, object constancy, the Oedipal conflict, and object love, i.e., attachment to people who are seen as separate from oneself. The narcissistic line of development is a normal developmental unfolding that proceeds parallel to the object line of development. When patients evidence disturbances of self and of archaic objects connected with narcissistic libido (self-objects), they are arrested in narcissistic development. These patients remained fixated at an archaic grandiose self configuration and/or an archaic, overestimated, narcissistically cathected object.

Under optimum developmental conditions, the exhibitionism and grandiosity of the archaic grandiose self are gradually tamed, and the whole structure ultimately is integrated into the total personality and supplies the instinctual fuel for ego-syntonic ambitions, the enjoyment of activities, and important aspects of self-esteem. Under similarly favorable circumstances, the idealized parent image, too, becomes integrated into the personality. The idealized superego is introjected and becomes an important component of the psychic organization. However, if the child suffers severe narcissistic trauma, then the grandiose self is not integrated into the personality but is retained in its unaltered form. It continues to strive for the fulfillment of its archaic aims. If the child experiences traumatic disappointments in the admired adult, then the idealized parent image, too, is retained in its unaltered form; instead of being transformed into a tension-regulating psychic structure, it remains an archaic, transitional object necessary for narcissistic homeostasis (Kohut, 1968).

Descriptive Characteristics

Narcissistic imbalance results in symptomatology such as an insatiable need for grandiosity as a compensatory striving, large amounts of unneutralized aggression which contribute to excessive hypochondriacal anxieties, and superego disturbances that cause an overdependence on approval from outside, contributing to the oft-observed symptom of self-consciousness (Reich, 1960). "Unsublimated eroticized manic self-inflation easily shifts to a feeling of utter dejection, of worthlessness and to hypochondriacal anxieties. Narcissists . . . thus suffer regularly from repetitive violent oscillation of self-esteem" (Reich, 1960, p. 224). The phase of lowered self-esteem is characterized by anxiety and feelings of annihilation, but not by guilt feelings.

Kernberg (1970) notes that "narcissistic" has been abused and over-used as a descriptive term; in his view, narcissistic patients are those whose main problem is a disturbance in their self-esteem or self-regard, in connection with specific disturbances in their object relationships. These patients show an unusual degree of self-reference, have a great need to be admired, and, despite their inflated self-concept, are dependent on tribute from others. Kernberg notes that such patients have a shallow emotional life and little empathy for others; their behavior is envious, exploitative, and parasitic; and they evidence grandiosity and severe ego and superego pathology. Feelings of inferiority and insecurity alternate with feelings of greatness and omnipotence.

Kernberg likens narcissistic patients to borderline personalities—the distinguishing feature is the relatively good social functioning and better impulse control of the narcissistic group. In addition, he cites a

> pseudosublimatory potential, namely, the capacity for active, consistent work in some areas, which permits them partially to fulfill their ambitions of greatness and of obtaining admiration from others. Highly intelligent patients with this personality structure may appear as quite creative in their fields: narcissistic personalities can often be found as leaders in industrial organizations or academic institutions [pp. 53–54].

However, despite talent and promise, there is often a lack of depth in their work, a banality to their productions, and an underlying incapacity for grief, mourning, and guilt, coupled with ruthlessness, coldness, and frequent hypochondriacal preoccupations. Kernberg (1975) believes that these patients generally have a poor prognosis, although it is better for those who manifest some capacity for depression, mourning, and guilt feelings.

Kohut's view (1971) of narcissistic disorders is quite different from Kernberg's, in that he believes the narcissist has attained a "cohesive self." He sees the central pathology as based on "cohesive and more or less stable narcissistic configurations which belong to the stage of narcissism" (pp. 31–32). He does not make the diagnosis of narcissistic personality disorder on the basis of presenting symptomatology or even life history, but rather, on the basis of the nature of the "spontaneously developing transference." In his view, patients who evidence psychosis or borderline states cannot form narcissistic transferences (i.e., mirror, merger, and idealizing transferences); rather, they experience fragmentation due to their fixation at a stage of fragmented self. Thus, developmentally, Kohut's designated narcissistic group is more advanced in terms of psychological structure then is Kernberg's narcissistic group. In addition, Kohut's are not subject to total regression and disintegration, in that they are nonpsychotic, nonborderline, and therefore analyzable.

Rothstein (1979) raises questions about Kohut's delineation of a group of patients based on the form of their transference potential, and suggests that narcissistic transference potentials may be "ubiquitous"; that is, they may appear in neurotic or psychotic forms. Rothstein suggests that the narcissistic personality disorder can be seen in psychotic, borderline, neurotic, and normal states of structural integration. He proposes that "the narcissistic personality disorder be defined by the predominant mode.of investment of narcissism in the self-representation, . . . not on a transference phenomenon" (1979, p. 906). Rothstein's definition of the disorder is intended to complement other diagnostic considerations that reflect nonnarcissistic issues.

Kohut (1966) suggests that clinicians make value judgments about the developmental position and adaptive value of narcissism, rather than retaining an objective view. In his view, some forms of narcissism are not merely primitive forerunners of object love, but also independent psychological constellations. He believes that "the reshaping of the narcissistic structures and their integration into the personality— the strengthening of ideals, and the achievement . . . of humor, creativity, empathy and wisdom—must be rated as a more genuine and valid result of therapy than the patient's precarious compliance with demands for a change of his narcissism into object love" (1966, p. 270).

In sum, while Kernberg is rather pessimistic about the prognosis for narcissistic patients, emphasizing their rage in response to frustration and their defensive denigration of objects, Kohut's view is more optomistic. The differing views on patients, prognosis, and treatment goals offered by Kohut and Kernberg, both major figures in the study of narcissism, are understandable if one considers that they are focusing on two very different groups of patients.

Treatment Interventions

Effective treatment of children exhibiting narcissistic pathology is predicated, on clarity of diagnosis. Tolpin (1978) cites Anna Freud (e.g., 1968, 1970b, 1976), Greenacre (1971), and Kohut (1971, 1972, 1977) to remind us of the serious consequences of mistaking the symptomatic manifestations and transferences of patients with faulty structure formation for the faulty conflict solutions, compromise formations, and disguised derivations of the repressed infantile neurosis of neurotic children. Anna Freud (1968, 1970b) describes how a neurotic superstructure can obscure more serious psychopathology.

Tolpin (1978), a child analyst and representative of the Self Psychology group empahsizes that "for patients with structural deficits, genetic reconstructions and interpretations of conflicts are ineffectual because these interpretations bypass and obscure the central psychopathology; and they inadvertently repeat childhood psychological injuries which lead to artifacts and regressive transferences" (p. 181). Furthermore, patients with faulty self-esteem tend to manifest a neuroticlike superstructure and a variety of self-object transferences, which must be differentiated from neurotic symptomatology and the classical transference neurosis, respectively. Tolpin sees the recognition and interpretation of mirror and idealizing transferences and transference resistances as essential to the working-through process. Gradually, these transferences are replaced with a new psychic structure that can maintain cohesion, self-esteem, a sense of direction, and the wherewithal to pursue ambitions and to follow inner ideals. These changes in psychic structure go hand in hand with the filling in of structural deficits, and constitute the goal and outcome of successful analytic work with self-object transferences.

Tolpin's analytic insights may be applied to analytically oriented psychotherapy with narcissistic patients. Neither short-term work aiming for symptom reduction nor ego supportive work pushing for better reality testing and healthier object relations constitutes an effective treatment plan for these patients. Because they rely on the therapist as a self-object, these patients require long-term therapy in which a sustained merger with the therapist allows them to make the internalizations necessary for their further growth and development. Being responded to as a part object or an idealized object requires a new therapeutic stance by the therapist. Frequently, apparent separation anxiety and dependency in these patients are secondary to their faulty regulation of self-esteem; that is, separation is experienced as the loss of part of an already fragmented self (Mishne, 1979).

The Self Psychology approach to the treatment of the narcissistically disordered patient has created an exciting ferment in psychoanalytic circles, with reverberating spin-offs affecting numerous analytically oriented clinicians. As psychoanalytic theory moved from an id psychology based on drive theory to an ego psychological perspective, new vistas, theories, and techniques became incorporated by clinicians of all disciplines. Most recently, there has been a new shift in the theoretical stance of some analysts and clinicians, with resultant modifications in treatment goals and treatment techniques, based on what is known as Self Psychology, or reconsiderations of internalizations in self/self-object configurations. Many clinicians have shifted their focus from drive, conflict, and ego development to self development and the shifting selves throughout the life cycle. Self Psychology has evolved out of recent explorations in the realm of narcissism. Kohut's controversial new conceptions of self-object transferences, namely, the mirroring, merging, and idealizing transferences, are a marked departure from classical conceptions of displacement onto the analyst of feelings related to past objects. Likewise, his emphasis on patient deficits which he sees as the result of impoverished and problematic childhoods, has sharpened our sensitivities to pre-Oedipal personalities with less than fully developed structure and a lack of cohesion.

Spirited discourse and discord centers around questions such as the relationships of Self Psychology to classical psychoanalytic theory. Is Self Psychology based on deficits and thus at odds with traditional conflict-based theory? Other major questions revolve around Self Psychology's deemphasis of insight, interpretation, and Oedipal conflicts and castration disorders—the major foci of traditional treatment—in favor of therapists' empathic introspection of their feelings toward, responses to, and communications with, patients, in a treatment relationship embodying optimal empathy rather than the traditional optimal frustration. Through a sensitive understanding of patients' subjective states and special vulnerability, therapists offer themselves as part objects to facilitate patients' structure building.

Many critics of Self Psychology state that this approach has offered little in the way of new, different, or revolutionary techniques. They believe that the "new" practice focus is in fact a reiteration of the traditional focus on sensitive clinical work. Some critics suggest that Self Psychology is not a separate kingdom—that it is basically restating traditional views on drives, object relations, ego development and arrests, and narcissistic reactions to stress and trauma. Kohut and his followers are often accused of giving scanty attention to major life traumas in the childhood of patients, and of focusing excessively on parental empathic ruptures, with the result that the analyst is called upon to provide maternal (parental) functioning rather than traditional interpretations.

Kohut and other Self Psychologists focus on a large population of patients who are considered untreatable, unreachable, and unresponsive. In Kohut's view, these patients have suffered pre-Oedipal injuries that profoundly damaged their self-esteem and thwarted their development. Treatment focuses on patients' ambitions, ideals, values, and humor; more attention is given to their daily lives than to transference interpretations, drive manifestations, and insight-induced restructuring.

Treatment of narcissistically disordered children might include several of the following interventions: individual outpatient treatment for the child; direct work with the parents; residential group care (if the child cannot be kept at home); and an intermediary intervention such as a day treatment program or therapeutic day school. Given the narcissistic patient's vulnerability and paucity of empathy, the more confrontational interventions such as family therapy and group therapy generally would be contraindicated.

Case of Joy

The case of Joy presents a child with poor regulation of self-esteem, grandiosity, and an unusual degree of self-reference. She was perceived as presenting a narcissistic personality disorder, based on the merger and mirror transference manifested in therapy and the evidence of a "cohesive self" (Kohut, 1971, pp. 31–22). Per Kernberg's criteria (1975, pp. 53–54), Joy showed creativity and a pseudosublimating potential. Other clinicians might differ with this diagnosis and label Joy a borderline child, based on her poor impulse control and inadequate separation-individuation.

Diagnostic Evaluation

REFERRAL

At age four and a half, Joy M. was referred to the hospital by her mother, who had been a patient in the adult clinic there. Mother described Joy as having the following long-standing difficulties: hyperactivity; incessant talking; defiant, provocative, sassy behavior; bossy, hostile interactions with peers and adults; and night fears that caused her to insist on sleeping with mother. It was hard to assess why mother sought help at this point, as the problems had been chronic. Other data suggested that the nursery school was urging mother to obtain help. However, the material in the diagnostic interviews suggested that mother's own need to ventilate and obtain some cathartic relief precipitated her contact. In the interview, she mainly talked about the pressures of managing her child, working, and obtaining adequate housing. Mother was obsessed with her housing problems; it was only with great difficulty that the diagnostician could glean any information about the child. In addition to this area of concern, she focused on her marriage and divorce, and her relationship with her parents. In a rather narcissistic fashion, after the diagnostic interview, mother walked into her former therapist's office unannounced. In spite of her knowledge of hospital procedure, she acted as if she were unaware that the therapist might be occupied.

HISTORY OF COMPLAINT

Joy had had colic until she was 10 months old, and sleep problems in early infancy, which resulted in her insistence on sleeping with mother at 18 months of age. Mother described the child's reactive distress to the stresses in the marriage and the parental separation when Joy was only four months old. Because of mother's need to work, Joy was cared for by sitters at 3 months, and by a nursery at 20 months. With only occasional glimpses of what the child might feel, mother described Joy from the somewhat narcissistic stance of how she experienced Joy's problems. Mother reacted to her child's problems with anxiety and helplessness. Mother's treatment apparently lessened her anxiety somewhat by the time Joy was three years old.

THE CHILD TODAY

Joy was intellectually very advanced, able in school, animated, and very articulate. Her adult verbal manner, which sometimes was sassy or sadistic, seemed to please mother unconsciously until the aggression was directed at her. Because Joy acted like a little adult and was bossy, she had no real friends. She rejected any friendly overtures. At the same time, she was immature, could not wait her turn, and was constantly impatient and nagging when frustrated. Mother stated that Joy always succeeded in wearing her down. Because mother was employed, Joy was in year-round nursery day care; at the end of the day, she would not let mother out of her sight. Joy presented as a feminine child with a feminine self-concept, mirroring and undifferentiated from her mother. Mother felt that Joy was easier since their recent move to larger quarters. However, Joy still threw fits, was impatient and nagging, and still had to sleep with mother. Mother's current major theme was Joy's intellectual precociousness; she seemed to need to deny any problems, concurrent with presentation of complaints.

DEVELOPMENTAL HISTORY

Mr. and Mrs. M. were married when she was 22 and he was 31. Mr. M. was described as a heavy drinker who womanized and was only marginally employed. In contrast, Mrs. M. was always employed (except during pregnancy). Their marriage of seven years was characterized by constant fights, separations, and reconciliations. Mrs. M. had five miscarriages prior to the birth of Joy. She hoped that a child would improve the marriage. Mr. and Mrs. M. moved from hotels to apartments to the homes of relatives. They fought physically, generally over money and Mr. M.'s involvement with other women. When Joy was four months old, they separated permanently. Shortly after this separation, they met on the street and Mr. M. threatened to kill Mrs. M. and Joy. Some weeks later, he kidnapped Mrs. M. off the street and kept her a prisoner in his car for six hours at gun point. Mrs. M. described him as a psychotic who heard "voices" telling him to kill her.

While she was captive, he alternately threatened to kill her and gave her the gun and begged her to shoot him. Mrs. M. jumped out of the car, almost killing herself, to get away. Following this harrowing incident, she and Joy moved out of town, returning fourteen months later.

The pregnancy with Joy was stressful; Mrs. M. described nine miserable months of harrassment by Mr. M.'s other women, who phoned and visited him at home. Despite a difficult delivery, Joy's birth was normal and there were no complications. Mrs. M. didn't feel well enough to nurse Joy. Mr. M. did not take her to the hospital and was not there when Joy was born. When Mrs. M. returned home, she found notices that the electricity was being cut off and that insurance and car payments had lapsed. Mr. M. occasionally appeared with lady friends. Mrs. M. left him when Joy was less than three months old; they were reconciled briefly and finally separated when Joy was four months old.

Joy was a fretful, colicky infant. No nursing was attempted. Mrs. M. stated that Joy "weaned herself" from the bottle at one year. A night bottle was used until age two. After the colic subsided, she settled into a better schedule and slept more. Mother felt that Joy ate fairly well, but could not remember when she went on solids, or started to sit, crawl, or stand. She thought Joy walked at ten months of age. Mother described Joy as an alert, active, responsive baby who articulated sounds early, spoke words before 17 months, and showed rapid motor and intellectual development. Joy never sucked her thumb until very recently, "and it's occasional and to annoy me." Joy was toilet trained at 18 months.

Mother stated that Joy wore her down with her tantrums. Currently, she insisted that mother take her somewhere after work, no matter what the weather or how tired mother was. The child seemed to resist being closeted in their small apartment. Mother and Joy were locked in a symbiotic relationship that had the flavor of two siblings interacting in a sadomasochistic fashion. When mother was home, Joy never let her out of her sight, insisted that she and mother have the same bedtime, and refused to close her eyes till mother went to bed. Mother had no life to herself and let Joy accompany her like a peer in their meager social contacts.

No privacy was observed in the home; Joy witnessed mother dressing, bathing, etc., continuously. She had raised questions about her mother's breasts and pubic hair, but had not queried about babies. Recently, she and a little boy were kissing and playing "house." Joy had no contact with her father and infrequent contact with Mrs. M.'s brother and father. Thus, she had not developed a sense of genital differentiation. There was no evidence of a real triadic relationship with the relatives, who served as semiremote father surrogates.

POSSIBLE SIGNIFICANT ENVIRONMENTAL FACTORS

Beyond her colic as an infant, and tonsillitis and sore throats at age four, Joy had not had any of the usual childhood diseases or any unusual medical illnesses.

Family Background and Personal History

PARENTS

As father's whereabouts were unknown, only mother was interviewed. Mrs. M. had one brother, who was two years older; he was in his second marriage and made a comfortable living in public relations. They did not see each other frequently, but were on good terms. Mrs. M. described her brother as their mother's idealized and favorite child. At the time of the referral, Mrs. M.'s mother was 55; her father, 57. After numerous and often lengthy separations, her parents had gotten a divorce when Mrs. M. was 11 years old. Her father was described as a good provider who never missed work. He had a chronic drinking problem that made him jealous and suspicious of her mother. The parents' physical fights were frightening, but the children themselves were never physically abused. Mrs. M. described her mother as a complicated person who had somewhat decompensated in recent years, as manifested by her series of alcoholic boyfriends, suicide notes, moodiness, and dramatic scenes that frightened Mrs. M. and her brother. Mrs. M. received help from her mother when Joy was tiny, but now avoided contact with her mother when "she acted up." She stated that her mother was very interfering in her marriage. Currently, Mrs. M. had more contact with her father, whom she used to blame for everything; she felt that her mother had placed her in the middle following the parents' divorce.

Mrs. M.'s former therapist felt that she had benefited from therapy but had not resolved specific issues. He stated that she denied both her problems with her parents and her anxiety and fear of men. Mrs. M.'s traumatizing, sadomasochistic marriage replicated many features of her parents' marriage. Her current status as a black ADC recipient/employee creates financial and emotional stress for her and Joy.

INTERVIEW

After clarifying where mother would be waiting for her, Joy seemed to separate easily from mother. She was a dainty, small-boned, nicely dressed black child with a distinct femininity about her. She pondered the clinician's name and proceeded to explore the office boldly. In response to the clinician's comments about why she was there, she said that she and mommy argued sometimes. She then said that she also argued at school. She focused exclusively on the teacher, whom she saw as a frustrating person. Her comments implied that she wanted all the attention and resented not getting it. She also described wanting to teach with the teacher: "I know all the rhymes, my numbers, letters, and colors." She thought being the boss and being in charge was fun. She asked if she and the clinician could play school. All the above was said as she walked around the office touching the furniture and the clinician in a strangely intimate and egocentric fashion.

She sat down with crayons and paper. First she became the teacher giving a drawing assignment; then she became the student fulfilling the assignment. As she drew, she commented that her drawing was her mommy's bed where they both slept. She explained that sometimes mommy seemed afraid or cried, so it was best that they sleep together. She then defended against saying any more and spoke about the physical aspects of the bed, pillow, sheets, blanket, etc.

Next, Joy suggested giving a play. The clinician was supposed to be the mommy who worked in the office and took the little girl with her. She walked around humming, "Oh What a Beautiful Morning" and began to caress the clinician's face in what seemed to be an eroticized maternal fashion, saying that the clinician should really be the mommy and take her home to play all the time and have fun. She showed a overt discomfort here and spoke of daddy being gone. She said that she didn't remember him, but that someday some man mommy knows might be her daddy. She said she didn't like not having a daddy. She also didn't like fights with mommy and she didn't know why they happened. She could not describe any effect of the arguments on her or mommy.

Joy said she would change the play to a dance and she began to improvise a ballet, talking about a TV program (seemingly "The Nutcracker Suite") as she danced. She became "The Sugar Plum Fairy," and then, "A Snow Flake Queen," saying that "the snowflake other dancers have shiny, shiny snow costumes like me, but I have something better—a shiny, shiny crown with pinpoints of snow and sparkle."

The clinician began to put things in order, commenting that their time was almost up. Joy helped in a fashion, humming to herself and no longer involved with the clinician. She was bland and imperturbable as she said goodbye, and seemed egocentric as the clinician took her to her mother.

DIAGNOSTIC FORMULATIONS—ASSESSMENT OF DEVELOPMENT

Joy's ego apparatus seemed to be intact. There were no signs of primary defects. Her memory, ability to learn in school, reality perception, and control of bodily functions were appropriate. Her ego functions, however, reflected weakness and shakiness. Their lack of synthesis resulted in poor impulse control and frustration tolerance. Defenses of denial and identification with the aggressor were prominent and interfered with neutralized age-appropriate object relationships with mother, teachers, and peers.

In terms of drive development, Joy seemed to be in the sadistic anal ambivalence phase of preobject constancy; thus, she had not achieved separation-individuation. Her quasi-phallic interests were meager and she had not advanced beyond the pregenital stage. Object cathexis and self-cathexis remained ambivalent, reflecting dependency longings as well as rage. Joy and her mother were nondifferentiated; both were frightened by their mutural rage and lack of self-soothing mechanisms. This lack of self-control exacerbated their poor sense of self-esteem. Joy discharged with great intensity, grandiosity, and omnipotence to defend against her lack of a separate, cohesive self. She had not achieved adequate control of aggressive impulses. She acted out at home and school, interacting with others in a hostile, sadistic mode. Oral components were reflected in her oral aggressivity. Constant anal power struggles were also present. Both the aggressive drive and the libidinal drive were predominantly anal in character.

Because superego development was weak and shaky, aggressive and libidinal impulses toward mother were out of control; thus, the constant fighting, provocativeness, and need for punishment. Joy experienced internal and external conflicts in terms of affects of opposite quality (i.e., love and hate, active and passive, and perhaps emerging masculine and feminine trends). She had significant external conflict with peers, school, and mother. There did not appear to be conflict between drives, as both aggressive and libidinal drive development were at the anal level.

The parents' gross marital problems, the father's psychotic behavior, and the financial duress created immediate postnatal deprivation and narcissistic injury for Joy. Her mother's need to be employed prevented consistent early mothering. Further, mother's high level of anxiety made her frantic and ambivalent with the child. This, plus the paucity of real ties with friends and family, made Mrs. M. ambivalently hold onto Joy, preventing her normal separation and individuation. Joy had only partially progressed from dependency to self-reliance in an as-if precocious fashion. At great cost to herself, she had become proficient at academic learning. However, she could not interact with peers and didn't let mother out of her sight once she came home from work. She and mother had power struggles over food, although she ate with greater calm at the day care center. Bladder control was not consistent; Joy sometimes wet at night. Bowel control had been achieved. Joy had not moved much beyond a position of egocentricity toward peer companionship. She had advanced to work activity in school and could learn, produce, and conceptualize in an apparently effective fashion.

The major problem for Joy did not appear between structures (i.e., ego, id, and superego), but rather, in the mother-child relationship. Therefore, simultaneous treatment of mother and child would be necessary to facilitate separation and individuation. Engaging mother might be problematic. Joy presented disturbance in regulation of her self-esteem, wanting constant admiration from others (e.g., teacher, mother, and peers). Others were to admire, obey, and gratify her, and Joy had little sense of the feelings of others (e.g., mother's fatigue at the end of the day, and peers' interests and wants). She demonstrated a compelling need for the self-object, and thereby reflected a narcissistic personality disorder.

Addendum

Joy was successfully treated in biweekly analytically oriented psychotherapy over a two-year period. During that same time, her mother was seen in therapy/parent-guidance, which enabled her to be very supportive of Joy's growth and development.[2]

[2]The reader will find additional references to this case in Chapters 14 and 17.

Character Disorder

Definition

Individuals who have not made a genuine entry into the phallic-Oedipal phase of development, i.e., reached a neurotic level, and who present inflexible behavior patterns without experiencing subjective discomfort, are best defined as personality or character disordered. Cameron (1963) notes that such distortion of the personality develops early in life and persists as one's characteristic style of coping with the environment and defending oneself. The resultant habitual inflexibility of behavior patterns without guilt, pain, or anxiety defends the individual and takes over the entire personality. In the more highly structured normal or neurotic individual, discrete areas of the personality reflect symptomatic involvement. By contrast, the character-disordered individual's entire personality is affected. The ego functions, affective responses, and object relations are completely skewed, as intrapsychic conflict has been resolved by rigid reaction patterns that permit partial gratification of instinctual wishes, rationalization of motives, and idealization of pathological behaviors.

The symptoms of such disordered children and adults are ego-syntonic; that is, they are unaccompanied by anxiety and guilt, and so do not generally motivate these individuals to change. These patients do not suffer the inner anguish, self doubts, and pain of the neurotic, whose symptoms and pathological behavior patterns are experienced as ego-alien. In fact, their behavior is disturbing to others, but not to themselves. Parents, teachers, the community, spouses, sibs, etc., often are distraught and worried in the face of the bland, unconcerned, unyielding stance of the character-disordered individual. The disorder may manifest itself via fatigue, inhibitions in certain areas, the generally cramped and rigid nature of these patients' adjustment, or the breaking through of warded-off impulses.

The DSM-III (1980) classification names the following personality disorders:paranoid, schizoid, schizotypal, histrionic, narcissistic, antisocial, borderline, avoidant, dependent, compulsive, passive-aggressive, and atypical, mixed, or other personality disorders. Most child psychiatrists and child therapists are reluctant to utilize these diagnoses. Meeks (1979) notes that "they seem to imply a static and fixed condition, with a relatively poor prognosis" (p. 482).

The GAP classification of disorders in children is considered more satisfactory in presenting the continuum of disturbances while acknowledging the fluidity of the evolving child's developmental process. "The personality disorders category is recommended only when the total personality configuration fits the degree of relative permanence and inflexibility of adaptive patterns implied in the diagnosis" (Meeks, 1979, p. 483).

In clinical practice, we see children with overly dependent, oppositional, asocial, impulsive (acting-out), and mistrustful personalities. Behavioral, and/or conduct disorders in the child population include stealing, running away, vandalism, cruelty to animals, lying, defiance and disobedience, provocative behavior, outbursts of rage and violence, and manipulative behavior. In Rutter's discussion (1975) of aggression, overactivity, and delinquency, he notes the higher frequency of these disorders in boys and the perception of many such children as unpredictable, unmalleable, and impulsive. Their assertiveness and aggression seem to exist in tandem with a lack of feelings for others.

Etiology

There are varied explanations of the etiology of character disorder. Thomas et al. (1968) stress the importance of temperament as a causative factor in behavior disorders: the mismatch or poor fit of the child's temperament and the environment results in ineffective parental management techniques. Organic or constitutional factors may be critical in the development of personality disorders and antisocial behavior. For example, children with known central nervous system damage demonstrate impulsivity, hyperactivity, and distractibility, which may lead to the development of a behavior or personality disorder. Meeks (1979) emphasizes that while organic or constitutional factors may play an important role

> this should not obscure the fact that they are basically psychological problems. Many of these disorders are the direct result of individual and family psychological conflict. Moreover, regardless of the inception of the difficulty, all problems in adjustment to social reality eventually demand resolution in terms of intrapsychic dynamics. Treatment approaches for any established behavior disorder are unlikely to be successful in the absence of an understanding of the typical motivations, defensive maneuvers and the styles of relating which characterize this group of youngsters [p. 515].

Those who view psychodynamics as the primary causative factor emphasize the experiential etiology and note gross pathology in the environment. This pathology used to be considered a lower-class phenomenon (i.e., only parents who were criminals, alcoholics, and the like, produced such children). We now clearly see that the disorder crosses all class lines. Those emphasizing psychological causative factors note the universal absence of mature and consistent parental love from one or both parents of the character-disordered patient. Parental love is distorted and inconsistent, creating a disturbed environment throughout the patient's childhood. Aggression, often expressed via uncontrolled and unpredictable hostility, is prominent. Frequently, character-disordered children have been witness to, or victims of, unrelenting anger and violence, with resultant feelings of helplessness. Some such children appear to internalize their counteraggression and become chronically fearful and dependent, while others act out their counteraggressivity at home, in school, or in society. These children often come from broken homes and evidence pathological narcissism, chronic anxiety, overwhelming tension, and superego lacunae. Children's superego lacunae may mirror and correspond to those of their parents, in that "parents may find vicarious gratification due to their own poorly integrated superegos which sanction forbidden impulses in the acting out of the child" (Johnson and Szurek, 1952). Parents who are unconsciously permissive or inconsistent in specific spheres of behavior allow their child to act out repeatedly. For example, parents may rationalize their own sadomasochistic impulses by condoning the same in the child, which the child experiences as parental acceptance of the unacceptable impulses.

In addition to superego lacunae and unconscious parental permission, "disturbances in superego development, in which an archaic superego with little tolerance for any impulse gratification overrides the ego and allies itself with the id, may lead to massive destructive acting out as a defense against intolerable feelings of guilt" (Rexford, 1978, p. 325). Thus, it is a mistake to assume that the child who acts out and presents severe personality or character disorder patterns has no superego. Rather, there is often a faulty, stunted, or primitive superego that relentlessly condemns the child and generates excessive, inappropriate guilt that causes the child to seek punishment repeatedly.

Descriptive Characteristics

The personality development of character-disordered patients is impeded by serious ego and superego distortions. In their description of character-disordered children, Redl and Wineman (1951) cite an inability to cope with boredom, frustration, or aggression, due to poor handling of insecurity, anxiety, and fear; sublimation deafness or a lack of creativity; distorted interpersonal relations; and a poor perception of reality. They describe a 13-year-old boy who was caught stealing; he was indignant at his victim for carrying so much money. The poor grasp of reality is further contaminated by wishful and magical thinking and omnipotent narcissistic fantasies that ward off low self-esteem, uncertainty about identity, and self-hatred. Children who are immobilized or overwhelmed by conflict over feelings of counteraggression and self-denigration are depressed, sullen, constricted, suspicious, fearful, and subject to intense free-floating anxiety. Redl and Wineman (1951) note that the most serious problem of children manifesting delinquent behavior is the great hatred resulting from parental rejection and/or mistreatment. Sometimes this hatred is markedly naked and primitive, due to the child's aggression never having been tempered and neutralized by a strong personal attachment that would have fused aggression and love.

Ekstein and Friedman (1957) suggest that acting out may be an experimental recollection of earlier developmental stages involving the expression, mastery, and use of impulses in problem solving. Grinberg (1968) considers acting out to be closely associated with inadequately mourned object loss and separation. Schwartz (1968) believes that acting out stems from a break in the mother-child relationship at the very height of the ambivalent phase of development (18–30 months) when only the presence of the mother and her tolerance make it possible for the child to express libidinal and aggressive feelings—love and hate of her—while gradually integrating and accepting the unavoidable frustrations and restrictions set by her. Malone and Bandler (1967) describe children from disorganized families and unfavorable sociocultural settings—who presented impulsive, action-oriented, and generally immature behavior: most conspicuous was their deficiency in object relations, manifested in a lack of emotional separation from their mothers.

Other authors emphasize the overt and covert behaviors of fathers of antisocial children. While the parents of antisocial children cannot be placed in any one diagnostic category, "the fathers resemble one another more closely than the mothers and display a strikingly similar attitude towards their sons. They tend to be passive-aggressive men with a high degree of dependency needs and confused sexual identification" (Rexford, 1978, p. 12). The fathers, further, seem to permit, aid, and abet their sons' aggressive activities, or to have poor communication, due to physical and emotional absences, or punitive, obsessive, controlling, and rigid responses to their children. Alcoholism and criminal and psychiatric records abound among the fathers of delinquents.

Frequently, conflicting parental attitudes, behaviors, and actions lead to a failure to establish a parental coalition and thus to a breakdown of generational boundaries where one parent makes a special ally of the child. Traumatic events in early childhood tend to be repeated in acting-out episodes. Greenacre (1978) states that "the acting out is most forceful and persistent when the child has suffered humiliation in the traumatic episode, being forced from a desired active position to a seemingly devaluated passive one" (p. 219). She stresses the following conditions as contributing to the production of delinquency:

> the conditions of strong stimulation of the very early aggressive and sexual drives of the young child did not permit a separation of the two, and . . . sexuality developed in the service of aggression and narcissism; further, . . . inconsistency of handling was such as to interfere with adequate object constancy to an extent which might strike at the roots of object relationship, promoting ambivalence expressed through action with a minimum of self-awareness. Is it possible that in certain cases of delinquency or criminality in which there is clearly a repetitive patterned form of the offending behavior, there might have been, in addition, a particularly strong fixation at the imitative stage, acting somewhat like an early imprint or engram on the developing child? [p. 231].

Treatment Interventions

Because the social, familial, and environmental factors loom so large in the life situation of many personality-disordered children, and because of the very early imprinting of character, treatment of these children remains difficult, frustrating, and taxing. Clinicians, youth authorities, probation officers, teachers, and others face a struggle in work with these deprived, disadvantaged, and frequently disorganized children. Actual engagement of this population is most difficult given their superficial mode of relating and apparent lack of genuine feelings. They frequently demonstrate a lack of care for, or trust in, people, as well as the inability to engage in peer friendships or meaningful ties with adults. Their inaccessibility is exasperating and often enraging to those trying to help them. Their lack of emotional response, concern, or anxiety, their patterns of seemingly pointless deceit and evasion, and their negativism, tantrums, and unrelenting delinquency portend enormous obstacles for therapy. In addition, the charisma and reckless verve that accompany the acting out of primitive emotions add to the extremely negative counterreactions and countertransference responses to these children.

OUTPATIENT PSYCHOTHERAPY

A variety of interventions are currently in use. Thomas, Chess and Birch recommend parental guidance for the young child exhibiting a behavior or personality disorder. Their focus is primarily on the child's temperamental style and the parents' management approach, rather than the psychological or motivational factors in the parents. More recent interventions of this type are parent effectiveness and behavior modification programs. Eyberg and Johnson (1974) note that although such interventions are beneficial, the parents must be reinforced for desired behaviors within these programs, as the child's behavior does not seem to be a sufficiently strong reinforcer in itself. Other behaviorists report that what works in one setting does not necessarily carry over to other settings (Patterson, 1974). A child might require a dual program at home and school for successful modification of unwanted behavior.

Meeks (1979) notes that outpatient psychotherapy is extremely difficult. However, he does not accept the findings of studies which suggest that it is of no value and notes that "these studies suffer both from the brevity and type of psychotherapy offered and the failure to distinguish diagnostically between impulse-ridden youngsters and those with neurotic behavior disorders" (p. 523). He suggests that positive treatment outcomes do occur with antisocial, acting out children when there is a preponderance of neurotic motivation for the antisocial behavior, relatively low family compliance with the antisocial pattern, and a good fit of therapist and patient.

Treatment techniques with behavior- or character-disordered children vary from those used with neurotic children. In contrast to the intensive, uncovering, more permissive analytic approach used with the neurotic child, limit setting and interpretation of reality are necessary with the personality-disordered child. Jackel (1963) states that an initial treatment aim is to make ego-syntonic traits and behaviors ego-alien, or ego-dystonic, in the context of building a relationship. Then, one hopes, behaviors will begin to correspond with reality expectations and the previously warded-off anxiety, depression, and discomfort will begin to surface and be better tolerated by the child. With these patients, clinicians should focus on the present, rather than the past, especially early in therapy. Obviously clinicians must avoid lectures, recriminations, moralizing, and parental attitudes with the child.

Children frequently test therapists, inviting them to break the rules, teasing them and calling them "square," "dull," etc. "The youngster attempts to cajole or intimidate the therapist into collusion in a deception of the child's parents or other authority figures and is rebuffed in the effort firmly but without anger" (Meeks, 1979, p. 524). Therapists must remain benign, secure in their integrity, and committed to an ongoing interest in and attachment to the child, with the goal of understanding the youngster's motivations, true feelings, attitudes, and values. Clarity regarding manifest and latent content is essential, in that an actually guilty child may come across as totally lacking in feelings and empathy for others, valueless, full of bravado, macho, and defiance.

Kohrman et al. (1971) caution regarding both the potential for regression due to identification with the patient and anger in the face of the child's resistance to interpretations. Proctor (1959) notes that action-oriented, acting-out children often cause therapists to counterattack via mobilization of the therapists' own infantile superego against patients' id, ego, and superego. This mobilization of the therapist's superego can result in punishment, hostile demands for conformity, or even violent rejection of the patient. As these patients can be maddening, it is crucial to sort out the realistic hatred they engender so that it can be dealt with in treatment. These patients project their own acrimonious self-rebuke (superego) and sadistically attack the therapist verbally or physically for supposed misdeeds, defections, etc. "The patient is then acting as sadistic superego to the therapist while at the same time, the therapist's id is being mobilized by the therapeutic uncovering of the patient's id impulses. This is most trying for the therapist, and it is of little help that the patient is projecting self-criticism and attack by his own superego" (Proctor, 1959, p. 301). Because these children frequently do not want therapy, it begins in a negative phase. Often therapists intellectually grasp these children's fears, resistances, etc., yet emotionally respond as if all behavior could be controlled by the children if only they would try. All of these dilemmas may produce nihilism, hostility, and rejections on the part of therapists. These trying patients seem intent on forcing therapists to engage with them in a drama which may not only undermine treatment but may even be threatening to therapists' professional and personal identity (Giovacchini, 1974).

Despite all these vicissitudes, a trusting relationship and therapeutic alliance are required and achievable in the treatment of many character-disordered children and adolescents. Surviving patients' tests, being sensitive to their low self-esteem, remaining calm, committed to and respectful of them, and keeping a sense of humor can carry the clinician forward in the difficult task of engaging such youngsters. Because of the interpersonal nature of these children's symptomatic behavior, it is rarely possible to work with them in the absence of a fairly intensive alliance with their parents. This may be achieved through collaborative treatment of the parents, regular and periodic contacts with the entire family, or concurrent treatment of the parents and the child in separate sessions. (Most therapists find concurrent treatment technically difficult and potentially disruptive to the therapeutic alliance with both the child and the parents.) The child's "opportunity for an intensely satisfying dyadic relationship which provides . . . ego strengthening, repair of self-esteem, and the internalization of a positive identification figure offers the chance to correct the core disabilities in the behaviorally disordered child" (Meeks, 1979, p. 524).

In addition to individual psychotherapy, group psychotherapy has proved to be of value in work with character-disordered children and adolescents. Group composition suggests a balance: some youngsters in the group will have relatively strong egos and good frustration tolerance while others will have relatively weak egos and poor frustration tolerance. Young children are frequently placed in "activity" group therapy that offers a structured group play situation. One hopes that acquisition of social skills and ego strengthening are accomplished through the children's identification with the leader and interactions with peers. Older children often are treated in "rap" groups which offer some educational and/or vocational focus. Outreach work with delinquent adolescents attempts to engage them in socially accepted activities and projects.

Family therapy is another modality frequently employed with character-disordered children, as the primary intervention or as an adjunct to individual or group psychotherapy. This technique often permits recognition of the important pathological modes of communication, alliances, roles, etc., within the family. From a therapeutic point of view, the family approach seems to be particularly appropriate when the child's symptomatology is "embedded in a state of neurotic family homeostasis. This includes youngsters who are severely scapegoated, the superego lacunae parents described by Johnson and Szurek, and some cases where the antisocial behavior appears to represent a maladroit attempt at separation from a "binding" or symbiotic family entanglement" (Meeks, 1979, p. 525). There are many situations where family therapy is contraindicated. Offer and Vanderstoep (1975) note the following: (1) when parents have made a firm decision to divorce; (2) when one or both parents present severe psychotic depression, hardcore psychopathology, or severe masochistic character; and (3) when the child or adolescent states emphatically that he or she does not want to be in therapy with parents or only wants group treatment with peers.

INPATIENT PSYCHOTHERAPY

If and when interventions have failed and the child's problems have become too disruptive or dangerous to the child or others, inpatient treatment becomes necessary. There are a number of residential facilities, e.g., children's psychiatric units in a hospital, residential treatment institutions, therapeutic boarding schools, and group homes. Treatment approaches and philosophies vary; some settings are closed while others are open, with appropriate children selected to attend public schools off grounds. The range of interventions encompasses milieu therapy, behavior modification and a system of rewards and punishments, and psychodynamically oriented group, individual, and family therapy. Psychoactive medication is frequently used, often excessively so in closed, understaffed facilities. Some facilities offer long-term treatment while others offer only crisis intervention or short-term placement. Ongoing parental involvement with the placed child—which includes visits, calls, and passes home, plus ongoing therapeutic work with the parents—is based on the treatment philosophy and the long-range plans for the child. Such plans may include eventual return home or re-placement in a foster home or school.

Currently, placement dilemmas arise out of funding limitations, the cost of care, and staffing problems. Childcare counselors or psychiatric aides vary in their competence, educational level, and degree of sophisticated psychological mindedness. The variables are tempered by the philosophy of the setting, and the nature of the supervision and consultation provided to the paraprofessionals employed there. In other countries, where childcare workers have had extensive academic and practicum training and are not considered paraprofessionals, they are given greater responsibility, status, salary, and input into the administration and treatment planning of the setting. Given the trauma inherent in separation, it is generally considered prudent to use an inpatient approach only as a last resort, when other interventions have failed and/or the child is in danger or it too disruptive to be handled in the natural home.

The intensity of residential treatment stimulates greater countertransference than does outpatient treatment, and it may arise between staff members, staff and children, and staff and parents. Adequate staff communication and supervision (e.g., sufficient staff meeting time) mitigate against the universal tensions and stresses inherent in such a complex and charged system.[3]

Case of Mike

The case of Mike depicts a character-disordered child who has not made a genuine entry into the phallic-Oedipal phase of development. Mike presented pervasive ego-syntonic inflexible behavior patterns, minus guilt, inner anguish, or anxiety. The early protracted disruption in maternal care created fixations and arrests in his pre-Oedipal phases of development.

Diagnostic Evaluation

REFERRAL

When Mike T. was ten years old, the social worker at his school referred him to a child psychiatry clinic for an evaluation. Mike was described as a bright

[3]For further discussion of these issues, see Chapter 11 (residential treatment).

child who read far above grade level but refused to produce in school. He refused to participate in class discussions or to interact with peers, and the school planned to fail him on the basis of his refusal to work. In previous years, he had been passed on the basis of his obvious intellect. It was not clear why the parents sought help at this point, in that the problem had been long-standing. The parents projected Mike's problems onto the school and various teachers; after making inquiries, they felt the cost of private education to be prohibitive. Though they described problems at home, their conscious perception of the situation was that their son was of superior intellect, was bored in class, and had been mishandled by teachers. Father was concerned about Mike's manliness, due to his dumb "unhearing" affect and his refusal to defend himself with peers.

HISTORY OF COMPLAINT

When Mike entered kindergarten at age five, he was "disappointed" at not being taught to read. The parents stated that he complained about coloring projects and the "curriculum"—or lack thereof—but did well socially. In the first grade, his teacher had to leave prior to the close of school. Following this loss of his teacher, Mike complained that he didn't like school anymore, and he stopped doing any work. In the second grade, he obtained good marks, but only because he had been forced to work: on more than one occasion, he came home with bruised buttocks and descriptions of paddling. His teacher complained that getting him to work was like pulling teeth. The parents were most upset about the spankings and contacted the teacher. However, they skirted the issue of the punitive handling of Mike, as they were preoccupied with the sudden death of the maternal grandmother from a stroke.

Mike changed schools in the third grade and was placed in a combination second- and third-grade class. He complained of having to repeat work he'd had the year before. Despite his resistance and refusal to comply with any assignments, he passed. The year before his referral, when Mike was in the fourth grade, the school failed him on the basis of his refusal to work, despite the parents' claim that he was reading on the seventh-grade level. Mother said the school faculty members, who felt very frustrated with Mike, couldn't decide whether Mike should repeat the fourth grade or be skipped to the sixth grade. Over the summer, the parents forced Mike to participate in summer school, hoping that he could avoid repeating the fourth grade.

THE CHILD TODAY

Mike was an attractive, well-built black child who came to each clinic appointment overly dressed up in the same outfit of patterned bellbottoms and a matching ruffled shirt. He had a slow, cautious smile, conducted himself like a little adult—ignoring all toys—and talked nonstop, finding it difficult to end each interview.

Mike's own account of school concurred with the description given by the referring social worker and his parents. He was bored in school and had not made any warm attachments to teachers or peers. He was openly fearful of peers, got bullied, and was unable to let go and defend himself. He was aware of his father's anger at his cowardliness; it made him feel ashamed. He could not even defend himself against one of his high-spirited younger sisters. He was closest to mother and planned to study piano (her profession). He had few good friends; in fact, he referred to only two nonthreatening peers in the neighborhood: one was a younger boy and the other was a crippled boy with whom he spent much time. There seemed to be little pleasure or mastery in play or in school. Summer school was seen as better than regular school because of a variety of interesting trips. However, there appeared to be no consistent, internalized pleasure. Fear of his parents' tempers, as well as his own temper, was a major theme. Mike conveyed a lonely, angry, and fearful self-concept—that of a "sissy" who strongly repressed his anger and self-assertion, profoundly feared his father, and identified with his mother, whom he favored.

DEVELOPMENTAL HISTORY

Mike's father, Mr. T., was an attractive and vital, humorous, warm black man. He had had less formal education than his wife and worked as a traffic manager and a part-time TV repairman. He worked long hours, getting home late four evenings a week. He was rarely home except on weekends, when he slept, watched sports on TV, or ran some errands. He and his wife made a rather incongruous couple. She was very light-skinned, tense, and intellectual while he was earthy and more open. The family owned their own home and struggled to manage financially, with mother giving piano lessons at home. Mother stated there was no time or money for socializing with friends. The family appeared to be socially isolated.

Mr. and Mrs. T. had been married eleven years earlier, when she was 20 and he was 30. He had been married before, when he was 17. This first marriage had lasted 11 years and produced 5 children; the oldest was now 23 and the youngest was 16. Mr. T. stated that his first wife frequented taverns all night after their fifth child was born; she would take money from her wealthy father and leave him home with the laundry and the care of the five children. She had her father buy them a lavish home and pay for maids while she caroused drunkenly, had affairs, and smashed up cars with her drunken driving. Her sisters raised the children, although Mr. T. said he was actively involved, paying child support and seeing them several times a week. He stated that four of his five children turned out well; only the youngest one had problems. He was described as unreachable, stubborn, and rebellious. Mr. T. stated that he finally terminated his first marriage out of fear that he would go out of control and beat his wife. He said he had always struggled to control himself—at age 13, he had broken a boy's jaw in a furious fight. He maintained relationships with his in-laws from his first marriage and in fact was employed by his ex-father-in-law. At the time of his separation and divorce, his night school studies were interrupted.

He met Mrs. T. at work and courted her. He was happy that his second wife was a homemaker who was involved with her children, although she was a "temperamental musician." Both Mr. and Mrs. T. seemed to have preserved the marriage at a cost of much repression and denial. Finances were a chronic problem. Mrs. T. generally criticized Mr. T. for overspending on cars, clothes, a boat, and toys for the children. Mrs. T. kept her income separate, using it for household and personal items.

Mike, who was conceived immediately after the marriage, was not planned but "accepted." Mother continued working as a bookkeeper through a comfortable pregnancy. Delivery was full term with a normal labor lasting seventeen hours. Mrs. T. nursed Mike for five to six months. Mike was described as a quiet baby who slept through the night at two to three weeks of age. He was very responsive and mother was not nervous with him as she was with her second child, who had been a very "fussy" infant. Mike never used a pacifier or sucked his thumb. He went on solids by five to six weeks and was initially weaned from the bottle at a year. However, his maternal grandmother gave him the bottle again at 14 months, when his first sister was born. He used it for four to six more months. Mike was curious but not jealous of the new baby and he played gently with her. When Mike was six months old, mother returned to work and he was cared for by the maternal grandmother. After time off for the birth of his first sister, his mother again returned to work; Mike was then 17 months old.

Mother stated that her employment was necessary, as father had to support three of his five children from his first marriage (two had been adopted by his ex-wife's sister). Mr. T. was still involved with these children, who visited him every Sunday. Mrs. T. felt that her own mother's care of Mike was healthy, in that grandmother was very lively and had 6- and 7-year-old children of her own (Mrs. T. was the oldest of six children). For the last three years, Mrs. T. had worked at home teaching piano. She said she never got out of the house except to buy a newspaper. She spoke of her enjoyment and frustration with music; she had been a child protégé who began piano lessons at age three, at which time she also learned to read. By teaching at home, she saved money on lunches, sitters, and carfare, and could better supervise the children. This arrangement was also a source of conflict and frustration, as she would have preferred to get away from the home more often.

When Mike was five months old, he sang and babbled. He copied sounds at 6 to 10 months and said words at 10 to 12 months. He walked at 13 months and spoke in sentences at about 18 months. Toilet training was started at 15 months and took 6 months to master. Mike was a serious, curious, and inquisitive toddler who could entertain himself with puzzles, books, and picture books. He never had tantrums; nor was he defiant or stubborn in his toilet training. Mike was never jealous or resentful of his three sibs, but rather, was suspiciously reasonable and protective. He did evidence discomfort about mother's week of absence during her hospitalizations. Other than these hospitalizations of mother, there were no separations. Mike had roseola as an infant, measles at two and a half, ear and throat infections up to age three, and mumps at age nine.

Mike conveyed some sense of genital differentiation. He felt less pushed for masculinity from mother and turned to her for protection, especially in the face of father's wrath. He was open in expressing his fear of father and his resignation that father had no time for him. Mike showed no conscious awareness of his own passive-aggressive gratification. Because of Mike's own more feminine identification, as well as father's consistent absence from the family, a true genital differentiation and triadic relationship with parents were probably lacking. Mike did relate to each parent in a differentiated fashion and conveyed a sense of his father's dissatisfaction and lack of esteem for him and his mother's better communication with him. However, his sense of his parents' relationship with each other was questionable.

There seemed to be no appropriate move into latency, with the necessary cathexis of peers, games, sports, school, and the like. Mike could not master latency-age tasks and seemed preoccupied with anal withholding and stubbornness, especially at school, an area of profound importance to his parents. His self-assertion was passive-aggressive: he was aloof, dawdled about and daydreamed, and turned a deaf ear to all adults. He could not yet move into any masculine identification or surrender mother. Mike's tie to mother was like that of a much younger child.

POSSIBLE SIGNIFICANT ENVIRONMENTAL INFLUENCES

Due to the family's financial situation, mother left Mike and his sibs with the maternal grandmother when they were only infants in order to work. She had only been teaching piano at home since Mike was seven years old. The four children came in rapid succession (one every two years), which further diluted mother's attention to Mike. In addition, the presence of older half-siblings from father's prior marriage drained parental attention and energy. Father had little time for his family, as he worked day and night; he was too exhausted on the weekends to do much with Mike. There were no unusual medical illnesses or hospitalizations. The sudden death of Mike's grandmother coincided with the onset of his school problems.

PARENTS

Mrs. T.'s painful history had affected her handling of her own children. As the oldest of six children, she had had little privacy and was never allowed to express any anger. She was smacked by her mother if she slammed the door. (She tearfully acknowledged that her current even temper and blandness in public were a cover-up; in private, when she was upset, she threw dishes, pillows, etc., kicked furniture, slammed doors, and cried.) Her parents fought a great deal about money and father's jealous suspicions about other men who never existed. Her second sister, who had an explosive temper, hit her a lot and threw things; the parents never stopped her. Mrs. T. said she always had been precocious intellectually and had received much in the way of monies for dancing and piano lessons. She was close to her mother, who encouraged her in her interests. She won a music scholarship to a college, but had to give it up and go to work after one year. She never returned to college and gave her earnings to her parents for a downpayment on a house. While working, she met Mr. T. and they were married after a year's courtship. Mrs. T.'s sibs had had some college but none had degrees. She stated that none of them were encouraged as she was. Since her mother's death two years earlier, Mrs. T. has been depressed and concerned about her younger, high-school-age sisters, who had refused to live with her and had been left unsupervised, as their father abandoned their care in pursuit of a string of women.

Mr. T.'s traumatic history had also adversely affected his involvement with his children. His father had died when he was four months old; his mother went on relief and later worked as a maid. He was raised jointly by his mother, aunt, and grandmother, whom he described as Southern, superstitious, and church going. He was made to participate in church activities such as selling flowers and churning ice cream for church banquets. His aunt had five boys who were like brothers to him. His aunt was separated from her husband; although she was strict in disciplining the six boys, Mr. T., who was the baby, got away with a lot. At times, his aunt was warm and indulgent with him; she also taught him to read at age three. However, she also gave him severe beatings. Finances were meager and he worked at age six, selling coal and ice for movie money. When he was nine, his mother remarried a quiet, church-going man who earned a meager living in the steel mills; his mother continued working. His stepfather had a son four years older than Mr. T. whom he described as mean and selfish. The two boys had little contact, as Mr. T. always worked after school. He left home at age 13 and lived in a room, going to high school and seeing his folks once a month. He was unable to give any details about this period of his life. When he was 16 or 17, his stepfather died of a stroke. His mother moved in with cousins while he lived and worked in a nearby hotel; he saw his mother for meals when he wasn't out socializing and gambling. He didn't dare drink for fear of losing his temper, but he made a lot of money playing pool and cards. He did well academically and had plans for college. He had many girlfriends but avoided male friends, stating that boys his age were interested in drinking, dope, and drifting, whereas he stayed in his room, studying and listening to opera. In his fourth year of high school, he got a girl pregnant, quit school to work, finished high school at night, and married the girl at age 17, as described earlier. Father recounted much of this with humor, zest, and a pride that he got through it all; however, holding back his anger was a recurrent theme and a profound necessity, especially in fights with his stepfather.

INTERVIEWS

Mike, a well-built, attractive black child with a self-conscious and cautious smile, was seen for two interviews. His attire was too immaculate and dressy, given the hot summer day and his attendance at summer school. He entered the office easily, sat down and talked steadily and rapidly, and found it difficult to end the interview. He evidenced no interest in any toys or drawing equipment, but presented himself in an adult fashion. He did not "test out" the therapist. His outpouring of relevant information was surprising given the history of his chronic, stubborn passive-resistive withholding in school and at home. In the second interview, Mike continued the style and content of the initial interview, adding specific and pertinent details.

He began with little assistance and spoke freely of his problems at home and at school. He knew that he was there because he had failed the fourth grade despite being bright and reading above grade level. He found school and all assignments boring and that was why he didn't do them. Summer school was better because the students took trips to places like the zoo. Mike showed no guilt, but rather, some unconscious pleasure over his teachers' and parents' concerns. However, he showed appropriate affect as he spoke of fear of other kids and his inability to fight back when pushed on the playground or in the cafeteria. He described in detail a twitching sensation he got in his back and arms when he wanted to hit back and could not do so. His arm didn't actually twitch, but he felt scared and paralyzed when he wanted to get angry.

He didn't do much at home. He had toys, and played and watched TV. He saw only his two friends and avoided all other peers. He was supposed to start piano lessons soon. He went into much detail about his mother's musical abilities. He wanted to take lessons from one of her friends. Dad and he did little together. They had gone to a baseball game recently, but that didn't happen too often, since Dad worked so much. His brothers and sisters weren't much fun and they didn't play together much—except for Monopoly.

Mike knew why he was coming to the clinic and thought maybe it would be a good idea to come regularly by the fall. He had been prepared for psychological tests and referred to having them at his school in the past. Mike's outpouring did not seem related to the clinician, but rather, to the freer situation as compared to the structure of the psychological testing situation, school, or the daily routine expectations at home. He was obviously an intelligent boy, articulate and communicative. He was aware of his problems around aggressivity, but was not aware of how they manifested themselves in academics.

PSYCHOLOGICAL TESTS

At age 10 years, 3 months, Mike was given the following tests:

Bender-Gestalt Visual Motor Test, Standard Procedure
Wechsler Intelligence Scale for Children (WISC)
Sentence Completion Test (SCT)
Thematic Apperception Test (TAT)
Rorschach
Draw A Person (DAP)
Kinetic Family Drawing (KFD).

Clinically, Mike gave the impression of a very anxious latency child who took a passive-aggressive stance to minimize anxiety conjured up by threatening stimuli and circumstances. He performed adequately under minimal stress, but on confrontation of challenge in a novel situation became readily threatened, uneasy, and hostile. Retreat and aggressive passivity were bulwarks against both external circumstances impinging on his psychic structure and intrapsychic keyed emotions that were increasingly called into play. Fantasy and denial seemed to be prominent defensive maneuvers in the effort to cope with anxiety-arousing stimuli. He found no help or support from close objects such as parental figures.

Mike was highly concerned about his oral needs and was threatened by a situational demand for differentiation of identity. Denial of anger and feelings of vulnerability and helplessness became so frightening as to call for distancing via fantasy or paralyzing passivity.

In the WISC, he functioned at the bright-normal level, corroborating his insistence that he was a capable boy. He earned a verbal IQ of 110, a performance IQ of 121, and a full-scale IQ of 117. Mike was exceptionally capable in abstraction and concept formation as well as logical thinking. General scatter deviations suggested, however, that there was impairment in learning ability since the fund of verbal information and general range of his ideas were limited; anxiety might have constricted informational input. Performance deviations suggested difficulty in planning, anticipation, and interpretation of social situations. Furthermore, despite his capacity for abstraction, he failed to perceive and recognize whole or total situations. Organization and planning might have been too threatening, causing him to resort to trial-and-error methods to secure success.

Completed items in the SCT suggested difficulty in dealing with affect: "Sometimes I feel like a rock." Though he readily reminded one of his intellectual gifts, at a deeper level, he felt afraid, lonely, and "different," alienated by marked feelings of inferiority. Part of this poor self-concept was his view of himself as unable to fight or run fast like other boys his age. He had strong oral needs, as seen in statements such as: "My body is hungry." Denial of the totality of body parts was evident, suggesting a lack of differentiation due to their anxiety-arousing content: he didn't know what to make of them or what to do with them. His attitude toward his parents was one of external acceptance, but he felt closeness only on an activity level; there was little affective display, and this was missed sorely. He often projected feelings of self-disgust and inferiority into learning situations, claiming that most teachers were "boring." There were also ambivalent feelings toward peer interactions and social demands—he experienced fear and vulnerability, with a wish to regress to the security of dependency and fantasied achievement; on the other hand, there was a strong wish to perform well, to be powerful and successful.

The DAP and KFD were strikingly lacking in differentiation and affective expression. Parental figures as drawn indicated the patient's oppositionality and response to their rigidity, but also possibly an aggressive wish to mutilate himself and others. Emphasis on the breast of female figures suggested oral concerns. Castration anxiety, although not primary, was evident.

The unstructured tasks of the TAT revealed underlying personality dynamics. His distinct resistance and overt stubbornness in producing sufficient data were partially overcome only when the examiner took a firm, strong stance and insisted he "get to work." Structure provided support for his insecurity; emerging themes in the picture-stories centered on broken objects, competition, distanced inquisitiveness, and loneliness due to oral deprivation. Acting-out aggressive behavior was often disguised as accidental. In addition, pictures suggestive of closeness and affective interaction were very anxiety arousing. Fear of the dark and feelings of being puzzled, chased, and frightened were elucidated. Feeling alone, hurt, and confused by conflictual impulses, Mike saw himself as "driving on a race track, trying not to crash while everyone's going past."

Inferiority revolved around his inability to differentiate or understand his need for close, loving relationships and his destructive, hostile impulses, especially those called forth by a budding masculine competitiveness. There was some unconscious recognition of a concerted and costly expenditure of ego energy to contain these impulses threatening ego breakthrough. In a competitive environment, he felt pressed to give and take simultaneously, to "win the race," and was disgusted about being placed in the painful situation at all. The challenges of adolescence and differentiation of sexual identity were foreboding tasks for the immediate future. Fear of disintegration, self-destruction, and isolation forced him to maintain ego controls, particularly of the aggression stemming from the budding attempts at autonomy. He was pressed by peers and situations to become a unified, differentiated self, but lacked the affective assistance of a firm male model and the encouragement of a warm, supportive maternal figure. He thus emerged as frightened and insecure, claiming he was starving to death because he had no parents.

Especially prevalent in the Rorschach were strong aggressive feelings— he saw the world as hostile and attacking, and his vulnerable self needed to take on monstrous dimensions to defend itself against these attacks. Major defenses, again, included fantasied achievement, denial, and repression; when these were insufficient, hostile passive aggression took hold. Since he found interaction with people extremely threatening, he restricted himself to producing animal percepts. On occasion, percepts were distorted to produce fabulized consistency of his aggressive impulses with reality; however, when distortion did occur, it was generally countered by firm recovery. There was none of the bizarre, illogical thinking characteristic of disintegrated states.

In sum, Mike was a passive-aggressive personality tossed about in a developmental crisis, forced by peer interaction and societal demands to take on an autonomous masculine role. Insecure and resentful of this pressure, he determined to differentiate himself and "make it" to preserve himself from attack by the hostile aggressors, but inferiority feelings made this desire tenuous. A serious need for personal, affective warmth, concern, and understanding from powerful close authority figures was evident. He felt helpless, vulnerable, and confused. Anxiety in the face of a hostile world increased aggressive impulses to the point where ego resources found it difficult to cope with them. In an attempt to secure narcissistic needs, to receive protection against unreasonable societal demands, and to obtain suitable close objects for identification, he resorted to passive-aggressive behavior in school activities and in personal interactions.

DIAGNOSTIC FORMULATIONS

Mike's ego was intact. There were no signs or symptoms of primary defects there. Nor were there signs of primary deficiencies in his ego functions. His memory, reality testing, speech, and secondary-thought process reflected intactness. He was an intelligent boy who learned in school and scored very well on achievement tests but withheld and would not produce. There was important secondary interference of his defense system with many of his ego functions. His defense organization consisted of repression, fixation, and regression to anal levels; reaction formation; marked passivity; dependence; and turning of aggression against the self. These defenses seemed to be a response to his totally inadequate (or nonexistent) Oedipal resolution and masculine identification. This ineffective defense organization caused anxiety and ego regression. Thus, there was interference with social and academic adjustment. His learning was not impaired, but his refusal to produce in school and at home infuriated the adults in his environment and resulted in emotional and physical abusiveness and a sadomasochistic interpersonal mode of relating.

Either Mike entered the phallic-Oedipal phase and regressed to an anal level, or he was fixated at the anal level of development. His profound anal withholding in school supposedly began after a teacher's "abandonment." The grandmother's sudden death was probably the actual significant abandonment. The rapid succession of siblings might have made Mike conflicted about becoming competent, growing up, and severing dependency ties; that is, mother could only be kept via inadequate functioning. The intensity of Mike's anal withholding seemed great and all pervasive. His self-cathexis seemed to be impeded; he turned his aggression against himself.

Mike had reached the stage of object constancy, but there was constant interference due to regression to and/or fixation at the anal level. Mike withheld at home, at school, and in any testing situation. In the clinical interviews, where there were no pressures or expectations, he poured out profound amounts of material, almost in a verbal diarrhea fashion, discharging pent-up emotions, fears, and anxiety. Both the aggressive drive and the libidinal drive seemed fixated at or regressed to the anal level. Mike only discharged aggression via passive-aggressive means and by turning it against himself. He feared his parents' aggressivity and hid behind his passivity, getting others to act out aggressively toward him and upon him; these were all characteristics of an anal sadomasochistic pattern. His superego seemed regressed. Conflict was both externalized and internalized. Binding in aggressivity was a parental theme; the parents' prohibition of open, easy expression from Mike led to his passive-aggressive behavior. Their explosiveness frightened Mike from open expression in a safe environment. Further, Mike had introjected their authority into his superego; his ego constantly defended against and surrendered to his punitive superego via defenses that had become rigid and maladaptive. Thus, there was a constant need for punishment.

Mike experienced trauma as a result of his mother leaving him with grandmother when she went to work, the rapid succession of sibs, and grandmother's sudden death when he was seven. Mother was warm, intelligent, and involved in his intellectual and cultural development, but was also frightening due to her explosive temper and depression. He thwarted her hopes for his academic success and seemingly could not maintain a positive inner image of mother. Instead, he was clinging, controlling, and withholding. He appeared regressed to or fixated at the anal phase and was unable to identify with his reproachful, generally absent father, who was angry and impatient and often severely spanked Mike. Mike had not been able to enter at all appropriately into latency. Thus, a dynamic and structural assessment would indicate external conflicts between aggressive drives and the object world, and internal conflicts between the ego and superego, both arousing fear of the object world.

Mike had not progressed very far from the dependent position or toward age-appropriate object relationships. He had to be prodded to get up, get dressed, and get in motion. He dawdled and showed little independence. He presented isolation rather than peer companionship. He learned seemingly by osmosis, withholding any compliance with routine schoolwork. Adults were infuriated by this bright boy's refusal to participate. He used to be involved with projects and study (e.g., a rock collection) but currently had no hobbies or evident interests. Sports were avoided. His conflicts with his environment were profound. Little would be accomplished by simple environmental manipulation (e.g., a school change). Clearly, work with the parents—especially the mother—was a necessary adjunct to any realistic treatment of Mike. It seemed that this bright boy could be engaged in a therapeutic alliance. Long-term fairly extensive psychotherapy was indicated; it was likely that Mike would become stubborn and withholding, testing and provoking the therapist. It might take him some time to establish a relationship of depth. He was diagnosed as a character-disordered child, passive-aggressive type.

Addendum

Mike was treated successfully over a three-year period in biweekly or triweekly psychoanalytically oriented psychotherapy. His parents were resistive to any extensive or regular clinic contact, but were able to use parent guidance contact productively. Thus, they maintained an alliance with Mike's therapist.[4]

[4]The reader will find additional references to this case in Chapters 14, 15, and 17.

CHAPTER 9

Psychoneurosis

Definition

Fenichel (1945) states that psychoneuroses are based on the neurotic conflict and that "the neurotic conflict by definition is one between a tendency striving for discharge and another tendency striving to prevent this discharge. . . . Therefore the general formulation would be: the neurotic conflict takes place between drives, that is, the id and the ego" (p. 129). Thus, the presence of an emotional disturbance caused by *internalized conflict*, rather than presenting symptomatology, is the key to a diagnosis of psychoneurosis. Children's various presenting problems, which may include feeding, speech, and learning problems, nightmares, and phobias, cannot be equated with an actual internalized conflict. In the recent past, this equation was all too frequently made, and thus, a child who presented obsessive-compulsive symptoms, such as handwashing, bedtime rituals, and school phobias, was always assumed to be neurotic. In addition, manifest acute anxiety, hysteria, and hypochondriacal symptoms were regarded as hallmarks of neurosis. Kessler (1966) suggests that clinicians are eager to make a diagnosis of psychoneurosis because of its favorable prognosis relative to other psychopathologies.

Anna Freud (1977) emphasizes the need for a thorough investigation of the child's personality to pinpoint the relevance of each presenting symptom to developmental level and structure. "In short, manifest symptoms may be identical so far as their appearance is concerned, but may differ widely in respect to latent meaning and pathological significance" (p. 35).

Tolpin (1978) cautions against "cases of mistaken identity" and notes that disorder of structure formation is regularly mistaken for the infantile neurosis in both child and adult patients. She refers to the work of Anna Freud (e.g., 1968, 1970b, 1976), Greenacre (1971), and Kohut (1971, 1972, 1977), and warns us of the

> serious consequences [that] result from the analyst's mistaking the symptomatic manifestations and transferences of analytic patients with faulty structure formation for faulty conflict solutions, compromise formations, and disguised derivatives of the repressed infantile neurosis which return in a classical transference neurosis—the structural deficits, faults, and failures which stunt and impair the personality from childhood on remain essentially unchanged by the treatment, and so do the deficits in self-esteem, self-reliance, autonomy and object constancy which are their hallmarks [p. 168].

Anna Freud and Greenacre have described nonpsychotic and nonborderline individuals whose deficiencies and deficits go beyond the infantile neurosis. Anna Freud (1968, 1970b) suggests that a "neurotic superstructure" built on structural faults, deficits, defects, and failures creates confusion, in that neurotic problems and symptoms more or less obscure the critical psychopathology. Some years before these clarifications, children with developmental deficits who presented neuroticlike symptoms were often treated via insight-oriented, uncovering, anxiety-inducing approaches, which only gave rise to unmanageable and overwhelming anxiety. Tolpin (1978, p. 181) states that for patients "with structural deficits, genetic reconstructions and interpretations of conflicts are ineffectual because these interpretations bypass and obscure the central psychological injuries which lead to artifacts and regressive transferences."

Advances in ego psychology and child development have broadened our understanding of pre-Oedipal, pregenital fixations and arrests. We now have a better understanding of the "less than neurotic" child, who in fact presents borderline pathology and gross disharmony between developmental lines. These children may evidence age-appropriate intellectual functioning parallel with poor ego functioning. They lack self-soothing mechanisms, cannot tolerate frustration, evidence a meager capacity to handle anxiety, and have minimal potential for sublimation. They have not achieved separation-individuation and thus have not obtained object constancy.[1]

These critical milestones in development are necessary for the child's progress toward the phallic-Oedipal level of development. The move out of the primary dyad toward a triadic mode of relating, which includes child, mother, and father, is essential for actual entry into the phallic-Oedipal phase. Object constancy connotes enduring emotional attachment to the mother, irrespective of frustration or gratification. The attainment of self- and object constancy is predicated on a fusion of the good-mother/bad-mother, i.e., the fusion of the aggressive and libidinal drives. The attainment of object constancy parallels the attainment of self-constancy and thus indicates achievement of clear self/other boundaries. This demarcation of self and other provides a cohesive and stable self-representation that is not subject to the overwhelming inner tensions associated with the fragmentation, narcissistic rage, free-floating (disintegration) anxiety, and depletion (empty) depression described by Tolpin (1978). Thus, the neurotic child has achieved considerable psychic and structural development.

Nagera (1966) emphasizes that only when the child has reached the phallic-Oedipal level of development do we see an actual infantile neurosis, which is an attempt to organize all the previous neurotic conflicts and developmental shortcomings. This compromise solution is predicated on the child's relatively high degree of development, which includes the achievement of separation-individuation and object constancy. Anna Freud (1971) also emphasizes the positive degree of personality growth. She notes that while the infantile neurosis belongs to the realm of psychopathology and in extreme forms can create severe and crippling difficulties, it also appears regularly in many children whose future adaptation to life is successful. Furthermore, the conflicts underlying it are normal ones. From a developmental point of view, then, the infantile neurosis represents positive personality growth, a progression from primitive to more advanced reaction patterns (Anna Freud, 1971). While neurosis connotes suffering and discomfort because the well-developed ego is disturbed, psychosis does not always result in acute suffering because the ego is too impaired or inadequate to register reality, affects, etc. Anna Freud (1971) presents the "well-known formula" for the formation of neurosis: conflict causes regression; regressive aims arouse anxiety; anxiety is warded off by defense; conflict solutions are reached via compromise; and symptoms are formed. The conflict causing the regression may be a traumatic event that cannot be integrated by the ego. The extent and nature of the

[1]See also Chapter 8 (borderline syndrome).

traumatic event or constellation of events must be understood over and beyond manifest content. For example, the birth of a younger sibling need not be traumatic but becomes traumatic for the child who already has been sensitized by mother's previous miscarriage and depression, which made her unavailable.

Etiology

There are varied explanations of the causative factors of childhood neuroses, and most researchers and clinicians suggest that the etiology is imperfectly understood. Adams (1979) discusses three etiological foci: (1) predisposing or hereditary conditions, which include biological factors such as the child's temperament, physique, intelligence and gender; (2) environmental factors such as the parents' patterns of child rearing and communication; and (3) psychopathology. Many aspects of each variable can be scrutinized. Shaw (1966) believes that we have little substantial evidence that "neuroticism" per se is inherited. He notes that some children are born with almost no capacity to adapt, children who would be placed at the extreme end of Chess's scale of "adaptable-nonadaptable. [1965]" Even after receiving excellent care and affection in a normal family surround with normal sibs, such children are fearful, maladjusted, and unhappy. Infant studies examining the subtleties of interaction between mothers and infants point to the not infrequent mismatch between an active child and a mother's preference for a quiet, passive child.

The familial environment is different for each child in the family, given the child's temperament and the parental response to the child. The latter will vary with the child's gender, birth order, and the state of the marital dyad; thus, each child enters a "different" family. Shaw emphasizes the emotional tone of the family, the overt and covert distortions and mishandlings, rejections, excesses of love and attention, and projections, including the lethal combination of excessive frustration and overgratification. Some parents are unable consistently to maintain a homeostatic balance that embodies continuity, parental empathy, and delight in the child, offered in an atmosphere that presents "optimal gratification" and an "average expectable" environment.

Adams (1979) points to precipitating events or mobilizing factors, which include physical ailments, psychic traumas, and broad sociocultural disruptions in the life of the child. Bender and Schilder emphasize central nervous system immaturity, infections, and other organic insults which could aggravate or induce a neurotic reaction, and Anna Freud (1965) emphasizes the same in regard to hospitalized children. Earlier, Anna Freud (1952) examined the impact of bodily illness over and beyond separation anxiety caused by hospitalization.

She noted the change of the child's emotional climate, given altered parental attitudes and affects (e.g., parental anxiety in response to the child's illness, the child's renouncing ownership of his or her body due to medical and nursing care, the ill effects of restrictions in diet and movement, and the trauma of intrusive surgical operations). She emphasized the child's mental interpretation of pain, and the impact of pain and anxiety. She compared deprived children who cared for their bodies in identification with their lost mothers and adult hypochondriacs who overcathected their body with libido after a withdrawal response from the object world.

Adams (1979) notes necessary and sufficient causes and conditions, the impact of events at specific critical and vulnerable phases, and the specific patterns of intrafamilial interaction, all of which may trigger anxiety or evoke an emotion unacceptable to child and parents. Systems theory emphasizes the differential impact of family actions, events, and reactions on the components of the system—that is, on the members of the family. Thus, family events create a different impact on each child in the family unit, depending on the child's age, life experiences, and varying resources, talents, intelligence, sublimatory channels available, vulnerabilities, and temperament.

Considerations of etiology are not complete without some reference to learned behaviors, family style, and parenting patterns that produce the child the parent consciously or unconsciously needs. Shaw (1966) suggests that counteraggressive acting out is generally noted in children whose families display aggressivity. Such children have actually been taught to fight, to participate in the family style and manner of handling emotions. Conversely, the inhibited, repressed, and constricted child most often has grown up in a rigid and overcontrolled family characterized by moralistic, strict, repressive parents. Passive, dependent children often are responding to the overprotective mother who has not allowed the child independence and normal social relationships with peers. Sick and complaining parents not uncommonly produce hypochondriacal children. Often, delinquent and acting out children have been unconsciously induced and seduced by parents who get vicarious enjoyment out of their children's delinquency. Johnson and Szurek (1952) suggest that this phenomenon arises out of parents' superego lacunae, (i.e., holes, deficits in the parents' superego), whereby parents unconsciously sanction the unacceptable acting out of their children.

Descriptive Characteristics and Symptoms

Unhappiness, anxiety, and irrational ego-alien behaviors are characteristic of neurosis. In children, the two most common neurotic symptoms are anxiety and academic failure. In addition, depression, apathy, isolation, oppositional behavior, aggressive behavior, sleeping and eating disturbances, enuresis, phobias, and irrational fears are often present. The diagnosis usually is based on the clinician's observation of anxiety, plus the child's distinct capacity for a relationship and frequent acknowledgment of inner suffering. The developmental history should show evenness of development prior to the onset of neurosis, negotiation of separation-individuation, attainment of object constancy, and entry into and/or partial or faulty resolution of the phallic-Oedipal phase. In the latency-age child, genuine superego structure should be apparent, though we assume that the final superego structure comes into being only after the resolution of the Oedipal conflict. The neurotic child has not achieved resolution of the Oedipal period, and Oedipal conflicts with marked castration anxiety may induce regression. In defining regression, Nagera (1964), says that "the drives have at one point or another reached a higher level of development but were, as a result of conflicts at these higher levels, forced back to earlier developmental positions" (p. 224). Nagera emphasizes that precise attention to the phase and subphase of the regression aids in our understanding of earlier overt and covert conflicts between the child and significant environmental figures such as the parents. These earlier conflicts evolve into intrapsychic ones as the child internalizes environmental standards and represses internal drives.

The intrapsychic conflict between id and ego, and/or id and superego, is based on the child's fear of breakthrough of instinctual expressions. Because such expressions are seen as dangerous, they are generally inhibited or disguised via symptoms, which are substitute expressions of the instinctual drive or urge. The ego, the mediator and assessor of reality, makes clear the unacceptable nature of the id impulse; the superego threatens punishment or induces guilt in the child. For example, a girl's death wishes and murderous impulses toward her younger brother are expressed in vivid dreams of her baby brother lying dead on the sidewalk after crawling out of the window of their ninth-floor apartment. After she awakens from this recurring nightmare, she checks his crib and can't sleep. In her daily routine, she is most solicitous of and attentive to her brother. She is attempting to undo the terrifying and unacceptable wish and impulse via the defense of reaction formation. The common neuroses of childhood are presented below according to Kessler's schema (1966).

Anxiety States

Anxiety states are manifested by sleep disturbances, reluctance to go to sleep, and nightmares. Anxiety suggests a fear that is not justified by the external reality or that is an excessive reaction to a disturbing situation or event. The child may or may not be aware of the anxiety. Often the symptom encapsulates or defends against anxiety.

In discussing anxiety neurosis, Adams (1979) speaks of unvarnished fear bursting forth in recurrent attacks of panicky feelings when it is not defended against with the ego's defense mechanisms. Resultant affective states and behavioral problems stemming from anxiety neurosis include feelings of inadequacy, impending doom, indecisiveness, insomnia, irritability, restlessness, and school problems. There may be accompanying somatic symptoms such as nausea, stomachaches, sweating, dizziness, and diarrhea.

Childhood Phobias

Phobias can be mild and transient, or fixed. A phobia is an all-consuming fear that the child knows is irrational. The most common childhood phobias are of animals, storms, transportation, and school. Severe phobias can be disabling, creating great social disadvantages, whereas milder phobias create anxiety and anticipatory fear. Freud's classic case of Little Hans (1909) documented a small child's fear of horses, which was caused by the child's projection and displacement of his own frightening impulses. A phobia starts with repression of an unacceptable idea, wish, or impulse. In the case of Little Hans, the wish to attack his father was projected, so that the father was perceived as the attacker; but the father was then so frightening that he had to be made less dangerous, so the fear was displaced onto horses.

Phobias generally screen aggressive or sexual feelings. In the "less than neurotic" narcissistically damaged children described by Tolpin (1978), phobias may be the neuroticlike symptoms masking structural deficits, narcissistic rage, disintegration, and fragmentation. Treatment approaches for such children are vastly difficult. The therapist serves as the child's prestructural self-object, rather than the Oedipal object of the neurotic child. School phobias have been viewed as a form of separation anxiety; the child's fear of aggressive acts is projected onto mother and then displaced onto the school.

Hysteria in Childhood

According to Kessler (1966), this lable is rarely affixed, as hysterical symptoms frequently are short lived and transient. She suggests that "hysterical symptoms appear when repression breaks down and the unconscious thoughts emerge in some guise seen as (1) isolated emotional outbursts, (2) disturbances of sensation or motility, (3) alterations in consciousness, or (4) temporary loss of sense of reality" (p. 243). Proctor (1958) notes these symptoms are more florid in specific cultures and geographic areas dominated by religiosity, primitive and repressive attitudes dealing with faith healing, magic, etc. Given the recent influx of Hispanic immigrants, such phenomena are seen more frequently in urban child guidance and mental health clinics.

An example of the effect of culture on diagnosis and treatment is the "Puerto Rican syndrome," or "ataque," described by Joseph Fitzpatrick (1971). He quotes Berl as saying that ataque is a culturally expected reaction to serious stress and that Puerto Ricans manage it as an ordinary occurrence. The clinician not familiar with the cultural background could interpret ataque as a symptom of a more serious mental disturbance. Proctor (1958) suggests that extreme inconsistency between action and word is the fertile ground for hysterical reactions; for instance, the child's sexual feelings and Oedipal wishes are kept alive by the parents' conscious seduction while at the same time sexuality is decried. The child then cannot accept or admit sexual feelings but is prevented from repressing them by constant stimulation. This occurs in households where children share beds and bathrooms with parents. The critical diagnostic dilemma is the assessment of actual psychic development; many individuals with basic structural deficits who have not achieved separation-individuation mask their pregenital problems in a sexualized guise. The same reservations hold for a child's presentation of hysterical hallucinations, despite the paradigm of repression, projection, and displacement. Esman (1962) suggests that repeated visual exposure to sexual scenes and adults' genital organs are characteristic variables noted in the histories of children suffering from visual hallucinations.

A developmental assessment combined with a knowledge of cultural and ethnic customs and life styles is of particular relevance in work with clients whose backgrounds are dissimilar from that of the clinician. The dangerous effects of racism and stereotyping in clinical work are effectively discussed by Cooper (1973). She details the errors made by clinicians who not infrequently superimpose their own highly emotional attitudes on clients.

> White therapists influenced by a culture rampant with racism and unfamiliar with the intricacies and nuances of the lives of ethnic people may, even with the best intentions, fail to recognize when social and cultural forces predominate in clinical work. Ethnic therapists are vulnerable to the opposite sort of clinical error. Because they are so centrally involved, they may exaggerate the importance or impact of ethnic factors, thus replacing ethnicity with ethnocentricity. In both color blindness and ethnocentricity, patients tend to lose their individual richness and complexity; there is a danger of no longer treating people—only culture carriers [p. 76].

Obsessive-Compulsive Neurosis

This neurosis occurs in combined form; that is, the child presents behaviors and symptoms which are predominantly compulsive or obsessional. In the predominantly obsessional neurosis, there is an ideational disturbance with recurrent, incessant ideas rather than affects, actions, or bodily sensations. The intrusive and disturbing thoughts and mental preoccupations frequently cause secondary interference with learning, memory, and ability to concentrate, and thus, cause academic problems. The compulsive neurotic child is engaged in actions—due to internalized preconscious or unconscious conflicts in regard to dirtiness and cleanliness, rebellion and submission, and activity and passivity. Kessler (1966) notes that "compulsive symptoms vary, but they often have to do with cleanliness (e.g., compulsive hand washing), safety (e.g., checking and rechecking door locks and gas jets), or superstitious rituals (e.g., doing things in a certain order, counting to a particular number, or touching things a certain number of times)" (p. 250). Despite the child's awareness of the irrational nature of his behavior, he cannot control it and feels overwhelmed by anxiety if compelled to stop. Magical words that must be uttered and stepping over cracks in the sidewalk "lest you break your mother's back" are common examples of compulsive symptoms. Adams (1979, p. 205) describes an 11-year-old boy fighting to the point of exhaustion his compulsion to step on imaginary dots on the floor; he usually did not feel "undriven" until he had gone through a three-time ritual. Differentiation of the obsessive-compulsive neurosis and childhood schizophrenia is critical. Although a child burdened with obsessive and/or compulsive symptoms can become very handicapped and constricted, as long as he or she is aware of the unreal and unreasonable nature of the obsessive thoughts and compulsive acts, the self-observing ego is still operative and there is no break with reality. Severity of symptomatology does not indicate psychosis; rather, the critical indicator is the patient's awareness and insight. Despert (1955) suggests that mistaken diagnoses of schizophrenia are more common than the literature indicates. Kessler (1966) suggests that while children frequently display obsessive-compulsive symptoms, "they do not acquire the total rigidity of the (adult) obsessive compulsive" (p. 254).

Character Neurosis

Pearson (1949) subdivides character neurosis into two types: (1) those in which the ego imposes numerous restrictions via defenses such as reaction formation to placate the severe superego, with resultant rigid self-control; (2) those in which the ego's restrictions are insufficient to bind in drive expression, with resultant rebellion and opposition. Too frequently, the "very good," adultlike children of the first type are overvalued, in that parents, teachers, and other adults enjoy the child's obedience and perfectionistic standards. Oppositional and aggressive behavior is a more frequent cause for referral of a child and is manifest either in overt rebellion or in covert manipulation, withholding, evading, and arguing. Both overt and covert forms represent expressions of hostility towards parents who themselves respond with "anger, frustration, resentment, helplessness, and indignation" (Shaw, 1966, p. 145).

Depression

Shaw (1966) describes the two general types of depression in children.

> The first occurs in infants under two years of age and results from separation from the mother. . . . The other type of depression is seen mainly in children of six years and older and presented is a picture of sadness, disinterest and a general psychomotor dimunition. In the neurotic child, depression seems to result when the child, finding no escape from his conflict, finally gives up the struggle. It may be in reaction to a variety of situations in the environment which the child views with hopelessness. Dynamically, as in adult depression, it may represent the loss or threat of loss of a love object [p. 146].

The literature suggests that depression in children is not as chronic, disabling, and resistive to treatment as in adults, but rather, is more transient, reactive, and fluctuating and is often manifested by a range of affects, (i.e., apathy, lethargy, somatic symptoms or aggressivity and delinquent behavior). In contrast to adults, children may become energized during depression, striking out at the environment and available objects, instead of or in addition to engaging in punitive self-punishing, self-injurious behavior. In addition, Adams (1979) suggests that children whose self-concept or self-esteem is impaired or threatened are at risk for a depressive neurosis.

Treatment Interventions

Anna Freud (1968) believes that analytic therapy can help psychoneurotic children and states that the infantile neurosis has shown itself eminently amenable to analytic therapy. Conflicts, unsuitable defenses, fixations, anxieties, regressive moves, and severe repression of aggression rooted in the child's history prevent an inner equilibrium as they prevent adaptation to the demands of external reality. When the child's conflicts are acute and phase specific, the decision for treatment cannot be clear-cut. Some clinicians advocate waiting for the ego's spontaneous compromises to provide some solidification; they suggest that coping with the overwhelming anxiety of a crisis takes all the child's resources and makes the child less available to treatment. Others recommend immediate analytic treatment to avoid additional fixations and regressions, and lasting harm to the child's further chances of normal growth. Likewise, with adolescents, some clinicians advocate immediate analytic intervention while others suggest waiting until late adolescence or early adulthood before attempting to undertake an uncovering, anxiety-producing mode of treatment. Bernstein and Sax (1978) note that intelligence and psychological mindedness are necessary factors for the successful analysis of psychoneurotic children. "Furthermore a degree of frustration tolerance, impulse control and intact reality testing are necessary requirements for an analytic process. Children who are overwhelmed by the strength of their instincts should not be analyzed until it is determined that the interpretation of their defenses would not lead to overwhelming panic" (p. 98).[2]

Analysis and intensive, uncovering treatment are contraindicated for children who are victims of the external circumstances of their lives. When damage is caused and maintained by active ongoing environmental influences, child and therapist are frustrated by the important unmet developmental needs of the child. In addition, the parents must indicate an ability and willingness to allow the child to begin and maintain analytic treatment. "Unstable parents who provide a threatening or excessively stimulating or depriving environment constitute a contraindication to psychoanalysis. Also, parents' statements about their children must be evaluated in the light of their own psychopathology. Parents may unconsciously propagate their child's symptoms or they may mislead the consultant, especially if they view the child as an extension of themselves" (Bernstein and Sax, 1978, p. 97). The importance of the parents' stance is emphasized by Anna Freud (1968) in her reflections on the impossibility of successful therapy for the child, when the threat, the attacker, or the seducer is a real person, or where the pathogenic influences are embodied in the parents.

Child analysis is most clearly indicated when the child's turmoil is a product of the child's inner world, as in the psychoneuroses. However, due to the time, investment, and expense of classical analysis, most psychoneurotic children are treated using other approaches, such as

---

[2]The problematic issue of the child's capacity for transference is discussed in detail in Chapter 13 (transference, the real relationship, and countertransference).

analytically oriented psychotherapy, parent guidance, direct treatment of the parents, and family therapy. Sours (1978l) suggests that

> general neurotic conflicts which do not seriously interfere with libidinal or ego development can be treated with one of a variety of psychotherapies. If the balance between wishes and repressive forces of the ego is not upset, internalization of conflict is minimal, and there is a preponderance of external conflict, the effectiveness of psychotherapy is greater than when these factors are absent. If there is a preponderance of internalized conflict, in general, psychoanalysis is indicated. Children with internalized neurotic conflicts who are not potentially psychologically minded or whose general intelligence is lower than what analysis requires should be treated by a psychotherapy in the range of supportive to expressive [p. 625].

Adams (1979) suggests that child psychiatrists do not have a complete and objective overview of neurotic children, since those who receive medical attention are preselected according to socioeconomic and educational class. He states that many lower-class neurotic children who are "identified as fearful, anxious, depressed, phobic, hysterical, obsessive compulsive and otherwise neurotic . . . [are] probably seen exclusively by pediatricians and general family practitioners. That is, referral to child psychiatrists never takes place. Hence, it is reasonable to conclude that some forms of . . . drug treatment (frequently) occur at the hands of nonpsychiatric primary-care physicians" (p. 231).

In addition to the direct therapies noted above, indirect treatments not involving the child per se have been historically recommended. Sours (1978a) surveys the literature on indirect therapies, citing attitude therapy (Levy, 1937), family therapies (Szurek et al., 1942), casework techniques (Hamilton, 1947; Coleman, 1949), and recent parent effectiveness therapies and crisis intervention. He discusses Furman's method (1957) of treating children under five through the parents and notes some of its hazards.

Case of Rick

The case of Rick shows the suffering and discomfort of a child who demonstrated considerable structural development and ego strength. However, at the time of referral, he had not resolved his Oedipal conflict and presented internalized conflict that was causing academic decline, poor peer relationships, and temper tantrums. He was eager for help and demonstrated considerable psychological mindedness in discussing his difficulties.

Diagnostic Evaluation

REFERRAL

Rick K., age nine, was referred by his fourth-grade teacher at a private, university-sponsored school. His parents were receptive, as they had been having considerable difficulties at home with Rick. They described him as a "problem child" since infancy, and seemed to be seeking consultation at this point because of the urgings of the teacher and the now public nature of Rick's difficulties. Rick was described as shy, and alternately aloof and hostile with peers, playing roughly and really hurting other children. His academic work had declined sharply and was at a poor level. His homework was never done and assignments were generally found in his jeans pocket at laundry time. At home, Rick was rude, defiant, and given to temper outbursts and serious combative exchanges with siblings. He swore, stomped, and was most difficult around mealtimes and bedtime. He was particularly adverse to church, which he scorned, and to sports and games, from which he withdrew. He talked at length about child criminals, child murderers, and other such chilling topics. Father was estremely anxious about Rick's negativism toward math (father's field) and the Catholic religion.

The K.'s were New Zealanders; they were only here for the academic year, as father was a visiting professor at a university. He was a noted expert in a rare specialty of mathematics. In June, the family would return home; prior to their departure, the K.'s wanted a diagnostic evaluation to offer them guidelines. The parents were highly sophisticated and intelligent people who were knowledgeable about psychological matters. They sought the diagnostic evaluation because of their helplessness, anxiety, and frustration over their increased awareness of their son's unhappiness.

HISTORY OF COMPLAINT

The parents dated Rick's first major difficulty to age ten months, when he was upset by the family's move to a new city, where father was a visiting professor at a university. Rick became a finicky eater and wanted only a limited diet of milk, bananas, and eggs. Mother had tried to coax him matter-of-factly, assuming that the fad would pass. Father had been frenzied, forcing meat and vegetables on Rick. Rick had resisted, refusing to eat meat until about age two. Toilet training had been difficult, with enuresis until age six, and occasional enuresis at age eight. Rick always had been anxious about school and socially isolated; his academic work had been superior until the year preceding his referral.

The parents always had worried about their eldest son but, until this evaluation, had handled his problems by changing his schools. Although their handling of Rick was inconsistent, in general, they were permissive, worried, and exhausted. Father described his futile lectures to Rick about ethics, morality, and Catholic doctrine. Rick evidenced awareness of his lack of friends, and ineptness in sports and math. He did not overtly correlate his behavior with his social isolation and presented feeling justified in his conflicts with his parents and siblings. All the moral preachings he and his parents described might have buried appropriate guilt on his part.

THE CHILD TODAY

Rick was a slight and slender boy with bright blue eyes. His speech added to his presentation of himself as a little adult, rather than a child. He worked hard in the interview and was very anxious initially. He was obviously of superior intellect and interacted with the clinician on a highly advanced intellectual and conceptual level, keeping affect very much repressed.

The past year had marked a sharp decline in Rick's academic performance. Earlier, his grades had been superior. He described profound confusion in New Math, and evidenced a total collapse in the permissive atmosphere of the private school after his prior, rigid parochial Catholic schooling. However, Rick said he enjoyed this school's lack of rules, uniforms, and "mean" teachers. Nevertheless, his work was mediocre and unsatisfactory. Rick had never been interested or able in athletics and withdrew from such peer contacts. He had always been a loner, having a friend or two at most. He was very attached to the neighbors' children at home (abroad), but both his parents strongly disapproved of the family. Relationships with adults were characterized by rudeness, anger, and rebellion, which was in sharp contrast to his need to be his parents' favorite. He wanted this preference to be overtly stated and demanded much individual attention from his parents. He talked late into the night with his father about spacecraft and the like and often followed mother in her daily housework, firing questions about rockets and spacecraft. He had a general dislike of teachers.

Rick had established a clear masculine identity, but he had a sense of hopelessness about his competence. His self-concept appeared to be that of an angry, lonely child who would never measure up and succeed. He felt doomed to failure due to his current deficiency in math (related to his father) and his long-standing lack of mastery of social and athletic skills. His self-concept seemed to be an enactment of his father's identification with him: "Rick is just like me, inadequate in the same areas and doomed to misery."

DEVELOPMENTAL HISTORY

Mr. and Mrs. K. were active, practicing Catholics who, according to their description, were members of the intellectual Catholic community. Father was currently in a profound personal struggle about every aspect of his religious identification. The intensity of his turmoil and struggle seemed symptomatic, going beyond actual religious questions. Mrs. K. seemed to be in less religious turmoil, except in relation to her differences with her husband regarding school placement for the four children; in the past, the K.'s had argued about birth control. The parents had had extensive marital difficulties. Periodically, Mrs. K. contemplated a divorce, but she feared taking such a step. Because she regarded her husband's difficulties as beyond his control and not willful, she hoped his return to therapy would alleviate some of their problems. She planned to enter therapy herself, due to her unhappiness and the depreciation by her husband. Mr. K. gave frenzied descriptions of his melancholia, anxiety, and chronic hypochondriacal state. Mr. and Mrs. K. described social discomfort caused by Mr. K.'s tension and inability to converse with ease at parties, which led to his excessive drinking, sexual excitement, and lecturing of people. When high, he would get excited and make sexual overtures toward other wives or shout at his wife about mistakes in her bridge playing.

Mr. K., who apparently possessed considerable professional competence, was not at all satisfied with his research and publication output. It appeared that he was well thought of at the university, yet he was very concerned about the family's position in the academic community. In addition to dissatisfaction with his own progress, he was displeased by his wife's lack of intellectualism and her lack of an advanced degree. She had attended a two-year teachers' college and taught school prior to her marriage. Mr. K.'s income was good, yet the K.'s had little savings, what with their extensive travels and the financial aid given to Mr. K.'s parents. The K.'s traveled continuously, if not obsessively, with Mr. K. guest lecturing at a myriad of American universities. Their travels from New Zealand to the U.S. were also interspersed with extensive travel throughout the U.S. and Europe.

Rick had been wanted, but not planned. The parents described themselves as delighted and thrilled about the pregnancy, which was normal and comfortable, with a full-term, normal delivery. Mother nursed Rick for nine months. He was colicky for the first three months, which mother felt was due to her nervousness and ineptness with her first child. She said she was not tense when nursing and feeding Rick, but was nervous when bathing him and changing his diapers. After three months, she and the baby settled down and become more relaxed. Rick, from three months on, is described as a contented baby who slept well and was responsive. He did not use a pacifier, but sucked his thumb till age four and a half, which concerned his parents. He crawled at six months and walked at ten and a half months. Because of poor enunciation, he was hard to understand. He was late in getting teeth, which began to appear at nine months.

When Rick was ten months old, the family moved, as father was to teach in this country. He became alarmed by the Cuban missile crisis and returned the family to their home, where they had to live with the paternal grandparents, as they had rented their house. At this point, Rick's anxiety about the changes were manifest by the food fads and a refusal to eat anything but milk, bananas, and eggs. Father became frantic about this and attempted to force meat and vegetables on him. He interfered with and criticized mother's more matter-of-fact approach. Living with the paternal grandparents for several months had been most stressful for Mrs. K.; she described her profound upset and its impact on Rick. Mr. K.'s mother, who had had several psychiatric hospitalizations, was described as "difficult, depressed, and hypochondriacal." For the next eight months, the family rented a house and then, when Rick was about 22 months old, the family moved back to the U.S., as father had secured another lectureship at another university. Immediately prior to this move, when Rick was 17 months old, the second child, M., was born. While mother was in the hospital, Rick was cared for by the housekeeper, whom he hated; he showed his resentment of mother's absence by rejecting her at the hospital and glowering for two weeks, the length of time the hospital insisted on keeping maternity cases. Mother described ignoring her new baby and bending over backwards to reassure Rick. The move to the U.S. when Rick was 22 months old was described as more exhausting than previous moves. That academic year was described as pleasant, due to easy living and friendly neighbors.

Toilet training was given a tentative try at eight months and dropped. Mother said she never pushed or was insistent. Bowel control was achieved at two years, eight months. Rick was dry during the day by two years, six months. Enuresis seemed constant, especially when Rick began school, which made him upset and tense. He also wet the bed occasionally at age eight.

When Rick was two years, eight months, the family left the U.S. and toured England and Europe for twelve weeks; they then returned to the U.S. and settled in still another university town where father was engaged for the academic year. K., the third child, was born there, when Rick was three years, one month. He showed little reaction to this sib's arrival and helped with some of the care. When Rick was almost four, the family left the U.S. and returned home, where they resided almost five years. They returned to the U.S. when Rick was nine.

Mother reported loving Rick "so much" and delighting in his development. She thought she was probably overanxious about his reaction to the rapid succession of siblings. She described Rick as her center of attention; she was overinvested in and overindulgent with him, always trying to compensate for the intrusion of the other children. The birth of the last child when Rick was four had produced the strongest overt reaction: "His behavior became so objectionable; he was always wanting and still wants all the attention." Mother was exhausted by his overt insistence on being her favorite, his endless questions about his siblings falling out of a car or a plane traveling 1,000 miles a minute, and his frustrated swearing or provocative chanting of obscenities. He rarely was with friends and seemed eager to see her after school, when he began his harangues or endless gibberish space questions. Mother clearly was unable to handle Rick's feelings of rivalry and always engaged in literal answers to his questions, especially about the outcomes of accidents involving his sibs. She could not respone empathically to the latent themes and feelings he presented.

Mrs. K. saw her husband in the child: "He and his father have temper outbursts, moodiness, and fears of death and cancer." She conveyed great alarm at this similarity and despaired about what she could do to intervene in what she saw as Rick's progressive deterioration. In the interview with

Rick, he could make little reference to his mother and ably expressed resentment that she did not protect his tops and models from his sibs' breakage. He was more open and angry about his father's lectures on math and religion. Father acknowledged his frustration and sermonizing, which were the result of his rage at the child's chronic misbehavior and seeming lack of remorse or guilt. Father saw himself in Rick; as a youth, he had been lonely, angry, and inept with friends and in athletics. He acknowledged a preoccupation with Rick in contrast to a most casual attitude toward the other children. He conveyed being in a literal frenzy, wanting to force sports (like food, when Rick was ten months), religion, and mathematics on Rick. He viewed math as the key to professional success. To listen to him, one could forget that he was discussing a 9-year-old child of superior intellect who had done excellent academic work until recently.

Rick acknowledged much turmoil and taunting in his relationships with his sibs. He delighted in warfare and the changing alliances among the four of them, as well as in uniting as a force against the parents. He referred to his and his sibs' slowness in making friends. They were together a great deal in the apartment, where they only had access to the janitor's children, whose English was meager. With all family members, Rick conveyed a sadomasochistic exchange and the feeling that he never got enough or was treated unfairly.

Rick seemed clear about genital differentiation. He was engaged in a sadistic and distorted form of the triadic relationship with his parents, relating to each in special and different problematic ways. He commented on the bedroom arrangements of the family. Just as he wanted to be mother's favorite and divert her attention from sibs, nightly he succeeded in separating mother and father by staying up late and engaging father in scientific discussions, with the consistent result that mother retired, and he and father talked late into the night. He used anal and sexual words when swearing, but it was not clear what his sexual understanding and fantasies were. It seemed that Rick was not clear about the marital relationship. Mother referred to her husband and oldest son as "two poorly controlled, hypochondriacal babies." Father harangued mother about her bridge playing, her driving, and her lack of advanced education, and Rick about his rudeness, math skills, and religious matters. It appeared that Rick and father competed for mother as sibs.

Rick had not made an appropriate move into latency. He had not lessened his drive urgency, nor had he adequately transferred libido from parental figures to contemporaries and teachers. Remnants from the phallic-Oedipal phase were exemplified by his fears of castration, cancer, and death, as well as his death wishes. There was no discernible evidence of quiescence; instead, there was increased aggressivity, which was vented in the more permissive school atmosphere.

POSSIBLE SIGNIFICANT ENVIRONMENTAL INFLUENCES

There were no unusual physical illnesses or problems in the family. However, there was an abundance of psychiatric illness in the extended family and the parents were clearly fearful of mental illness, manifested by the similar problems Rick and his father presented. Mrs. K.'s youngest sister's acute paranoia over the last five years had resulted in two hospitalizations. This sister was described as strange and withdrawn since the age of 12, when she had begun to stare into space and daydream. Mrs. K. believed that her sister's rheumatic fever at age six altered the way the parents handled the sister. Mr. K.'s mother's chronic depression and hypochondriacal fears had led to repeated psychiatric hospitalizations that included shock treatment. Mr. K. had sought psychiatric treatment for himself and was seen prior to the family's last move. He gave little information about his therapy, except to say that it had been helpful and that he intended to resume it upon his return home. It appeared that Mr. K. was fearful of his own agitated depression, which was reminiscent of his mother's illness, and of Rick's problems, which reminded him of his own childhood. Mr. K.'s younger brother had led what appeared to be a marginal schizoid existence, constantly shifting his career focus without success. Currently, he had a nonmetastisizing cancerous tumor of the arm which might necessitate amputation of his arm. This fact seemed to have exacerbated Mr. K.'s cancer fears.

Rick had been acutely anxious at the separation from parents when he entered school. He was described as "white around the gills, frightened, and nauseated," and at this point enuresis reappeared. He always spoke with fear about the "mean" nuns who in fact, according to the parents, did much frightening and threatening to control a class of fifty. Mr. K. had intervened and been criticized by the parish priest for being the "fancy professor intimidating helpless nuns." The boys had transferred to a supposedly more progressive Jesuit school where discipline and the strap reigned nonetheless.

PARENTS

Mr. K. described an extremely traumatic childhood in New Zealand, characterized by his parents' severe marital discord, precarious finances, and religious conflicts. His father was an uneducated man who forever changed jobs and failed in each business venture. Because of their financial straits, his mother had to work and he was sent to his grandparents at age one. The Depression made the family situation more acute, and he lived with his grandparents till age four. His mother, who was very upset about having to give him to her parents, visited him during the entire placement. Father's work instability continued. His violent temper made Mr. K. seek refuge behind his mother's skirts. His parents had serious religious conflicts over the church and birth control. Their fighting was often physical and was set off in part by the crowded conditions in which they lived, generally surrounded by mother's relatives, all attempting to pool their monies for survival.

Mr. K. described himself as a terrified child. He wet his pants daily through the fourth grade because he was too frightened to ask the teachers to let him go to the lavatory. He was poor at sports but good in arithmetic. He was preoccupied with fears of death and with mother's threats to give him to a local beggarwoman or to the local state institution, which she would often pretend to telephone, until he would cry and beg to be kept at home. Mr. K. was unaware of his rage toward his mother until he was 26. His mother always worked except for a brief period when he was six, at which time his brother was born. Emphasis was put on the boys' education and Mr. K. felt guilty about the scrimping and sacrifices that were made to keep him and his brother in private parochial school. Following most successful academic achievement in high school, he won scholarships to college and graduate school.

Now, due to his guilt and sense of obligation, he contributed to his parents even though, since age 26 when he left his family to attend graduate school in England, he has had overt conflict with them, especially with his mother, whom he described as "cloying, impossible, and pleading." His parents still fought, with the mother constantly asking for Mr. K.'s intercession. It appeared that avoidance of this situation might have been one factor that kept Mr. K. out of his native country, moving about.

Mrs. K., also a native New Zealander, described a more secure background. She was the second of three girls and had a younger brother. Despite her parents' lack of education, the family was secure financially. The father, a lathe operator, owned his own business. Her parents were strict but warm and sent all four children to college. Mrs. K. described herself as shy and sometimes sulky, but never rebellious. Despite their verbal battles and door slamming, her parents appeared to have a solid relationship. The greatest stress described in her growing up was her younger sister's withdrawal and avoidance of all duties, which her parents accepted. After graduating from a two-year teachers' college at 19, Mrs. K. returned home, where she taught school and enjoyed a busy social life for seven years. At 25, she moved to a larger city where she shared an apartment with friends.

During her two-year courtship with Mr. K., she never anticipated their subsequent marital problems around sex and birth control, which induced such profound guilt in her husband that he would rush to priests continuously. This frenzied consultation with priests still persisted, but now concerned school placements for the children. Mrs. K. expressed a desire for therapy for herself when they returned home, to deal with problems that had resulted in her permitting her husband to browbeat and depreciate her. She spoke of gaining cathartic relief from her contacts with the clinician. Her tension had been heightened by the total lack of good friends during this last academic year. She described the academic community as reserved and rather cold, and herself as too upset to make overtures.

The diagnostician had a warm, positive reaction to Mr. and Mrs. K., who were attractive, intelligent, warm people. They were very worried about their problems—mother in a most appropriate fashion, father in a more dependent, engulfing, frantic way. He wanted detailed advice and clearly was in urgent need of therapy.

INTERVIEWS

Rick was seen for two interviews. He arrived at the first one looking disheveled, with his shoes untied. His manner was that of a little adult, and this stance was intensified by his extraordinarily sophisticated way of conversing. He seemed tense initially, but quickly relaxed and talked steadily in a scrupulously polite way, ignoring the nearby toys and art equipment. He answered questions easily, independently brought up material, and was significantly resistive to leaving at the end of the interview.

The initial focus was on Rick's understanding of why he was at the clinic. He had an intellectual grasp of the evaluative nature of his most limited contact with the clinician, but he also seemed to evidence magical wishes for relief. Initially, Rick said he liked his new school better than his old parochial school, with its rules, uniforms, and strappings for punishment. He described the family's frequent moves in obsessive detail, stating that he missed the neighbors at home. Gradually, with the clinician's help, Rick moved into discussion of current uncomfortable areas. He acknowledged his problems in school, especially with New Math. His previous superior grades were discussed, and he said his decline was due to his problems with math. He indicated little overt worry and put it on his father, who

> gets terribly excited about religion and math. He's a medium famous mathematician throughout the world and he says I'll never get anywhere without math. I can never be a scientist or a doctor without math. I'm not sure what I want to be when I grow up; maybe a scientist, because now I'm very interested in spacecraft, rockets, and the planets. Anyway, I can never be as good in math as he is.

Rick sounded very sad as he spoke of how inept he was at sports.

In answer to the clinician's questions, he spoke of his lack of friends with evident loneliness and pain. He parroted his mother's comments, stating that not until late in the year did they learn of the school custom of inviting kids over to play after school. He had started to do that recently with two boys in his class. He said of himself and his sibs, "we're slow to make friends." Rick did not acknowledge his part in not making friends. He blamed his parents for not giving him more spending money to buy rocket models, like the other kids at school. After extensive discussion about fights with his sibs, he referred to fights with peers. No guilt was evident; he blamed the problems on his sibs or parents. "K. makes vulgar noises; she's very much a brat who always wants her own way. She also tattles and I am the one always blamed. S. breaks my toys and mother isn't careful to keep him out of my things. M. sometimes is OK. Often he is a tattletale though."

Rick was sick of church and his father's lecturing. "Dad talks all the time about Christian ethics, and how I should be guilty for the things I do. I'm not. He talks on and on about hell and sin and love and I'm sick of hearing him. He's always angry about what I do at home." Rick gave no indication of his own temper outbursts. He went on to describe his lack of privacy at home; he feared that his toys and models would be damaged by his sibs and blamed mother for not safeguarding them. Mother didn't lecture, but she was "too busy and not smart" about rockets, planets, and the like.

Rick spoke about his endless, obsessive talks late at night with his father about spacecraft and the planets. The clinician's questions about late night discussions and sleep enabled Rick to talk about "some bad dreams," including a recurring one in which "I'm alone in a spacecraft, high in the sky and traveling a trillion miles an hour. A mistake happens and I'm ejected and am falling, lost and alone. I never seem to land, but keep tumbling through the clouds." Rick acknowledged that this dream frightened him. He apparently attempted to master his fears through the obsessive creation of rocket models and endless calculations about spacecraft travel. He said he liked talking to the clinician and wished she knew about rockets and could discuss them with him. The clinician replied that she didn't know what rockets and such meant to him; she thought it must be hard to talk easily to a person one couldn't continue seeing. Rick agreed and said, if the clinician thought it best, he would talk to a "therapy person" at home. He had been prepared for psychologicals, and made reference to the tests and picture games that would be scheduled before his next interview. Rick was terribly polite in saying goodbye; he shook hands and was extremely reluctant to leave the office.

At the second interview, Rick eagerly entered the clinician's office, sat down, and began talking, again ignoring the toys. The clinician discussed treatment recommendations with Rick. He understood and approved of the idea of seeing a therapist when he got home. He wondered if it would be like his talks with this clinician. He also wondered if this clinician would have seen him if he lived here—he would have liked that. She replied that she would have liked it, too. The clinician thought that perhaps he was a little worried about a new person. He agreed, looking very sad and scared, and asked about the tests.

He was pleased and a little surprised to learn that he had superior ability and that eventually, with therapy, he should find school work easier. There was much talk about his capabilities and long-standing problems with friends, sports, and family. The clinician suggested that moves, school changes, etc., were very hard. Rick agreed, but said he wanted to change schools at home. He asked if his father had talked to the clinician about "math and religion," especially parochial school. He clearly indicated awareness of his parents' conflicts over his school placement and commented on their wish to consult his future therapist before enrolling him. He wanted to go to the public school, even if it wasn't as fancy as the parochial school. He didn't want to go back to a place where they strapped boys. He wanted to go to a school with his neighborhood friends, whom his parents disapproved of for religious reasons. In Rick's complaints about his father, he denied his own provocativeness and tantrums, taking no responsibility for, and showing no guilt about, disappointing his father.

Rick then said math hadn't been as bad since he had seen the clinician. He also talked about two friends at school. Apparently they acted out together, but Rick showed no discomfort about this, only pleasure in some peer contact. It came through that they had succeeded in getting their teacher angry at times. His affect changed as he spoke of his profound sadness at leaving this city. He would be glad to get back to his own house, but he liked this school much better than the one at home. He looked very pained when he talked about saying goodbye to his teacher and classmates. The endless separations he had experienced were "so hard."

In addition to empathizing with his sadness, the clinician offered some support and help with the move. Picking up on his pleasure about home, she asked about it and Rick talked with some enthusiasm about the yard, his bike, and the spaciousness of the house. He drew a "blueprint" of the house, which he explained in detail. He then talked about two friends at home whom he had written to this year. Only one boy had answered, and Rick had written him about his return home. With anxiety, he began to obsess about the time span for letters, and whether the boy who hadn't answered should be written another letter and, if he answered, whether he should be told the date of Rick's return. It was noteworthy that the K.'s were departing for home in only five days. Finally, he flatly said he wouldn't write him since he had never answered his letter. He acknowledged his disappointment about this.

His affect reversed suddenly and he spoke of writing present schoolmates about the trip home. In great detail, he described the plane, the itinerary, and the length of time the trip would take. There were some obsessive features in his description, which were obviously a means of handling his anxiety. The clinician wished Rick well and felt this anticipatory discussion of the move had been somewhat helpful to him. Rick again demonstrated reluctance to separate and leave the office.

DIAGNOSTIC FORMULATIONS

Rick's ego apparatus appeared to be intact. There were no symptoms or signs of primary defects there. There were no signs of primary deficiencies in his ego functions, either. He was a most intelligent, imaginative child (verbal IQ of 137, performance IQ of 110–114, full-scale IQ of 126–128), who up until this year (in a permissive school, in contrast to his previous authoritarian school) had done superior academic work. However, there appeared to be considerable ego weakness, manifested by defective control of motility, long-standing and recurrent enuresis, an inability to delay or tolerate frustration, and a lack of synthesis, so that he was unable to bind and unify perception, affects, and defenses. Rick demonstrated defenses of denial, projection, obsessive intellectualization, and regression; as a result, his defense organization was not age adequate, balanced, or effective and caused secondary interference with other ego functions.

Rick had reached the phallic-Oedipal phase, but seemed to have very strong fixation points at the oral and anal levels. He had had serious eating disturbances till age two, had been forcefed, and to this day was a finicky eater. He demonstrated sadistic anal power struggles. Latency-age tasks were grossly impeded by lack of a proper resolution of the Oedipal conflict. His fear of and competition with father made it difficult for him to identify with him. The rapid succession of siblings had heightened his competition for his mother, and he continued to long for her undivided attention and his prior exclusive position. Self-cathexis reflected interference, low self-esteem, inhibition, and diffidence. He felt inadequate and vulnerable, and thus was isolated and withdrawn. Rick had reached the stage of object constancy, but it had been interfered with by early fixations at the oral level caused by multiple traumas at that point (i.e., father's anxieties and forceful intrusion on the maternal role, the move to a new country, and the birth of a sib).

Rick had not achieved adequate control or neutralization of his aggressive impulses, which frequently broke through and were discharged outward onto parents, siblings, and peers at school. Superego development appeared weak and immature. Rick seemed consciously comfortable about projecting his conflicts totally onto others. His superego seemed to be externalized in his authoritarian father and rigid Catholic school. It was possible that Rick's superego was buried under all the lectures on morality, Catholic doctrine, and guilt. Regardless, the superego basically was immature, harsh, and punitive, and was unable to control sadistic and aggressive outbursts.

Rick and his environment were at cross purposes. His ego seemed to have sided with his id to pursue need and drive fulfillment. Control of the id had been taken care of by outside authoritarian figures. Rick's aggression seemed to be a defense against castration fears and fear of loss of parental love via mother's exhaustion, father's outbursts, and expectations of further parental criticism. A dynamic and structural assessment indicated external conflicts between the id, ego agencies, and the object world.

Rick had not progressed very far from the dependent position, or toward age-appropriate object relationships. Body independence was meager, in that rational eating was not consistent and occasional enuresis still occurred at age eight. He presented egocentricity rather than peer companionship. He had regressed in his academic performance this year and took little responsibility for this, as there were no external school punishments to be faced. He was described as reading voraciously and being isolated, inept at and fearful of sports, and mainly preoccupied with his own study of spacecraft, rockets, and planets. Long-term, fairly extensive psychotherapy seemed indicated. Rick seemed most receptive to at least an intellectual discussion of a treatment program for him. The parents were motivated to secure treatment for Rick and father planned at least a three-year stay in New Zealand before taking any more lectureships out of the country.

Initially, a diagnosis of character disorder was considered for Rick. However, because he never acted out in school until this year, his aggressivity didn't seem to be all pervasive and ego-syntonic, but rather, defensive and realistic, especially given the continuous family upheavals and moves, and parental psychopathology. Thus, a diagnosis of obsessive neurosis was made.

Addendum

Rick's parents sought an evaluation immediately prior to leaving the United States. They were alarmed by their child's difficulties and needed support in the face of yet another family upheaval. Ongoing therapy clearly was not possible at the time of the clinic contact. They did accept the findings and recommendations of the diagnostician and requested that the material be forwarded to Rick's new therapist at home.

PART IV

Translating the Assessment into a Treatment Plan

CHAPTER 10

Therapy with Children

Individual Therapy

Kessler (1966) describes the emergence and evolution of the child guidance clinics as due to a myriad of factors.

> First, there was a new interest in child psychology at the turn of the century. The feminist movement, which worked for many social reforms, was thereby opening the way for the century of the child. Laws against child labor were sponsored and passed. As compulsory education gained ground, children with problems could no longer be hidden away at home. In fact, judging from the reports of their activities, the first clinic created specifically for children . . . was primarily concerned with the adaptation of children to the school situation [p. 369].

By 1921, a number of clinics emerged, attached to courts, schools, social agencies, and mental hospitals. Kessler (1966) notes that the first child guidance clinics emphasized a team approach to the diagnosis and treatment of children's problems. The clinical team included a psychologist and caseworker, both of whom worked under the direction of a psychiatrist.

Prior to World War II, based on the pioneering work of Anna Freud, a theory and technique of child analysis was conceptualized, and from this approach various forms of child psychotherapies emerged. The approaches involved a time-limited format, focused play therapies, and direct environmental manipulations. Casework efforts focused on educating the parents as a prophylactic measure for the children. However, the problem-solving orientation of casework has proved to be disappointing. Rather, child psychoanalytic psychotherapy still relies heavily on modified child analytic techniques, offering direct and indirect therapies (i.e., direct work with the child and indirect work with parents).

Analysis Versus Psychotherapy

Child psychoanalytic psychotherapy and child analysis have been compared and contrasted in detail earlier; a brief recapitulation is offered here.[1] First of all, analysis involves four or five sessions a week, while psychotherapy involves two—or, at most, three—sessions a week. Second, the goals of child psychoanalysis and psychotherapy differ. Child analysis aims for a reconstruction of the personality, with changes in the balance and nature of ego, id, and superego; child psychoanalytic psychotherapy aims for symptom resolution, behavioral modification, some degree of structural personality change, and a return to the normal developmental path. In addition to the differences in objectives and frequency of appointments, there are technical differences between analysis and analytically oriented therapy. Differences in focus and interpretation are crucial. In analysis, the transferences and displacements are analyzed as fully as possible, with consideration of past and present. In therapy, the emphasis in on the here-and-now and the child's relationships in general; in analysis, the primary focus is on the inner conflicts of the child and the transference and displacement in the treatment situation.

Speech and play are the primary modes of communication in child analysis and child therapy. Both modes of intervention begin with a careful perusal of resistance and affect, followed by interpretations of the defense against warded-off affects. Conflicts are not interpreted until later. Defenses cannot be assaulted and frightening id content (disturbing aggressive and sexual impulses and wishes) must be approached cautiously (Sours, 1978b).

Indications for child analysis and child psychotherapy have been fully discussed elsewhere.[2] To review briefly, neurotic conflicts that do not seriously interfere with development can be treated via therapy,

[1] See Chapter 1.
[2] See Chapter 9.

and, by contrast, if there is a preponderance of internalized conflict, analysis is the treatment of choice, unless the child's intellect is poor or the child lacks psychological mindedness. Severe parental pathology is another contraindication for child analysis. Because it provides more structure than analysis, psychotherapy is often the treatment of choice for children with "less than neurotic" symptomatology, structural ego defects and deviations, preverbal disturbances, and failures in individuation-separation. Children with blatant psychotic, perceptual, and cognitive defects cannot be treated with psychoanalysis, particularly if their ego and self boundaries fragment under aggression in unstructured situations. Psychoanalysis is contraindicated for children in certain developmental phases. For example, many preadolescents cannot undergo analysis because their defensive organization is too rigid. Finally, since analysis requires a supportive environment, it is generally contraindicated for children who have serious problems within their community (Sours, 1978b).

Given these indications and contraindications, it is obvious that individual psychotherapy is the optimal treatment plan for the vast majority of child therapy cases, in that it is the suitable intervention where others are viewed as inappropriate.[3]

Psychotherapy is appropriate for the more severely disturbed child, the child in a traumatic home situation, and the child who presents habit disorders in eating, discipline, toilet training, and sleeping related to lack of appropriate parental direction and/or environmental structure, limits, and boundaries. Many children do not require open-ended, insight-oriented interpretive treatment by analysis, but rather, need a more pointed, goal-directed therapy. For example, children with adequate personality development who have experienced trauma (e.g., surgery, divorce, and/or death of a parent) can be helped via a brief psychotherapy contact aimed at helping them master the recent unsettling situation.

In addition, psychotic (e.g., schizophrenic) children are suitable child candidates for individual psychotherapy rather than analysis. Ekstein et al. (1978) note that these patients use the treatment relationship very differently from other patients:

> The psychotic patient often feels incomplete and uses contact with the therapist to complete himself. A fantasized introjection or other means of identification makes the patient feel more comfortable for the period he retains the image of the therapist and keeps contact with him. . . . The patient's mechanisms of defense and adaptation are primitive, and involve fantasized fusion with the therapist. . . . He may advance past autistic and symbiotic functioning as he undergoes separation-individuation. However,

[3]Also see Chapter 9.

maturity and a sense of separateness produce anxiety and loneliness. The child regresses to the use of autistic and symbiotic mechanisms. Experiencing fusion during the symbiotic state may result in fears of engulfment. This in turn leads to an autistic retreat which is itself regressive, adaptive, and frightening. Attempts to separate once more appear only to create anxiety [pp. 676–677].

Thus, work with these children is to avoid uncovering and rather is, slow, indirect, lengthy, supportive, and empathic, with the emphasis on building identification and introjection, and more mature defensive and adaptive mechanisms. Identificatory efforts must be made in work with borderline and schizophrenic children to adjust to their special modes of relating and communicating (e.g., their play with metaphor and simile, their indirect way of talking, and their different stage of language and play development [Ekstein et al., 1978]).

Insight-Directed Psychotherapy: Indications and Contraindications

There is a spectrum of individual therapies running from supportive treatment at one end, to intensive, insight-directed, uncovering psychotherapy at the other end. The latter, though close to analysis, is nevertheless different, given the less frequent appointments, the lesser attempt at restructuring, and the minimal focus on primary-process unconscious material. Supportive therapy puts more emphasis on symptom relief, the here-and-now, and improved age-appropriate adjustment.

Insight-directed psychotherapy is aimed at conflict resolution, the development of new modes of adaptation and personality reintegration, and maturation to whatever degree is possible in the particular patient, considering the limitations of the treatment method. Insight-directed psychotherapy therefore will usually involve a significant investment of time, effort, sacrifice, and emotional significance if it is to be successful, and it frequently represents a long-term venture for the patient and the therapist [Dewald, 1964, p. 109].

Thus, insight-directed therapy can provide major and lasting change beyond simple symptom reduction. One goal is to bring into consciousness specific unconscious and preconscious conflicts, modes of thinking, and defense patterns. Careful interpretation of resistances and defenses, with well-timed reflections and the use of metaphors such as the child's play, will gradually enable the child to relinquish defenses and become aware of what was defended against. This surrender of defenses can arouse considerable anxiety until the material becomes more fully conscious, and thereby more integrated and controlled, and less frightening. These defenses may concern the recall of repressed memories. The child's relationship to the therapist and the therapist's interventions combine to bring previously unconscious conflicts to the patient's awareness in an emotionally meaningful way. That is, the therapeutic situation recreates the earlier conflicts that resulted in the neurotic symtomatology or character traits. However, because patients are now at a more advanced stage of development than they were when the conflict first arose, their ego generally will have both a greater tolerance of anxiety and frustration and a greater potentiality for conflict resolution. The patients are simply older; they have more experience, a greater potential for independent functioning, and a greater capability of adjusting to and dealing with their conflicts.

Another difference between the original pathogenic conflict situation and the current therapeutic situation is that, in the former situation, patients had to deal with their problems alone. Therefore, they had "a greater need for prompt resolution, and there was greater likelihood of an attempt at repression and exclusion of the conflicts from consciousness as quickly as possible. In the therapeutic situation, however, [patients have] the aid and alliance of the therapist, and thus, a greater capacity to tolerate the anxiety and frustration that will be mobilized in the attempt to deal with the previously unconscious conflicts" (Dewald, 1964, pp. 103–104). Although the therapist is supportive, identification per se is not encouraged; rather, the child's efforts at independence and self-development are promoted. Of course, some identification with the therapist generally takes place, and "it is often necessary to deal with this as a manifestation of resistance and defense against the development of a more independent sense of identity" (Dewald, 1964, p. 105).

Insight-directed therapy requires specific ego strengths of the patient, similar to those needed for more intensive, analytic uncovering work. The child or adult patient must be able to handle frustration, tolerate and contain anxiety (including that aroused in the treatment situation), and deal with specific life tasks. Patients who present severe ego regression and decompensation are not suitable candidates for any sort of uncovering treatment that is, by its nature, a less supportive, more frustrating intervention. Required is the patient's willingness and ability to establish rapport and trust to work for a considerable period of time towards a desired goal. This is predicated on the patient's life capacity to maintain emotionally significant relationships. Motivation, or the conscious wish to understand recurrent difficulties, requires psychological mindedness and a willingness to change. Many children do not present motivation, but rather, a wish for relief, or the hope that their parents will change. Certain reality factors, such as time, family support, and a home milieu that is not disruptive, chaotic, or traumatizing, are prerequisites for successful, open-ended, long-term, insight-oriented treatment.

Dewald (1964) notes that the reality of clinical practice frequently presents us with an admixture of positive and negative factors and forces that must be considered carefully, in terms of their strength and significance. Even when a full evaluation indicates that treatment is likely to be long and difficult, with a relatively poor prognosis, "an attempt at insight-directed therapy may still be warranted . . . on the basis that if the individual is to have any chance of success or stability in his life, he must modify or change underlying conflicts and disturbances" (Dewald, 1964, pp. 127–128). When patients have an unconscious need to get into trouble, or when introspection is impaired due to neurotic inhibitions, a longer and more difficult therapeutic course is generally indicated.

Goals may change if new factors or unrecognized issues become apparent.

> Not uncommonly, after the original assessment has been made and therapy has begun, a patient's motivation may change, the reality situation may be altered, or there may be factors previously hidden from the therapist which now come to light and indicate that the previously set goal is no longer the one of choice. It may be that the previous goal was too ambitious, or that the previous assessment of the patient proved to be overly pessimistic, and a more ambitious goal may now be possible [Dewald, 1964, p. 129].

Continuous, ongoing assessment or diagnosis is critical in the course of therapy. The therapist should have a clear conceptualization and understanding of treatment goals, based on a conscious, explicit, rational appraisal. When treatment goals and strategies are not clearly understood, therapy often becomes vague and aimless.

Supportive Psychotherapy: Indications and Contraindications

Supportive treatment permits repression to be maintained; the patient only deals with more available conscious or preconscious material. Such treatment provides the opportunity to ventilate, share, and seek symptom relief and overt behavioral change without attempting a basic personality change or a resolution of unconscious conflict. Resistances and defenses are supported and maintained within the boundaries of improved reality testing and self-appraisal. The therapist must determine which of the patient's defenses can most effectively be introduced, strengthened, encouraged, or reinforced. Generally, the patient is allowed to maintain those defenses already in use, unless they result in seriously destructive symptoms or behavior. Important defenses must not be altered too quickly. The therapist helps the patient to use preexisting defenses more effectively, rather than introducing new ones. When the therapist does introduce new defenses, they must be compatible with the patient's overall ego structure and major defenses (Dewald, 1964).

At times, in supportive treatment, the therapist must actively assume certain ego functions that patients ordinarily would handle themselves. This may involve giving active advice, making decisions, and intervening in a patient's life. A therapist may have to serve as a child's advocate in situations where the child cannot successfully and independently communicate with the parents. Supportive work requires a more active stance by the therapist, less nondirective listening, more structuring, and more efforts to improve rational control, minimize anxiety, and reinforce secondary ego processes. Stuart (1968) stresses that attention should focus on the present, with minimal discussion of the past. While an understanding of the present is important for borderline patients, "a rehashing of the past . . . often leads to a recurrence of guilt and despair" (p. 290).

Dewald notes the advisability of supportive treatment with patients who suffer from a failure to establish meaningful object relationships, who show patterns of remoteness, or whose suspiciousness requires a long period of testing objects before investing trust in them. The clinician may have to employ a variety of supportive techniques with such patients, as they often cannot develop a meaningful therapeutic relationship in the therapeutically neutral atmosphere of an insight-directed approach (Dewald, 1964).

Other suitable candidates for supportive treatment include those who deny the existence of a physicological illness, or who come for help only because of referral and pressures of community authorities or family members. The patient who projects all difficulties onto others or who only desires quick relief from pain or symptoms, with no understanding of causative factors, is best treated by a supportive approach rather than an insight-directed one. In some instances, this stance changes and the patient's trust in the supportive relationship gives him or her the courage and strength to look more deeply, to try to get to the bottom of recurrent troubles and pain. Enhanced self-esteem may facilitate maturation.

The "Less than Neurotic" Patient

Considerations of problems of self-esteem and borderline conditions confront us with the current analytic controversies revolving around the proper diagnosis and treatment of adult patients; these issues have not yet been thoroughly integrated into child therapy and/or child analysis. However, they certainly are relevant to clinical work with children. The aforementioned traditional criteria of analyzability and patient suitability for insight-oriented treatment are now being challenged. "We have seen that the extension of psychoanalytic practice beyond the classical psychoneurosis to the treatment of severe characterological, narcissistic, borderline, and psychotic disorders has made it necessary to distinguish between psychopathology that is the product of intra-psychic conflicts and psychopathology that is the remnant of developmental voids, deficits, and arrests" (Stolorow and Lachman, 1980, p. 171).[4]

Much recent research on the treatment of developmentally arrested ("less than neurotic") patients has shown that "correct" interpretations actually can be countertherapeutic. With our increased knowledge of the psychology of developmental arrests, it is no longer satisfactory to assume that treatment failure is due solely to the patient's guilt, resistance, unreachability, etc. In accord with Kohut's position, Stolorow and Lachman (1980) suggest that "many therapeutic impasses and disasters are the product of a specific failure in empathy, wherein the analyst misunderstands and misinterprets the meaning of the patient's archaic states by amalgamating them to his own much more differentiated and integrated world of self and object representations" (p. 190).

In addition, with the exception of the Self Psychologists, few have questioned the clinical intervention of confrontation. Levy (1976) suggests that honesty and candor require modulation, noting that "confrontation is as capable of harm as it is of good. It makes discriminating use especially necessary because it can have shattering consequences for the client. No truer words are spoken than are sometimes uttered by a sadist, an authoritative person, or a controlling individual whose confrontation may be motivated—perhaps unconsciously—less to accelerate a client's needed change, than to disturb his equilibrium" (pp. 140–141). The child client, unstructured and not fully consolidated, clearly is vulnerable, and thereby a most inappropriate patient for this approach. Confrontation is often used by the well-intentioned clinician who wants to make the patient see reality. Despite this good intent, such interventions will be interpreted as a gross failure of empathy, and will constitute a traumatic narcissistic injury. Ideally, in work with developmentally arrested children, the therapist will offer empathic communications that clarify the content, affect, and function of the patient's self-object configurations, which resurface in the face of threats of regressive fragmentation and dissolution (Stolorow and Lachman, 1980).

[4]See Chapters 8 and 9.

While the recent contributions and controversies raised by Self Psychologists may create more questions than answers for the reader, this prespective is included to make child therapists aware of current issues in psychoanalytic writings and research relevant to work with the "less than neurotic" client. Those treating children are witness to an increased child patient population that lacks well-defined neurotic structure and evidences developmental arrests, incomplete structuralizations, and thus, precarious self- and object representations.

Group Therapy

Group therapy, an intervention for work with parents and children, often is the treatment of choice. Latency-age children can benefit from the range of interpersonal connections and relationships provided by the group experience. Parents who start therapy because of their troubled children can gain clarification, support, and empathy working with a peer group of parents. Diagnostic criteria are the critical determinants for selecting any form of therapy. Josselyn (1972) warns against professional bias toward a single modality of intervention for all patients. She notes instances in which adolescent patients were placed in a group without an initial screening and/or in which the group therapist believed that group therapy was *the* therapy of choice for all adolescents. She concludes that while group therapy can be a positive mode of intervention, it can also be a dangerous one. She describes patients who actually became more acutely disturbed by the group experience; they were threatened by the experience or acted out a previously repressed, defended against conflict. This group evidenced profoundly depleted ego strength; a critical factor was ego exhaustion caused by the group therapy sessions. Josselyn suggests that this phenomenon might have been due to the inexperience or limitations of the group leaders. In other cases, according to Josselyn (1972), even the most skilled group leader could not have avoided a crisis, as group therapy was the wrong form of therapy for the patients. Obviously, these clinical observations about adolescents are also pertinent in considering child and adult clients.

Freud (1922) thought that people in groups regress due to the revival of old patterns, with individuals seeking consolation and reassurances of infantile anxieties. Members can experience transference phenomena to peers as sibs, and the leader as parent, thereby exhibiting blind devotion or profound disappointment. Freud's cautions do not suggest negation of the value of group experiences. He himself believed that successful immersion in a well-functioning group could inhibit and even cure neurotic functioning. Buxbaum (1945) emphasizes the "submission and rebellion" phenomenon in group process. She further states that group experiences are crucial in development as a "medium between the dependence of the child and the independence of the adult" (p. 365). While concurring with the value of group experience for children, adolescents, and adults, she underscores the need for caution in recommending group therapy. Such a recommendation should be based on a screening or assessment process.

Indications and Contraindications

The criteria for determining indications and contraindications for group therapy are many and varied. In considering potential candidates, one must be clear regarding how they have handled or mishandled their developmental tasks. One may look at individuals' "(1) emancipation from parental attachments, (2) development of satisfying and self-realizing peer attachments, with ability to love and appreciate the worth of others as well as one's self, (3) an enduring and sustaining sense of identity in the family, social, sexual and work-creative areas, and a flexible set of hopes and life goals for the future" (Berkowitz and Sugar, 1975, p. 3). Berkowitz and Sugar further suggest that a sound recommendation for group treatment depends on the availability of a suitable group. For example, it is dangerous to mix nonacting-out adolescents with severely acting-out adolescents. The common practice of grouping individuals of all ages together on the basis of a common label, e.g., foster children, obese children, delinquent youth, etc., is not recommended. Rather, clients should be grouped based on an appraisal of their ego functions and developmental level. (i.e., highest level of functioning presented).

Usually, highly narcissistic individuals who lack empathy and are fixated in struggles regarding self-esteem or self-regard are inappropriate candidates for a group therapy experience. They may require individual therapy first, to help them make successful relationships in a group. Clients with deficient control, such as the inpatient still immersed in the resistance phase with no therapeutic identifications with staff, may cause contagion or resistance to other members. Heacock (1966) notes as unsuitable for group therapy "the severely delinquent and hyperactive boy who 'acts in' during the sessions. His disruptive behavior spreads to the others who are quite responsive to this, and so therapy becomes impossible. Suggestible patients who are easily led would be stimulated to more acting out by the therapy" (p. 41).

Ginott (1961a) enumerates several criteria to exclude specific children from group therapy. For instance, he recommends excluding children experiencing intense sibling rivalry and sociopathic children who present shallowness, cruelty, persistent stealing, selfishness, impulsivity, and a lack of empathy.[5] Ginott (1961a) also excludes children with accelerated drive expression, and highly sexualized and/or extremely aggressive children. Children who have been eroticized via exposure to critical perverse sexual activities are not suitable for group treatment. Likewise, children who have been traumatized by overt catastrophe have an immediate need for the more supportive individual modality.

Goals

Currently, there is a wide array of group therapy approaches that vary not only with respect to the planning and handling of the treatment, but also with respect to the theoretical model on which they are based. Kaplan and Sadock (1971) note that every school of personality theory and psychopathology is represented in group practice. However, the model of developmental ego psychology has retained its emphasis on the dyadic relationship.

Anthony (1971) notes that there has been very little work on the development of the ego's capacity to create and maintain a group relationship. He believes that a conceptual developmental model could be very useful in group psychotherapy. Specifically, children find aid and often some effective solution to the conflicts rooted in the infantile phases of psychological growth if they are free to go beyond the protective nest of the family. Interpersonal relationships are enriched when children become a part of the nonparental social world of their peers. The assessment of each and every maturational step is most clearly delineated by a developmental perspective.

Psychoanalytic group therapy is not a new group therapy technique. A presentation of the history of this intervention is beyond the focus here. However, it should be noted that this modality has much the same roots as individual analysis, i.e., the understanding of latent material, and the search for unconscious motivation, which lead the patient from the here-and-now into historical determinants, and from the interpersonal to the intrapsychic (Wolf and Schwartz, 1971).

Group work has modified the goals of psychoanalysis. Specifically, less regression is encouraged than in analytic treatment, and the focus is more on the interpersonal process among group members, and between members and leaders. The time perception is frequently the here-and-now, rather than the unresolved early infantile conflicts. The leader assumes a more active supportive stand than does the nondirective analyst. The goal is not restructuring the basic personality, but rather, enhancing ego functioning (e.g., increasing the capacity for real-

[5]In this text, the sociopathic child is referred to as the narcissistically disordered child.

ity testing, strengthening object relations, and improving drive modulation). Group work with parents and children dates back to the early child guidance clinics as well as to the imaginative, prescient, and pioneering efforts of Slavson (1958). Some of the methodology offered is interactional, some deals with cognitive material, and some is educational, but all of it is in the service of ego building.

The Setting

Groups conducted by clinicians for rehabilitation purposes are located in such varied settings as public schools, mental health clinics, correctional institutions, hospitals, child welfare agencies, settlement houses, community centers, and the offices of private practitioners. The setting becomes an integral part of the group experience and group purpose. For example, it may determine whether services are long- or short-term, problem-focuses or open-ended. Schwartz and Zaba (1971) note that the agency or host setting has a stake in the proceedings, in that its own tasks and foci are involved and become an integral part of the group experience. They suggest that two sets of tasks, those of the client group and those of the agency, converge to create the terms of "the contract" between clients and agency. This contract provides the frame of reference for the work that follows: for understanding when the work is in process, when it is being avoided, and when it is finished. Schwartz and Zaba (1971) assert that the moving dynamic in the group experience is work.

Agency function is clearly articulated by Smally (1970), who believes that the first step is to determine whether the agency's services fit the potential client's needs. Agency function introduces a focus, a partialization, a difference that serves as a dynamic in the clinician-client relationship. Thus, agency function and focus suggest the kind of services offered and the range of clients served. Recently, group approaches such as rap sessions, parent education groups, and drug abuse education in schools have been used in attempts to prevent deviant behavior among groups of children or parents.

Agency function and focus suggest a spectrum of approaches, the three most important being educational groups, management groups, and clinical groups. An educational group may be six to ten parents in an ongoing group examining early childhood development. Management groups are frequently used in hospitals and residential centers to aid children's admission and discharge, to examine day-to-day program planning, and to deal with group problems such as scapegoating and vandalism. Clinical groups with therapeutic goals should be carefully selected to insure appropriate group balance, should meet for regular intervals on specified days to insure the development of group interaction, and should aim at the improvement of specific psychological or interpersonal problems. Children's play therapy and activity groups and parents' therapy groups fall under this category. It must be emphasized that educational groups and management groups often provide therapeutic input and contribute to the well being of the members, the structure and predictability of the setting, and the enhancement of communication among members and/or between members and staff. While the lines separating these groups often are very fine, the distinctions are essential if the practitioner is to delineate the group's focus and purpose.

The physical surroundings and staffing pattern deserve some consideration and discussion. The physical setting is of the utmost importance in conducting group meetings. Meeting rooms should be in a location that is comfortable for the group members and the leader. The setting should be as conducive as possible to spontaneous group exchange. This would include a cheery and sufficiently ample room with comfortable seating arrangements and fresh and well-cared-for furnishings. Rooms that are too small force members into too close proximity, which causes frustration and irritation. In planning for children's groups, Ginott (1961a) states that "forced propinquity engenders hostility and intensifies defenses; in cramped quarters isolated children withdraw further into themselves and aggressive children attack others. A very large playroom is also undesirable; a big room invites wild running and rough play in aggressive children and permits withdrawn children to avoid contact with the therapist and the group members" (pp. 63–64).

Similarly, parents fare badly in a crowded room, or one that is excessively large, as it interferes with group cohesiveness and interchange. Furniture should be sturdy—and for children's groups, adequate, appropriate creative materials, tables, and chairs should be available. A nearby bathroom is often crucial. Parents should not be seen in children's therapy rooms. The small furniture and toys prompt regression and feelings of childishness, and exacerbate authority/submission in leader/member relations. Groups should not be convened in messy and disheveled rooms. The implicit disrespect may cause a serious contagion of chaos, particularly with clients lacking sufficient inner structure and stability.

One may be forced to utilize a less than optimal setting, and the professional must compromise and accomodate to the host setting. It is not unusual for a mental health clinic, school, or social agency to be lacking a suitable space. In judging whether or not to begin, one must consider the ecology and the environment. It is unsound to begin a venture that is doomed to fail. Frequently treatment must be delayed until organizational procedures (e.g., the requisition of reasonable furniture) have been accomplished, or until the needed arrangements and collaboration with a nearby setting (e.g., a church) have been made. Sometimes one must accommodate to budgetary constraints as part of the environmental reality. For example, in a settlement house or mental health clinic with precarious funding, one must often be creative and innovative. Organizing children to participate in the creation of an attractive meeting space may effectively engage hard-to-reach youths; thereby the improvement of the physical surroundings may serve several therapeutic goals. Minimally, one should aim for a closed area to insure confidentiality, no disruptions and interruptions by other staff .and clients, and no distracting noise.

The appropriate length of meeting time is an issue frequently raised. This must be tailored in accord with the setting, the purpose of the group, and the age and ego structure of the clients. For instance, while preschool children and impulsive, young latency-age children might not be able to tolerate more than an hour of meeting time, adolescents and parents may well benefit from an hour-and-a-half session. However, there are obvious exceptions. Acutely psychotic children may become too agitated if sessions go beyond forty minutes. So, practice wisdom, experience, and consultation serve as sensitive guidelines for structuring sessions. It is recommended that members be expected to prepare and clean up any refreshments, creative materials, etc. One must allow time for these procedures.

Group Composition

The importance of employing diagnostic criteria for determining the composition of groups cannot be stressed enough. However, group composition is also a function of the setting and purpose of the group. On the one hand, *where* the group is held and *what* the group's goals are influence the selection of participants. On the other hand, individuals *seek out* particular groups in particular settings. A screening or assessment interview should be a requirement, regardless of how potential group members are initially found. Beginner therapists may have difficulty with this prerequisite, as often they do not have sufficient people to populate their group. At other times, they are pressured by work conditions to recruit all individuals within a certain category to join their group. Glass (1969) warns new practitioners against starting with large numbers; even three children can constitute a group, and a group consisting of all the troublemakers from a class may find it hard to outlive its designation. The pressures of waiting lists, however, are not always surmountable. However, understanding ego development through an assessment of ego functioning can at least serve as a means of understanding the interactions among members.

Level of object relations, considered by many to be the surest indicator of the structure of the ego (Kernberg, 1976), is manifested in the type of friendships and interactions children have with others. Ginott (1961) regards children who suffer intense sibling rivalry as poor candidates for group work. These characteristics typically are revealed in initial individual meetings and on TAT, CAT, and Rorschach tests. However, the level of object relations is not always easy to ascertain (Blanck and Blanck, 1974).

Activity and art therapy groups for latency-age children and adolescents offer an alternative outlet for drive derivatives that may not always be expressed verbally. Groups have been described as providing a more permissive atmosphere than that provided by individual consultation (Ginott, 1961a). It should be noted that impulsive individuals might not be able to tolerate the limit setting necessary for their maturation in groups. That is, whereas the group might be conducive to growth for the repressed, it can be counterproductive for the impulsive.

In part, the degree of focus on reality required by group members is a function of the type of group and the age of the group members. For example, psychoanalytic groups frequently pay primary attention to dream and fantasy material. Young children in play groups engage in make-believe with very constructive outcomes. Reality testing is basically fostered in groups through exchanges with other members. Inappropriate responses receive rapid reactions from group members. New ways of behaving can be tested out in comparatively safe surroundings. Shared feelings and thoughts can provide support to those uncertain of the basis of their emotions or ideas.

The earliest ego function described by Freud was the defense. Defenses are mechanisms used to deal with unconscious drive derivatives. Moreover, they are employed unconsciously, although they are recognizable in one's behavior. Defenses can be understood developmentally. The young child employs primitive defenses such as denial, projection, and splitting. Splitting also occurs in adults who cannot contain disparate feelings about others simultaneously.

Once the potential group members have been assessed, the group composition must be determined. Yalom (1970) provides some evidence that both homogeneous and heterogeneous groups are effective, but for different purposes. Yalom believes that heterogeneous groups have advantages over homogeneous groups for intensive interactional group therapy. However, homogeneous groups seem to "jell" more quickly, become more cohesive, and offer more immediate support, including more rapid symptom relief. While the homogeneous group is better attended and less conflict-ridden, it tends to remain at a more superficial level than the heterogeneous group, and thus, is an ineffective medium for altering character structure. In sum, composition depends in part on the group's purpose.

Yalom (1970) notes that grouping people homogeneously does not necessarily result in "a truly similar mix." Often clinicians working with groups organized along a single symptom criterion such as academic underachievement or acting out discover that, in terms of dynamic conflicts, descriptive diagnosis, and psychosexual stage, every member is different. Depending on the goals of the group, this may or may not be helpful.

Usually the heterogeneous group creates the most productive atmosphere for resolving problems. Heterogeneous selection allows for a balance of members' personality characteristics, with both active and passive styles included. Glass (1969) believes that, in general, beginners should start with more homogeneous groups made up of individuals with average or above average intelligence. However, some heterogeneity of personality should be permitted to insure interaction and interest in the group. One always should attempt to provide homogeneity for children's groups with respect to age and grade. In all groups, within the realm of possibility, there should be some matching of intellectual strength and interests. Yalom (1970) reports on a technique for eliminating group isolates while allowing for heterogeneity. It includes matching and is called the "Noah's Ark" principle of forming groups, as every member is paried with a comparable peer.

At the birth of group treatment, it was said that its main advantage was economy. However, group psychotherapy is no longer viewed as the poor man's substitute for individual psychotherapy (Kessler, 1966). Group therapy's special value is that it stimulates age-appropriate social and role behavior. Both ongoing group therapy and the group as a diagnostic mode of intervention have proved to be effective in work with children and adolescents of all ages, as well as with parents. For some patients, group therapy is the sole mode of treatment; for it is used in tandem with individual treatment or family therapy.

Case of Judy: Helping a Hospitalized Child Use Group Therapy

9/29

Judy, a 4-year-old, was admitted to the hospital because of a home accident. A bookcase fell on her as a result of her sister climbing upon it. The parents are divorced. Father and maternal grandmother live with the children. The grandmother was with the two children at the time. The diagnosis of the child is quadraplegic.

11/5

Since her admission, Judy has been in traction. She was alone until just recently, when she was moved to a room with other children. She became quite depressed, which could be attributed in part to the fact that she was lying face down on a frame with a window looking out onto the floor for this six-week period. Judy has refused to talk to anyone except her grandmother, who comes to the hospital every day. At first, Judy reacted quite negatively to the clinician who saw her. When the clinician talked to her, she shook her head slightly, indicating "No." After *regular* contacts, three times a week over a month's period, the clinician still met with the same negative response. While in her room today, the clinician noticed that Judy reacted to the janitor with a series of mewing noises. When the clinician then tried mewing to her, Judy immediately mewed back. This mutual mewing was their only communication for awhile.

11/8

The clinician tried to invite Judy to the group meeting, as she felt she might be ready to be helped by the group. The clinician explained very carefully what the group did. Judy listened very attentively, still not speaking. The clinician told Judy that she would return for her decision about joining the group. Judy's grandmother tried to dissuade the clinician from taking her to the meeting. The clinician explained to her that the doctor had okeyed Judy's attendance and that the group might help Judy a great deal.

11/10

When the clinician returned for Judy's decision about coming to the group, she greeted her with more positive feelings. She nodded that she would come to the meeting, although she was still afraid to risk talking.

In the meeting, she was very quiet; she had not yet talked to the worker or to the children. In order to reach out to her, the clinician asked the group if any of them knew what Judy knew how to do best. The immediately reply was, "make cat noises." The clinician then involved the group in a game whereby members took turns making animal sounds while the other members tried to guess what animal it was. Finally, one girl said, "Glug, glug!" No one could guess what the sound was. After a few moments, Judy surprisingly stated that it was "a fish." The whole group reacted very warmly to Judy's correct answer and to her actually speaking. This increased Judy's ego strength somewhat. When the meeting finished, Judy talked to the clinician in full sentences for the first time. She asked, "Would you bring me a glass of water and would you take me to the meeting next time?"

11/12

There was no meeting today. When the clinician went in to see Judy, she greeted her by asking, "Look, I don't have to be an animal anymore, I can move my arm." She asked the clinician to take her to the meeting, as she wanted to show the group how she could move her arm. The clinician told her that she would indeed take her to the next meeting so that she could show the group. She wanted the clinician to read to her and show her some pictures. In the pictures, Judy saw a mouse and stated she was no longer afraid of the mouse as she was when she was a baby, and that now she was big. She commented that she would soon outgrow her *new* bed. (She had been moved to a regular-sized bed after coming out of traction.) The clinician asked her what she would most like to do. She replied that she would like to play with her 5-year-old sister, walking with her and riding on her tricycle. The clinician commented that it was a good thing to wish, but it might be a while yet. Then the clinician introduced Judy to her neighbor. She was able to respond to her new found friend extremely well.

When the clinician told the doctors and nurses what had happened in the meeting and in her visits with Judy, they were quite amazed. Judy's doctor had told the grandmother that Judy might never move again. He had become quite angry when the grandmother had given Judy false reassurance that she would be walking. He had reprimanded the grandmother in front of Judy, telling her of Judy's serious condition. Part of Judy's great excitement regarding her ability to move her hand might have been related to this conversation.

11/15

There were many new patients at the group meeting. After introductions and discussions of why each was in the hospital, some singing together, and the telling of a story by one member, the clinician said that Judy wanted to show them something. Judy showed them the movement of her arm. The clinician explained that she could not move her arm before and now she could. The group accepted her action quite warmly. Judy could not risk verbalizing in this meeting because of the new members, but she was keenly observant and participated as noted.

11/22

Judy regressed during the week, refusing to talk to her grandmother or to others on the floor. She greeted the clinician with her mewing sounds. Finally, as the clinician talked to her, she asked the clinician to take her to the meeting, much to the delight of all around her. The clinician asked her if she would like to do anything special in the meeting, and she stated that she would like to listen to stories.

In the meeting, Judy was more at ease with the children in the group than she had ever been before. As introductions were made, she again showed the group how she could move both her arms. One of the children asked her why she had to stay in bed. Judy did not answer, so the clinician said that Judy could not move and had to stay in bed. The questioner said he did not think this would be so hard. Immediately, he was attacked by the other children, who all agreed that this was very hard indeed.

The clinician then described more fully how Judy had been very sick and had not been able to move for more than a month and a half; and how she had been getting better and had been moved to a regular bed after the traction had been removed. This was to help July become more aware of her problem, and understand that she had improved greatly. Judy listened intently; when the cliniain asked if this was the way it had been, she nodded her head, "yes."

11/24

Judy cried in her room just before the meeting was about to start, because a nurse was dressing her and she was afraid that she might miss the meeting. She participated by watching the group and was present for only half the meeting as she was taken for an appointment with the psychologist.

11/29

Judy requested that some of her storybooks be brought to the meeting. She insisted that the clinician read to the group, rather than having one of the members do it. After the meeting, when the clinician asked her why she did not talk in the group, she said that she was too "chicken" to talk, meaning that she was still afraid to verbalize before the others. She was still the youngest in the group.

12/1

Judy verbalized in this meeting and interacted with the other children. When one child said he was homesick and wanted to go home, and another commented that everyone wanted to get out of the hospital, Judy said that soon she would walk and then she could go home. When the clinician asked how she knew about this, she replied that the doctors were making casts for her so she could walk. The clinician said she knew how eager Judy was to walk, and that the casts would help her arms and legs, but that she would have to learn to move her legs before she could stand. She remained quiet for awhile. None of the other members said anything. All of a sudden, Judy said she would like to bring her slide projector into the meeting. Her father had brought this to her. It was brought in, and Judy asked the clinician to close all the shades. All the children enjoyed seeing the comic strips.

12/6

The clinician discussed with the physical therapist her concern over Judy's saying she would soon be able to walk. The physical therapist said Judy had been misinformed by someone when her new casts were being considered. She felt the encouragement should be in helping her to sit rather than walk.

In the meeting, paper and crayons were distributed to each child. Judy asked the clinician to come to her and help her to color. She asked the clinician to hold her fingers and push her hand along. She stated, unrealistically, that her fingers were too small to hold the crayon. Her will to color was tremendous; she showed little concern for what color she used or what picture she made, as long as someone was helping her to color. When the clinician needed to help another child, she asked one of the boys to help Judy. He was afraid of hurting her when he realized he had to squeeze her hand to hold the crayon. Judy reacted by saying that she could not feel anything on her fingers and that it was all right for Rich to sqeeze her hand. Rich went to Judy's room after the meeting and continued to help her color.

12/8

Before the meeting, Judy told the clinician that she did not want to talk in the meeting. She could not give a reason, but the clinician accepted this. The clinician knew she had seen her sister for a short time the evening before, but Judy changed the subject when questioned about this. She participated in the meeting by observing.

12/13

In this meeting, Judy's increasing difficulty in accepting limits was manifested. Throughout her hospitalization, the tendency of personnel was to give in to Judy's wishes. As her relationship with the clinician has developed, she has become increasingly insistent and demanding of her time and attention. However, she was able to accept limitations from the clinician during the meeting as she verbalized more of her needs and desires. The clinician announced that the group would meet once more before her two weeks away from the hospital.

12/15

This last meeting was a Christmas party. The children made gay paper hats decorated with Christmas stickers. Judy was given the title "official sticker licker" by one of the boys, because she suggested that she could lick the stickers in making her hat. She stuck her tongue out while the clinician placed the sticker there, and then she told the clinician where to place the sticker on her hat. She became silent when the clinician announced again to the members that she would not be meeting with them for two weeks, stating that some of them would be going home before then. The clinician asked who thought they might still be in the hospital. Judy said she would be here because she would not be able to walk by then. The clinician said that this was true, but there would be Christmas in the hospital, too. She said she would see the group on Friday before she left for her vacation.

Judy demanded to be taken back to her room at once after this discussion. This was the first time she had ever wanted to leave a meeting early. The clinician told her that she knew Judy was angry that the group was not going to meet for awhile, and that the clinician was sad to say goodbye to the group, too. The clinician said if Judy would be patient, she would take her back to her room at the close of the meeting. She nodded in agreement.

12/18

Judy handled her separation anxiety by being very cool toward the clinician when she went to tell her goodbye. The clinician sensed her pleasure over a small doll she presented to her, but Judy gave no verbal response.

1/5

After the clinician returned from her vacation, Judy's demands on the clinician intensified. This continued in the meeting, as she wanted the clinician to get her gum and water from her room. She could accept limits, however, which the clinician felt were most important for her to learn at this time. She participated fully with the other children in a discussion about her fears of X-rays.

1/10 AND 1/12

In these two meetings, Judy began reaching out to other children and relating to them in very significant ways. She verbalized freely with them about happenings in their room at night and about other situations in the hospital. Her ability to risk talking substituted for her need to gain attention. She identified in a positive way with James, a paraplegic who had joined the group in the January 10th meeting. When one of the children asked if Judy were paralyzed, the clinician explained that neither Judy nor James could move their legs, that James had been in a wheelchair, and that Judy was going to begin to sit in a wheelchair. At the close of this meeting, Judy and James were left in the room, and Judy said she was glad not to be in a frame like James was in during the last meeting. She told him he must be very lonely in a room by himself. When the clinician pushed Judy back to her room, she asked her to take a piece of gum and give it to James. The next day, Judy was put into a wheelchair for the first time since her hospitalization.

1/17

Judy was to be transferred to the Rehabilitation Center. The clinician told her there would not be a meeting that day. She took her for a ride in her wheelchair. Judy told the clinician her father told her she was going to another hospital. She then asked her to build something out of blocks for her, and to be very careful not to knock the castle down. When the clinician left her with one of the children she liked, she hesitated to say goodbye and looked away when she finally said it. The nurse told the clinician the next day that Judy had cried before leaving the hospital where she had been for so long.

The work with Judy clearly indicates the great need to reach out to children who are deeply depressed in an effort to gain their confidence and trust. This frees them to use their strengths for coping with their illness. Through the group, they can be helped to function better, both as individuals and with others, in mastering their environment and their illness.

Family Therapy

Since the 1950s, family therapy has steadily gained impetus and has achieved the status of a therapeutic model in a myriad of psychiatric and social work settings. Full discussion of this ever-burgeoning school of theory and therapy, with its manifold approaches, is obviously beyond the scope of this chapter. However, in consideration of therapeutic work with children and parents, the family therapy approach warrants careful consideration as a potentially useful intervention and, dependent upon assessment and evaluation, in some cases proves to be the treatment of choice.

Schertz (1970) suggests that experience in the treatment of individuals, with its successes, shortcomings, and failures, plus the ever-pressing need for effective means of working with troubled people, led clinicians to explore new treatment modes, such as group, milieu, and family therapy. In many instances of individual treatment, goals were not realized because of interfering relationship forces within the family. For example, a husband might influence his wife to resist change or to leave therapy because he sensed the increasing marital disequilibrium and feared for the maintenance of the marriage. Parents might sabotage a child's treatment unconsciously because they feared loss of control over the child, opposed the child's growing self-assertion, or shared similar symptomatology. The well-known tenacity of the schizophrenic process did not lessen, in all too many cases, until the family was brought into direct therapeutic interaction with the schizophrenic family member.

The developments in ego psychology and the works of Hartmann and Erikson broadened the view of adaptation and identity and brought into clear perspective such dynamic elements of the environment as role, class, and family structure. Sullivan's focus on the meaning and use of interpersonal relationships, Jackson's work on communication, Parson's contributions in regard to socialization and the interactional process, plus other researchers' theories of the process of small groups have stimulated and contributed to theories of family development and family therapy. A basic theoretical conceptualization is that the family as a system, is always affected by changes in any one of its units or parts (i.e., family members). The healthy family is an open-ended system that members enter and leave in the course of the family's life cycle; under the influence of numerous biological, social, and cultural forces, and in the context of the members' personality structures, the system develops roles, rules, patterns of behavior and communication, patterns of coping and emotional reactions, values, and unique modes of managing the instinctual drives and impulses of its members. Family therapists focus on complementarity, coalitions, collusions, secrets, myths, and reciprocity patterns, and look at how these conscious and unconscious agreements are communicated between family members.

Family Functioning: A Systems Perspective

Disturbed relationships commonly are characterized by rigidity and repetitive, circular, predictable transactions that often contain several messages; in these double binds, words say one thing, but behavior and intent say another. Two examples are the engulfing, infantilizing parent who holds on while verbalizing the wish that the child will mature and become autonomous, and the neglectful, abandoning parent who verbalizes concern for the child but shows none. In the family system, parents commonly turn to children, who develop symptoms that express their own and their parents' conflicts; the children then actively enter the marital projection system. Thus, children pay a high price for maintaining the marital or family equilibrium. In some disturbed families, children suffer as a result of parental strife but are not drawn into it. Kessler (1966) states that "in theoretical respects family diagnosis and psychotherapy are an extension of the concepts of Adelaide Johnson and her co-workers who view much child psychopathology as the result of the unconscious parental conflicts, e.g., the 'super-ego lacunae' unconsciously fostered by the parent whose delinquent youngster vicariously gratifies the parent's forbidden impulse" (p. 392).

Schertz (1970) notes that family developmental tasks parallel individual developmental tasks in the realms of self-control, intimacy, distance, separation-individuation, responsibility, etc. Thus, a systems perspective suggests modes of evaluating the family's functioning in terms of how the family system copes with developmental phases and stress points, which require new identifications, alliances, transitions, and family rules, all in keeping with the age-appropriate tasks of the members. In addition, shifts in family structure may be produced by death, divorce, serious illness, or economic stress.

Schertz (1970) enumerates the major assumptions about the family and marital system which are at the base of family therapy as follows:

1. Whenever one member of a family is in trouble, all members are in trouble, as they all are producers, collaborators, gainers, and victims in the family system.

2. The family structure (i.e., its identifications, object relations, collusions, alliances, and roles) is a significant index of family functioning and is influential in terms of individual members' development. The parental ability to change the nature and strength of marital and parent-child relationships during the child's various developmental phases is crucial; it enables the child to separate emotionally for age-appropriate tasks while remaining an integral part of the family. Disturbed families, as noted above, are closed and rigid systems where parents lack the flexibility to adapt to the changing needs of their children. In addition, troubled families evidence unhealthy collusions that undermine a family member, an inadequate parental coalition, distorted object relations, problems in emotional and physical separations, role reversals, blurring of generational boundaries, and acceptance of pathological role assignments, all of which breeds severe symptomatology, anger, and guilt. Such rigidity and distortions in parental role functioning have been termed the "mass undifferentiated ego family" (Bowen, 1966).

3. Communication in the family is via roles and rules, and processes of identification and differentiation, to manage tasks and conflicts. Communication may be clear or distorted, explicit or implicit, verbal or behavioral, conflict free or conflict laden, straightforward or shrouded in family taboos, secrets, and myths. Each of these styles forms a stable, predictable pattern of communication. Disturbed families demonstrate distorted modes of communication marked by impulsive actions and/or an inability to hear correctly.

Family Assessment and Diagnosis

Schertz (1970) advocates a clinical approach to treatment based on an assessment of the unique family relationships; while this approach is rooted in psychoanalytic personality theory, it differs in that it views the individual as part of the family system and thereby focuses on the what, how, when, and why of intermeshing family behavior. This perspective conceptualizes family therapy as a three-pronged approach based on (1) content or data, (2) the processes of interaction and transaction, and (3) the family structure (i.e., family rules, roles, identifications, alliances, and collusions).

Ackerman (1958) recommends making a family diagnosis based on history taking, home visits, and office observations by a clinical team, to evaluate marital and parental interactions, and to serve as a guide for the evaluation of the child's personality in the here-and-now. The diagnosis also may indicate the sequential stages of the child's development." Of special importance in family psychiatry is the evaluation of the personality of a child here and now, the determination of the child's level of emotional maturation, and the correlation of this data on child behavior with the diagnosis of the family group" (Ackerman, 1958, p. 138).

Ackerman (1958) offers detailed guidelines for collecting and organizing the data for a family diagnosis. He begins with a general outline of the data that must be gathered, broken down into the following categories: (1) nature of, and attitudes toward, the presenting problem; (2) identifying family data (i.e., family composition, physical setting, sociocultural patterns, special problems); (3) internal organization and external adaptation of the family as a group (e.g., family identity and stability, family-community relations, and interplay between intrafamilial and extrafamilial roles); (4) current family functioning (i.e., current parental interaction as marital partners and as parents, and current parent-child interaction); (5) personality of each family member (including any pathogenic interference with a member's functioning and integration within the family); (6) relations with primary parental families; (7) developmental history of the primary patient; and (8) summary interpretation of the mental health of the family group, and of interrelations between the mental health of individual members and the family group.

Ackerman further details the criteria for evaluating the marital and parental interaction. He begins with the history of the marital relationship (i.e., meeting, courtship, and marriage), examining each phase of the marriage in terms of the spouses' shared identity, stability, and reciprocal role adaptation (i.e., emotional, social, economic, sexual, and parental complementarity, as well as sharing of conflict patterns and mutuality of support). The same criteria are applied to the current marital and parental interaction.

Ackerman then looks at parental achievement and goal fulfillment, both collectively and individually. Next he turns to the interrelations between the parents' personalities, on the one hand, and their marital and parental roles, on the other. Finally, he deals with the neurotic aspects of the marital relationship, beginning with an identification and evaluation of the specific neurotic patterns and their consequences, and concluding with an examination of patterns of restitution.

Ackerman emphasizes the urgent clinical importance of estimating the balance between the pathological and the relatively healthy aspects of the marital relationship and offers pertinent questions to guide the diagnostician in this task. Adequate diagnosis of the marital relationship enables the therapist both to focus on damaged areas of functioning and to reinforce and strengthen the relatively healthy areas of functioning.

Finally, Ackerman offers guidelines for evaluating the child in the here-and-now. He begins with an assessment of the child's intelligence, physical appearance and general health, and symptomatology. Next, the diagnostic evaluation of the family group is examined, followed by observation of the child's adaptation to external reality, interpresonal relations, and attitude toward himself/herself. The quality of the child's affects, including richness and depth of emotions, spontaneity, stability, appropriateness, and flexibility, is detailed. The child's anxiety reactions, patterns of control over emotions and impulses (including capacity for pleasure, tolerance for frustration and pain, and functioning of conscience), and defenses are closely observed. The final evaluative step involves the formulation of the child's central conflicts, at a conscious and unconscious level, with the role of the conflict and its associated symptoms defined in the context of the overall functioning and adaptation of the child. The relation between the conflicts and the child's self-image and defenses is specified, and the interrelations of the conflicts and the child's development and family experience are delineated.

In contrast to Schertz's and Ackerman's emphasis on diagnostic assessment, many family therapists appear to view the medically oriented disease-treatment schema as foreign and inappropriate. For example, Haley (1971) believes that the diagnositic evaluation is merely a device to deal with the therapist's anxiety; he recommends replacing it with active intervention.

Opinions also differ regarding indications and contraindications for family therapy. Haley (cited in Offer and Vanderstoep [1975]) believes that the whole issue is irrelevant, a "non-question," since psychopathology is defined as a relationship problem and the unit of diagnosis and treatment is no longer the individual, but is the family" (p. 152). Offer and Vanderstoep (1975), in considering indications and contraindications for family therapy and in reviewing the literature, divide family therapists into systems analysts and psychoanalysts (or psychoanalytically oriented therapists). Per this schema, systems therapists find disease and psychopathology irrelevant; instead, the critical issue is the potential mutual evolution and change in the two intermeshing systems, the therapist's system and the patient's system. Unterberger and Whitaker, two systems anaylsts, reflect this disinterest in diagnostic assessment. Unterberger believes that discussion of whether or not to do family therapy can be an externalization of the therapist's self questions, while Whitaker believes that the most crucial indication for family therapy is the presence of a skilled family therapist (Offer and Vanderstoep, 1975). McGregor (1972, personal communication to Offer) believes family therapy is indicated when the family can be convened and is not indicated when the family cannot be brought together. Bell and Vogel (1968) treat personality as an undifferentiated system that has interchange with the various subsystems of the family.

Structural Family Therapy

Minuchin (1974), the proponent of structural family therapy focuses on the patient within the family rather than the patient per se. Structural family therapy focuses on "the feedback" between people and their circumstances. This approach is a therapy of action aimed at modification of the present; it does not explore or interpret the past. Thus, the target of intervention is the family system, and the therapist joins that system in order to transform it; by changing the position of the system's members, the therapist changes their subjective experience. Minuchin (1974) examines family structure, which he describes as invisible sets of functional demands that organize the way family members interact, the family being a system that operates through transactional patterns. The structure of the family relies on two systems of constraint: one is idiosyncratic, involving the mutual expectations of particular family members, based on years of explicit and implicit negotiations; the other is a power hierarchy, based on complementary of functions (e.g., a husband and wife who accept their interdependency and operate as a team).

The concept of boundaries is also important to the structural approach, as boundaries protect the structure and differentiation of the system. Boundaries must be clear and flexible for proper family functioning, in that extremely diffuse or rigid boundaries indicate areas of probable pathology. The therapist often functions as a boundary marker, or arbitrator, clarifying diffuse boundaries and opening up inappropriately rigid boundaries.

Psychodynamic Family Therapy

In contrast to the systems analysts, the psychoanalysts and psychoanalytically oriented therapists, as represented by Ackerman, Jackson, Kramer, Wynne, and Williams,

> hold to a nosological psychiatric classification system and conceptualize individuals and families along psychodynamic and psychopathologic points of view. For them, doing a diagnostic family interview enables the psychotherapist to diagnose psychopathological processes and thus arrive at both the family and individual diagnoses. With a diagnosis at hand, one can then select the most appropriate treatment or group of treatments" [Offer and Vanderstoep, 1975, p. 146].

Family therapy is perceived as especially helpful in situations involving here-and-now struggles with interpersonal conflicts (e.g., marital disorders or disturbances in the parent-child relationship).

Psychodynamically oriented family therapists note the following contraindications for family therapy: the presence of severe psychotic depression, severe masochistic character, certain types of schizophrenia (there is some difference of opinion here), or hard-core psychopathy, perversion, or criminality; the lack of a structured treatment setting; the unavailability of a skilled family therapist; a firm decision to divorce or to break up the family in some other way; deeply rooted dishonesty in one or both parents; and the existence of unyielding cultural, religious, or economic prejudice against family therapy (Sugar, 1975).

There are many approaches and techniques used for ongoing family therapy; the focus here will be on family therapy that proceeds from diagnosis. Kessler (1966) points to Ackerman as having done the most to apply family therapy to child patients. She notes that Ackerman was a psychoanalytically trained psychiatrist who worked closely with social work students and family service agencies. His approach to family therapy involves separate sessions with the patient interspersed with sessions that include other family members. This flexible approach is predicated on Ackerman's belief that at certain phases and stages it is appropriate to see mother and child together, parents together, and the whole family together to ascertain distortions in members' perceptions of one another. "From one stage of therapy to the next, as the balance of reciprocity in family role relations shifts and the focus of pathogenic disturbance moves from one part of the family to another, the therapist must be ready to institute corresponding shifts of the level of therapeutic intervention into the family disturbance" (Ackerman, 1958, p. 307). Ackerman's approach does not use clinical staff working in isolation with individual family members; rather, it uses a clinical *team* that meets together periodically with the entire family group. The team approach has been modified recently by some practitioners, who work with a colleague or cotherapist in variations of Ackerman's suggested format.

Bell (1975) cautions that the cotherapist model runs the risk of the family pushing the therapists into parental roles, particularly if one is male and the other female. The children are likely to set up the cotherapists as substitute parents; a great deal of effort has to be directed towards preventing the children from seeing them as mother and father. Bell suggests that the male clinician seems to threaten the father, who then tends to be the last to participate. As might be expected, a female therapist can stir up strong feelings in the mother.

Bell (1975) emphasizes that useful diagnostic understanding comes through actual exposure to the family, and that "diagnosis and therapy go along simultaneously even up to termination" (p. 113). He notes that predicting how many sessions will be required is not easy, though he suggests that eight to twenty sessions is his norm. He suggests that children under nine years of age are not suitable candidates for family therapy, except in unusual cases. With the younger child who uses play materials, the focus remains on the child; this is not family group therapy, but individual treatment of the child in the presence of the whole family and with the help of all the adults.

The participants in family therapy vary with therapist bias, conviction, research interests, etc. Some family therapists work solely with the nuclear family while others include relatives who reside in the household, or who reside separately but are actively involved with the family. Some therapists also include domestic household help. Family therapy with hospitalized patients sometimes involves bringing the whole family to the hospital to live. Though family therapy typically has favored better educated, more affluent, and more urbanized families, some therapists attempt it with more chaotic, disorganized families that have multiple problems, struggling with the practical realities of sporadic and inconsistent attendance by some members. Some clinicians are not put off by families with poor verbal communication skills, as much can be communicated nonverbally (Bell, 1975).

Introduction and orientation to family therapy are generally followed by some specificity and structure of sessions. Bell (1975) delimits the content of discussion, which he sees as productive only when it is focused on solving certain kinds of problems. Specifically, Bell suggests that the therapist support direct family discussion about how members are getting along with one another, while blocking discussion of extrafamilial relationships. (Alternatively, the therapist may direct attention to the family implications of talking about outsiders). While individual members may report preoccupations of their own inner life and problems, clinicians do not pursue the history, form, and personal implications of this material, as they would in individual therapy. Rather, they follow the consequences in the group of the reporting of personal content (Bell, 1975).

It must be noted that family interviews can be very exhausting and demanding, especially for the beginner clinician. Some clinicians believe that this modality of therapy should only be undertaken by seasoned therapists who have had substantial experience in individual therapy. Whatever the skill of the family therapist, it must be emphasized that to do family treatment, one must be aware of identifications with various family members and must be able to register family currents, undercurrents, conflicts, and defensive patterns. Family therapists have to phrase their interventions so that they will be acceptable to several different people simultaneously. Of critical importance in all interventions, but particularly challenging in family therapy, is the question of conflicting loyalty. The general rule is that therapists must guard against criticizing the parents or endorsing the child's indignation over something the parents have done. One can say that the child's indignation is understandable—adding that perhaps the parents did not fully understand the situation, or maybe their action was their way of showing love and concern (Kessler, 1966).

Conclusion

In conclusion, careful assessment is necessary in determining treatment modality; clinical experience and practice wisdom have demonstrated that no one modality serves all well. Unfortunately, the bias of an agency or a professional too frequently determines a universal mode of treatment.

Emphasized is the need for a *family perspective* in considering any form of child therapy. The child cannot be treated in isolation, independent of the reality of the parents, the home milieu, and the needs of the sibs. Given the young child's complete dependency on home and family, the supports or obstacles within the family must be regarded as most significant. This reality changes as the child matures—it no longer applies to the adolescent who has separated and individuated from the parents. Most clinicians can cite cases of adolescents who made therapeutic gains in treatment despite parental opposition or noninvolvement. However, one rarely, if ever, sees this independent use of therapy on the part of young or latency-age children.

CHAPTER 11

Placement

Residential Treatment

Despite today's welcome emphasis on strengthening family life, there will always be some children who temporarily, or for extended periods of time, will need group care. In his request for funding for the Group Care Project of the Child Welfare League of America, Joseph H. Reid, its former executive director, stated:

> Institutions are coming under stringent examination in various parts of the country. There is considerable question about the effectiveness of the programs, about their cost and the relationship of the services to other child welfare services, and a host of other questions and issues. It is believed that the quality of services currently offered varies from extremely questionable to excellent. Some observers of the field estimate that perhaps as many as a third of the children are receiving care which is of poor quality, or actually unsuitable for their developmental needs. Improved group residential services and the development of other effective resources are essential for the future of this half million children [Reid, 1977, p. 7].

Mayer et al. (1977) sum up the major questions of the Group Care Project. First and most fundamental, is group care necessary? Advocates of "deinstitutionalization" are concerned about the possible depersonalization and alienating effects of group care on the child. Can group care provide the psychosocial ingredients necessary for the child to function in the outside world? Are children moved out of group care in accordance with their developmental needs and progress, or is their placement more a matter of administrative expedience (e.g., filling empty beds)? Are institutional staffs overprotective of their charges? Certainly residential care has been horribly abused and misused at times, and graduates of state training schools do have a high rate of recidivism. What does this say about the effectiveness of group care as a whole? Is group care in this country harmful for the poor children at public or voluntary institutions, but helpful for the rich children at prestigious boarding schools? That is, is there inadequate, ineffective group care for the majority and "elitist" group care for the few? Finally, is it group care per se that draws criticism, or the class structure of group care?

While most all the literature on group care states that the home is the best place for the child, reality requires the professional to face the indisputable fact that there are many children who have no home, or only a dysfunctional home, to return to, or are too severely damaged to be adoptable. Too many severely disturbed children and emotionally limited adoptive parents have been linked in the legalities of adoption, which then are disrupted by the need for separation and placement of the children in residential treatment facilities. In "deinstitutionaliza-tion" and "permanency planning," the reality fit of adoptive home and child is often overlooked, as is the inability of some children to relate to the intimacy of family life.

Mayer et al. (1977) ask whether such planning policies

> are based on romanticized and fictitious images of the family and the com-munity, on a fictitious diagnosis, [or] a fictitious concept of the state of the art of treatment. . . . Is our bias against group care predetermining our use of foster homes . . . so that, finally, after a string of failures in foster homes, a child comes to group care in a state of emotional disarray that defies any kind of treatment? Although use of group homes as alternatives to institu-tions whenever possible is favored . . . the indiscriminate use of such facil-ities was questioned by many. Do we force too many acting-out and aggres-sive children into small community-based facilities that cannot control them, and thereby not only jeopardize these youngsters' development but endanger the continued use of group homes for children who can benefit from them? [p. 16].

One must question the perception of planners who request short-term placement facilities, in small community-based units, to serve "the most difficult children" (including murderers, psychotics, and children with suicidal tendencies). Short-term placement is pre-posterous and damaging for children needing so much more.

Many questions can be raised about the overall child welfare system regarding the funding and cost of group care, the survival of group care under voluntary auspices, and the nature of public-voluntary relationships and the linkage system (among foster, group, and natural homes). Then there are the treatment issues: which form of group care is best for a particular child? How and where should emergency care be offered? How should the violent and/or psychotic child be treated? Mayer et al. (1977) state that "these children become 'revolving door children' whose treatment is fragmented between short stays in mental health hospitals and short returns to their own homes, foster homes, group homes, and treatment centers. They become nobody's children and everybody's children—the 'victims' of rigid, perhaps well intentioned legislation, statutes, and executive orders" (p. 23).

Child Rights

Many contemporary questions are raised about the rights of the child, and must include consideration of whether the rights and the needs of the child are identical or even reconcilable. Does the disturbed child's right to treatment include a right to refuse treatment and placement? If so, what are the emotional costs to the family, and the dangers and economic costs to the community? These questions pose the "labeling" issues; e.g., is the distinction between status offenders and delinquents psychologically sound?

> Is the assumption of 'normalization' underlying the approach to some status offenders indeed justified, or is there a point where quantity (for instance, number of assaults or runaways) changes into quality and where normal behavior becomes abnormal? Is the child rights movement taking sufficient cognizance of the many ambivalent feelings and conflicting needs of the adolescent, such as the need for freedom *and* authority, independence *and* dependence, group participation *and* privacy?" [Mayer et al., 1977, p. 25].

Mayer et al. ask whether child rights advocates and institutional operators each see only one side of the adolescent dilemma; that is, do the former stress only the freedom and independence of the child while the latter keep the adolescent in a dependent state?

As the child rights advocates have created significant legal and ethical questions regarding the nonvoluntary confinement and treatment of children, similar questions have been raised in regard to mentally disabled adult patients. While recognizing the need to correct abuses of the confinement process, many question the trend in legal reform (i.e., the legal barriers to involuntary hospitalization). Stone (1979) notes that such legal requirements fail to consider whether the person is treatable. "Confining dangerous persons who are not treatable in a hospital is surely a bankrupt exercise of legal authority. [Further] the presence of a critical mass of such dangerous and uncooperative persons transforms the best of hospitals into a prison" (Stone, 1979, p. 564). Stone notes that state mental hospitals have become more dangerous and oppressive for treatable inpatients.

Families no longer can use legal intervention in planning treatment for the nonvoluntary patient. As a result, growing numbers of schizophrenic patients wander the city streets or live in welfare hotels. This reality is replicated in the troubled child and adolescent populations, who are often unprotected, unserved, and on the loose. Their repeated acting out may become increasingly profound and injurious, with their aggression turned inward onto themselves, and outward onto family, peers, and society.

A Continuum of Services

Kamerman and Kahn (1976) note that the deinstitutionalization trend revives the old "institution-versus-foster-home debate." However, despite this debate, states and cities are finding that they must reinstitutionalize increasing numbers of violent youth. Needed are intermediate child welfare services falling between those of large institutions and foster homes (e.g., day care, day treatment, specialized foster homes, group homes, group residences, and residential institutions).

Traditionally, the juvenile justice system has taken responsibility for children who needed care and treatment because of their behavior while child welfare agencies have served children who needed care because of family neglect or family problems. These categories are now recognized as overlapping. In 1967, federal policy brought dependent and neglected children into court, and the federal government agreed to share the costs of foster care for families in financial need and for court-placed children. These youngsters were designated PINS (persons in need of supervision) and CAINS (children in need of supervision), respectively, and these groups were added to the delinquency and neglect categories. Despite recognition and "improved" labels, white children are still more commonly served by the child welfare system while low-income minority children are served by the juvenile justice system.

In the sixties, the juvenile justice system's concern about labeling and negative self-fulfilling prophecies focused on "diversion" to prevent and minimize children's entry into the juvenile justice system. This approach offered counseling and concrete services in the realms of health, education, housing, employment, and case advocacy. Probation, rather than commitment to a correctional facility, became the preferred intervention, though currently it is viewed as an inadequate deterrent for many disturbed and violent youths.

It must be emphasized that residential group care is only part of the childcare system. Mayer et al. (1977) stress that prevention of placement of the urban minority child in substandard custodial care is the first and foremost task of the child welfare system. There is a need for more good group care facilities, especially group homes and other alternatives to institutionalization. While group residential care is the focus of this chapter, it is only part of a coherent system that offers preplacement, placement, and postplacement services. The child welfare, child mental health, and juvenile justice systems are plagued with fragmentation and profound disorganization of services. The various polarizations along policy, practice, political, and funding lines gravely impede quality and continuity of care.

The chronic dilemmas plaguing these systems are rooted in a basic inability to intervene before a child winds up in an institution; that is, a lack of community work with parents is the real problem (Jacoby, 1977). A most serious problem is the quality of the management of the child welfare programs. Staff personnel are overworked and undertrained, and frequently are unable to assess the child properly at intake. The intake worker must be able to determine whether placement is necessary and, if it is, what intervention and facility are appropriate. A substantial number of facilities are faced with children whose disturbances cannot be dealt with by their programs.

Diagnostic Indications for Placement

Severely aggressive, disturbed children are of special concern to clinicians in residential treatment centers. Their placement should be based on a diagnostic decision related to the psychopathology of the child, the family situation, and the available resources, though in reality many children live away from home because of family inadequacies or pathology rather than the severity of their own emotional disturbances (Kessler, 1966).

Wineman (1972) describes the psychopathology and placement of the ego-disturbed child. Such hyperaggressive, destructive, highly impulsive children externalize all their problems, pushing their primitive impulses upon outer reality. Their symptomatology is on an expressive level. Their symptoms represent conflict patterns with societal demands rather than conflict patterns between parts of their personalities. Wineman believes that such children need to be placed away from home for any treatment to "register." They are usually too disturbed for foster home placement but behaviorally ill-suited to a closed institution such as a psychiatric ward or a training school for delinquents. These children really need 24-hour year-round treatment in a controlled but flexible environment that permits just the right amount of community-style experiences.

Such children have failed to develop adequate ego structure and thus are fixed on primitive action symptomatology as their mode of instinctual expression. Treatment must be tolerant of their symptomatology and allow time for appropriate ego development while holding to the expectation that they begin to accept and internalize reality demands. "Therapeutic recreational programming for such disturbed children is thus built around the principle of suiting the activity to the need of the child. In this way activity planning becomes a life net for the ego. It dispenses direct therapy through the provision of reality openings for expression. It gives structure to the ego by tying impulse demands closer to reality demands" (Wineman, 1972, p. 178). Because these children always manifest distorted object relations, the adults in a therapeutic milieu must respond with clarity, firmness, and empathy. Commonly these children are handled by harassed, exhausted, biased, rejecting adults.

Therapeutic Milieu

Bettelheim and Sylvester (1972) define a therapeutic milieu by its inner cohesiveness, which permits the child to develop a consistent frame of reference. The child becomes part of a well-defined hierarchy of meaningful interpersonal relationships.

It is important to recognize that, unlike less disturbed outpatient children, severely disturbed children cannot be approached through interview technique initially because no part of the conscious personality is free to detach itself from the manifest behavior for purposes of self-observation. Through endless reality clarifications and demonstrations by staff, these children are slowly made aware of the discrepancies between reality and their responses.

Fritz Redl (1959) developed the "life space interview," an on-the-spot means of responding therapeutically to children's explosive temper outbursts, fighting, vandalism, etc. The life space interview was "performed by an 'out-of-role' person who had direct life-experiential meaning for the child on reality, values, and libidinal terms" (pp. 55–70). For the child in placement, this person would be the house parent or childcare worker in charge of the immediate situation. Redl (1959) suggests that the therapeutic milieu in a placement facility consists of the institutional staff, the role of the group, the group living experience, and the management of daily activities.

Obviously, programs will differ in accord with the types of children served, the budget, the professional staff, and the setting's orientation. There are institutions for the long-term or permanent care of severely handicapped children, such as the psychotic or retarded. There are programs for aggressive, acting-out delinquent children, children and adolescents with self-destructive symptoms (e.g., anorexia nervosa), those with psychosomatic disorders, and those who present life-threatening suicidal behavior. There are very long-term programs specifically for schizophrenic and autistic children. Kessler (1966) notes that despite differing populations and other variations, all (noncustodial) institutions utilize (1) individual psychotherapy with the child and parents, (2) remedial education, and (3) a therapeutic way of life.

Maier (1972) describes residential treatment as "a therapeutically designed round-the-clock living-in experience, the purpose of which is care and treatment. Its clinical components are an integration of functions, structure, physical setting, and immediate social environment. . . . Residential treatment involves the temporary replacement of family living with group living in a controlled environment" (p. 154).

Children with severe disturbances such as autism and schizophrenia are bewildered and terrified by the environment; they need a highly controlled, structured, predictable environment, with as few staff changes and schedule irregularities as possible. That is, they need the epitome of the predictable safe surround that offers a stable frame of reference in a gratifying environment. Goldfarb et al. (1969) provide a climate of corrective socialization for schizophrenic children that is responsive to children's needs, but is "adult directed." Through active, assertive management, the adult creates an environment that guides the child toward appropriate behavior. Boundaries of time, space, and activity are clear and predictable, and adult expectations of the child are consistent. Goldfarb et al. believe that in a more permissive, nondirected milieu, schizophrenic children would create a very constricted world for themselves. Thus, they recommend energetic, positive intervention in the context of a stable adult environment for such children.

In addition to milieu and group living, residential treatment for children and adolescents who are unable to benefit from ordinary reflextive and relationship therapy may encompass special education classes; vocational training for some adolescents; recreational activities for youngsters unable to sublimate themselves in academics, athletics, art, drama, music, etc.; and psychotherapy (usually a combination of individual, group, and/or family therapy). Typically, social workers and other therapists serve as the "transference parents" while cottage staff serve as the "power parents" (Mayer, 1972) who supervise daily life and discipline and coordinate treatment care plans (those involving cottage, school, recreation department, social service, the child's "real parents," etc.). Teachers, volunteers, and maintenance and dietary personnel usually complete the staff of residential institutions.

The Violent Child

Institutions serving nonpsychotic populations note admission of an increasingly disturbed child population. Many facilities struggle to handle the violent child. Mayer et al. (1977) point out that the needs of the violent, acting-out child can only be met if the child is controlled. They believe that this need for control has been minimized in some of the literature. Further, since the frustrations of staff who deal with violent children often accelerate failure, such children should not be accepted by agencies that don't have the staff and means to control them. An agency must have staff available to spend time alone with the child—to manifest concern, interest, and commitment; to help the child over crises; to rebuild the child's self-esteem—in short, to demonstrate faith and conviction in the child's rehabilitation. Nonpunitive measures of coercion and limits on the child's actions and movements must also be available. It is not realistic to presume to treat the violent child without limits and coercion, but the latter must be implemented without staff anger, hostility, or punitiveness.

Mayer et al. (1977) cite problems of control created by misconceived state regulations. These regulations, which were aimed at correcting abusive coercion, have so tied the hands of staff members that the latter now fear the violent child. This fear is a serious barrier to treatment, as violent children can be helped only if they know they can be controlled and, ultimately, can control themselves. Agencies and group homes must assess how many violent children they can accept at a given time, keeping in mind the effect of these children on the environment.

Staff and the means to control such children needs elaboration. The staff/patient ratio must be such that one-to-one coverage is available for the agitated child as needed. It must allow for the comfortable management of the total group. It is generally essential to have male counselors for violent male and/or female adolescents. In situations where staff is inadequate in number and/or skill, punitive measures too frequently are resorted to in desperation, thus recreating the child's original home environment of abuse and violence. A locked unit where a wildly acting-out child can be segregated to avoid group contamination and fear is necessary. Some institutions have quiet rooms stripped of furniture where a violent child can be contained and supervised continuously by staff. Leaving children unattended in isolation is inhuman and unethical and has grave consequences.

Some group care institutions with physicians on staff utilize medication to calm a child. There are some "untreatable" children who cannot be contained even with adequate staff and means. These children move from aggression to assault, to repeated crimes—most commonly repeating their violent, abusive, chaotic early childhood. Such children are shunted from natural homes to foster homes, to institutions, to hospitals, to the street, often winding up in jails or correctional schools. This dismal fate is frequently avoided only via placement of such severaly damaged children in very small, secure, closed settings, with a very high ratio of staff to residents. Such a setting is expensive, and therefore frequently unavailable. With contemporary funding cutbacks, it is increasingly dubious that this more humane intervention will be available.

The Child with Severe Narcissistic Pathology

Another similar group of hard-to-reach youth who present therapy dilemmas are nonviolent children with severe narcissistic pathology. These children also evidence the long-range effects of early neglect and unstable parenting. They are also initially resistive to conventional treatment approaches, in that they seemingly lack warmth and the capacity for relationships. Their relationships are all too often superficial, without real feeling; they have no capacity for empathy, emotional connectedness, or true peer friendships. They are frequently inaccessible, infuriating, and draining for staff. They generally have no emotional response to situations where it is normal to be concerned or anxious. Pointless, constant deceit and evasion permeate their interactions with others. Without relationship feelings, primitive emotions such as fear, anger, and pleasure often are expressed in raw, unneutralized, explosive form. These children seem unconnected with human emotions of love, sorrow, joy, and loneliness. Kernberg (1970) describes these patients as follows:

> Haughty, grandiose, and controlling behavior is a defense against paranoid traits related to the projection of oral rage, which is central in their psychopathology. On the surface these patients appear to present a remarkable lack of object relationships; on a deeper level, their interactions reflect very intense, primitive, internalized object relationships of a frightening kind and an incapacity to depend on internalized good objects. The antisocial personality may be considered a subgroup of the narcissistic personality. Severe superego pathology is always present [p. 52].

Such patients use and exploit others, often depreciating them. This behavior reflects their own hungry, enraged, empty selves. They are frustrated, angry, and fearful of a world they perceive as hateful and vengeful.

Kohut (1966) cautions against therapeutic overambition and mis-guided treatment goals. We cannot be so governed by the

> improper intrusion of the altruistic value system of Western civilization in that such value judgments exert a narrowing effect on clinical practice. Some clients cannot be treated or assisted into our normal conceptions of object love. In many instances, the reshaping of the narcissistic structures and their integration into the personality—the strengthening of ideas and the achievement, even to a modest degree, of such wholesome transforma-tion of narcissism as humor and creativity must be rated as a more genuine and valid result of therapy, than the patient's precarious compliance with demands for a change of his narcissism into object love" [p. 270].

How does one facilitate this "transformation of narcissism" in a setting predicated on older notions of relationship therapy, with a child population unable to make relationships and threatened by closeness? Institutions have become increasingly convinced that, for a sizable number of children, conventional child therapy is contraindicated and enrichment in the milieu and daily living situation is necessary. Pleas-ant surroundings and more outlets for creative expression are necessary to help such children defend against their primitive impulses. No long-er can the institution rely on caring, well-trained adults, responded to by some of the children as phobic objects. So many children need to keep a safe distance and avoid closeness at all costs. Many children who are unreachable via any mode of supportive relationship psycho-therapy are more accessible via photography, dance, art, and music therapy, which aim to provide "forms and transformation of narciss-ism" (Kohut, 1966).

Therapeutic Recreation

Recreation consumes the major portion of a child's waking hours in a residential treatment center and must be effectively integrated into the total treatment milieu. Beyond gainful occupation of a child's time, play is essential for ego integration; a child's play is equivalent to an adult's work, as they both reflect the degree of ego development.

Children with severe ego defects that cause lack of time orientation, feelings of omnipotence, and confused concepts of cause and effect rely on primitive defenses such as denial and projection. These ego defects, together with an impaired superego, seriously interfere with the child's ability to sublimate or otherwise control aggressive impulses. Thus, the child's aggression is constantly expressed—either directly or indi-rectly, through resistance, avoidance, and passive defiance. One goal of any treatment program for such children must be that of helping them to develop inner controls through ego development and integration. In this way, they eventually can develop a meaningful self-identity.

Thus, the recreation worker's primary responsibility is to provide children with ego-supportive play experiences that nurture the child's self-worth and self-esteem. Successful play experiences, can help develop internalized controls, as well as a productive relationship with the worker. Recreation becomes "recreation therapy" only when it provides the aggressive child with a positive means of contact with adults. Alt and Grossbard (1949) point out that the childcare worker only becomes meaningful to the child when he or she is a real being identified with concrete activities and experiences in the child's daily life. Crafts, sports, games of lower organization (e.g., capture the flag, monopoly, cards, chess), games of higher organization (e.g., team sports), and off-campus excursions (e.g., camping, hiking, and trips into the community) must be planned carefully in terms of proper group composition, sufficient staff coverage, age-appropriate activities, etc. In recreational activities, it is essential to reduce competition and pressures to succeed to manageable doses. Activities must be geared to help disturbed children handle their aggression through relationships with others.

It is significant to note that 40 percent of the "high-level programs" covered in the Hylton study (1964) indicate little or no special attention given to the development of therapeutic recreation for children in residential treatment. Given the problematic engagement of placed youths in relationship psychotherapy, institutions are well advised to be less reliant on this aspect of their program. In fact, it is imperative that "leisure" activities be taken seriously as a treatment modality (Green and Clarke, 1972).

Institutional Staff

The variations in staffing patterns and modes of organization of residential institutions raise questions regarding centralized and decentralized systems, bureaucracies and democratic staff structures, high and low professionalization, and charismatic leadership. Whatever the formal structure of the setting, it works best when there is a common ideological base among staff, esprit de corps, clear channels for communication, and an open atmosphere that allows staff members optimal input of their own skills, ideas, and personality.

The living group is the nucleus of institutional group care and ideally ranges from eight to fourteen children in institutions of fifty or less children. The activities and interactions of the living group are the major ingredients of the group living process. The counselors or childcare workers responsible for the living groups spend the most time with the children, and thus are the builders and backbone of the milieu. In some cases, these counselors also see children in individual therapy sessions. Bettelheim's description (1950, 1955) of some such sessions suggest that the focus is on the relationship, rather than on ego defenses and unconscious conflicts.

In contrast to the professionals' well-defined functions (i.e., the diagnosis, education, and treatment of the children), the functions of the sizable childcare staff are far from clear-cut. These workers are extremely important, as they live with the children and take care of their daily needs (e.g., meals, dressing, bedtime). Further, they generally participate in treatment conferences and are acquainted with the history and record; in some settings, they also work with parents and contribute to care planning. The degree of authority that counselors or cottage parents exercise varies per institution, but, almost universally, the treatment program rests on these staff members, in that they must provide the following: "(1) need fulfillment at the most primitive levels, (2) acceptance of primitive expression of need and feeling from the children, (3) working through some conflicts in 'marginal or (life space) interviews,' and (4) working through other problems in specially scheduled individual interviews" (Kessler, 1966, p. 472).

Qualifications for becoming a childcare worker vary per setting, and there is no uniform pattern regarding personal and/or educational credentials. Maier notes (1972) that neither childcare work nor parenting have so far been defined or explicitly researched, despite the reality that these activities encompass the largest occupation in the world. In residential facilities, they occupy the hub of the wheel. The implementation of the entire institutional program depends on them. Nevertheless, with a few notable exceptions (e.g., the Sonia Shankman Orthogenic School of the University of Chicago) they tend to be at the bottom of the hierarchy of decision making and, most important, the institutional policies and procedures tend to bypass them in the allocation of prestige. Childcare is a low status occupation, in terms of education expected, salary paid, and power permitted (Maier, 1963; Hromadka, 1966; Schwartz, 1968). In contrast to Canada and Europe, in this country there are meager preparatory educational programs or professional organizations for childcare workers.

Because of the paucity of formal training, it is critical for institutions to provide supervision and inservice training. Many settings have attempted to link with colleges and universities to develop programs that award college credits toward an accredited degree in childcare. There has been research on the marginal role of, and strains on, the childcare worker. Barrett and McKelvey (1980) note that, until recently, Littner's classic book, *The Strains and Stresses on the Child Welfare*

Worker (1956), was the basic text for staff and supervisors, with the emphasis on the vulnerable position created by emotional stress. "Littner focused on the client role in stress and strain on the worker; more recent literature tends to focus on organizational issues and personal stresses on the worker" (Barrett and McKelvey, 1980, p. 277). Barrett and McKelvey recommend that staff's personal efforts to identify and cope with stress may well be facilitated by the supervisor—via adjustment of caseload and rotation of responsibilities—and that supervisory responsibility should include limiting unnecessary stress.

Despite research, recommendations, etc., the high turnover of child-care workers has consistently plagued residential institutions. Fant and Ross (1979) cite a recent study that indicated several factors contributing to this high turnover. "Job stress and compensation were not, in many cases, the reasons for leaving the job. A lack of sufficient nurturing was a major factor" (p. 640). In addition, formal and on line supervision are required, and nurturance needs to be provided by the direct supervisor *and* the organizational system. As in most systems, organizations, and bureaucracies, there is a "parallel process": the director establishes a certain climate that is then passed down through the hierarchy; thus, for the child patients—those at the bottom of the ever-descending spiral—to receive attention, those above them need the same.

The situation is analogous to the parental coalition established within the family via mutual respect, nurturance, empathy, and support between father and mother. The concept and model of parental coalition is critical in comprehending the needed components of sound residential care for children. These youngsters frequently come from one-parent homes, or intact families that have been marred by collusions, inappropriate alliances, and the various pathological modes of the family.[1] Given such familial training, plus basic ego deficits, children in care often are, or become, masters at splitting, first in relation to their parents, and later in relation to staff members. Relationships among staff members must be characterized by open, respectful communication and reflection, to counteract borderline all-good/all-bad split-object relationships.[2] Staff in an institution must not distort presentations of colleagues, undo the discipline set forth by others, or undermine one another to curry children's favor, placate, or bid for peace at any price. Polsky's classic *Cottage Six* (1962) documents the terror-filled cottage environment created by house parents' abdication of authority to the child patients.

[1]See Chapter 10 (family therapy).
[2]See Chapter 8 (borderline syndrome).

Education in Residential Facilities

Most children requiring residential placement have had serious problems in school, and not infrequently have been excluded for behavioral, management, and/or academic problems.[3] Kessler (1966) notes that the learning problems of institutionalized children differ from pure learning disorders. Some of these children are paralyzed by a fear of failure or success; some are too emotionally exhausted and apathetic—or too hyperactive and unfocused—to learn; and others fail to learn to "defeat" teachers and parents and/or to punish themselves and thereby relieve their unconscious feelings of guilt.

These children require an educational program and approach geared to their intellectual potential and dynamics. Classes generally should be small, to provide regular, supportive one-to-one instruction, a controlled environment, and individualized expectations for progress and acquisition of skills. Teachers need to collaborate and confer regularly and frequently with childcare staff and therapists. Often as children improve and acquire age-appropriate academic skills, they can gradually reenroll in public school settings while continuing to reside in care, if need be. It is obvious that academic progress promotes ego growth and improved self-esteem; often it is the first index of improvement and reestablishes the child on a progressive line of development. It is exhilarating for child and staff to observe the child's increased reading and comprehension skills, which reflect ego growth of memory, synthesis, perception, etc.

Psychotherapy in Residential Placement

Most residential settings provide several modalities of therapy: usually some combination of individual, group, and/or family therapy is used. Most children in residential care who are seen in individual therapy need the opportunity for a "corrective identification" (Alpert, 1957). They need a long-term, supportive, intimate relationship that focuses on working through current problems, rather than on uncovering unconscious conflicts. These children rarely manifest solely internalized conflicts; they are primarily at odds with their environment, and only secondarily with themselves. Thus, relationship therapy and ego support (i.e., support of their highest level of ego functioning) seem most appropriate.

The living group has already been described as a major ingredient in

[3]For further discussion of learning disabilities, see Chapter 7.
[4]See Chapter 10.

the therapeutic milieu. In addition, many settings provide clinical groups, in contrast to management or developmental groups. Management groups focus on cottage life, child-staff relationships, stealing, scapegoating problems, etc., while developmental groups support children's developmental transitions (e.g., return to the home and/or public school). Clinical groups are not unlike those described earlier, and may include activity group therapy, play therapy, or insight-oriented interventions. Family treatment can be a most appropriate approach for the child in residential care, as it preserves a sense of family ties and helps to prepare child and family for the child's discharge and return home.

Parents: The Role of the Family of the Placed Child

Thus far, very little has been said about the child's natural family. Despite the universal recognition that the role of the family is critical, parents receive more lip service than real service in the majority of settings. Many institutions try to sever parent/child ties, view the parents in negative terms, and presume to "rescue" the child. Other settings are not supportive or expectant of parental cooperation and involvement (i.e., regular visits, letters, and collaboration with the staff of the institution).

Children in residential placement usually have not had the long experience of nurturance and security essential to their development of identity and basic trust. Frequently, the family has suffered breakdown because of separation, divorce, death, imprisonment, or physical or emotional illness. Mandelbaum (1972) notes that the severely disturbed child "cannot relate to his parents without demanding infantile, primitive gratifications. He explodes with rage and aggression when these needs are frustrated. His world is filled with glaring hatred, disorganized behavior, wildly fluctuating ego states, bizarre symptoms and distorted realities. . . . Because of the illness within him and in the parent-child relationship he requires residential treatment" (p. 386). In residential placement, children repeat their past, replicating the distorted relationship with their parents with cottage staff, teachers, and therapists. It is crucial that staff members resist stepping into the role of the hostile, exhausted, ambivalent parent and instead handle the inevitable countertransferences and counterreactions that crop up in response to the child's outbursts and provocations.

Ideally, considerable work with parents is done prior to the placement. Facing the need for placement is painful; parents feel guilty, angry, helpless, and fraught with fear of loss. If appropriate preplacement work is done, grief reactions and depression over separation can be expressed, rather than acted out later by parents. Further, they can come to feel positive about securing the necessary treatment for their child. Excluding parents makes them fearful and distrustful of staff, creating severe loyalty conflicts for the child. Parents become alarmed by their child's complaints and requests to be returned home. For successful treatment of children in placement, the parents must establish a bond of trust, an alliance with the staff of the institution.[5] This is made poignantly clear when one looks at attempts to work with the child without including the family. Albert et al. (1965) comment on a volume of the *Journal of the American Academy of Child Psychiatry* devoted to a symposium on the treatment of the child without the family; the findings were "far from optimistic."

Barnes (1972) notes the all too common practice of referring a child for inpatient treatment or residential placement with little or no consideration given to the child's overwhelming need for genuine guardianship. Barnes believes that often when children are placed in inpatient care, the hospital or training school is expected to be the "parent." The community thus abdicates all responsibility for these "bad" children, leaving it to the hospital or training school to make them "good." Barnes finds this approach wrong, impossible to implement, and "morally inhumane." Such children cannot be ignored or gotten rid of; sooner or later, they will return to the community. Barnes emphasizes the child's sense of abandonment and vulnerability over the initial parent loss. Robinson (1950) recommends working out a parenting plan before seeking any kind of treatment. Likewise, Barnes (1972) states that "in the case of a child without a family, proper guardianship comes ahead of treatment. Parents are more important to a child than doctors, and treatment cannot be effective unless proper guardianship is established first" (p. 139). Child welfare agencies that act as guardians need to exercise their parental obligation more firmly and consistently. Unvisited children seen by a procession of ever-changing workers are all but doomed to an unsuccessful stint in residential facilities, followed by a series of unsuccessful, "revolving door" placements.

Appropriate work with parents in residential care, be it individual and/or group, increases parents' identification with the treatment process and diminishes their ambivalent conscious and unconscious reactions to their child's improvement. There is decreased sabotage and increased cooperation by parents. Some residential settings have experimented with parents in the role of treatment partners. Many authors emphasize that an integral aspect of the placement should be a sustained focus on helping parents learn child management skills since what happens to the child upon discharge may be more important than

[5]See Chapter 12.

what happens in the program. Childcare programs without parental involvement are unlikely to effect lasting change; given the declining funds for long-term placement planning, this reality becomes an increasingly important consideration.

Krona (1980) reports a model of extensive involvement of parents as partners in residential care, whereby the parents make assessments, and treatment and discharge decisions; they receive training to help their children in the program and to maintain and develop behaviors once children have left the program. Stressed is communication over and beyond the child's individual counseling session and one family session per week. The parents are contacted weekly by staff and receive weekly written reports on their child's behavior. Any major disciplinary action is discussed with them. Staff members are available for consultation with the parents in regard to problems at home (e.g., marital conflicts, the placed child's behavior on home visits). In addition, parents and staff confer with the public school regarding the child's progress. The staff remains available for months after discharge to provide help in crisis and to offer general support.

This extensive involvement of parents appears to be predicated on both agency philosophy and the reality of fairly intact parents and children. This model, which employs behavior modification techniques, is not universally applicable, but does demonstrate a radical departure from the historical pattern of all but total severance of child and family. However, all children can benefit from an atmosphere of teamwork and open communication founded in mutual respect between parents and staff.

In conclusion, it must be noted that residential care of children is only one of several interventions that may be used according to the needs of the child and the family. It is a radical recommendation and must warrant the reactions to separation. Children's and parents' depression, fear, panic, and anxiety should not be underestimated. Feelings of rejection and separation anxiety are common and expected responses initially. All this notwithstanding, after all other efforts at outpatient treatment have failed, residential care frequently becomes the sole alternative.

Mayer et al. (1977) note that new forms of group care have replaced or supplemented some of the old ones; new ideologies have been applied to group care, and social and educational theories have gained influence beside psychodynamic concepts as the guiding principles of group care. Whittaker and Trieschman (1972) are convinced that "there is no one 'right' way in milieu treatment. Our ultimate goal is a model for treatment that is open to new ideas, basically eclectic in regard to theory—and most important of all—a model that will bear both the test of time and that of the children" (p. 4).

Case of Jason: A Violent Child in Long-Term Residential Treatment

Reasons for Placement

Jason, age nine, had a lifelong history of severe temper tantrums; he was referred to a children's hospital for psychiatric testing following a period of disruptive behavior in school. He was then transferred to a long-term residential treatment facility. This very handsome, light-skinned child of a black father and white mother was shifted from mother to maternal grandmother to boarding home during the first five years of life, as his father was in prison. His mother had three other children by a black lover while the father was in prison. When Jason was five, his maternal grandparents were granted custody through Family Court; at this time, mother was charged with prostitution and neglect of her other three children.

Jason had poor impulse control and was very immature emotionally. However, his superior intelligence (his tested IQ was 132, and this figure was probably below his true potential) enabled him to appear far more intact than he actually was. He had learned to manipulate his mother and grandparents by setting his own rules and resisting the inconsistently set limits. He behaved outrageously to get what he wanted, and his grandmother constantly showered him with gifts. Recently, Jason's father, who had been in jail since Jason was an infant, was released from jail and resumed his relationship with his wife. His interest in seeing his son precipitated a family upheaval and an opening up of racial conflicts (Jason had been raised as a "white" boy; when he behaved badly, grandparents would call him a "nigger," "black bastard," etc.).

Residential Treatment of Jason

For the first few months of his residential treatment, Jason did not open up about his past experiences or current situation. Outside of therapy, he was very manipulative and had temper outbursts when he didn't get his way. He played checkers and chess with the therapist and built models during sessions, but was reluctant to talk.

The therapist received a phone call from Jason's father, who had been released from prison and wanted to visit Jason. Jason had not seen his father since he was an infant, with the exception of a Thanksgiving four years earlier, when he had seen his mother and father at home but had not been told that the man was his father.

The therapist met with the father prior to his visit with Jason. He was very anxious and voiced his concerns about the meeting. The therapist reassured him and explained that she planned to be with them both the whole time to help make the visit as smooth as possible. She explained that Jason was very ambivalent about the visit and might be somewhat upset and/or resistant.

The father said he was prepared for this and would not be surprised if Jason refused to see him.

When the therapist picked Jason up at the cottage, he was quite tense. Jason refused to get out of her car when they reached the building where the father was waiting. The therapist fetched the father as quickly as possible, fearful that Jason would flee. When she came out with the father, Jason had indeed run a few hundred yards. She tried to retrieve him, but was forced to call Security, who brought him back within five minutes and firmly told him to go into the conference room with his father and therapist. In the conference room, Jason was very agitated and tried to climb out the window. The father noticed that Jason had a deck of cards in his pocket and asked Jason if he played cards. Jason replied that he did, and the two of them played poker for money for about half an hour. Jason relaxed considerably and even laughed at times. He was not very talkative, but did respond to his father's questions.

The therapist took Jason and his father for a ride to get some ice cream (at the father's suggestion). On the way back, Jason asked his father if he would like to come to the gym with him to see a play, which he did. Jason also showed his father around and worked on a crafts project with him; the cottage parents said that Jason was in excellent spirits and showed his father around with pride.

Despite considerable tension surrounding the father's visit, and Jason's tremendous anger and resentment toward his father, the visit went smoothly. The father was sensitive and understanding in his approach to his son; he reached out to Jason and accepted his responses. He told the therapist that Jason seemed quite a bit like him and that he would have behaved the same way had he been in Jason's shoes. The father was very pleased with the visit and was looking forward to seeing him again when Jason came for a weekend visit in a couple of weeks. Jason had expressed an interest in seeing a lot more of his father.

At Jason's next session, he and the therapist played chess, but he was very reluctant to talk about Sunday's visit with father. When the therapist said that she wanted to explain why it had been necessary to have Security go after him on Sunday, he shouted, "I don't want to talk about it!" She told him that he didn't have to talk about it but that she had to tell him why it had been necessary to send for Security. He again said he didn't want to hear it, but she explained that he had been brought back to the administration building for his own protection, because he had been feeling upset about meeting his father. Jason became upset and shouted, "Play the game, play the game, I don't want to talk!"

Jason objected to a chess move that the therapist made; she said that they had to play by the rules. Jason got angry, jumped out of his chair, and began to destroy some puppets on top of the game chest. The therapist said that if he was upset, she hoped he would talk about it. He said no, he wanted to ruin the puppets. She again told him that he couldn't do this and he picked up an object to throw at the window, announcing that he was going to break it. The therapist grabbed him by the arms and told him he couldn't do this because it was destructive and he might hurt himself. She told him that if he was angry and couldn't talk about it, they could go over to the gym where he could work off some of his energy. He said no, he wanted to break the window, and he quickly went out of control.

There ensued a half-hour struggle, during which time the therapist managed to keep Jason under control for the most part; however, he wrecked the entire office as he struggled furiously in the therapist's hold, telling her he hated her and would kill her. She repeatedly told him that if he could not control himself, she would have to control him. The therapist wanted to avoid calling for outside help at all costs and told Jason that if he quieted down, they could talk about it and work it out. However, as soon as she released him, he tried to throw a heavy ashtray at her. Eventually, she informed Jason that she was going to have to call Security, which she did, still holding him with one arm. Only once during this struggle was the therapist aware of expressing anger toward Jason: this occurred when he almost succeeded in biting her. When Security arrived, Jason immediately calmed down. He was not visibly upset as he left and, according to the cottage parents, was fine for the rest of the day. He did not require any medication.

The therapist conferred with Dr. A. concerning her encounter with Jason. He was very supportive of what had transpired, stating that Jason often could not control his impulses and actively sought external controls. He added that though many workers are reluctant to get involved with a child in this way, it is a very necessary part of treatment with such children. He advised the therapist to have another worker nearby in the future to help her control Jason when he became violent. Jason needed and sought such external control to contain his impulses; in the past, his tantrums had been used as a means of manipulating all the adults around him.

Foster Care: Practice and Policy Implications

In recent years, significant changes in orientation have taken place which have redefined the tasks facing child welfare agencies. It is no longer considered sufficient to place children in a benign environment that meets their basic needs in terms of shelter, food, and clothing. In addition, children must be assured *permanency* in living arrangements and continuity of relationships. The recent notion that all children should be living with natural or adoptive families and that foster care should *not* be a permanent arrangement has taken on the force of a small revolution in the child welfare field. This radical change has been facilitated by the increased success in placing older, handicapped, and minority children for adoption; the increased assertiveness and organization of foster parents and adoptive parents; the changed view of the rights of the natural parents and the child; and the periodic court review of foster care cases that has resulted in a significant number of adoptions. Further, continuity of relationship has become a critical criterion in deciding where, and with whom, children should reside (Festinger, 1975; Fanshel, 1977).

A serious issue facing the child welfare field is the quality of the management of programs. The profound disorganization and fragmentation of services, and the polarizations along policy, practice, political, and funding lines, gravely impede implementation of the goal of permanency for children. While many children receive reasonably good care in substitute living arrangements, many languish, locked into the system; horrifying case records document these "law made tragedies" (Goldstein, 1975).

A thorough understanding of these problems requires a review of the history and characteristics of foster care.

History and Characteristics of Foster Care

The foster home movement began in 1853 with Charles Loring Brace's efforts to place homeless children with families in the West. His concept generated considerable debate during the last half of the 19th century. There was much justified criticism of this practice, because the distant foster homes were virtually unsupervised and children were often mistreated. Bernard (1973) notes that "although most child welfare leaders by 1900 supported family care of some sort, as opposed to institutional fare, it would be a while before the institutions felt the competition of the new movement" (pp. 37–38).

While foster care now is generally viewed as preferable to most methods of institutional care, especially for children who have not reached adolescence, its efficiency has been much debated. Nevertheless, it is the routine child welfare intervention applied to neglected and dependent children, especially those under the age of six. Jenkins and Sauber (1966) describe the range of conflicting childcare solutions, which encompasses institutional care, foster care, and preventive services aimed at keeping children in their natural homes. Clearly, foster care cannot be viewed as an isolated area in the field of child welfare, or even as separate from the total range of national socioeconomic problems. "Families with children in foster care are families in trouble. The need to place children stems (in part) from the dysfunctioning of the family caused primarily by the failure of our social and economic systems" (Jenkins and Norman, 1972, p. 1).

Jenkins and Norman question the traditional focus of foster care on the child; they believe that family-centered care is more effective in the long run. They note that while insulating children may be easier than rehabilitating their natural parents, the majority of children return to their natural homes after foster care.

Lay people and professionals alike know that many preventive interventions have been well conceptualized, but not actualized. Such
programs go beyond the foster care or child welfare system, and depend
on allocation of the nation's resources to adequate family maintenance,
education, housing, employment, improved homemaker services, and
the like. Although a discussion of the needed social and economic
reforms is beyond the scope of this chapter, the interwoven nature of
the above problems must be stressed for any accurate view of the total
picture. Suffice it to say that child welfare and foster care traditionally
have had a low priority in American politics.

Alfred Kahn (1973) suggests an alternative to foster care: give families the money that otherwise would be spent in placement of the child
and help them to use it productively to maintain the family intact.
However, while much lip service has been given to the concept of
prevention of placement, the quantity and quality of preventive and
supportive services are most questionable. Family maintenance requires a combination of office interviews, home visits, and a range of
auxiliary services. However, the amount of money most agencies allocate for preplacement work with families is negligible. Given the
paucity of services and monies for the macrosystem of social and child
welfare, it comes as no surprise that the actual foster care programs are
inadequate, inappropriate, and chaotic in their operations. This dismal
reality stands in bold relief against the backdrop of sophisticated, sensitive research and knowledge about how to improve the system.

Briefly stated, the growing major problems of foster care in this
country are: (1) the paucity of genuinely therapeutic foster home placements; (2) the poor standards in assessing applicants and the tolerance
for, and approval of, inadequate and/or disturbed people as foster parents; and (3) the meager state reimbursements to foster parents. It is
surprising that, in view of the widespread preference for foster family
care, this mode of placement has not been developed more successfully
over the years. One wonders why more efforts have not been made to
recruit foster parents from different strata of the population and to pay
them an adequate fee or salary, particularly since the special problems
of the children referred to foster family care require special alertness
and skill on the part of the foster parents.

In his study on foster care in Massachusetts, Alan Gruber (1973)
found a number of very serious shortcomings. For instance, three-quar-
ters of the foster parents were either completely unaware, or did not
realize the extent, of the foster child's disability at the time of placement. Less than one-quarter reported receiving training prior to receiving a foster child. More than 93% reported that they regularly had to
use their own resources to cover expenses for their foster child. Obviously, there has to be relationship between the fees paid to foster

parents and their availability. Rein et al. (1973) point to the persistent stereotype of the foster mother as the lower-middle-class or upper-lower-class unemployed woman, whose fulfillment in having a child is her compensation, and whose financial renumeration is not payment for her work, but rather, "pin money" that rarely covers the child's expenses.

The economic liabilities plus the strain of caring for foster children give little incentive to foster parents, and placement becomes a selection of the lesser evil. Rein et al. (1973) point out that such negative choices create great instability in foster home care. The majority of children in foster care change homes frequently, sometimes living in ten or more foster homes before being institutionalized.

Wolins's research (1963) further clarifies the predicament regarding the selection of foster parents.

> We found rules and divergence from them. The rules were abandoned in the face of pressures and personal idiosyncracies. Workers in agencies with large case loads, low board rates, and small rejection rates (probably indicative of low supply/demand ratios) were likely not to be applying their own ideology. Such personal interpretations are understandable enough when the rules of the game are not completely clear or when pressures are so great that the rules are abrogated [pp. 147–148].

Meager payments to foster parents seem to be a tradition, and not simply an issue of economic priorities. The fact that many children have been taken for profit and grossly neglected lingers in the minds of many. Thus, an ideology has developed that caring for a child and being paid decently to parent a foster child are incompatible. Significantly, no one suggests that staff members in institutions care for children less well when they are decently paid.

Temporary Versus Long-Term Foster Care

There are two major modes of foster care: temporary care and long-term care. The conditions characterizing the need for temporary care were identified by Jenkins and Sauber (1966), who found that when physical illness of the mother was the immediate cause of placement, placement was usually brief. In such cases, which were often single-parent welfare families, there were strong, close family relationships. Brief or temporary care was the initial conception of foster care; after this short-term separation, the child was supposed to return to the family or be placed for adoption. The "reality experience of foster care agencies does not support this either/or approach which failed to take into consideration the range of interrelated social and psychological factors that cause long term placement, and those that indicate the need for continuation of the plan until the child reaches a stage of relative or complete self-reliance" (Klein and Overstreet, 1972, pp. 51–56).

Klein and Overstreet (1972) identify the conditions that usually point to the need for long-term foster care, in which restoration of the family cannot be anticipated. Indications for long-term treatment include: chaotic family life, parents with defective ego functioning, chronic family instability, and major developmental and/or psychosocial problems in the child resulting from the disturbed parent-child relationship. Long-term foster care can become permanent foster care that substitutes for legal adoption under conditions that either preclude or contraindicate adoption. One example is the older child who requires a prolonged period of treatment, but whose age makes future adoption unlikely; another example is the child whose parents retain a relationship with him or her without making any progress towards the reestablishment of a home, and who eventually accept the foster home as permanent.

The effects of separation and loss are well understood and the literature of all the helping professions abounds with research and case studies that document the massive psychological impact on placed children and their parents. Given this powerful response, one would expect such a momentous decision to be made only after careful consideration and evaluation of the family's needs. However, in actuality, untrained workers burdened with massive caseloads often rush into ill-thought-out actions. "For the majority of children and their families, placement is an emergency, an unplanned traumatic experience, and full knowledge of why children come into care cannot be found in the entry records" (Jenkins and Norman, 1972, p. 259).

Anna Freud questions current custody and placement procedures. She notes that

> children are not adults in miniature but beings per se, different from their elders in their mental nature, their functioning, their evaluations of events, and their reactions to them. . . . Their needs may contrast with those of their biological parents, their foster parents, or the social agencies concerned with them. For this reason, their rights cannot be represented adequately by the advocate of either the adult claimant or the adult defendant. They need party status in any court proceeding concerned with their fate, . . . [and] their own advocates need to be knowledgeable about the specific characteristics which govern any child's specific needs for more or less unhampered growth and development" (Freud, 1972, p. 625).

Supporting Anna Freud's concerns, Goldstein (1975) criticizes foster care for failing to promote continuity in the child's relationship with the natural parents or, in cases of permanent foster care, with the foster parents. Further, multiple placements for a single child keep the child "familyless" throughout childhood." Goldstein explains this dilemma as due to apparently conflicting values. On the one hand, family privacy, and the rights of both the natural and the adoptive parents to raise their families free of government instrusion (except in cases of neglect or abandonment) must be respected. Kahn (1963) notes the long tradition of parental power over children, and the reluctance to bring in outside intervention. On the other hand, once a child's placement appropriately becomes a matter of state intervention, the child's needs must come first (Goldstein, 1975).

Jenkins and Norman's research (1975) indicates that, in the majority of cases, the best interests of the child and of the natural family are complementary, rather than conflicting. However, "it is an archaic conception to assume that the worst own home is better than the best foster home or institution. There are in fact, numerous cases in which placement in foster care may represent the optimal plan for a child and possibly for his family" (Jenkins and Norman, 1972, p. 259). Long-term placements might best be described as "foster care with tenure"; they can provide the child and the foster parents with the kind of continuity generally associated with adoption (Goldstein, 1975).

Foster Care, Adoption, and Child Welfare Dilemmas

Insufficient recognition has been given to the fact, that foster parents are the backbone of any foster care program. While the literature abounds with accounts of the inadequacies of most foster parents, little has been done to rectify the situation. Much could be done to recruit and adequately compensate more appropriate foster parents and trained staff workers. Investment in these areas undoubtedly will initially prove more expensive than current practices, but will result in substantial long-term economic savings in terms of: (1) less staff time spent in spit-and-glue efforts to hold together inadequate foster placements; and (2) less shifting of children from inadequate foster home to inadequate foster home or to expensive residential institutions.

In many cases, although a discharge objective is discernible at intake, no plan is formally recognized and implemented, leaving case management in eternal limbo. Many foster care cases demonstrate how "temporary" separations in foster care become permanent, without creating permanent relationships between children and caretakers. Lash and Segal (1976) ask the important question, "How well geared is the foster care system for providing adoptive homes for the children for whom adoption has been designated as the long term objective? Are there situations where foster parents have moved (or can be helped to move) in the direction of adoption?" (p. 72).

Lash and Segal (1976) report that the number of children accepted for adoption dropped 45 percent from 1971 to 1974. They cite the need for a "massive campaign" to facilitate the move from foster care to adoption. Before such a campaign is implemented, however, existing resources should be more widely used. They note the boon of the adoption subsidy, which has been available since 1968 to foster parents who wish to adopt their foster child. Childcare agencies have not sufficiently absorbed the realities of the ever-increasing need for long-term care; they still focus on their original model of "temporary" foster care. Further, agency staffs are not trained for the difficult adoption task. It is not uncommon for courts to order agencies to explore adoption with foster parents when agencies have failed to do so on their own.

The need for adoption subsidies and increased maintenance allowances for foster children is a national problem that most severely affects the minority child placed out of the home, given the lower family incomes of minority foster homes. Since 1970, black and Puerto Rican children have accounted for more than 75 percent of the total New York City foster care population. Although the percentage of all New York City children in foster care has been increasing, a black child is three times as likely, and a Puerto Rican child more than twice as likely, as a white child to be removed from the natural family. Similar findings occur in all urban communities. It would appear that these foster homes could be greatly improved via more careful selection backed by substantial financial reimbursements for care rendered. A sounder economic base might enable low-income foster families to move more readily into adoption or tenured foster care of their foster child. Again, these initial expenditures would benefit children's needs for continuity of care and decrease the multiple placements and/or institutionalization of such vast numbers of minority children.

In addition to the expenditure of adequate monies to provide sufficient numbers of experienced, professionally trained staff members and decent foster homes, adjunctive services such as treatment are frequently needed. Overwhelmed child welfare agencies cannot continue to ignore newer ways to provide needed services when the services are beyond the capacity of their own staff. Truly adequate foster parents do not require endless ongoing scrutiny by the placing agency; they are capable of seeking help for their foster child. The concept of "purchase of services" can be extended beyond the traditional purchase of institutional care into more frequent purchase of outpatient psychological treatment. This kind of payment customarily has been granted only for physical ailments and medical care.

It is significant to note that while care is routinely provided for visible and physical disfiguration, psychological pain and disfigurement receive scant attention until the child is in crisis, when it already may be too late. Often, costly institutional care is the ultimate outcome for such children.

Few preventative approaches are used in a widespread fashion to halt the overt and covert development of psychopathology, despite recent lip service to the contrary. Insufficient attention is paid to the reality that the best treatment provided late can do little to reverse the inordinate psychopathy the current foster care system is actually promulgating. The finger of accusation should not be leveled at the overburdened, understaffed public agencies, but rather, at the politics that allocate inadequate monies for programs. Changes in law, policy, and funding to offer more combined services for the child in public agency foster care can provide the child with "a home and continuing membership in a family where he (or she) feels wanted" (Goldstein, 1975, p. 662). Unfortunately, such suggestions are rarely put into general practice due to a "penny wise, pound foolish" mentality. Societal priorities and pressures create procedures that seem to save money but eventuate in greater emotional and financial loss, i.e., greater treament expenses for children who have been made more disturbed since they entered care away from home (Frank, 1977).

Fanshel's findings cite "return to bio-parents as the largest source for assuring "Permanency"—and that regaining the child is highly correlated with parental visiting. The unvisited children are often simply abandoned to the system" (Fanshel, 1975; Fanshel and Shinn, 1977). What worker activities support parental visiting? Issues such as this point to the need for improved staff qualifications and skills, updated training for the newer adoption approaches, better foster homes, and improved management of the programs. It is particularly important in foster care/adoption programs (1) to distinguish between temporary and permanent foster care placement and (2) to determine the feasibility of adoption. Reduction of children's time in limbo is the prime objective in pursuit of permanency.

The effectiveness of foster care/adoption services is measurable in terms of evaluation critera. Evaluation criteria require highly individualized case by case planning, and then monitoring, to see if the intake and discharge objectives are being implemented. Cases too frequently fall between cracks without suitable systematic accountability systems. New legislation and new methods of record-keeping are aimed at correcting these chronic problems. Estimates of progress are based on length of time in placement, and comparison of actual and stated discharge objectives. For example, with a group for whom adoption was the stated discharge objective one must determine how many children were actually freed for adoption, how many were placed in preadoptive homes, and how many adoptions were finalized. With return home the stated objective, one must evaluate whether parenting capacities have improved and whether children have improved enough to be able to manage at home. Research findings regarding the natural parents note that "(1) the higher the frequency of visits when the worker is involved in contact with the child and his family, the greater the likelihood of discharge within the first year of placement. In the second year there is a positive relationship only if the child is discharged from long term care. From the second year on, there is no relationship. (2) The more experienced the worker during the first year of placement, the more likely the child was to be discharged" (Shapiro, 1976, pp. 20–28). Thus, case effectiveness is measured in terms of worker skill and actual case activity, and the progression of the child within the system.

Other measures of effectiveness come from sources outside the immediate child welfare system. Outside audits by interested parties are accruing. Foundations interested in child development, the press, and officials in local and national government are initiating public hearings, audits, and studies to evaluate foster care programs. Other sources of pressure and evaluation are various citizens' groups, such as foster parent groups, adoptive parent groups, and the Citizen's Coalition for Children.

The dilemmas of foster care/adoption practices and legislation mirror many of the dilemmas of uneven welfare reform. The child welfare situation is further complicated by the competition of other self-interest groups, such as the aged. Since children do not vote, their interests have not sufficiently captured the attention of the federal government. Children are captive clients, and work with them is more complicated than work with independent adults, in that services must go in so many directions (e.g., to the child, the parents, and the surrogate parent figures) and attention must be given to educational and legal issues. This causes disorganization, fragmentation, and endless divisions of responsibility.

There are complex political and financial conflicts of interest of public and private agencies, where opinions differ regarding the benefits of long-term foster care, versus adoption, versus return to the natural parents. The monies no doubt contribute to professional opinions and convictions on these issues. Currently, there are legislated monies for preventative and early interventive work with families to avoid placement. This legislated reality does not alter the fact that agencies are plagued by staff too rapidly turning over, being overworked, and often, undertrained.

With the recent emphasis on accountability, child welfare agencies have come under increased scrutiny. Financial urban crises and mounting public pressures in this country point to the urgent need for a "revolution" in child welfare; time is running out for agencies to make significant alterations and reforms in the direct practice and overall system of foster care. Values and professional attitudes complicate the judicious gathering of accurate data necessary for an in-depth analysis of foster care practice. Complex ethical questions of privacy, confidentiality, paternalism, coercion, and social control surround each case decision. The lack of sufficient staff currently endangers the moral dilemmas inherent in case management, creating compromises of professional practice standards. Thus, the child welfare system remains one of the most draining and stressful systems serving children.

Case of Karen: A Child in Foster Care

The Child at Termination

Karen, age 13, was a very attractive and appealing white child with long blonde hair. She had experienced massive trauma and deprivation, the details of which are not known, given the lack of continuity of care and caretaking persons, and the conspicuous lack of information in the cross country placement records about this child. To date, Karen was in her seventh foster home, with initial placements on the west coast, and subsequent ones in the Midwest. She had lived in an extraordinary and superior foster home for the past four years, the longest she had resided anywhere; it was her current foster parents who had sought treatment for her.

Natural Family

The natural mother was described as a prostitute who abandoned Karen and a half sister seven years older than Karen. The police located Karen's natural father and placed both children with him. He could not care for the children and a temporary foster home was arranged for them, all before Karen was four years old. Her current foster mother stated that she was convinced that Karen had received initial warm care because of her early demonstration of affection and her ability to relate.

The natural father remarried when Karen was six, by which time she had been in three foster homes (one home from the age of four to six, and two subsequent homes for a period of several weeks). After a brief attempt to maintain Karen and her half sister with him following his remarriage, father placed Karen in another foster home for emotionally disturbed children because of her conflict with her stepmother. She was described then as explosively acting out, cutting curtains, ripping her clothes, smashing lamps, and being locked out of the house by stepmother. Following the California earthquake, father reclaimed her and moved the family to the Midwest. Father and stepmother had a 6-year-old child of their own and stepmother had several children from her own prior marriages. Karen's half sister managed to remain with father and stepmother until she eloped as an adolescent. However, the stepmother attempted to hospitalize Karen in a state hospital, describing her as a "sexually perverted child, who would be like her natural mother." The hospital refused admission, stating that Karen was not psychotic, and referred the family to the local child welfare agency, who placed Karen in a special diagnostic home while trying to involve the parents in treatment. Efforts were made to work with Karen and her parents and to facilitate her return home, but the parents could not, or would not, sustain this contact or accept Karen at home. Thus, Karen was placed in her seventh foster home at age nine. Per agency plan, Karen was to see her natural father every five weeks, but he often canceled or failed to show up for visits, and months rolled by with no contact.

Father and his current family were described as lower-class, unskilled, migratory white people. Father currently worked in a gas station but frequently had vague ideas about moving to a warmer climate. He and his second wife lived in a house in a blue-collar community and maintained what appears to be a stable though conflict-laden marriage characterized by stepmother's children coming and going, disorder, disorganization, fundamentalist religiosity, and extremely erratic contacts with Karen.

Foster Family

The foster family was a decided contrast to the usual foster family. They were not obtained via any agency recruitment campaign, though policy questions can be raised regarding recruitment possibilities of more such homes for children needing foster care. The foster mother acknowledged that her need to mother more than her one natural child stimulated her desire for a foster child. (She had a series of miscarriages after her first child but gave birth to a healthy second child during Karen's treatment.) She also had considered that her own needs, related to her own shared history, stimulated the wish for a foster child, much the way personal needs stimulate people to enter specific professions (e.g., child therapy, psychiatry, social work, childcare). Thus, with considerable insight, she concluded that she could fulfill her own creative needs by becoming a foster mother.

The foster father was a professor at a university, and the foster mother had been employed on a part-time, flexible basis as a research assistant, though she currently was unemployed and was considering future graduate education in one of the helping professions. Their marriage was stable and gratifying, and foster father had supported the foster plan, though he frankly stated that such an idea would never have originated with him. From the onset, the child welfare worker and therapist were astounded by the strengths of the foster parents and by their striking interest, empathy, and commitment to Karen. The foster mother intuitively knew how to soothe this child, and one could only be amazed at her capacity to convey warmth, acceptance, limits, and discipline, all with firmness and tenderness.

At the time of referral, the foster parents described Karen's significant improvements since entering their home. Her explosive temper tantrums had ceased, and poor control only occurred during times of change, e.g., trips abroad. In addition, Karen no longer was exhibitionistic; formerly, she had run naked in the home in front of the foster father and male visitors.

Despite the above improvements, the foster parents were greatly concerned about Karen's social isolation, unsuccessful interactions with peers, accident proneness, constant losing of things, and—most serious—long-standing learning disability and total inability to read.

Diagnostic Formulations

Karen's ego apparatus was intact, and there were no signs or symptoms of organic defects. (This was substantiated via subsequent neurological examination.) However, she presented a picture of serious ego deficits. She was not able to sublimate aggressive impulses, her learning and memory were grossly impaired, her frustration tolerance was poor, and she had not learned to read. She did not evidence consistent synthesis, but rather, weakness of secondary-process thinking and defenses of wishful thinking, denial, and reaction formation. Libidinal drives evidenced anal and phallic components. Her recently relinquished exhibitionism was reminiscent of a toddler in the toilet training stage and evidenced phallic and sexualized expressions of excitement caused by the overstimulation of her natural parents. At some preconscious level, she apparently had some awareness of her natural mother's prostitution, which had occurred in the home (some memories and fantasies substantiated this speculation). In addition, Karen showered with her natural father during her erratic residences with him. Her stepmother's reference to this child as "sexually perverted," no doubt, was due to her recognition, at some level, of the overstimulated, driven, and eroticized quality about the child.

Karen's strong aggressive drives were both turned against herself, manifested by her accident proneness and provocative behavior, and discharged outward onto peers, parents, and teachers. She exploded and fragmented like a helpless infant and, due to erratic early mothering, lacked self-soothing mechanisms. Superego development could not be considered due to the lack of psychic structure and failure to make a genuine entry into Oedipal conflict. Object constancy had never taken place due to the clearly documented, erratic early mother, who actually abandoned Karen. The attachment to her natural father might well be viewed in the realm of a maternal substitute. Because of the unevenness of the drives, the arrest in object relations, and the impairment in ego functioning, she was diagnosed as a borderline child, in desperate need of individual intensive treatment.

Treatment Recommendations and Implementation

Fortunately, the foster home was excellent and would effectively support a course of therapy. Because of her arrest in object relations and her conflict over the "good" and "bad" mother, she needed to be seen intensively, biweekly at least, to be effectively engaged in therapy. Her inability to learn at age ten made it imperative that therapy not be put off, or offered in a diluted fashion, if this child was to achieve any competence in the area of learning. She was obviously bright and articulate and desirous of learning and mastery. The Wechsler Intelligence Scale for Children yielded the following results: Verbal IQ = 91, Performance IQ = 122, Full-Scale IQ = 107. Evident in this evaluation was a fear of failure and a very poor self-concept. Verbal functioning was within the average range, whereas nonverbal ability was within the superior range. On verbal items, Karen did poorest and significantly below age level when a response was dependent on adequate social judgments. Items related to learning acquired through schoolwork also were slightly below age level. These factors and her emotional problems depressed her IQ scores considerably. Karen appeared more at ease with the therapist than during the psychological testing. This might have been due to her greater ease and verbosity away from the structure of the test situation.

Before attempting to describe the course of the therapy, it is essential to clarify the circumstances that resulted in Karen's treatment with a private practitioner, rather than at the agency or a community clinic. The child welfare agency responsible for her placement was an enormous public agency, overwhelmed, understaffed, and unable to provide any direct treatment beyond case management, placement of children, and coordinative efforts among the agency, institutions, and natural and foster parents. Attempts to secure treatment at three community child psychiatry clinics proved fruitless: one setting had an enormous waiting list and could not even offer evaluative services; one clinic insisted upon regular contacts with the natural father, who refused to be involved; and the third setting unilaterally refused services to any children in foster care due to their prior experiences with unplanned and sudden shifts of children from one foster home to another, inadequate foster home milieus, etc.

The foster parents, obviously well educated and sophisticated, were determined to procure services and, unintimidated by bureaucratic structures, they clearly and emphatically made their wish for a private practitioner known to the public agency. They were supported by the public agency worker, who, like Karen's foster parents, was atypical. He was a mature, older individual, extremely well educated, sensitive, and dedicated. He had been at the agency six years, longer than most staff members, and was committed to stable relationships with those on his caseload. He had remained the sole worker for Karen since she entered the agency four years ago. Thus, private treatment was given administrative sanction on the rationale that the costs would be less than those of a residential institution, which would probably be necessary in the future if Karen did not receive help now. Justification for this plan was also based on the reality of a total of seven foster homes to date.

Summary of Treatment

The following summarizes four years of work with Karen.

Karen was well prepared for therapy and highly motivated in regard to her wish to preserve her current placement, as well as to improve her academic functioning. Despite her conscious wish for change, she was naturally cautious and mistrustful in establishing a relationship and in sharing painful aspects of her life. She was charming and cooperative, obviously wanting to gain the therapist's acceptance in order to please her foster mother. She seemed to put her best foot forward, as though sensing that her foster home and her survival were at stake. She exhibited the too ready affection and lack of testing in foster children and institutionalized children. For many months, she only presented her most appealing and adequate side and wanted to "play and be happy" with her therapist. Gradually, she made considerable strides in forming an alliance and an ever-deepening relationship with the therapist. She became increasingly trusting and confident that the therapist could tolerate anything from her, especially her hostility, aggressivity, and infantile demands.

Any separation such as a vacation was stressful for Karen, yet the work and interpretations about the fact that all separations do not constitute abandonment were helpful. Karen also displayed concern about the foster mother's pregnancy and her security in the placement. She slowly began to share her thoughts and feelings about her natural father, his erratic, unpredictable contact with her, and the futility of romanticizing him with her unrealistic hopes.

Many sessions were devoted to academic and social concerns. Karen was able to face and share her social isolation and her prior preference for tomboyish activities with boys. She could talk more easily about school as a stressful situation, and could recognize how erratic her memory was; she remembered things selectively, often quickly forgetting school-related tasks and skills. Karen's loss of her belongings, of words she once could read, and of multiplication tables she once knew, made sense in light of Anna Freud's comments (1967): "A further even more far reaching motive comes into view, identification, passively with the lost objects which symbolize themselves, actively with the parents whom they experience to be as neglectful, indifferent, and unconcerned toward them as they themselves are, towards their possessions" (p. 16).

During the first year of treatment, appointments were increased from two to three times a week, at Karen's request, in regard to her expressed anxiety about the foster mother's pregnancy, and her concerns as to whether she was still wanted in the foster home. Karen's intense attachment to the therapist was most discernible, and at times she articulated a wish for seven appointments a week. Karen had no friends or companions other than her peripheral, unsatisfactory contacts at a "Y" swimming and gymnastic program, and at art classes. She clearly preferred coming to therapy over playing after school. This lasted until the last eight months of treatment, when her social relationships improved considerably and she could enjoy invitations from other children. Earlier, her hunger and provocativeness had spoiled things and resulted in total rejection by her peers. Karen often seemed to desire the presence of the therapist as a part of her self who would observe, reflect, and participate in her selected activities (i.e., artwork, acrobatics, the creation of craft productions, and the knitting of a blanket for the foster mother's new baby). Karen had a need to "buy" relationships the first two years of treatment, via endless presents to peers and members of the foster family. She made these gifts in treatment and, as she came to experience security and permanence with her foster family, she could give up this activity. The 57 wool dolls and other presents she made created a rebirth fantasy, an umbilical cord between her and her therapist.

Surprisingly early in treatment, Karen began to read, haltingly but accurately, but only in the presence of the therapist. In six months of treatment, she moved from complete illiteracy to a 1.9 reading level. Math skills seemed to be acquired more easily, in that Karen understood concepts; but for a year or more she could not memorize multiplication tables and instead would count laboriously to find the answer.

As her third year of therapy concluded, she was in a regular 7–8th grade classroom, thrilled to no longer consider herself a "dummy or a retard" in a special remedial class. Concurrent with the marked academic strides, her improved self-esteem also could be seen in her improved peer relationships, and her responsible management of some jobs. These improvements came slowly but surely, as she articulated her pleasure at just being with the therapist and living in the foster home. She could describe feeling good in the presence of the foster mother and/or the therapist, even "when I draw and we don't talk much." Karen referred to her four mothers: two "good" ones—the foster mother and therapy mother; and two "bad" ones—the natural mother and stepmother.

Karen's foster parents were committed to keeping her with them permanently, and viewed their four years with this child as most taxing but gratifying. They were empathic and consistent parent surrogates, psychologically sophisticated, and never overwhelmed or ready to give up. Their intuition guided them effectively, though often there was a need to confer and blow off steam (e.g., over Karen's prior impulsivity, temper, stealing bouts for several months, power struggles, and short frustration tolerance). Because of her vast improvements in these and the aforementioned areas, they were increasingly confident and comfortable, and had a decreasing need for contacts with the agency and/or the therapist.

As this case was concluded via a planned termination, Karen felt and had been told that her foster home was a permanent one. She did not want to be adopted, as she did not want "never again to be able to see her natural father," but she was very realistic in her surrender of her prior unrealistic expectations and idealized view of him. She realized she could not rely on him for any simple continuity, regularity, or predictability in contacts, and now could frankly describe the joylessness, boredom, etc., during brief visits in his home. She, her foster parents, and the worker recognized her father's relief at her permanent placement and the progress she had made. Karen is an excellent example of a child for whom foster care placement was the optimal plan; her long-term placement might best be described as "foster care with tenure," which provided the child and the foster parents with the continuity generally associated with adoption.

Conclusion

The success in Karen's development seemed due to her good constitutional endowment, the oustanding foster parents and the continuity of four years of excellent care in their home, the assurance of permanence and continuity of her relationship with her "psychological parents" (Goldstein et al., 1973), and the consistency and commitment of the agency worker and the therapist. Upon intake to the foster home department, the agency worker immediately recognized the effects of Karen's early years, and the unreality of her eventual return to her natural father. He ascertained her lack of object constancy and her need for stable parental surrogates. He wisely chose to maintain his own continuity of contact and to find a stable, caring foster home that could tolerate this child's acting out and sustain the placement. His match of this child and this foster home is based on his accurate initial assessment and the availability of such unusual foster parents. After her traumatic early years and seven foster homes, Karen finally received the best and most enlightened of child welfare services. The foster parents, the worker, and the therapist worked well and closely together on Karen's behalf.

Karen needed permanence; her caring, committed foster home milieu alone could not have sustained this placement. Like so many children in foster care, she also needed individualized treatment to enable her to utilize, rather than sabotage, this home. This combination of services is not innovative or unique; its success has been amply demonstrated. Changes in the laws, policies, and funding of foster care are needed to facilitate the provision of such combined services, which can offer many children in foster care a home and a stable family where they feel wanted.

CHAPTER 12

Therapeutic Work with Parents

The process of referral sets the tenor and tone of the ongoing work with the referred child's parents. Kessler (1966) believes that an effective referral should communicate genuine concern for the child's welfare, rather than portray the child as a disruptive nuisance. It should emphasize the child's and parents' inner feelings, pain, and confusion and involve the parents in preliminary work that deals with their initial resistances and objections. The latter frequently are related to fear of stigma or handicap, concern about confidentiality, parental guilt, etc. The preparation of the child and the various objectives and steps in the process of assessment have been detailed elsewhere.[1]

During the assessment or at the beginning of treatment, it must be established that parents and therapist have the same psychological conception of the problem. A beginning alliance between therapist and parents evolves out of assessment activities such as history taking; educational explanations of behavior, normality, symptoms, and defenses; and provision of preliminary advice and recommendations regarding methods of discipline, age-appropriate behavior, recreational activities, etc. All of this is easier said than done. Kessler (1966) enu-

[1]See Chapters 3–5.

merates some frequently encountered causes of parental resistance: jealousy and rivalry with the therapist, displacement of conflict with the spouse onto the therapist, child and parent sharing the same constellation of defenses or symptoms, the need to fail per masochistic character traits, and/or anxiety about the results due to fear of the unknown. Some parents present an ongoing transference conflict, expressed as resentment of authority, professionals, and experts. Some clinicians advocate working through these resistances before beginning to see the child. Too often these resistances are ignored and the treatment begins only to conclude prematurely.

There have been many perspectives on how and why one works with the parents. Hamilton (1947) stressed the necessity of clarity about the dynamics of family life. She noted that the objective in work with parents is to help them see the connection between their own problems and those of their child and thereby to enlist them in the search to remove obstacles from the child's path. Chethik (1976), with a similar view, describes helping parents to understand and gain some perspective on what they are reliving through the child. This approach does not entail referring the parent for direct personal psychotherapy; rather, the child's therapist commonly works through these temporary impasses.

Chethik (1976) notes that we lack an extensive body of literature on work with parents. The explanation he offers is that parent work historically has been considered low-status or second-class psychotherapy—traditionally handled by the social work staff of child guidance clinics—while the "glamorous" work was the psychiatrist's direct work with the child. This author concurs with Chethik on the error of this pejorative aura and tradition, in that work with the parents is the most taxing, requiring great skill and sensitivity. Further, it often constitutes the success or failure of child therapy cases.

This rigid historical division of labor in child guidance clinics seems to have been mirrored by equally rigid approaches to parents. For example, the psychologist would test the child, the psychiatrist would treat the child, and the social worker would share recommendations with, and give direction to, the parents. Parents were expected to transport the child, pay the fees, and modify the environment as directed. Then the child guidance movement did another pendulum swing, and all parents were referred for personal therapy and designated as patients. This approach underwent modification as we came to recognize that we cannot assume that treatment of the parents' problems is essential to the therapy of the child, because their treatment in no way ensures their ability to support their child's treatment. The idea that parents must be problem-free to work effectively with their child has yielded to the reality that many parents cannot work effectively even with therapy while some disturbed parents can be extremely help-ful despite their own problems or refusal to seek personal treatment.

Lane (1980) notes problems in establishing a "good enough" (Win-nicott's term) working relationship with parents, the people most re-sponsible for the child's well being.

> Sometimes the potential for establishing this relationship is sabotaged in its inception by the therapist and/or agency foisting on the parents an often impossible demand: that they be in treatment in their own right if they want a therapist to work with their child. I am not referring here to the offer or suggestion of child guidance assistance for parents in dealing with specific situations. Nor do I refer to instances in which parental ambivalence or denial of their child's need for treatment must be worked through before it can proceed. More difficult are those times when the clinician perceives aspects of the parent's personality which are judged deleterious to the child's psychological development but about which the parents themselves are not uncomfortable" [Lane, 1980, pp. 122–123].

Some parents desire and support growth and change in their child only as long as this process does not demand more of them than they are willing to give. Lane believes that respect for such parents' need to remain relatively uninvolved is the basis of a cooperative working rela-tionship without which therapy cannot proceed.

Anthony and McGinnis (1978) also emphasize the importance of respect in counseling very disturbed parents, noting that borderline and psychotic individuals often feel unworthy and have low self-es-teem. They suggest that such counseling has to be a "human," rather than an institutionalized, contact. The clinician must be available al-most on demand, offering "consistency, reliability, concern, and deep involvement in the welfare of the family and its everyday problems. The degree of investment necessary to maintain the contact over time varies with the adaptive and supportive capacities inherent in the fami-ly" (Anthony and McGinnis, 1978, p. 333). These authors also empha-size flexibility, living with the unexpected, patience, and a gradual nonconfrontational approach. Disturbed parents often relate to the pre-sent as if it were the past, thereby resisting a here-and-now real, ra-tional, and supportive approach. Thus, the clinician must be sensitive to tendencies of regression or withdrawal. The weak ego boundaries and primitive defenses of the disturbed parent cause symbiotic merger and, frequently, an overwhelming need to be taken care of completely. Despite the vicissitudes in work with very disturbed parents (i.e., their frequent trivial preoccupations, obsessive questions, recriminations, erratic handling of appointments, prolonged phone calls, and 24-hour demands for help at all hours of the day and night), the work of a resiliant, patient, and skilled clinician can be most productive. Resi-dential placement, realistically difficult to obtain, should be the intervention of last resort, after all else has failed. Anthony and McGinnis caution that "a sharp break with the sick parent would leave a residue of unfinished business" (1978, p. 340).

Considerable controversy remains regarding the parent-child therapist relationship. This controversy evolved out of the questions related to the child analyst-parent relationship. Some child analysts advocate seeing the parents as rarely as possible (Weiss, 1964). The reasoning behind this point of view is that the analyst-parent contact obstructs development of the therapeutic alliance. Children may feel that the treatment is really for their parents. They may worry about the analyst revealing their secrets, and/or their fusion of analyst and parent may be reinforced. Finally, parents may lead the analyst astray by distorting facts about children's history or current situation (Glenn et al., 1978). This perspective mirrors the parameters of adult analysis and suggests independent work with the child, without parent contact; this approach is applied to the child endowed with considerable intelligence, ego strength, and a tranquil home milieu.

Despite child analysts' relative agreement on which children are suitable analytic candidates,[2] considerable disagreement remains about frequency of meeting of analyst and parents. Glenn et al. (1978) believe that the therapeutic alliance is enhanced when the child learns that parents and analyst are working together on the child's behalf. The child should know that meetings with the parents are held to provide additional history and information. The one-way policy of confidentiality is explicated: that is, children should know that the content of their sessions will not be revealed but that they are entitled to know what the parents discuss. If parents confuse their child too much, the analyst can diminish contact with them. While seeing parents may produce some interference with the development of the transference, many researchers believe that intense and prolonged transferences are rare in child analysis due to the immaturity of the child's cognitive development and the child's involvement with parents (Glenn et al., 1978). Anna Freud (1922–1970) notes that the child lives with parents who provide care and many needed gratifications.

These authors contrast child analysis with adult analysis: the adult lies on a couch, not viewing the analyst, and received a minimum of stimulation or gratification, while the child patient is up and about, engaging in play with the child analyst and involved in a highly gratifying interaction. Kay (1978) suggests that gratifications are inherent in the child analytic situation. As children advance from primary- to secondary-process functioning, they feel a sense of thrilling triumph. Together, the child and analyst explore and solve hidden, frightening

[2]See Chapter 9.

riddles; the analyst helps the child to articulate what has been chaotic and wordless. The child comes to trust the analyst as a result of this shared searching, receiving pleasure and gratification from the relationship with the analyst. The personal rapport between child and analyst is an important component of the child's gratification.

Those who advocate analyst-parent contact underscore the need for advice and explanations to parents during the course of a child's analysis to help them understand that the goal is insight and restructuring rather than symptom reduction alone. Sours (1978b) believes that in the treatment of children of midlatency age or younger, parents should be seen regularly so as to increase their understanding of the child's behavior and pathology. He feels this is the only way parents can change their own attitudes toward and interactions with the child. "Direct advice to parents is seldom effective, particularly early in treatment, unless the parents' attitude towards the child is empathic and their understanding is sufficient to enable them to interact meaningfully with the child. . . . Direct prohibitions to the parent, specifically in matters of sexuality and seduction, is not effective and may be disruptive to therapy" (Sours, 1978b, p. 624). Not all child psychotherapists concur with Sours's universal advocacy of parent-therapist contact. The therapist-parent controversy parallels the analyst-parent controversy noted above, but is less of an issue in child psychotherapy than in child analysis. A brief example of an approach involving ongoing parent-therapist contact follows.

Case Example: Treatment Involving Parent-Therapist Contact

A series of disrupted consultations and treatment attempts of Sally (see Sally, Borderline Child, Chapter 8) was begun when this child was six and first manifested separation problems. Initially an agency worker urged the mother to handle Sally very firmly in regard to school attendance, and immediately provide separate sleeping arrangements for Sally and her brother, who was three years her senior. Neither recommendation, offered prematurely, could be heeded, and agency contact was abruptly terminated. At age ten, Sally's separation problems became full blown, and a school phobia interfered with any school attendance, till mother accompanied Sally to school and spent the full day at the school, volunteering in the office, thereby sustaining the child in the classroom via her presence in the building. Over a two-year span there were a series of therapeutic contacts with three child psychiatrists and one social agency, all of which were terminated after prolonged attendance, due to mother's revulsion at the idea of hypnosis, physical force, or nonadvice.

A fourth clinician was sought who offered weekly sessions with Sally as well as mother, and bimonthly sessions with father and this therapeutic contact proved successful, alleviating Sally's symptoms in a surprisingly short time. These sessions provided the following new information. In addition to the school phobia, Sally had a myriad of other phobias; her phobia of elevators caused social isolation and considerable disadvantage unless mother would accompany Sally up and down the elevator of their apartment. Sally once had been stuck in an elevator and claimed this experience was the precipitant of her fear of elevators. She had seen an account on television regarding rescue measures for choking—when food became lodged in the windpipe—and developed ever-expanding food phobias. The child's suggestibility caused her to fear leaves on the street possibly getting into her throat and causing strangulation; choking on popcorn at the movies; etc. Thus at the time Sally began to work with her therapist, she was most self-restricting in her diet, choosing only soft foods like eggs, cheese, and ice cream. Of superior intelligence, Sally had always excelled at school, but interference was reflected in her recently diminished reading scores on schoolwide testing day, when she complained of acute anxiety, lack of patience with the questions, and problems in concentration.

In addition to Sally's extensive symptomatology, parents acknowledged their chronic marital strife over a twenty-year period, which had exacerbated in the last year to the point of contemplation of divorce—a solution both parents are averse to. The parents recognized the futility of their bickering, endless recriminations over minutia, and set about to manage their time together with greater patience and self-control.

For some months prior to working with the fourth therapist, with cooperation from school personnel, mother had been deceiving Sally about her all-day presence at the school. She would depart surreptitiously and go home to do housework, etc., and return and accompany Sally home as if she had been at school all day. Gradually, with support from the therapist, mother could be firmer and more matter of fact, and openly state her resentment over being at the school all day. Sally began to attend independently, and, to both their surprise, could maintain herself all day in class. This precocious child had hidden her problems from her friends, felt shame and discomfort, and previously had consoled herself that "lots of people, even adults, feel scared away from their mothers." She began to experiment with eating new foods and joyously shared in her weekly sessions the new accomplishments of eating foods she had previously avoided, and her growing ability to move away from mother (e.g., going to the park with father and brother on Sundays to play tennis).

The work with Sally's parents involved much listening; the emphasis was less on advice than on education and support for their highest level of ego functioning as it related to their sound, perceptive views of Sally's behavior and its latent meaning. Ongoing work with child and parents obviously was needed and provided despite recent symptom reduction.

Parent Education

While work with parents is aimed at ego support, clarification, and education, it is generally offered in the context of several differing models. Parent education is offered via mass media, group discussions, parent education groups, and individual guidance sessions.

Some parents find the educational experience enriched through group support and sharing with peers. Parent groups affirm the importance of child rearing and the crucial nature of the parental role. Factual information is transmitted, helping parents to know what to expect and to learn some basics about child development. Group members may offer recommendations on empathic effective handling, interpretations about the latent meaning of children's behavior, and observations of the variations on "typical" development, or the symptomatic behavior that is reactive to normal stress (e.g., a family's move, birth of a sib). Barnes (1965) lists the following common foci of parent education groups: feeding problems, sleep disturbances, toilet training difficulties, discipline, and the handling of jealousy and aggression. She notes that clinicians have the most influence with parents when they work continuously with a study group over a long period of time or counsel parents together regularly in settings such as a dynamically oriented well-baby clinic, a child development center, or a social agency concerned with the well-being of children. Barnes refers to Anna Freud's paper, "Work with Parents," in which she takes a stand against the widespread assumption that no mother will change her handling of her child without something changing in her personality. Mothering is viewed as more than a result of "instincts"; it is also influenced by tradition and public opinion, both of which are open to change. Clinicians engaged in parent education must have a sound knowledge of child development and childhood behavior, and be sensitive to the pathological as well as the normal. They must be able to distinguish whether a behavior is reactive, brief, and not serious (e.g., brief regression in toilet training after birth of a sib); a normal transitional stage in development (the normal sleep disturbance of the 2-year-old beginning to negotiate separation-individuation); or the result of an internalized developmental conflict between defense and drive.

Treatment of the Child via the Mother

Recognition of the varied etiology of children's fears and symptoms has led some clinicians to consider treatment of the very young child via the mother, following Anna Freud's guidelines, when the mother is intelligent, willing, and fairly normal herself, and where the child's problems are not too severe. Furman (1957) notes that this approach keeps the focus centered on the child and aids the mother in understanding her child emotionally; and she helps the child by the use of direct and reflective advice. Because of the mother's uniquely close bond with her child, with help, she can become capable of perceiving many of the child's thoughts, defenses, and unconscious feelings. Furman emphasizes that this approach is only profitable when the mother's deep unconscious conflicts are not mobilized. The clinician suggests interpretations that the mother can offer the child. This procedure is predicated on the clinician's possession of extensive historical and auxiliary information.

Chethik (1980) notes that this mode of intervention capitalizes on the close unconscious communication between the mother and the young child, based on an unconscious bond and identifications. Once the mother is free to observe her child, the intimate symbolic understanding of the child is particularly useful in the treatment process. The mother often understands the developing conflicts before the therapist can infer them, and the clinician affirms and corroborates the mother's intuitive impressions. Thus, with help, mother can intervene at home in the "life space" of daily family interactions.

The Mother in the Consulting Room

Another mode of work with parents of very young children involves the mother in the sessions. Like treatment via the mother, this model is predicated on the reality that the mother is the most important person in the young child's life, and her presence in sessions provides a good opportunity to study the emotional interplay between parent and child, and to see how it may contribute to the child's disturbance. Schwartz (1950) suggests that this shared experience enables the mother to cope better with the troubled child at home. For the child, the presence of the mother acts as a reassurance of her approval of the therapist and the ongoing work. After some time, as the child develops a positive relationshp with the clinician, mother and child can be separated, each having separate sessions. Schwartz emphasizes a synthesis of therapy and education with the far-reaching aim of having the mother ultimately identify with the therapist in efforts to understand the child. Mothers and children with strong symbiotic ties may find this approach palatable and less threatening than conventional approaches involving separate sessions and/or separate therapists. The mother of the young child is frequently grateful for being allowed to participate in her child's treatment and relieved that the child has not been taken from her. She forms a very positive relationshp with the analyst which is capable of weathering later restrictions or frustrations imposed by the child's needs (Schwartz, 1950).

This approach also may be appropriate with an older child who has experienced heightened anxiety followed by regression. The precipitant may be a change in the home situation, or an emergence of separation difficulties due to intrapsychic conflict or severe trauma (e.g., illness or death of a parent). When threatened with removal from the home, some children cannot sustain themselves in sessions without the presence of the parent. "Understanding of the child, his age, his developmental stage and the immediate precipitating cause of the behavior determines whether or not it is appropriate for . . . discussion to take place in the presence of the child's parents" (Glenn et al., 1978, p. 421).

One caution raised regarding treatment of the child via or with the mother is that after treatment, parents may continue to interpret to the child, with pathological consequences (Olch, 1971). "The child may react with intense hostility to the parents' comments and institute excessive and maladaptive defenses, or . . . believe the interpreting parent is urging him to carry out acts which are usually forbidden. Further, the child may think the parent can read his mind and is a powerful omniscient being. This can interfere with normal separation-individuation" (Sours, 1978b, p. 624). Barnes (1965) cautions that some mothers mistakenly give in to the unreasonable inner world of the child, seeking to make everything pleasurable for the child. Barnes calls such efforts a misapplication of analytic theory, based on the fallacious notion that problems will diminish by avoiding all frustrations and imposing few limitations.

Parent Guidance

Parent guidance is counseling that helps the parent to help the child. Weisberger (1980) notes that although it has features in common with both psychotherapy and casework, it has its own special approach, in that it helps the parent while remaining focused on the child. Its goals are to mobilize the familial environment to support better parental functioning, thereby relieving unrealistic and unhealthy pressures on the child; to offer information about growth and development; and to give practical help with management. In essence, this approach offers parents advice, support, counsel, clarification, information, and supportive psychotherapy to help the child indirectly. Arnold (1978) suggests that current approaches have progressed beyond the simplistic blaming of parents for children's problems. He reminds us to keep the following factors in mind when confronted by parents' bewildering and/or resistive behavior.

1. The parents have been attempting to improve the child's situation for longer than the professional has.
2. There is usually some reason for the parents' doing whatever they did, no matter how ill-advised it may at first appear.

3. Any successful intervention will require the parents' cooperation.
4. Before the parents can cooperate, they need to understand and accept what is recommended.
5. It is unlikely that any recommendations will be understandable or acceptable if the professional making them does not first understand empathically "where the parent is coming from."
6. Failure to reconnoiter the parents' predicament from the parents viewpoint will impair the professional's ability to tailor interventions to the specific needs of that family and will expose him as an impractical dispenser of canned advice [Arnold, 1978, p. 4].

Arnold (1978) defines parent guidance as one intervention on a continuum of interventions with parents. Obviously, the choice of intervention is based on what practice wisdom indicates is necessary, given the child's presented problem, the parents' personality and strengths, and the obstacles to effective parenting. The inadequacy of an intervention quickly becomes apparent and the professional can escalate to the next level of complexity. If the problem seems deeper than can be handled via supportive parent guidance, a referral for personal psychotherapy can be offered.[3]

Treatment of the Parent-Child Relationship

Although Chethik (1976) suggests that treatment of the parent-child relationship is psychotherapy within the guidance context, it clearly falls somewhere between advice/guidance and total treatment. Chethik remarks that surprisingly little has been written about such "in-between" areas of work. He notes that Levy (1937), Cutter and Hallowitz (1962), Slavson (1952), and Fraiberg (1954) are among the few who have dealt with the subject. Chethik describes his approach to treatment of the parent-child relationship as a process of "ego clarification and limited insight therapy where unconscious or preconscious meanings that a child represents to parents can become evident. Despite the fact that interpretations and uncovering interventions are used, this process contains important boundaries which limit the transference and controls transference regressions" (1976, p. 1). Parents suitable for this mode of intervention do not need referral for personal therapy. The scope is much more restricted than that of open-ended therapy. For example, parents may be helped to see that in their rela-

[3]Eugene L. Arnold's anthology, *Helping Parents Help Their Children* (1978), New York: Brunner/Mazel, includes sections aimed at helping parents cope with specific problems of children—e.g., mental retardation, physical handicaps, autism, and delinquency—as well as chapters about parents who have specific problems—e.g., abusive parents, adoptive and foster parents, separated and divorced parents, teenage mothers, and stepparents.

tionship with their child, they are reliving problems they have had with their own parents or siblings. Interpretations are related to the effect of such previous conflicts on the relationship with the child. In order to use this limited insight therapy, parents must possess sufficient ego intactness and psychological mindedness to desire modification of difficulties, and sufficient affective self-observation to achieve this change.

We have heard much about the dangers of accepting the child as the identified patient, in that parents often mask their family, marital, or individual problems by making a child the repository of all the problems and pathology. Chethik's approach deals with the pathological interplay within the family while also responding to parents' wish for a child-focused therapy to enable them to become more effective parents.

> This technique is explicitly a form of sector psychotherapy with delineated goals that particularly meets the developmental needs of children. We are aware that in order to minimize pathology we need to intervene early, as close to the affected developmental phase as possible. Often even effective individual personal psychotherapy of a parent comes too late, because though they might make significant gains over the years, the child is beyond many of the significant developmental stages. Treatment of the parent-child relationship as a technique attempts to immediately focus on the interlocking struggle between parent and child so that fixations will not become entrenched and reinforced [Chethik, 1976, p. 463].

Division of a Case: Separate Therapists for Parents and the Child

The question of whether to use separate therapists for parents and child rests on the age of the child, the degree of parental involvement, timing, and other factors. Hamilton (1947) suggests that indications for division of a case are strengthened whenever there is overt hostility and aggression between parent and child. Some children are too insecure about their parents' attitudes toward them to form a relationship with the clinician who sees the parents. The strongly ambivalent attitude of adolescents toward adults in general, and especially toward all parental figures, usually makes it desirable for them to have their own therapist. A practical consideration is that a very punishing, rejecting, or abusing parent inevitably will arouse negative counterreactions in the therapist who sees the child suffering. Since the abusing and punishing parent also needs support and an alliance, it is best that this parent have his or her own therapist. When parents have a great need for extensive contact, the child's sense of an exclusive and private relationship with the therapist may be threatened; in such cases, a case may be divided.

The frequency of collaborative conferring between the child's therapist and the parents' therapist is an individual matter that must be
determined on the basis of the child's chronological and emotional age
and stage of development, and the precipitants of the symptomatology.
As noted earlier, confidentiality becomes more problematic as the frequency of such conferring increases. Obviously, the child's private concerns, fantasy material, unacceptable wishes, etc., are not shared with
the parents' therapist or counselor, though the overall course of therapy
and the child's age-appropriate and special needs should be shared.
Similar collaborative sharing is operative in collaborative work with
schools, other agencies, and multidiscipline settings such as hospitals,
group homes, residential centers, and day treatment programs.[4]

The need for ongoing work with both parents must be emphasized.
Traditionally, work with parents at child guidance clinics has been
limited to work with mothers. The outreach to fathers, including clinicians' attitudes and the frequent necessity for evening appointments,
still is far from commonplace in child treatment agencies. Conviction
falters profoundly in the case of children of divorced parents, and the
numbers of such children in therapy are rapidly increasing. Leader
(1973) notes that the conviction of the worker about contact with divorced fathers out of the home is often the decisive factor in successful
parent contacts. The treatment of choice may be family therapy, or
separate treatment of parents and child. It is essential for clinicians to
recognize that "despite any formal divorce status, there is usually considerable interaction going on between father and the rest of the family—strong bonds, ambivalent feelings, severe reactions, problem behavior, and actual contact with the children in their own home"
(Leader, 1973, p. 14). Effective child rearing requires a high degree of
family solidarity and cooperation, which is difficult enough to achieve
even in intact homes. To prevent divorce from becoming abandonment
of children, the therapeutic interventions discussed above must be
used with both fathers and mothers.

Consultation with Parents Resistive to Referral

In considering the nature of therapeutic work with parents, something
must be said about the "unreachable" parents, those who refuse referral by the child's pediatrician, school psychologist or social worker,
etc. Earlier, mention was made of respecting and honoring the parents'
decision to decline referral for direct treatment for themselves and/or
their children. However, even the aborted referral may bear fruit at a
later date. The tone of this preliminary contact is most important, as it

---

[4]See Chapters 10 (group therapy), 11 (residental treatment), and 16.

sets the stage for later contacts with parents who were initially fearful or preoccupied. The following examples present resistive parents.

Case Examples: Parents Resistive to Referral

The mother of 8-year-old Jim had protracted evaluation contact with the school social worker and formed a therapeutic alliance. She used her time well in the course of the diagnostic study and could share the acute family tensions due to the financial crisis and the pending divorce. Between working full-time and caring for four children, she was under much pressure. Her wealthy and aristocratic family had disapproved of her marriage and refused emotional or financial support during this crisis. She responded to this and to her husband's refusal to move out by hysterical outbursts and by sleeping in Jim's bed with him. Her overstimulation of her youngest child was contrasted with her neglect of him after school. She left him alone and unsupervised until she returned from work. Goals with her were modest, but significant and successful. The school social worker referred her for long-term evening supportive therapy at an adjacent family agency and helped her arrange for after-school child care until mother finished work. Further, during the extended evaluation contact, the worker helped mother to make other sleeping arrangements. Mother had no emotional energy to arrange therapy for Jim, and could not take any time off from work to transport him. The agency treating her did not offer evening sessions for children.

The parents of Bob, age eight, had been divorced a short time. His mother worked part-time and struggled to manage housing, health difficulties, work, and two aggressive, rebellious children. She was genuinely concerned about Bob's learning disorders, but could not refrain from nagging and overindulging him and was unable to set any limits or maintain order in the home. The children were up until 11:00 and 12:00 p.m. every night, watching TV and bickering. Mother was in a stupor a great deal of the time due to excessive drugs used for her colitis condition. She weighed ninety pounds and was on special soft diets which she often did not follow. She previously had had some questionable psychotherapy in another city and initially was resistive to referral. Finally she did accept referral to an analyst, whose special interest was colitis patients and who accepted her at a very low fee. She had initial difficulty in establishing an alliance with him, and tried to continue to see the school social worker, whom she viewed as "cheaper and closer." Ultimately, she accepted the analyst, as she understood that he was better able to treat her symptoms than was the social worker. Bob was not seen in treatment, but he improved as mother made productive use of her own therapy.

The young, uneducated parents of 8-year-old Phil were overwhelmed by their five children, all of whom were having problems. They were very threatened by the principal's referring them to the psychologist. They could not formally come into the office, but chatted informally in the hall. They stated their initial preference to discuss things with their priest, which they did. This seemed to calm them and eventually, sure of confidentiality, they did request a single appointment. Their priest had referred them to Catholic Charities and they wanted aid in securing teacher reports. They kept the psychologist posted and in an informal way apprised him of the various steps they were taking. Several of their children previously had been expelled from a parochial school, and they had been reprimanded and often chastised by various teachers. Thus, their fears and apprehensions in this new school were understandable and had to be respected.

John, age eight, showed low academic achievement; he did not work anywhere near his potential and seemed preoccupied, restless, and passive, with recurring bouts of hyperactivity. His social adjustment was superficial, with a paucity of relationships. However, he did not act out aggressively and his parents appeared unconcerned and insensitive to him. They were well to do and had had John, who was unplanned, late in life. They made it clear that they thought any concern about John was unnecessary, "and if he needs a jolt to improve his grades, we'll send him to military school." They put in an appearance during the evaluation, but could not be engaged by school pupil personnel staff. Father traveled a lot and mother was preoccupied, attempting to lead the pleasant leisured life of a well-to-do matron who had already raised her family. Their lack of awareness of the boy's loneliness and ongoing distress seemed to indicate that they would not be engaged until forced to do so by some crisis, such as an adolescent upheaval.

The above examples suggest that some parents need to handle things completely independently, others make environmental changes without therapy, some achieve modest preliminary goals without treatment of the child, while others need to avoid the reality of their child's problems as long as possible. Frustrating though it may be for the clinician, parents' refusal of referral often must be accepted and honored. The ethic of client (and parent) self-determination does not hold, however, for cases where child abuse is suspected. The most contemporary legislation insists on the reporting of such cases by clinicians, teachers, school nurses, and all those directly or indirectly working with, or on behalf of, children. Chronic problems of resistive parents and child abuse are most frequently found in correlation with parental drug and alcohol abuse.

PART V

The Treatment Process

CHAPTER 13

The Treatment Relationship

The Therapeutic Alliance

The therapeutic alliance is seen as resulting from the "child's conscious or unconscious wish to cooperate and his readiness to accept the therapist's aid in overcoming internal difficulties and resistances" (Sandler et al., 1980, p. 45). The alliance does not arise solely out of the child's wish for pleasure in the treatment situation, but "involves an acceptance of the need to deal with internal problems . . . in the face of internal resistance or external resistance, as from the family" (p. 45). The child-therapist relationship includes nontransference elements, some of which belong to the therapeutic alliance. It is difficult but necessary to differentiate the therapeutic alliance from the transference.

Some authors question the validity of the distinction between the transference and the therapeutic alliance. Arlow and Brenner (Arlow and Brenner, 1966; Brenner, 1980) believe that it is neither correct nor useful to distinguish between the transference and the therapeutic or working alliance. Based upon examination of clinical evidence, Brenner (1980) concludes that the concept of the therapeutic alliance is not justifiable; it is simply one aspect of the transference. The terms "working alliance" and "therapeutic alliance" are borrowed from the field of adult psychoanalysis. Formulation about the therapeutic alliance dates from Zetzel's 1956 paper on transference. Greenson's later paper (1965) suggested the term "working alliance." Curtis (1977) notes that in the last twenty-five years, analysts have expanded their sphere of interest beyond the patient's intrapsychic life to embrace all aspects of the therapeutic relationship.

Much has been written about ego alliance, the therapeutic split in the ego (into the observing and experiencing egos), and the mature, rational part of the patient that wishes to change and alleviate suffering. Zetzel (1956) stated that mature ego functions (per Hartmann's outline of the development of mature ego qualities, or the capacity for object relations, out of primary and secondary autonomous ego sources and processes) are the basis for the therapeutic alliance. Collaborative efforts of patient and therapist emanate from the wish for cure and relief, the hope for more efficient and gratifying functioning, intellectual interests in self-understanding, and the wish for love, success, and approval. "The consistent and most reliable source of the cooperation between patient and analyst lies in the mature, realistic aspects of the analytic relationship which depend on the ego functions of reality testing, capacity for self-object differentiation, tolerance for tension and delay of gratification" (Dickes, 1977, p. 181). Dickes cautions regarding the danger of seeing the therapeutic alliance as an end in itself—that is, as a new and corrective object relationship—rather than a means to the end of enhancing the treatment process and overcoming resistances.

The child patient is motivated in the alliance by cognitive, rational appraisal of the painful situation, as well as by aspects of positive transference. "The analyst is the representative of the important adult whose lead is followed, who is trusted, and believed as a helping adult, and, as a consequence with whom the child is willing to work" (Sandler et al., 1980, p. 46). The child may experience the therapist as a new object who provides new understanding that arouses positive feelings. Children often enter treatment with fantasies and expectations, as well as distortions and false pretenses, which may enhance or impede the development of a treatment alliance. Children who present overriding wishes for care in the present cannot enter into a treatment alliance when their basic needs currently are unmet.

Sandler et al. and Anna Freud (1980, in Sandler et al., 1980) state that the treatment alliance contains elements that are neither libidinal nor aggressive, but are linked to the superego and the ego. Apart from the child liking and identifying with the therapist, and enjoying their shared activities, the alliance is based on the ego's accurate appraisal of a need for understanding, feelings of trust, satisfaction from the work, and gratification in being understood. "The superego causes the child to feel that he ought to come to therapy even if he does not wish to or is not in the mood" (Sandler et al., 1980, p. 49). The commitment to keep the appointment, even when resistance is present, plays a major role in the treatment alliance. The therapist must monitor counterreactions and countertransference to missed sessions, and not make what Keith (1968) describes as an "unholy alliance" with the superego by scolding and chastising the child.

Children will only look to therapy for relief if they have the capacity for self-observation and some awareness that there is an internal problem. Not all child patients have enough inner ego structure for self-awareness and self-observation.

Most psychotic and borderline children are able to form a symbiotic relationship with the therapist. This merging of ego boundaries means that for a long period of therapy the patient will use the therapist's ego as his own observing and synthesizing ego. . . . This merging of the therapist's and child's ego can be called a "pseudoalliance" since it does not represent a true therapeutic splitting (self observing and self experiencing) of the child's own ego. The therapist consistently and repetitively interjects his own secondary process and rational behavior into the treatment situation [Keith, 1968, p. 38].

Pseudoalliances also occur with less structured adolescent and parent populations.

Often children do not experience their symptoms as painful. When their maladaptive behaviors are ego-syntonic rather than ego-dystonic, they do not experience anguish or anxiety. Rather, the adults (e.g., parents and teachers) in the child's life suffer and force the child to enter therapy. In such cases, the parents are the first to make the treatment alliance. "When a positive alliance exists between the analyst and the parents they tend to bring the child to treatment when he will not or cannot overcome his resistance on his own, that is, when the treatment alliance between the child and the therapist is weak or absent" (Sandler et al., 1980, p. 51). In such situations, parents must have sufficient determination and fortitude to bring pressure to bear on the child.

Major treatment obstacles arise when there is either no alliance, or a negative alliance, with the parents. Some parents have unconscious needs to sabotage their child's therapy and/or to collude with the child's resistance; they may be competitive and jealous of their child's emerging relationship with the therapist. Parents may need considerable contact with the child's therapist or their own therapist to overcome their fears and resistances. Frequently, active encouragement of the alliance is crucial. The therapist must try to make the treatment situation attractive to the child; this helps to counterbalance resistance. Sandler et al. (1980) stress that therapy should not be all hard work for the patient.

Concluding Remarks

There are two definitions of the treatment alliance. The first refers to the composite of factors that keep patients in treatment during phases of resistance and hostile transference. The second, narrower definition is based on patients' awareness of their illness and need to do something about it, which are linked with their capacity to face painful internal conflict" (Sandler et al., 1980). Id elements (Keith, 1968; Sandler et al., 1980) are wishes for gratification of instinctual elements such as love or object hunger, and can be the basis for alliance and continuation in treatment even during phases of resistance. At other times, ego and superego elements of the alliance predominate.

Some children cannot enter therapy and make an alliance because of an overpowering wish to keep their private life private. They feel that no one has the right to intrude (Anna Freud, in Sandler et al., 1980). Even without an alliance, some children improve as a result of treatment, gaining symptom relief and reentering the path of normal development. Sandler et al. (1980) caution that such improvement may be "treatment compliance" rather than "treatment alliance." They suggest a number of factors to attempt to explain a basic *unwillingness* to enter therapy, which they distinguish from resistance to treatment. These factors include

> the existence of family secrets, loyalty conflicts, and deep-seated disturbances in object relationships. . . . [and may] also express the unconscious ambivalence of one or both parents about the child's receiving treatment. This is particularly the case when there are family secrets, or when the disturbance in the child is so tied to a disturbance in one of the parents that an unconscious collusion between parent and child is threatened by the treatment [pp. 55–56].

Mistrust and a basic fear of rejection interfere with a treatment alliance. Lack of trust does not always originate in the earliest months of life. It may develop relatively late—i.e., at the phallic-Oedipal phase—in which case there are positive characteristics in the patient's object relations that suggest that a trusting relationship with the therapist eventually will develop. Some patients are unwilling to enter treatment and an alliance because of the slow progress and lack of quick gratification inherent in the undertaking. Then there is the puzzling situation of the child who continues in therapy without any apparent progress in the office, but whose outer life shows marked improvements. Sandler et al. conclude that the sheer presence of a therapist with specific personal characteristics may be of more therapeutic importance than is generally realized.

The Therapeutic Alliance—Case of Ellen

Ellen, age ten, a white Jewish child of superior intelligence with initially poor social and academic adjustment, was open in expressing her need to deal with her internal and interpersonal problems. Having been in therapy for one year, she consciously wished to be seen regularly in treatment and could note that she had come to count on her sessions. Thus, she showed concern that several appointments fell on national holidays and, given her school commitments, rescheduling posed problems. "I really think it's important that we find another time. I am happier and calmer when I see you. I understand my anger at my brother better and I don't want to face those scary nightmares again. Remember, I get scared and worried that he's hurt and I can't sleep . . . or I have those terrible dreams." Clearly, Ellen had developed the belief that treatment offered her relief. She indicated her capacity for self-observation and recognized that there was an internal problem (i.e., nightmares about her brother being killed or hurt, related to her anger and competitiveness with him). Closeness to the therapist was based on the therapist's understanding and helping her put into words troubling feelings and affects.

At times, Ellen had taken the responsibility of phoning to request a rescheduled time and/or to insure that her parents remembered their appointment time with her therapist. "It's very important that Mommy and Daddy see you soon. I know that you will make them see that I need time with them, too. There's so much illness with my grandparents—and David, 'cause he's only four gets all the attention. I may be older, but I'm not all grown up." This statement reflected Ellen's trust, hopefulness, and relief in having someone available to help her and positively influence her home milieu. Ellen's constant cooperation with the therapist related to her wish for, and relief at, being able to communicate her problems and anxieties. She could articulate her enjoyment at having exclusive attention and having someone to play with: "I love to play school, but since I have this problem making friends, my students are my dolls and stuffed toys. You're my first live pupil." Later in therapy, Ellen could relate her play with the therapist to her increasingly successful play and interchange with peers. She could articulate her feeling that she was learning how to play, be less bossy, and relax. She wrote the therapist while away at overnight summer camp, noting her better social adjustment. "I'm getting on better—I really have some friends. They don't mind that I'm chubby and not great at sports. We play lots of imaginative games and I'm not teased 'cause I'm not preppy or because I'm a bookworm. Since I'm less scared of the kids, I don't try to boss them."

In a similar vein, Ellen related her greatly enhanced academic achievement to her therapy.

> This year since I'm now more patient and sure of myself, nearly all my grades were A's. But even you couldn't help me with this year's Hebrew class. My teacher is a very old and grouchy man that none of us understand. You see, he survived the Holocaust—so they keep him at the school and can't fire him, 'cause he's had such a terrible life. That's only fair, I guess—but no one learns a thing from him—and since my father isn't a rabbi, this class is a bust. You and I can figure out a lot of things together, but this is impossible. I'm glad my life wasn't like my teacher's, but I feel bad to think that way—I mean, to be so glad to have it better than him. . . . Even though class is terrible and he's impatient, that's one teacher I'm never sassy to, and I'd never argue with. You wouldn't respect me for being bratty to such a sad old man who survived a concentration camp.

Ellen's superego was evident in the treatment alliance, as she presented an ethical stance as well as the clear desire for the therapist's approval. In addition to profoundly improved academic and social functioning, Ellen stopped sucking her thumb and lost 17 pounds.

Transference, the Real Relationship, and Countertransference

Although transference and countertransference are psychoanalytic phenomena that do not appear in pure form in psychotherapy, non-analyst therapists need to have a clear understanding of them. There are difficulties in defining these terms, as they often have been misused as catchall concepts that encompass everything experienced and expressed between patient and therapist. The multiplicity of meanings must be further refined to delineate features pertinent to child patients in contrast to adult patients.

Transference

In his discussions of transference, Freud (1912, 1915b, 1916–1917) stated repeatedly that all people transfer unconscious libidinal aspects of their primal object relationships to current object relationships. The term "transference," which is derived from adult analysis, refers to the views and relations the patient presents about significant childhood objects, expressed in the patient's current perceptions, thoughts, fantasies, feelings, attitudes, and behavior in regard to the analyst (Sandler et al., 1980). In the course of work with children, the relationship between child and analyst is "often a complicated mixture of elements of a real relationship, an extension into the analysis of current relationships, and a repetition or even a revival of the past" (Tyson, 1978, p. 213).

In 1966, at a panel considering problems of transference in child analysis, there was general agreement that transference neurosis cannot take place in children until there has been sufficient structural development to allow for internalized intersystemic conflicts. Tyson (1978) states that this does not occur until the superego is independent of parental influence, which is usually around the age of puberty. In contrast, Blos (1972) believes that the infantile neurosis only acquires delineation and structure as a central unconscious conflict in late adolescence, with the consolidation of the personality and the formation of adult neurosis. Tolpin (1970) restricts the definition of infantile neurosis to the repressed conflicts of the phallic-Oedipal phase of patients whose earlier development has been normal.

Anna Freud (1971) reminds us that not every child's psychopathology assumes the form of an infantile neurosis. In extreme cases, the infantile neurosis can create severe psychopathology. But it appears in milder form in the childhood of many individuals whose future adaption to life is very successful. Looked at from the developmental point of view, the achievement of the infantile neurosis represents a positive sign of substantial personality growth, "a progression from primitive to more sophisticated reaction patterns and, as such, the consequence and perhaps the price which has to be paid for higher human development" (Anna Freud, 1971, p. 89).

In contrast to the Freudian view of neurotic conflict between different agencies (i.e., id versus ego, ego versus superego, and ego versus external reality), the Kleinians believe that the fundamental conflict is between the life and death instinct. The Kleinians consider the Oedipus complex an integral part of the depressive position of infancy. Thus, the question of transference is "a taxing one. . . . The Kleinian view is that a transference neurosis (or psychosis) is, in all cases, there from the beginning, and is to be found in all child analysis. Yet there cannot be transference neurosis if the case is not a neurotic one. But since the Kleinian view of neurosis is so radically changed from the Freudian, such a point can scarcely be expected to carry any very great weight" (Yorke, 1971, p. 152). Yorke further notes the Kleinians' neglect of reality factors and their lack of attention to the formation of a treatment alliance.

Many "less than neurotic" children with developmental failures remain arrested at a pre-Oedipal level of development. These children are diagnosed as on the border of very severe pathology, such as psychosis or mental deficiency. Due to constitutional defects, early deprivations, lack of suitable objects, and wrong environmental handling, these children have inferior object relatedness, weak identifications, incomplete structuralization, permeable id-ego boundaries, and distorted, deformed, and immature egos (Anna Freud, 1971). This population of severely damaged children, commonly seen by social workers and psychologists, constitutes the caseloads of public agencies, child guidance clinics, and mental health facilities. These children lack the capacity to form genuine transference. Even the more intact children seen in analysis present only a short-lived, circumscribed transference neurosis.

Tolpin (1978) emphasizes that "for patients with structural deficits, genetic reconstructions and interpretations of conflict are ineffectual because these interpretations bypass and obscure the central pathology" (p. 181). Such patients have faulty self-esteem, lack a sense of direction, and manifest anxiety, depression, and a lack of firm values and ideals; they develop self-object transferences that must be distinguished from the classic definition and understanding of transference. Self-object transferences (i.e., merger and mirror transferences) are not the displacement phenomena of classic transference, but rather a use of the therapist to provide for the patient a missing part of the self.

SUBTYPES OF TRANSFERENCE

Transference as manifest by children may be divided into the following four subtypes:

1. *habitual modes of relating* in which the child reveals various aspects of his character in treatment as he would to any person;
2. transference of *current relationships* whereby in treatment the child's mode of relating is an extension of, or defensive displacement from, the relationship of primary objects;
3. transference which is predominantly that of *past experiences*, i.e., when past experiences, conflicts, defenses and wishes are revived in treatment, as a consequence of analytic work, and are displaced into the therapist in the manifest or latent preconscious content;
4. *transference neurosis*, meaning "the concentration of the child's conflicts, repressed infantile wishes, fantasies, etc., on the person of the therapist with the relative diminution of their manifestations elsewhere [Sandler et al., 1975, p. 427;].

EXTERNALIZATION IN THE TRANSFERENCE

Furman (1980) discusses various forms of externalization (i.e., attribution of any aspect of the self to the external world) in transference. She cites Anna Freud's remarks on the tendency of children to battle with their environment and to use the therapist to represent a part of their personality structure.

Furman reminds us that externalization and internalization of superego attitudes occur at the onset of latency. Children may view benign parents and teachers as harsh because of their attribution of the harsh voice of their own conscience to persons in their environment. This defense is similar to projection, which Sandler et al. (1975) define as "the attribution to another person of a wish or impulse of one's own toward that person, and felt to be directed back against himself" (p. 413). In externalization, the superego wards off inner conflict, and the superego function is relegated to a potential authority whom the child defies but also "invites" to control or punish the displayed misdeeds (Furman, 1980). Thereby children tie themselves to those onto whom they externalize and from whom criticism will come. "However, the externalization not only changes an inner battle into an outer one; it also supplants a very harsh inner threat with a usually milder punishment from the outside. The visible misbehavior is seen as less of a violation than the inner forbidden activity or wish, i.e., masturbatory activity, or sexual or aggressive feelings toward forbidden objects" (Furman, 1980, p. 271).

Too frequently, educators, parents, and even therapists mistakenly fulfill the assigned superego role of harsh disapproval and punishment, or lower their expectations and offer reassurances of love that fail to help the child with the inner conflict and/or developmental struggle. Such handling frequently exacerbates the child's acting out, provoking bewildered adults in the environment into a cycle of overgratification alternating with manifest harsh disapproval. Furman (1980) describes the following pathological outcomes in such cases: stimulation of the child's regressive sadomasochistic strivings for ever-harsher punishments, failure to develop age-appropriate self-control, and establishment of maladaptive character traits.

Furman describes how the mistaken interpretation of externalization as transference exacerbates the defense and thereby causes deterioration and regression in the child. "Externalization of superego attitudes ceases to be a phase-specific, self-limited, early latency defense when its intensity or rigidity precludes progress towards mature and appropriate integration of superego demands" (1980, p. 274). When the latency-age child uses the defense of externalization excessively, misdiagnosis can easily occur. Such children may be seen as having inadequate superego development, when in fact their conscience is over strict and harsh. Seemingly guiltless, aggressive behavior is actually defensive, masking the push for severe punishment. Extensive use of externalization causes both ego and drive regression. Frequently, more developed, Oedipal-level children are misperceived as "less than neurotic" and lacking in any superego development.

The child's defensive externalization of superego attitudes has a significant relationship to the countertransference responses of child therapists. The therapist may indulge the child, encourage regressive behavior, and misjudge the child as incapable of internal controls, assuming that the child cannot look at inner conflict. The therapist may act out unresolved issues with the child or take on the role of the harsh punisher. In the following exchange, Bornstein (1948) demonstrates the therapeutic empathy and diagnostic skill called for in the face of a child's externalization: "One day a little boy had asked her what she [the analyst] would do if he stole something from her desk; she replied, I would think to myself, 'I wonder what has happened to make an honest person act as if he were a thief'" (pp. 691–697).

Transference as manifest by children must not be understood to represent displacement from old objects, in that the child residing with the parents most commonly presents current thoughts, behaviors, etc., about the parents in the therapy sessions. Thus, the child's current and ongoing dependent relationships present the therapist with the child's habitual modes of relating and reacting to adults. For this reason, there is nothing special or unique in the way the child relates to the therapist. There is spillover—often both ways—in that the child may act out at home as a result of treatment while simultaneously presenting the therapist with affects, defenses, etc., that originate in the parent-child relationship. The transference neurosis seen in more intact children involves three people: a subject (the patient), a past object (parent), and a present object (the therapist). These distinctions are rarely seen in a sustained fashion with child patients, even those who have achieved object constancy. More commonly, we see one or more of the subtypes of transference, i.e., *habitual modes of relating* and *transfer of current relationships* (Sandler et al., 1975). With the more damaged child, we see self-object transferences (Tolpin, 1978).

The Real Relationship

The real relationship, so essential throughout work with children and adolescents, is based on the child's realistic perceptions of the person and qualities of the therapist, and the therapist's genuine feelings of respect, compassion, and empathy for the child. (With adults seen in intensive insight-oriented therapy, the real relationship is generally reserved for the termination phase of treatment, when patient and therapist savor the special, private, and meaningful work accomplished together.) Tyson (1980) states that there are "nontransference ways in which the analyst's gender as well as other real factors (such as age or physical features) may very well determine the child's initial reaction and where the child's character might be highlighted in his habitual mode of relating" (pp. 324–325). The therapist can serve as a new object and developmental reorganizer, and variables such as age, style, sex, and character traits currently are increasingly recognized as significant. Tyson points out that gender of the therapist is also critical beyond the real relationship, as it "can provide possible foci for resistance to transference development, serve to exaggerate transference resistance, and work for the enhancement or attenuation of particular aspects of transference manifestations" (p. 337).

There are difficulties in keeping separate and distinct the two kinds of relationships in work with children (i.e., the transference relationship and the "real" relationship). Anna Freud (in Sandler et al., 1980) discusses the case of a boy who had lost his father. He was treated by a male therapist, who was seen as both father and therapist, creating a very mixed relationship. Sandler et al. (1980) emphasize that treatment complexities arise out of "the 'real' relationship between two people, on the one hand, and the distortion of that relationship through the transference, on the other" (p. 104).

Children may use the therapist as an intermediary between themselves and parents. This can create treatment barriers with children who explicitly demand that the external world be changed. They may want the therapist literally to take over the parenting role and provide need satisfaction, (e.g., they may demand a cure for a physically deforming illness, or the reunion of separated or divorced parents). When therapists are used as new love objects, they can become new objects of identification. "This identification is not transference, although in every new relationship there are also transference elements because nothing is uninfluenced by the past. . . . There may be identification with the role of the therapist as a caring person, with some idealized image of the therapist, or with some real personal attribute" (Sandler et al., 1980, p. 107).

The therapist also may be used as a modifier of the child's punitive superego and as an "auxiliary ego" that provides information and helps in actual problem solving. Children with ego defects use the therapist as a real person to defend against underlying impulses. However, no new here-and-now positive experience that ignores the past can provide a cure. Such a positive current therapy relationship is "correcting" rather than "corrective."

The nonanalyst child therapist who sees the child once or twice a week is the most likely to enter into a "real relationship" with the child. But, as stated earlier, the distinction between the "real relationship" and the transference relationship is not always clear-cut, as nothing is uninfluenced by the past. The child's previous and current object relationships will have more effect on the child's mode of relating than will the excellent qualities of the positive new object (the therapist).

The abused child who has experienced multiple foster homes and disruptions in significant ties may not relate meaningfully to the most skilled therapist.

Countertransference

Countertransference is distinguished by unconscious or preconscious forces within the therapist, that cause the therapist to react to the patient in ways inappropriate to the current reality of the therapeutic relationship. Such reactions are displacements from significant early relationships (e.g., with siblings and parents) in the therapist's life (Dewald, 1964). Marcus (1980) defines countertransference as having specificity to the patient, to the transference, or to other components of the patient's material; when used defensively, it interrupts or disrupts the therapist's "analyzing function." It "activates a developmental residue and creates or revives unconscious conflict, anxiety and defensiveness" (Marcus, 1980, p. 286). Countertransference can be a negative contaminant or a positive therapeutic tool to aid in the interpretation of patients' unconscious.

Marcus (1980) notes that the therapist's responses to young patients might be projective identification, a revival of omnipotent feelings and sibling or Oedipal rivalry with the child's parents. In addition, a therapist unconsciously may use a patient in relationship to professional colleagues, e.g., as a source of pride and praise, or a source of shame and criticism. Such feelings may be followed by controlling, manipulative behavior by the therapist. Patients may be used to satisfy drives of voyeurism and curiosity, or to gratify unconscious aggressive or masochistic needs. If a therapist is not in touch with unconscious and unresolved earlier conflicts, therapeutic understanding and handling will be greatly compromised. However, countertransference also can be a means of understanding the patient and the patient's communication. The affective reactions stirred up in the analyst may contribute important information about the patient's feelings.

Proctor (1959) notes that countertransference problems are greatest in work with impulsive, acting-out patients and highly narcissistic patients. Such patients tax therapists who attempt to defend themselves with counterresistance. Frequently, therapists are tempted to counterattack or mobilize infantile aspects of their superego against the patient's id. This mobilization of the therapist's superego can result in rejection, punishment, or hostile demands for conformity by the patient. Proctor uses the term countertransference to mean the reverse of transference: therapists displace their infantile object-relations patterns onto patients. With "less than neurotic" patients, interpretation of the therapist's own countertransference "can be a highly effective tool, but requires some finesse. Such interpretations must be correctly timed, and should be aimed at the most superficial level that is effective" (Proctor, 1959, p. 305). This use of self on the patient's behalf stretches the concept of countertransference for use with this very disturbed population. Blanck and Blanck (1979) state that the therapist "takes on more of an interpersonal role than was understood when countertransference, defined in its strictest sense, applied to neurosis alone. . . . Especially now that we understand that the therapeutic need for reorganization of the patient's subphase inadequacies calls for some sort of experiential interaction with the therapist, the therapist must be in communication with his own phase and subphase adequacies and inadequacies" (pp. 135–136).

During specific phases of their development and of the treatment process, children can be resistive to treatment, stimulating the therapist's countertransference or counterreactions. Weiss et al. (1968) describe how many children exhibit conscious, unconcealed, dramatic opposition. Such phenomena can stir up normal human emotions of despair and frustration. Conversely, interest in the patient and pleasure in the therapeutic work should not be misconstrued as unconscious overidentification. Marcus (1980) cautions that it is "untenable to view countertransference as all of the analyst's emotional responses; and as a general reaction which includes all unconscious and conscious attitudes, feelings and actions" (p. 288). Such an all-inclusive concept denies appropriate human and professional feelings toward patients and the therapeutic work. Warmth, affection, and respect for patients are not overemotional responses and therefore are not countertransference.

CHAPTER 14

Techniques of Play Therapy

Definitions and Characteristics of Play Therapy

Play is a general accompaniment of normal life and is seen in animal as well as human activity. Greenacre (1959) suggests that play often involves make-believe and even imitative action (e.g., children who play at being grown up). Thus, although play often is fun, amusing, spontaneous, and aimless, it also is a recreative, renewing or reviving activity.

Freud explained the repetitive nature of human activity and noted that the inner pressure to repeat significant and disturbing experiences is at the heart of neurotic development. He used the term "repetition compulsion" to describe this phenomenon. The repetition compulsion came to be seen as only one of many repetitive tendencies. Repetitions are due to recurring struggles between the repressed impulses and the repressing forces; traumatic experiences are repeated to achieve belated mastery. The repetition of trauma is seen most clearly in children's play, in dreams, and in the anxiety attacks of patients suffering traumatic neurosis. The painful tension of the original trauma is relived, under somewhat more favorable conditions (e.g., in play). Greenacre suggests that there is the illusion that the new situation is different, and thereby more favorable, and that now, everything will be all right. But the change is expected in the external situation, whereas it is the inner one which is usually more important. In children's play, the more favorable condition lies in the fact that the play apparently is under the control of the child. Further reassurance is formed in the reversal of roles, the child often in imagination or in acted out play, taking the powerful part and assigning the weaker, more passive or more suffering role to a toy, a pet, or another . . . thereby re-enacting in an active way, what he has previously experienced passively [1959, p. 64].

Thus, the child recovering from surgery repeatedly plays "doctor," performing endless operations on toys.

Greenacre and others note that repetition of experience is necessary in establishing a sense of reality. Alien and overwhelming experiences need to become integrated. Play may be based on the pleasure principle, the desire to be big and grown up, or the need for mastery of something alarming. Thus, the content and theme of the play activity are not casual or interchangeable. Walder (1933) suggests that when an event is too difficult or large to assimilate immediately, it must be chewed again and again; in this way, a passively experienced event is converted into an actively experienced one. The postoperative child who plays doctor becomes the active actor, repetitively dividing into small portions, or vignettes, that which was originally overwhelming; thus the child assimilates in piecemeal fashion that which was too large to integrate all at once. Walder (1933) notes that "play may be a process like a repetition compulsion, by which excessive experiences are divided into small quantities, reattempted and assimilated in play" (p. 217). Greenacre (1959) likens this attempt to allay anxiety by mastery of the situation that caused it. "The anxiety-producing problems of today in the child's life become the subjects of the play tomorrow, whether or not these problems have apparently risen from or even are much involved with maturational needs" (p. 66). Thus, play can represent fragments and bits of reality that have been altered and adjusted to fit the child's needs and wishes.

In contrast to Walder, Greenacre suggests that repetitions in play may not be so helpful, but in fact may help to establish overly strong neurotic defenses. Hendrick, author of the "Instinct and the Ego During Infancy" (1942) and "Work and the Pleasure Principle" (1943), and White, author of "Efficiency and Competence" (1963), developed the concept of an instinct to master that helps a child to develop a sense of competence. While Greenacre doubts the existence of a universal drive for perfection of skill, etc., she notes that play is "not merely pleasure at the relief of anxiety, but in the truer sense of pleasure in functioning, i.e., satisfaction of maturational potentials" (1959, p. 69).

In his article, "A Contribution to the Theory of Play" (1958), Alexander examines the relation of play to creativity and presents a view opposing that of Walder. Alexander stresses that in true playfulness, the solution of a problem is not imperative; thus, play can be differentiated from work. He notes a strong affinity between play and creativity, but makes no reference to unconscious motivations or fantasies. In his view, the creative aspect of play is the child's unlimited freedom of choice, which offers play an experimental quality.

Freud observed that all children behave like poets in their play since they create a world of their own or, more accurately expressed, transpose things into their own world according to a new arrangement of their choosing. Thus, play is a leave-taking from reality as well as from the superego, and strongly parallels fantasy and daydreaming (wish-fulfillment).

Erikson (1940) considers play an ego function and notes that child's play begins with, and centers on, the child's own body. This "autocosmic play" entails exploration by repetition of sensual perceptions, kinesthetic sensations, and vocalizations; it serves as the preamble to play with available persons and things. The next unit of attention is the "microsphere," i.e., the small world of manageable toys, which is followed by the "macrosphere," i.e., the world shared with others, in the child of nursery age, 3–4 years old. The nursery child can first treat others as things to be examined, bumped into, or forced to be horsie, mommy, or baby in the game. Learning and ego growth are necessary for the child to discover what content can be shared or forced upon others.

Peller (1955) emphasizes libidinal development as reflected in play, and cites the following libidinal phases in the sequence of childhood development. Narcissistic play is evident in the earliest months when the playing infant appears interested in body parts, functions, and products. Gratification and frustration relate to bodily needs and the earliest interest in toys is derived from body interest (i.e., movements of the child's fists, legs, etc., and later, vocal experimentation). Very young babies play with their fingers and toys, babble, and seek pleasure. Pre-Oedipal play evidences the child's attachment to mother; games such as hide-and-seek and peek-a-boo, and the hugging of doll, turn the passive experience of being left by mother into an active experience.

Oedipal play reflects inner conflict and awareness of sexual roles, but also blindness or denial of the age difference between the child and the parents. Peller (1955) notes that the Oedipal child "fantasies or acts as if he were his parents' full-fledged partner" (p. 179). Because the child is excluded from the pleasures of grownups, core fantasies focus on being big and powerful, and the child assumes the roles of father, mother, king, doctor, teacher, captain, etc. The Oedipal child enjoys toys that are replicas of adult tools or possessions—cars that can be driven, dishes, doll equipment, uniforms, dress-up garb, miniature stoves, etc. In contrast to early solitary play, the play of the Oedipal child can involve complex plots, themes, and scripts that cast peers into roles.

Post-Oedipal latency play involves social interplay and attachments to playmates. Rules are generally observed to the letter. Team participation and winning are critical in the often rigidly codified games of latency. Peller (1955) suggests that latency-age children "see their ego ideal in their playmates or in their leaders or in nationally famous players, and as long as they play in the same game, they partake in this ego ideal and this lessens the pressures of the superego. . . . Games thus provide gratification, but as they are prefabricated [and] run in traditional molds, the player remains rather anonymous and unexposed—to himself and to the others" (p. 182).

James (1977) notes that Rousseau was one of the first writers to advocate studying the play of children in order to understand and educate them. Piaget recognized the role of play in cognitive development and concluded that children must begin at the concrete level of experience before they can progress to the abstract. That is, children use play as a medium to concretize their emotional experiences, which they then generalize to a more abstract level. "It has been widely suggested that play is to the child what verbalization is to the adult—a medium for expressing feelings, exploring relationships, and reaching fulfillment. In play therapy children are provided an opportunity to be free, creative, and self directing" (James, 1977, p. ix).

Psychoanalytic Play Therapy

In comparing the methods and goals of adult and child psychoanalysis, Anna Freud concluded that since child patients rarely come in independently with conscious motivation, they require "wooing," and the establishment of rapport and a relationship. Toys and play are particularly valuable in work with young children in that, through toys, children can create their own environment. "In this play world, he is able to carry out all of the actions which, in the real world, remain confined to a fantasy existence. By using toys, the therapist has the opportunity of getting to know the child's various reactions, aggressive impulses, sympathies, as well as his attitudes towards the various things and persons represented by the toys" (Anna Freud, 1951, pp. 117–136). Play becomes the child's mode of free association, a relatively uninhibited expression of affects, defenses, traumas, relationships, wishes, and hopes.

Melanie Klein's view (the English School) differed from that of Anna Freud (the Viennese school).[1] She disagreed with Anna Freud's guidelines of adjustment and educability, and stressed "the fantasy aspect of the mother-child link [and] the intensity of the tension accompanying the love drive (and) using ambivalence as a theme, she stressed the scrutiny of the play of opposites in the conception of the object relationship" (James, 1977, pp. 6–7). Klein looked for symbolism in every act of a child's play, and used both toys and dramatizations as avenues for discovering the fantasy world of children. In her early practice, Klein would visit the child at home, so that initial play involved familiar toys. Then, after home observations, therapy was moved to the consulting room or playroom to facilitate the development of transference. Each patient's toys were kept in a separate box. This box and the toys in it, which were only exposed in analytic sessions, became an individual experience for each child and the play was interpreted as if it were an adult verbal production or offering.

The Kleinian interpretive approach confronted children with their unconscious, and centered on their anxieties and defenses against anxiety. Anna Freud offered a more cautious approach that did not assault children's defenses. Klein believed that very young children are capable of understanding and benefiting from interpretation, "especially if they are tied to materials and make use of the child's own expression" (James, 1977, p. 9). The Kleinian English School emphasized tracing the desires and anxieties in the current patient-analyst relationship to the first love objects of infancy—via a reexpression of early emotions and fantasies in safety—in order to reorganize these early relations and thereby diminish anxieties. While the Kleinian approach emphasized the development of transference, Anna Freud questioned its routine occurence in child analysis, given the reality that the child is still living with the original objects. In her view, the child-therapist tie is characterized by "respect and ideal, rather than transference" (James, 1977, p. 9).

In 1966, Anna Freud noted that the differences between her Viennese school and the Kleinian English school were far greater than they had seemed initially, and involved theoretical as well as technical issues. Anna Freud and her colleagues made alterations in classical technique "necessitated by the child's inability to use free associations, by the immaturity of his ego, the dependency of his superego, and by his resultant incapacity to deal unaided with pressures from the id" (James, 1977, pp. 51–52). The Freudians were struck by the strength of children's defenses and the difficulties of interpreting transference. By

---

[1]See Chapter 1.

contrast, the Kleinians did not feel the need to modify classical adult approaches with child patients because they viewed free play as the absolute equivalent of free association and the vehicle of transference. Thus, direct interpretations were made to the child. The Kleinian and Freudian views of child development were also very different. The Kleinians placed the struggle between life and death instincts, and the splitting of objects into "good" and "bad," in the first year of life. In contrast to the Freudian emphasis on the phallic-Oedipal phase, the Kleinians believed the events of the oral phase determine the main features of superego and character formation as well as the roots of mental illness.

Structured Play Therapy

Structured play therapy involves the therapist designing specific stimulus situations that the child responds to and plays out. "This type of therapy has been referred to by David Levy as release therapy; by J. C. Solomon as activity play therapy; and by Jacob Conn as the play interview" (James, 1977, p. 9). This approach is seen as an offshoot of the psychoanalytic school. Hambridge (1955) described the therapist recreating in dramatic play an event or situation similar to the one causing the child's stress, and helping and urging the child to abreact to that which has been precipitating and maintaining anxiety. Hambridge cautions that this technique be used selectively; with certain patients, it should not be used at all. Further, care must be taken to avoid frightening the child. The therapist must be sensitive to the child's integrative capacity. Flooding and resultant regressive and disintegrative states must be avoided. It is recommended that structured play be followed by free play that involves "direct manipulation of the dolls, relatively complete absorption in the play so that the child is practically oblivious to his surroundings while playing out the primary impulses involved" (Hambridge, 1955, p. 609).

David Levy (1939), another structural theorist, offers "release therapy" to provide the child relief. *Specific release therapy* is recommended when the symptom has not been evident for a long duration, when the child is younger than ten years old, and when the problems are uncomplicated by family difficulties. Following initial free play, the therapist introduces the structured situation with appropriate questions and uses play materials to reproduce specific episodes. *General release therapy* is used when the child's problems are seen as a result of excessive early demands. This approach does not entail the reproduction of specific experiences, and rather is aimed to modify social attitudes and infantile aims, and modulate aggression. Play situations are defined and presented to convey specific themes that have been overwhelming the child. Each scene involves toys selected for the given theme; e.g., to reflect sibling rivalry, a mother doll, baby doll, and self doll may be used while to unleash aggression, bursting balloons and punching bags may be appropriate.

Solomon, a pioneer in play therapy, devised an approach that emphasizes the primary importance of ego integration in the development of self. Solomon's play technique has been used as a diagnostic and therapeutic medium with children, and as a research device. In therapy, the concern is primarily with conflicts involving the primary motivations (instincts), the secondary motivations (superego), and the level of ego development prior to the onset of the symptom. Solomon suggests that "through play the child is able to express his own regressive tendencies, thereby lessening the need to act out such forms of behavior in his real life situation. Instead, he is afforded the opportunity to move forward towards more realistic solutions for his problems" (1955, p. 594). Via play, children can disengage from magical thinking, can clarify time, reality, and causality, and can enhance ego development. Solomon initially used created play situations, but later relied on the child's spontaneous responses to original play constructions.

Conn (1939) developed a structured play interview in which the therapist may play different roles. Although the therapist permits free play, the primary format entails planned situations, which have been based on the child's earlier use of the toys.

Relationship Play Therapy

James (1977) notes that relationship play therapy evolved from Rank's philosophy, especially his premise that the common trauma of birth results in permanent fear of individuation. This therapy perspective emphasizes the conscious cooperation of the patient and deemphasizes the patient's unconscious, past history, and transference phenomena. The here-and-now relationship and the concept of time are crucial.

In applying this approach to children, Allen focuses on the child's here-and-now daily experiences and most pressing concerns, in contrast to the concerns of therapist and/or parents. Moustakas (1959) advocates here-and-now active participation in the living process with the child, whereby the therapist conveys unqualified acceptance, respect, and faith, and focuses on feelings rather than causes or symptoms. The therapist's stance is one of active listening and following, as opposed to structuring, interpreting, or guiding the child's play. The aim is the development of a significant relationship.

Client-Centered Therapy

In describing the development of client-centered therapy, Dorfman states that

> from the Freudians have been retained the concepts of meaningfulness of apparently unmotivated behavior, of permissiveness and catharsis, of repression, and of play as being the natural language of the child. From the Rankians have come the relatively ahistorical approach, the lessening of authoritative position of the therapist, the emphasis on response to expressed feelings rather than to a particular content, and the permitting of the child to use the hour as he chooses. From these concepts client-centered play therapy has gone on to develop, in terms of its own experiences" (1951, p. 273).

Axline is most well known for adaptation of the client-centered approach to child therapy. She suggests that disturbed children are in a state of incongruence between self and experience, and when they "experience conditions of worth in an atmosphere of unconditional acceptance, an increase in unconditional self-regard will occur" (James, 1977, p. 22).

In describing her treatment philosophy, Axline states that "nondirective therapy is based on the assumption that the individual has within himself, not only the ability to solve his own problems satisfactorily, but also his growth impulse that makes mature behavior more satisfying than immature behavior" (Axline, 1964, p. 34). The basic aims of this approach are to provide the child with an experience of self different from all others which allows for the processes of reintegration, synthesis, and maturation. To provide this therapeutic milieu, Carl Rogers, who developed the client-centered viewpoint, emphasizes that therapists must hold a basic belief in the individual's capacity for growth, independent decision making, and maturity.

Axline's eight basic principles are guidelines for therapists involved in nondirective play therapy contacts.

1. The therapist must develop a warm, friendly relationship with the child, in which good rapport is established as soon as possible.
2. The therapist accepts the child exactly as he is.
3. The therapist establishes a feeling of permissiveness in the relationship so that the child feels free to express his feelings completely.
4. The therapist is alert to recognize the feelings the child is expressing and reflects those back to him in such a manner that he gains insight into his behavior.
5. The therapist maintains a deep respect for the child's ability to solve his own problems if given an opportunity to do so. The responsibility to make choices and to institute change is the child's.

6. The therapist does not attempt to direct the child's actions or conversation in any manner. The child leads the way; the therapist follows.
7. The therapist does not attempt to hurry the therapy along. It is a gradual process and is recognized as such by the therapist.
8. The therapist establishes only those limitations that are necessary to anchor the therapy to the world of reality and to make the child aware of his responsibility in the relationship [1947, pp. 55–56].

Axline's stress on the importance of recognizing the child's feelings and reflecting them back points up a distinction between reflection and interpretation. Interpretation connotes explaining the meaning of the play while reflection implies mirroring feelings and affects, and staying within the metaphor the child offers. Many writers caution that premature interpretations of children's play and dreams may frighten children; they may believe that their mind can be read or that awful ideas are attributed to them. This will produce more defensiveness, cessation of play activity and sharing of dreams, and possibly regression. The nondirective acceptance and reflection of feelings can permit the child gradual insight and freedom to express feelings in the safety of the relationship.

The Playroom and Its Toys

Melanie Klein (1955) suggested that the equipment of a playroom be simple and nonmechanical. The simplicity of the toys enables the child to use them in a large variety of situations and to express many different attitudes. How a child handles play material is of significance even in the initial session. "The touching of sand, the terse fingering of a book while probably studying the therapist, the throwing down of some puppets, any initial action, however arbitrary it may appear, should be considered as significant as the first dream brought to the initial analytical session in adult therapy" (Hellersberg, 1955, p. 485).

Despert (1945) emphasized the highly individualized use of play material. Some children will use the same toy over and over, repeating the same theme. Others may refrain from using specific toys because of concern over revealing too much. Some highly fixated and disturbed children cannot play at all or offer only repetitive, impoverished play productions. "Certain qualities of the psychotic play of children such as stereotyped repetitiveness, fragmentation, condensation, and other characteristics are striking and outstanding features, the observation of which permits inferences about the nature of the psychic organization of the child" (Ekstein and Friedman, 1959, p. 291). The psychotic child's play so very frequently reflects the child's inner struggle to maintain symbiosis and to wipe out the difference between self and the outside world in order to avoid painful insight.[2]

This broad range of reactions to toys in the playroom is most apparent with simple toys that facilitate varied and expressive responses. Doll houses, puppets, and small figures that represent parents and children, paper, crayons, pencils, and paints in a room with a washable floor, simple furniture, a work area, and running water create an environment conducive to meaningful expressive play. Some therapists use toy guns, clay, toy soldiers, sand, peg-pounding sets, etc. Axline (1947) notes that checker games have been used with some success but are not the best material for expressive play. Chess and checkers are often sought by latency-age children who desire rules, codified games, and distance from more repressed, unsettling drive derivatives. They are dissolving Oedipal ties, and cooperation with siblings, leaders, and followers is experienced as gratifying. Meeks (1970) stresses that the value of such games for latency-age children lies in their being realistic. In addition, Loomis (1957) suggests that a checker game is an excellent way for a child to play out and disclose resistances.

Ginott notes that the value of any toy or activity in child therapy depends on the contribution it makes to the objective of effecting basic personality changes. He (1961b) suggests that there are five major criteria for selecting and rejecting toys and materials for child therapy. One must determine whether they (1) facilitate establishment of contact with the child; (2) evoke and encourage catharsis; (3) aid in developing insight; (4) furnish opportunities for reality testing; and (5) provide media for sublimation.

The appropriate play items make it easier for the child to be expressive and for the clinican to grasp the language of the child. Proper materials provide less room for misinterpretation. Ginott cites the example of a child banging two blocks together. The child may or may not be banging two parents together, but if the child bangs two dolls together, the therapist will have little doubt as to the characters in the play. Play will relate to a child's fundamental problems. Ideally, materials will not evoke hyperactivity but rather, will aid in reality testing and provide fearful children media to work with that will not increase their fear of failure. Since the libidinal phase dictates the mode of play expression, (Peller, 1955) the child patient usually selects toys or activities not totally commensurate with reality and chronological age. For example, the young latency child may give ample evidence of fixa-

---

[2]Cf. the behavior of the neurotic child, Rick (Chapter 9), who declined to play during the initial diagnostic session because of his great anxiety; instead, he shared and ventilated his worries clearly and articulately.

tion/regression by repetitive play with the baby doll's bottle. Materials must vary with handicapped or disabled children, or children in special settings such as a hospital pediatrics ward.

Stephenson (1973) suggests using drawing, painting, and other artwork with slightly older children to illustrate and help work out feelings. He also mentions mutual storytelling, latency-age team and board games, and games with toy armies. Winnicott employs pencil and paper in his "squiggle" games, in which he draws with the child while simultaneously providing interpretations.

Limits in Play Therapy

Most clinicians are in accord that preadolescent children should not be in the position to receive or reject therapy. This decision is ideally made by the parents in consultation with professionals. This initial issue raises the ongoing question of adult-determined limits in the course of therapy. Ginott notes that in therapy, children will attempt behaviors akin to their previous behavior and relationship patterns; he suggests that from the very beginning it should be made clear that the therapeutic relationship will be different from other relationships the child has known. For some children, limits may need to be clarified in the initial session. Haworth (1964) notes that most clinicians concur that children should not be permitted to destroy property or to injure peers, themselves, their therapists, or anyone else. Within this basic postulate, each therapist interprets what consitutes injury and damage. Other pertinent questions arise, such as specification of limits in advance versus a wait-and-see stance; is it possible to have too many limits, and should we be concerned about the complaint child who never tests? If a limit is defied, what should be done? Should the therapy hour be concluded early and the child dismissed from the room? Why is a child fighting and combative, and what feelings thereby get aroused in the therapist? How can a child be stopped therapeutically? Is the child enacting the desire to punish or the need to be punished?

While Haworth's questions remain pertinent, all the existent literature on the subject is twenty or more years old, and some authors appear to parallel the permissive parenting practices of more than a quarter of a century ago. At that time, some leading therapists (Slavson, 1943; Schiffer, 1952; Rosenthal, 1956) considered unconditional permissiveness and unrestrained acting out primary and basic requisites for effective child psychotherapy. Dorfman (1951, p. 262) reports that most client-centered therapists use but one criterion for therapeutic intervention: they only limit activities that interfere with their ability to remain emotionally accepting of the child. Some of these therapists allow the child almost complete control over the therapy situation; the children may paint the therapist's face, take toys home, urinate on the floor, leave the playroom at will, miss sessions, or terminate treatment. "Permissiveness means the acceptance of all behavior as it appears in the [therapy session or] group, be it aggressive, hostile, destructive, sadistic, masochistic, etc., without reproof, censure, or restriction on the part of the therapist" (Schiffer, 1952, p. 256). Such therapists do not sanction such behaviors. They only permit them, with the obvious hope that the child's ego and superego growth and identification with the therapist will eventually promote appropriate guilt, self-control, and an ego ideal that will create autonomous management of self. This approach might have proved successful with the better structured neurotic child seen in child guidance clinics a quarter of a century ago. It is certainly contraindicated for the increasing numbers of borderline, impulse-ridden, character-disordered children treated in mental health clinics today.

In contrast to the above definition of permissiveness, which embodied tolerance of acting out, other leading therapists defined and operationalized permissiveness in very different terms.

According to the other approach, permissiveness means the acceptance of all *symbolic* behavior as it appears in therapy, be it destructive or constructive, without censure or restriction. All feelings, fantasies, thoughts, wishes, passions, dreams, and desires, regardless of their content, are accepted, respected, and allowed expression through words and play. Direct acting-out of destructive behavior is not permitted; when it occurs, the therapist intervenes and redirects it into symbolic outlets [Ginott, 1959, p. 148; author's emphasis].

As a rationale for the use of limits in individual and group play therapy, Ginott (1959) makes the following points.

1. Limits direct catharsis into symbolic channels, so that forbidden acts get translated into symbolic release, enabling children to transform incestuous and destructive urges into harmless outlets and to develop sublimations compatible with social demands and mores. The child with Oedipal entanglements cannot act them out on the physical person of the parent or therapist, but can do so with a puppet, doll, or artistic creation. The same is true of aggressive impulses and tolerance of the symbolic destruction of parents, teachers, and therapist.
2. Limits enable the therapist to maintain acceptance, empathy, and regard throughout therapy, by preventing physical assault on the person or office of the therapist, which could only lead to anger, anxiety, and rejection. The therapeutic controls always apply to behavior, never to words. Verbal and play outlets are used to express asocial or unacceptable impulses or wishes.
3. Limits assure the physical safety of the child and the therapist in the playroom.

4. Limits strengthen ego controls, in that without limits therapy may only delay self-regulation, encourage narcissism, and lead to a false sense of omnipotence. Further, the child is not overwhelmed with guilt. Ginott (1959) states that by "accepting the child's feelings and preventing his undesirable acts, the therapist reduces the child's guilt and at the same time turns his wishes in the direction of reality controls. Thus the child comes to accept and control impulses without excessive guilt" (p. 150).
5. Some limits are set for reasons of law, ethics, and social acceptability. Thus children cannot play sexually with one another or with the therapist and cannot urinate on the floor, but they can curse, use sexual and/or aggressive language, draw pornography, etc.
6. Some limits are for practical clinic realities; e.g., a child cannot stay beyond the time limit of the interview or take home toys.

Thus, research and inquiry suggest that child therapists show greater permissiveness in most areas than does society at large. Profanities, racial slurs, and all verbalizations, as well as play constructions of the outrageous, the forbidden, and the obscene, are allowed. Blatant physical aggression toward persons or the milieu and sexual acting out are not tolerated. Child patients are not permitted to yell profanities at other clients, staff, or passersby, however; these aggressive outbursts are only tolerated in the confines of the therapy sessions.

"The therapist always has to be ready to impose restrictions on the child for good reason: it is done to protect the child, the therapist, and the environment. By this protection it is hoped to keep the child safe, to prevent him from feeling too anxious and guilty about his behavior and to facilitate the continuation of the [therapy] (Sandler et al., 1980, p. 189). Anna Freud differs with the permissive notions of giving the child leeway and free expression. "On the contrary the analytic material is obscured and changed if the analyst permits a massive regression in this way" (in Sandler et al., 1980, p. 189).

Therapists disagree strongly about dismissing a child early from sessions. Bixler (1949) suggests the following steps in the setting of limits: (1) reflect the desire or attitude of the child, (2) verbally express the limit, (3) provide an acceptable alternative, and finally (4) control by physical means if necessary. Bixler and others recommend that when the child engages in physical battle with the therapist, after an initial warning, the therapist should terminate the session and put the child out of the playroom. Ginott (1959) objects to ejecting the child because it conveys rejection and shows the child he can defeat the adult.

It may well prove to him the suspicion that he is hopeless and helpless; since he can defeat all adults no one remains to help him. No blanket recommendations can be made on how to deal with the child's aggression. . . . (A child's size, strength, and intent cannot be ignored.) Some

> aggressive children cannot accept the therapist and his friendly overtures
> because they have never recognized or accepted any external authority.
> These children may need an experience of submission to an adult who is
> firm, just and strong [p. 156].

Every therapist has a different tolerance level for aggressivity and acting-out behaviors.

In "less than neurotic" patients we can readily perceive fears of
merger and/or engulfment that may cause aggressivity. Some children
with severe early traumas and distorted early object relations fear closeness to such a degree that they must recoil and fight, or take flight. Such
children cannot be treated in the one-to-one traditional mode, but
rather, require the safety and distance of a group or milieu approach.[3]
Such children predictably will test, provoke, and defy normal limits.

So much for the situation when limits are broken. Most therapists
believe that the entire subject of limits should not be mentioned before
the need for them arises. There appears to be no advantage in beginning
treatment by invoking prohibitions on actions that may never occur,
even if they have occurred in the child's previous therapy experiences.
"The listing of limits may serve as a challenge to the aggressive children and as catharsis—deterrent—to submissive ones" (Ginott, 1959, p.
155). Kessler (1966) recommends that in setting limits, therapists
should attempt to share and convince the child that the limits are
primarily for the child's benefit and safety, stating the restrictions with
calm conviction and firmness.

Aims of Play Therapy

The play activity of a child is a natural medium of self-expression. In a
therapeutic setting, play can be used for a variety of purposes. Play can
be used for diagnostic understanding of the child, as a supplement to
the history provided by the parents. Play is also used to establish a
relationship and alliance with the child patient. Play in the treatment
process provides child and therapist with material and opportunities
for deeper understanding of anxiety, fears, and defenses. Unconscious
material can be acted out, thereby relieving accompanying tension.
Thus, play therapy has a cathartic purpose. Play themes and all modes
of nonverbal communication enable a child to share, relive, reenact,
test reality, and sublimate, thereby improving ego functioning. The
play activity is a complex kaleidoscope of the child's conscious and
unconscious expressions. Erikson (1950) states that modern play therapy is based on the observation that an insecure child seems to be able to

[3]See Chapters 10 (group therapy) and 11 (residential treatment).

use the protective sanction of an understanding adult to regain some play peace, for to "play it out" is the most natural, self-healing measure childhood affords.

Case Example: Play Therapy (See Chapter 8, Narcissistic Personality Disorder—Case of Joy)

Most commonly, children express fantasies and concerns in play with puppets and dolls, or in role play. Content is expressed in words, actions, drawings, and motor activity. When referring to a "verbal" mode, the therapist should distinguish between vocalized and written material. The following case example illustrates the use of play in the treatment of a young child with a narcissistic personality disorder.[4]

Joy was seen biweekly for a two-year period, beginning at age four and a half. She was a dainty black child with presenting problems of hyperactivity, incessant talking, defiance, provocative behavior with adults and peers, enuresis, and insistence on sleeping with mother since 18 months of age. Joy proved to be of superior intellect, with the ability to play, draw, and evolve dramatizations and role plays with marked creativity. For the first year in therapy, she frequently required limits and restrictions from the therapist.

Excerpted Process Recording

In the seventh session, Joy had difficulty entering the office, and acted silly and defiant, running about the waiting room. Once in the office, she was most provocative, grabbing at the drapes and darting toward the cabinets and drawers of other children's special toys and drawings, ignoring her own drawer/locker initially. The therapist reflected that her problems coming in to the office were possibly related to another morning fight with mommy. Joy agreed and blurted out that she had been watching TV when her mother wanted her to wash up and leave promptly to catch the bus. The therapist noted that following such fights it always was hard for Joy to say goodbye to mommy in the waiting room and to come in for her own appointment. Seemingly ignoring that comment, Joy went to her drawer for drawing material and said she wanted to draw Easter baskets. Her drawing reflected her agitation, and she exploded and kicked the metal desk, yelling that the therapist didn't help her draw well and that she was leaving to find mommy.

The therapist said that she could not run out and that mother was having her own therapy session, but they could phone her if she needed to talk to her now. Joy began to scream and kick, and attempted to hit the therapist.

[4]The assessment and diagnosis of this child are discussed in Chapter 8 (narcissistic personality disorder).

She was stopped in this and became more and more furious, testing, but not completely out of control. The therapist held Joy's hands and told her that she would not let Joy hurt her, herself, or the furniture, and that they would do nothing until she was calmer. She shouted back that the therapist should shut up, that she would have a tantrum and would get her way. She struggled, kicked, swept the doll house off the shelf, and tried to bite the therapist and leave the office. The therapist pushed her chair against the door to stop Joy from dashing out and held Joy in her lap, facing outward to avoid her attempts to bite and spit. The therapist told her that she realized this was just like the scary fights at home that she and mommy had told her about, which always ended up with mommy giving Joy a severe spanking and telling her that she was giving her away to a foster family.

The therapist assured Joy—still writhing, but listening attentively—that she wasn't angry, and that this kind of upset was one of the most important problems for them to work on. The therapist indicated that, in her office, she was in charge and no one would be hurt. Joy yelled that she would tell her grandmother on the therapist, and that she wanted to go to an office where the therapist wasn't in charge. (She often taunted her mother in a similar fashion—as though they were sibs—and would threaten to "tell grandma on you.") After some minutes, Joy gradually became calmer, absorbed the reality of the situation, and said she was okay and would clean up the room. She wanted to phone mommy. The phone call was followed by a quick visit to the office where mommy was being seen. Joy reentered her therapist's office looking very relieved (that mommy hadn't left her) and went to play with the doll house, where she constructed "a mommy and a little girl having fun making dinner together and not angry anymore." When the therapist reflected on their working on these fights and struggles together, her serious response was "maybe I should come here every day."

Joy increasingly came to see and feel that her contact with the therapist was essential for her ability to assert and maintain self-control. In the 29th treatment hour—the last before the summer vacation break-she was anxious to make the therapist a picture as a present and wanted the exact spelling of her name to affix on it. When the therapist mentioned her vacation, Joy first responded with coy cuteness, but her face quickly crumbled and she began to cry, got into the therapist's lap, and insisted that the therapist take her with her—and said that her mommy wouldn't mind. She cried bitterly and asked the therapist why she needed a vaction—so much longer than other times when an appointment had been changed for a meeting. After the therapist reassured Joy of her understanding and acceptance of her feelings, she reiterated her previous promise to write her postcards and reaffirmed their first fall appointment date. Joy then attempted to draw a "lonely" clown, and sadly said she couldn't draw well today. The therapist wondered if Joy was worried about being lonely and about managing at home. She reassured Joy about the changes both she and mommy had made about handling angry feelings.

Once Joy's acting out had diminished, she could relax in treatment, play, and explore concerns such as her birth fantasies; her loneliness; and her wish for sibs, a father, a normal family life, and age-appropriate functioning. She dictated the following stories and poems.

Once upon a time, there lived a happily married king. He had a wife and he had a daughter. He had a boy and twenty children. He would like to have more children. He ask his wife is it all right to have more children. She said, "Of course, but we would have to move to a bigger house. When we have two more children, we will have twenty-four children, so we would need twenty-four bedrooms. So we could have more children if we like to." One day the wife went out in the garden to grow some flowers. The next morning they arose again in the garden. They saw the flowers growing—they had a daisy, a cactus, and a rose, and an iris, and a tulip.

Then they had another baby. Then they had twenty-five. Then they had three more, twenty-eight children. The fourth of July, it was the mother's birthday and the children fixed breakfast for her. They fixed toast, bacon, scrambled eggs, and orange juice. Then they had a new '74 Maverick. And they got up. Since it was the mother's birthday, they let mother drive. They took her downtown and bought decorations to throw a surprise party. The next day, the fourth of May, they had father's birthday. They fixed breakfast for father, the same as for mommy, toast, bacon, eggs, and some juice. We went downtown that day and got some more decorations to throw father a surprise birthday party. The next day, the fifth of January, it was sister's birthday. They fixed her breakfast. They had toast, bacon, eggs, and juice.

The king went to his palace. He saw a dirty dragon, scared the king out of his palace and frightened the daughter, too. The End.

Once upon a time there were some people who have jobs. Some people no jobs. Mary Poppins had a job. The job was flying with an umbrella. When she was a little girl she had a mother just like us. But did her mother bother her! Then when she grew up she got married and had a baby. She bought a crib for the baby. They had another one. It was a boy. She bought another crib. She had two babies. Then that very day she had another one. The end!!! They lived happily ever after!

The Name of this story is Mommy and Daddy

One day they went for a walk. The husband said to the wife, "Would you marry me again?" "I suppose that you want all the babies and children because you want all the babies and children. It doesn't mean anything. You are serious." "Yes. I am serious." "No, you're not serious." "Oh yes I am!" "You are not! You'd better not be! You take some of the babies! She'll take some too (whisper)!" Write it.

Babies grow in people's stomachs. They go in the hospital, sometimes the doctor cuts the stomach open and gets the baby out. My mommy told me when the baby comes out there's a little blood on it. You have to wipe it off. Babies take bottles. The mother brings them home from the hospital store. Some people have boys, some have girls. The difference is the girls have more hair. The girl wears girl shoes and the boy wears boy shoes.

(change of subject; Joy sobs about hair-braids and not wanting to look like a boy)

Boys have a penis. Girls don't have a penis. Mother couldn't cut it off I think—so girls never had a penis. Penises get stuck sometime.

A Poem
Once there were a little clown
His name was Tony
The little clown was lonely.
One day it was his mother
She had good news saying that she is going to the doctor
The doctor said that she expect a baby.
Then the clown shall not be lonely!
The End
They lived happily ever after!

Joy did many dramatizations and role plays of a mother and daughter, or of school. She made construction-paper costumes and props (e.g., hats, purses, and jewelry) to complement her scenarios, for which she sometimes wrote scripts by dictating lines to the therapist. At times, she cast the therapist into the role of mother, older sister, or school peer.

In summary, Joy manifested acute anxiety at the beginning of therapy, referring to "shots," patients sitting in their beds at the hospital, and mother abandoning her or giving her away to the therapist. In treatment Joy quickly mirrored her behavior at home with her mother, presenting ambivalence, testing, and requiring actual physical controls as she experienced temper tantrums in sessions. She went through months of provocative behavior, wanting to rifle through all the drawers in the office as well as mishandle the phone and the drapes. She tried to get the therapist to chase her, by dancing around the clinic and refusing to come into the office. Simultaneously, she expressed aggressive and libidinal impulse in therapy (e.g., wanting to kiss and/or hit the therapist) to see whether limits would be imposed on her impulses.

She responded well to being limited with firmness and consistency, and was able to abandon temper tantrums and attempts to destroy the office. She handled frustration in more appropriate ways, and mirrored the therapist's calmness, as beginning gains in regulating and self-soothing mechanisms were made. She used the therapy time to share areas of anxiety via play and endless, imaginative games, stories, and artistic creations. At times, Joy wanted to be a baby and climbed into the therapist's lap and lay in her arms. She seemed to want both to avoid any interpretations and to recapture a time when she had felt safe. She attempted to avoid anxiety in treatment initially via the infantile pose and/or repeated trips to the bathroom.

In play and actual discussions, Joy reflected her sibling relationship with her mother, their equal status, and her fear of her mother's rageful responses to her defiance. She also showed problems of fusion and control, and a fear of losing a part of herself if separated from the therapist and mother. Joy shared many fantasies about intruders and burglars, which seemed to indicate concerns about the therapist's private life (similar to her concerns about her mother's private life when she slept at grandmother's). Burglaries of the apartment were a reality and it appeared that her reality fit her fantasy and/or that because of her concerns she fashioned her fantasies out of reality.

In the course of treatment, Joy idealized the therapist and demonstrated her wish for the therapist's admiration and idealization of her. "If I'm your first customer today, am I your favorite of all the kids you ever see?" Joy demonstrated mirror and merger transference manifestations, was preoccupied with imitations of her therapist down to the minutest detail, and would articulate her fantasy of the perfection of the therapist and her ensuing perfection from their closeness. The activity of the therapist was empathic, with detailed attention to consistency, firm limits when necessary, and allowance of Joy's idealization. Fantasies about the therapist were sparse (that she lived in a hotel with her husband and cat).

Relating concerns about the therapist to questions and concerns about the lost object, the father, proved to be only minimally fruitful. Joy always denied not knowing her father. She stated she knew him well but at times would admit she really knew his photograph. "Daddy was bad. He didn't pay the rent. They fought all the time like a little boy and girl, the way mommy and I fight, like two kids." Subsequent fantasies and musings were shared: "Mommy and daddy fought all the time and he didn't take care of us, but maybe now he has a new family and other kids that he does take care of. One day he'll come to take care of me."

It proved more fruitful not to puncture or question Joy's grandiosity and need for admiration, expressed via the endless stories and plays she created and produced in therapy hours. Further, the need for idealizing the therapist was accepted. In accord with Goldberg's discussion (1973) regarding psychotherapy of narcissistic injuries, the therapist accepted the assigned role of narcissistic self-object because of the patient's need for the therapist to function as a part of herself.

Treatment also included contact with Joy's teachers, and regular educative and supportive contact with her mother. This latter contact, coupled with mother's own psychotherapy, helped her to become a more consistent, empathic parent and to understand Joy's alternating adoration and hostility, and idealization and devaluation of her, the surviving parent.

Verbalization and the Unconscious in Children's Communications: Dreams and Creative Productions

A child's main modes of expression are verbal, nonverbal, or a combination of the two. Special problems are presented by children who bring predominantly nonverbal material (Sandler et al., 1980). Nonverbal children who present gross muscular discharge and an inability to contain feelings and words pose serious problems in treatment. Katan (1961) notes that verbalization is considered part of our general education, and its importance is not confined to the treatment hour. She concludes that

1. Verbalization of perceptions of the outer world precede verbalization of feelings.

2. Verbalization leads to an increase of the controlling function of the ego over affects and drives.
3. Verbalization increases for the ego the possibility of distinguishing between wishes and fantasies on the one hand, and reality on the other. In short, verbalization leads to the integrating process, which in turn results in reality testing and thus helps to establish the secondary process [p. 185].

Anna Freud quotes her father: "My father once remarked on the philosopher who said that the man who first hurled a word of abuse at his enemy instead of a weapon was the founder of civilization. This is really what analysts are aiming to do in getting patients to verbalize" (Sandler et al., 1980, p. 122). Thus the question of treatability via "talking" psychotherapy or analysis relates to the child's capacity to bring material into sessions in a fashion suitable for the work of treatment. There is an implicit expectation that the child will move from primarily nonverbal modes of expression early in therapy to talking more to the therapist. Some children present verbal fantasy material while others only relate and describe reality events, and these differences are understood as reflecting the characteristics of a child's style of ego functioning (i.e., defenses, frustration tolerance, object relationships, resistances, and defensive maneuvers). Children present via flooding, bouts of silence, sharing of fantasy material, role play, and drawings. Some children's drawings and play reflect direct, easily perceived derivatives of their current life situation or past traumas, while others are shrouded in far more symbolism. Thus, communications serve a myriad of purposes—expression, communication, abreaction, and defense. One child's bathroom play and preoccupation may symbolize anal or urethral concerns, whereas for another the faucet and flowing water can illustrate anxiety about genitals, masturbation, and castration.

A child's appearance—well groomed or bedraggled—is another nonverbal source of material that serves as a barometer of the child's mood and/or the parental care of the child.

Case Example—Nonverbal Expression

Julie, a 10-year-old white Jewish child, was referred to the clinic by her parents at the urging of the school. Her teacher was concerned about her passivity, apathy, poor academic achievement, daydreaming, and preoccupation with drawing naked "Barbie doll" figures. The parents were ambivalent about seeking help. They acknowledged their concerns about Julie's performance at school, as well as her inability to hold her own with her younger sisters, her readiness for tears, and her general depression at home. The parents expressed both guilt and a defiant stance about their life style and past history as drug addicts, which had resulted in placement of the children with grandparents during the parents' two-year residence in a therapeutic community. The parents currently were directing a major drug abuse program, which entailed their supervision of a myriad of therapeutic residences and almost total absence from home and contact with their four children. Their life style entailed meager supervision of the children and an insistence that they not be asked to parent more actively, given their need for their work as their own life line. They expected the children to be pseudoadult and independent in having their needs met as "junior members" of the therapeutic commune-type residence near their home.

In the 71st session, Julie arrived in outlandish attire, wearing a pajama top under a vest, "because there was no clean laundry." She had a terrible rash—a swelling around her mouth and chin—and stated she hadn't gone to school today, but had seen a doctor who prescribed some ointment medication. She was unclear about the cause of the rash, but thought maybe she wasn't eating enough vegetables. She said she had had rashes before, but supposedly wasn't allergic anymore, and only rarely got the "old eczema."

She was very sad and said she didn't feel like talking much and was just glad to be here today. She silently went to her toy drawer and got out the numerous pieces of doll furniture that she had been constructing out of paper and clay. She resumed the unending project of redecorating the doll house, which involved recovering or reupholstering the furniture and making new pictures for the walls—activities that dominated her play. She and the therapist had discussed the relation of these activities to her wish to stave off the deterioration in her life; her parents' now precarious marriage; her wish for an intact family and a nice home; and her rage and despair over their ill-kept home and the teasing she experienced at school over her ugly, shabby, thrift-shop or hippie-type garb.

There are frequent shifts in a child's way of bringing in material. The therapist must be alert to progressive or regressive patterns, gross motoric expression that evolves into more symbolic play, and play content that demonstrates shift in libidinal and ego level.

Verbalization in the course of treatment puts into words what might have existed previously only on the level of symbolic play. Often, an enactment of the child's fantasy material is later worked through on a verbal level.

Some therapists have the misconception that material which comes verbally is more true, or shows that the analysis is on firmer ground than material which is brought nonverbally. Particularly in child [treatment and] analysis there may be times when nonverbal material, such as play enactment, reveals an unconscious fantasy more directly than a verbal communication could. So-called confirmatory verbal material may actually be a compliant echoing of the therapist's intervention, something found in adult analysis as well [Sandler et al., 1980, p. 121].

Case Example—Regression in the Service of the Ego

Jim, a 9-year-old white Jewish child, was referred by his parents upon the mutual insistence of the parents' respective analysts. Jim had never really been toilet trained, and manifested nocturnal eneuresis and, more recently, day wetting as well. Upon dismissal from school, literally when he reached his front door, he would wet his pants, and he wet his bed nightly. He sucked his thumb, whined, and was generally infantile and demanding at home, and most rivalrous with a precocious older brother. Jim demonstrated none of his infantile behaviors publicly (e.g., at school or day camp). At school, he was a superior student, an athlete, and was well liked and respected by peers and teachers. He could play a recorder, and handle calculus problems and complex academic questions. In play sessions, it was most incongruous to observe him sucking his thumb while doing advanced mathematical calculations on the playroom blackboard.

Jim's play simulated his varied ego states and libidinal levels of fixation. There was considerable disharmony in the lines of development, which seemed to mirror the uneven parenting he had received. His parents presented themselves as more attuned to Jim today, but still contending with problems of inconsistency and a tendency to excessive permissiveness to counteract their own strict upbringing. The most salient feature of the history presented was the mother's massive depression and incapacitation during Jim's first two years of life. She described feeling inert and almost suicidal until she entered a classical analysis that enabled her to mobilize herself, enter graduate school, and, later, work productively and most successfully, with home and children managed by housekeepers. Mother spoke of her profound discomfort at being "the worst mother in the world" with infants and toddlers, and her greater enjoyment of her children once they entered school. She expressed guilt over her unavailability to Jim in his earlier years.

Initially in therapy, Jim had a month or more of age-appropriate latency-age relating and sharing; he then moved into a more regressive stance. Upon entering each session, he would pop his thumb into his mouth and symbolically play out his apparent unconscious awareness of early traumas. For months, he was remote—a "space boy," as he titled himself—and he directed the therapist to communicate only via programming and pushing the right buttons. He would answer in a mechanical, jerky voice and play a robot boy with mechanical gestures.

Once Jim had related and connected to the therapist, "space boy" was abandoned and he entered a new phase of oral preoccupation, whereby he ran various kinds of restaurants and the therapist was the customer to be fed, tricked, or cheated. Jim would make endless meals out of play dough; some were vividly realistic, and others were "revolting" combinations concocted, to give the therapist a stomachache. Sometimes he would take great glee in charging $100 for a glass of water, or serving the therapist only frozen food.

His greatest amusement came from his later adoption of various foreign accents as he played the owners of foreign restaurants, and he demonstrated amazing mimic skill and perfect accents as he pretended to be the owner of a Chinese restaurant, an Indian restaurant, a London fish & chips place, an Italian restaurant, etc. He had a marvelous time with the accents and his imaginative preoccupation with various foods. The family's extensive travels had made Jim adept with foreign currency and credit cards, and he loved computing bills and figuring out currency rates of exchange. He "served" the therapist just as he previously had served his mother her morning coffee, as she was always very tired in the mornings (Jim's appointments were at 8:00 a.m., before school, and Jim would awake, get dressed, and get himself to sessions). That Jim was most deprived and unattended during the oral phase of his life was reflected in his unconscious communication in the play related to current day phenomena: serving mother coffee, much eating out, much travel abroad, and mother rarely the producer of family meals.

Anal play followed, concurrent with total cessation of day wetting. Following oral play and food as the foci, Jim spent several months preoccupied with the adjoining bathroom—its faucets and toilets. Night dryness did not occur so rapidly. Phallic, more genuine latency play emerged. Jim used tinker toys and Lincoln logs to construct fantastically well-engineered forts, castles, space centers, and the like. He would construct tall phallic towers out of the tinker toys while keeping up a running dialogue about the people in the buildings he made. Initially, he and the therapist journeyed together in the strange and mysterious lands and settings he created. Close to termination, his travel companions were peers.

At times, there were regressions back to earlier modes of play, which Jim showed awareness of in his play dramas of "taking a train back to Baby Land or taking an elevator to age fifteen, down to age two, up to age seven." While regression in the service of the ego was a major characteristic of treatment sessions, Jim also brought in age-appropriate activities (e.g., schoolwork and his recital pieces on the recorder). His regression never carried out of the session to school, a place where his achievements and adjustments continued to improve. The ultimate surrender of infantile behavior in the home came more slowly and less dramatically than his public achievements.

Sandler et al. (1980) point out that silent or internal speech can find indirect expression in drawing, play, or dramatization "as a derivative which conveys content that can be interpreted" (p. 121). Anna Freud looks at the "tools" of the ego, cautioning that verbal or symbolic expressions "should be examined in the general context of ego tools and ego means, keeping in mind that thoughts and words are a means of civilizing the individual and that putting into words can be a substitute for action" (Sandler et al., 1980, p. 121).

Case Example (See Chapter 8, Character Disorder—Case of Mike)

Mike was seen biweekly and sometimes triweekly over a three-and-a-half year period.[5] His major presenting problem was his refusal to produce in

[5]The assessment and diagnosis of Mike are discussed in Chapter 8 (character disorder).

school. Despite obvious superior intellectual abilities, he refused to participate in classroom discussion, academic work, sports, or peer interactions.
At the time of referral, Mike, the oldest of five children in a lower-middle-
class, intact black family, was ten years old. When Mike entered treatment,
he was not handling latency tasks—specifically, school, care of himself, and
appropriate peer interaction—effectively. He had to be prodded to get up,
dawdled constantly, and generally provoked adults in a passive-aggressive
way. He presented isolation, passivity, and femininity, rather than appropriate peer companionship; all group activities and sports were avoided. He
seemingly discharged aggression via passive-aggressive sadomasochistic
means, provoking peers, parents, and teachers to act out aggresively towards him and upon him. He could be so infuriating that teachers confessed
to spanking him and the clinic student psychologist ruefully acknowledged
yelling at and scolding him during the assessment process.

Mike brought material into treatment in various ways. He was very
verbal and articulate, and also spent much time drawing and ultimately
sharing fantasies and associations. Initially, he presented an excessive
amount of verbal content, much of which was a series of rationalizations,
intellectualizations, and projections. He resisted any comment, reflection,
or interpretation, and kept up his endless barrage, seemingly needing to
ensure control and to defend against his fear of expressing aggression, as
well as to keep the therapist at a safe distance. He clearly was struggling
with his wish for and fear of closeness, his sibling rivalry, and his fear of
failure. Much later in treatment, he acknowledged his wish to be the best
and favorite child the therapist had ever treated. He feared his own angry
impulses and externalized them into elaborate fears of tornadoes, floods,
fires, storms, and a plane crashing into the clinic. He did obsessive drawings
of airplanes, racing cars, and ships, and gradually shared his omnipotent,
megalomanic fantasies through the epics and stories he spun related to his
drawings or to a GI Joe doll he often brought into treatment sessions.

It is important to note significant gains after two years of therapy. Mike's
schoolwork improved rapidly and he achieved a superior level academically. He was less provocative at home and school and slowly began to
participate in swimming classes and a Little League baseball team. His peer
interaction slowly increased and improved. He demonstrated self-observing
capacities, and was able to verbalize feelings and fantasies, rather than keep
them confined to his solitary daydreaming and drawings. He could articulate that treatment helped him to figure things out,

> like my imagination baby games and heroes—full of monsters, racing cars, stars,
> and pilots. I used to like to lose myself thinking about those make-believe people
> because I'm the opposite, and want to feel good and forget I'm the shortest in my
> class, not popular, not a big shot, not a good athlete, and too frightened to fight
> and defend myself. I'm now an excellent student and it's the only thing in my
> control. I guess I'm just brains and no brawn.

In examining his fears in the 102nd session, Mike spoke about his dad as
"weird" and "unpredictable." "He's the coach now for our Little League
team and he cheers us up when we lose, buys us pop, but has little to say
when we win. I can't talk to him—or cross him." With a twinkle, Mike

related recently reading a book about Freud, in which there was a story about a grown man afraid of the dark because he was locked in a closet as a child. The man was also afraid of dogs, and the book, according to Mike, stated that the fear of dogs was really a substitute, or displacement. Mike then pondered his fears—of bugs, a baseball coming at him, anything unexpected—and laughed, insisting that he was not afraid of his father.

Children's communications and creative productions are not always expressed in symbolic play or related to fantasy, with a stamp of unreality. It is significant to note poetic and artistic creations related to reality concerns and reality pain that the child struggles to integrate and master. Sandler et al. (1980) state that some children can express in writing what they cannot vocalize.

Dreams unquestionably play a major role in adult analysis; in Freud's view, "The interpretation of dreams is the royal road to knowledge of the unconscious activities of the mind" (1932, p. 608). Greenson (1970) called the dream "exceptional and unique . . . the most intimate and elusive creation of the patient" (p. 545). However, as Harley (1962) notes, relatively little has been written about the role of dreams in child analysis, and what has been offered suggests opposing views: some believe that dreams play an inconsequential role in the treatment of children and are only incidentally related, while others attribute the amazing frequency and ease with which child patients are able to communicate dreams to the child's closeness to the unconscious.

Harley describes two types of latency children. For those children who present only sparse dreams, thereby protecting themselves against contact with their instinctual strivings, dreams should not be interpreted outright, but rather, should be used as a springboard for discussion of everyday events and feelings. The dream may also help to clarify or confirm preceding or subsequent themes in the treatment process, or to stimulate new and valuable play productions or daydreams. With such children, direct interpretation of unconscious material would be frightening and is contraindicated.

In contrast, another, smaller group of children can utilize dream interpretations. These children have been under considerable inner pressure with a corresponding weakness or weakening of defenses. With such children, the dream seems to serve as a safety valve for the discharge of instinctual strivings and thereby provides some distance from their unconscious. Dream interpretation should seek to clarify reality, examine magical thinking, and distinguish word, wish, and deed for the child.

Children who recount disagreeable and frightening dreams usually convey severe anxiety in their waking as well as sleeping hours. Their weak, overwhelmed egos cannot handle excessive stimulation. As interpretation would bring them too close to frightening material, empathic reflection of their affect is seen as appropriate. Treatment gains, i.e., a strengthened ego and improved functioning, generally parallel more relaxed sleeping patterns. The noninterpretive, reflective approach is based on greater respect for the defenses of the ego and the latency child's goal of secondary process. Thus, the therapist does not delve into the primary-process, threatening content of the dream in the context of psychotherapy. A child seen frequently in analysis might well have greater personal resources and therapeutic support to comprehend dream material more fully.

Sandler, et al., suggest that it is possible that external influences play a greater part in child analysis. In addition, in child therapy, toys, stories, role play, dreams, etc., permit the child a degree of displacement, so the approach to threatening mental content must be gradual. Anna Freud (1980) states that if "the analyst interprets too early a child's death wish against the parent or against the siblings, this arouses all sorts of unpleasures such as superego strictures" (Sandler et al., 1980, pp. 168–169).

Case Example—Dreams and Nightmares

Ellen, age ten, brought a scary, repetitive dream into therapy and, at mother's urging, sometimes phoned the therapist to relate it and seek reassurance. In her nightmare, she had a sense of terror and alarm that her baby brother was missing. She would go to his room to check his bed and would find the window grill missing, and her brother spattered on the sidewalk like a broken egg, having fallen ten stories from their apartment. In sessions, she would recount with pleasure and delight her 2-year-old brother's antics and her babysitting for him. However, because brother Daniel was very active and unruly, babysitting for him for even an hour was an overwhelming task for Ellen. Gradual reflections on Ellen's ambivalent feelings about Daniel proved to be helpful. Her love, irritation, and anger gradually were focused on and, slowly and hesitantly, she acknowledged her fury when he got into her things and/or pushed things through the window grills. Anger and irritation at younger sibs were accepted and universalized as normal feelings. Parent guidance with mother served to decrease Ellen's routine responsibility for her brother.

Thus, a gradual approach to the range of children's communications (i.e., dreams, play, drama, and creative expression) is important. The child's need for displacement must be respected and the pace that a youngster can handle must be honored. As the analyst or therapist slowly approaches the defended against content, the child comes to realize that he or she is not the only one who has ever thought such things, that these thoughts are not so terrible after all, and that it is possible to talk about them without getting criticized or feeling overwhelmed. To accept such feelings in oneself is a gradual process.

CHAPTER 15

Resistance and Working Through

Resistance, Defense, and Regression

Anna Freud (1978) refers to children's inability or unwillingness to embark on free association, their unreliable treatment alliance, their diminished sincerity and frustration tolerance, and their preponderance of action as opposed to verbal expression. All these characteristics of children can contribute to resistance in child therapy. Children's complaints about their irrational rituals and requests for reassurances must not be misconstrued as evidence of insight, or even as sure signs of therapeutic cooperation. Anna Freud compares and contrasts the adult and child patient, noting that while the resistances of the adult are lodged in the id, the ego, or the transference, the bulk of children's resistances "stems from their ego's age adequate preference for clinging to its own methods for safeguarding or reinstating well-being and for their inclination to reject all others" (p. 6).

Resistance

Resistance must be differentiated from basic unwillingness to participate in treatment out of no real wish for treatment (e.g., due to lack of interest in change or in forming an attachment to a new object). Resistance is defined as the opposition that develops in the course of treatment as a consequence of the treatment process. It is related to transference development and the use of defenses against the emergence of anxiety-invoking material. In adult analysis, resistances are to verbal free association, which is not found in child analysis. With child patients, analysts look for resistance to communication and cooperation in general. However, there is general agreement that resistance is difficult to define in relation to child psychoanalysis. "Some resistances are present from the very beginning of treatment and are inherent in the mental structure of the patient. These may be called 'character resistances'. As with adults, there is a type of juvenile patient who does not allow anxiety to find expression in thought or words but constantly negates it" (Sandler et al., 1980, p. 58). Character resistances must be distinguished from resistances that arise during the course of treatment. Resistance is expressed in accord with a child's stage of development and the content being defended against. In all resistances, the patient holds something back or unconsciously pushes something out of awareness (Sandler et al., 1980).

Anna Freud (in Sandler et al., 1980) reminds us that as long as there is internal conflict, there will be some degree of resistance against the analytic process. Thus, resistance to the acceptance of the treatment contract, to the entrance into the therapeutic alliance, and to the work of the treatment process all occur to varying degrees. Forgetting is a defense, but to look at the ego resistance is not enough; the content defended against must eventually be understood.

Dewald (1964) states that resistances that appear during therapy occur at varying levels of consciousness similar to those operative in ego defense mechanisms. They arise from the following three sources: "(1) out of the need to maintain repression of unconscious conflicts [in order to] . . . avoid the anxiety, guilt and the unconscious 'dangerous' situation, (2) out of the repetition compulsion and the patient's continuing wish for gratification of infantile and childhood drives and drive derivatives, and (3) out of fear of change" (Dewald, 1964, pp. 96–97). Dewald notes that patients experience fear, anxiety, and uncertainty when they attempt to develop new adaptive modes and behavior patterns. Resistances continue throughout treatment, varying in form and intensity, and not always recognized by the patient.

Greenson (1967) emphasizes the defensive function of resistances, in that resistances defend the neurosis or core conflicts, which are essentially in the unconscious portion of the ego and yet are accessible to the observing, conscious portion of the ego. All resistances operate through the ego and connote ego development. A total absence of resistance and defenses is an ominous sign suggesting a psychotic process. A defense entails a danger and a protecting agency while a resistance consists of a danger, a force impelling protection of the irrational ego, and a force pushing toward taking a risk. Thus, it is important to ponder why, what, and how the patient is avoiding, and not to assault the defenses by premature reflections or interpretations. In work with children and adults, the therapist must attempt to help the patient see and understand the defenses and resistances before looking at the id material being defended against. One is well advised to begin with ego, or surface content, before approaching id and superego content. Initially, the therapist attempts to strengthen the ego and expand its observing qualities.

Pearson (1968) recommends that therapists expand their understanding of resistance in work with children; this includes the resistance of the child before and during treatment, the resistance of the parents before and during treatment, and the resistance of the therapist. Children commonly feel they are "captive" clients or patients. Because they are not experiencing anxiety, they are not motivated for therapy. Many children are brought into treatment on their parents' or school's insistence, and have no wish to participate or cooperate.

Brody (1961) notes that children consciously assume the right to withhold information, to deny conflict, to project all difficulties onto parents or sibs, and deliberately to plan to speak, hear, and see nothing in the treatment setting. Because of the child's uneven mastery of instinctual drive derivatives, uneven maturity of ego functions, and unmoderated superego demands, resistances in child therapy present specific problems. The child commonly presents with ego-syntonic orientation, and an "energetic push to act out and to repeat, rather than to remember his unsatisfied emotional strivings . . . [and so he] parries, temporizes, holds back and battles with himself as to whether or not to speak his thoughts" (Brody, 1961, pp. 273–274). Brody states that however carefully interpretation is offered, it is hard for the child to accept because of the "essentially narcissistic investment in the child's defenses" (p. 255).

Because of children's conscious opposition to treatment and fear of stigmatization, many refuse to cooperate, which they perceive as capitulation and giving in. In an attempt to distance themselves from incestuous objects, children will refuse to submit, or will struggle against submitting, to another adult. They frequently fear that therapy and the therapist will make them over into the child the parent desires. There is a reluctance on the part of the latency-age child to share private thoughts and personal feelings. In addition to feeling concerned that "bad" thoughts and acts will be shared with the parents, children may be "caught between mixed loyalties to parents, i.e., the need to report to the [therapist] and still protect his parents" (Pearson, 1968, p. 361).

A child's physical stance and demeanor may reflect resistance. A youngster may be rigid and stiff, wiggling and hyperactive, or silent; he or she may reflect impatience, boredom, and resentment at being in the therapist's office. Material offered may be trivial, with an intentional avoidance of the current problems and realities at home. Lateness, missing sessions, fixation on board games, and an attitude of "putting in time" may characterize a child's discomfort and dislike of therapy sessions. Sometimes compliance and submission may constitute a more subtle form of resistance. The extent of a child's resistances and the way in which they are manifested depend on the child's age, stage of development, and psychic structure.

Parental resistances may emanate out of the parents' sense of guilt and stigma, or wish to keep family secrets. Often parents will avoid seeking help, taking a wait-and-see stance, or, if therapy has commenced, will reflect their ambivalence and resistance by forgetting the child's sessions, bringing the child late for appointments, taking vacations, etc. The therapist's resistances may evolve out of chronic problems with parents or discomfort with the special and unique demands of child therapy (e.g., facing children's fluctuating ego states, primitive expression, and primary-process material).

Case Example: Resistance

Arleen was 12½ years old at the time that her adoptive parents applied to a Family Service agency. The parents, especially mother, were eager for therapy for Arleen as well as parent guidance. Their presenting complaint was their anguish over Arleen's social isolation, underachievement in school, seeming masculine identification, and temper outbursts, which were only manifest at home in sadomasochistic interactions with mother. Arleen's only interest and area of manifest talent was horseback riding.

The parents, in their early fifties and unable to have children, had adopted Arleen as an infant via a private adoption. Mother, a school teacher, was employed part-time as a substitute. Father had long-standing problems in business; he owned a small grocery store in a ghetto neighborhood, which had chronic financial difficulty in competition with supermarkets. Father, the more passive parent, was very defensive about Arleen and rationalized and denied her problems as insignificant. He evidenced and verbalized his overgratification of his daughter, and his enjoyment of their mutually exclusive relationship. Despite these excesses, he was the parent who was consistent and nurturant. Mother, a diminutive and volatile woman, described her pattern of permissiveness and then explosiveness with Arleen, her resentment of her husband's undoing of any discipline, and her anguish over what she perceived as her daughter's unhappiness, loneliness, and lack of mastery and pleasure at school and with peers.

Arleen, a very tall and tomboyish looking girl, was in the throes of an ungainly adolescent development. She was somewhat overweight, self-conscious about her advanced physical development, and came for appointments most frequently in jeans and lumber jackets. Her hair was very short and boyish. Basically, she was most attractive, but this was well disguised by her attire and masculine stance. She was obviously of superior intellect. She belligerently and vehemently denied any concerns and discomfort with the present situation. Her only verbalized motivations for complying with the diagnostic study were to "tell her side" and to prove that her mother was the "crazy one." She expressed her wish that her mother be the client or patient, and be gotten off her back.

The developmental history highlighted precocious intellectual and motor development, no illnesses or separations, and much overindulgence and anxiety by doting parents. From age three to four, limit setting was a problem, and from that point on it was apparent that father could never allow the word "no" toward his "princess." Mother would displace onto Arleen her resentment of her husband, and the sadomasochistic pattern between mother and Arleen was well developed prior to school. Separation problems were apparent when Arleen was enrolled in dance classes. Attempts at nursery school were abandoned. Mother sought help at this point and was advised that it was a "phase," and that she should stay with Arleen in the dance classes. Upon entrance to a prekindergarten program, the separation anxieties again were clearly manifest. At age four, Arleen had to be kept at home after she severely burnt her shoulder and upper arm playing with matches.

During the diagnostic study, her plastic surgeon notified the parents of the readiness for starting the long-planned series of operations of skin grafting. Arleen had always been desirous of this procedure because of her self consciousness about the disfigurement. She totally denied any apprehension or anxiety.

For one and a half years, Arleen and her parents were seen separately in weekly interviews. The parents needed bolstering to sustain Arleen in therapy, since for eight months she constantly threatened to refuse to come to the agency. Because of certain resistance issues, the case was not split between two therapists, as was customary with many children's treatment cases. For purposes of this discussion, the focus will be on Arleen rather than the parents.

For eight months or more, Arleen would vacillate between presenting raving complaints about her mother and screaming at and threatening physical abuse of the therapist (She had in fact physically abused her mother several times). She also refused to listen to the therapist. She would make faces and sit with her fingers in her ears, or would read with her fingers in her ears, or would arrive with a transistor, which would be turned up full volume when the therapist opened her mouth. The therapist would verbalize what appeared to be issues at home, feelings about therapy, and feelings about the pending surgery. Arleen occasionally would talk with feeling and reason, or tears would appear, and the fingers in her ears were at times only gestures, in that she was clearly listening and not pressing her ears closed.

These times would always be short-lived, and the belligerence, sarcasm, and high-volume transistor would reappear. Sometimes child and therapist simply sat together.

At the time of Arleen's operation, the therapist sent flowers to the hospital, phoned her, and offered to visit, and was surprised when she did not refuse the offer. When she visited Arleen, Arleen was silent but not hostile; in fact, she was pleased by the visit. Her parents reported her overt denial of pain, despite her obvious discomfort. She "typically" was rude and demanding to her parents and the nurses, and strangely attached to the flowers sent by the therapist, keeping them after they were dead and dry, and then taking them home with her.

When Arleen resumed her appointments after the operation, she began to open up and talk sparingly. She would discuss horseback riding and then lapse into periods of silence and/or belligerent behavior. When Arleen's bas mitzvah was approaching, she invited her therapist in her fashion: "I'm sure that you wouldn't bother, and when not paid, wouldn't come in the evening to see me." Only partially concealing her astonishment, the therapist replied in a neutral and warm way that she would enjoy coming to see her.

Following this event, Arleen really made a commitment to treatment. She never could express any direct warmth, but did acknowledge something had happened. Fearful of failure, she slowly began to work in school, and in therapy shared some of her concerns, as well as two significant accomplishments. She opened up with peers and slowly began to form relationships with boys and girls. She went to some parties, lost weight, and began to change in her outer appearance, especially by moving into a more feminine identification. When she let her hair grow, and began to wear skirts and dresses, her demeanor shifted. She spoke of the future in a realistic fashion (i.e., going to college and being a gym teacher, rather than a stable hand), as well as things closer at hand, such as grade aspirations, school teams and committees, and the like. Arleen opted to terminate when she departed for summer camp. She saw the therapist for several subsequent months the following year about some academic concerns. Despite her belligerent and negativistic stance, she independently initiated this follow-up contact. She was belligerent and sarcastic during this period as well, although less intensely than before.

This child is described many years after her therapy, as her image remains vivid in the therapist's mind, in part because she unquestionably was the most difficult child the therapist ever treated. She made it nearly impossible to give to her. Communication often was nonverbal, via facial expression and gesture, as she shut the therapist out so much of the time. Humor expressed verbally and nonverbally proved effective. As obnoxious and provocative as Arleen could be, nonverbal therapeutic communications always conveyed mutual respect. It sounds strange perhaps to use the term "respect," but there is no other way to describe Arleen's expression when the therapist passed her various trials by fire, never exploding back at Arleen or allowing Arleen to frighten her.

This case underscores the need for the therapist's absolute respect of the child without becoming retaliatory in the face of unpleasant forms of resistance.

Defense

Defenses are manifest in a myriad of forms, i.e., via habitual modes of relating, acting out, and nonverbal expression. Defense is a general term used to describe struggles of the ego to protect itself against danger. The danger arises because of the threat of eruption into consciousness of a repressed wish that has become associated with painful feelings of anxiety or guilt, feelings that impel the ego to ward off the wish or drive. Defenses or defense mechanisms occur and operate unconsciously so that the individual is unaware of what is taking place. Not infrequently, when excessive defenses are called into action, there is a deletion or distortion of defense mechanisms.

The examination of defense organization involves assessing whether the defense is employed specifically against individual drives, or more generally against drive activity and instinctual phases. In addition, one must consider whether the defenses are age adequate, too primitive, or too precocious, and whether they deal effectively with anxiety or result in disequilibrium, lability, mobility, or deadlock within the structure. The defenses of patients who lack inner structure are due to ego deficits rather than fear and guilt. For example, the borderline child's impulsive acting out is commonly due to poor frustration tolerance, poor drive modulation, and a lack of internalized soothing mechanisms. The primitive defense of "splitting" mirrors the borderline child's defective object relations and lack of object constancy. Thus, objects are perceived as all good, all bad, or ever changing in terms of cathexis. There is a lack of tolerance of ambivalence, and attachment does not remain constant in the face of frustration. The child cannot remain irrevocably attached, irrespective of gratification.

Other important questions are whether and how far the child's defenses against the drives depend on the object world. It is always critical to note any secondary interference with ego achievement, i.e., the price paid by the child for the upkeep of the defense organization (Eissler et al., 1977).

As noted earlier, absence of defense is a serious danger sign. If defense against anxiety is lacking or completely unsuccessful, the child suffers panic states and full-blown anxiety attacks, both of which are harmful for the swamped and overwhelmed ego. "The occurrence of these [states] is indicative that the child's ego has failed to acquire the important ability to reduce harmful panic anxiety to structurally useful signal anxiety, i.e., to the much smaller amount which is necessary to set defense in motion" (Eissler et al., 1977, p. 45).

Denial is a primitive defense mechanism whereby the ego avoids becoming aware of some painful reality. The disagreeable or unwelcome fact is thereby erased. Projection is another primitive defense in which unwelcome thoughts or feelings are attributed outside the self. Splitting of self- and object representations is also a primitive and early defense. More advanced defenses commonly exhibited by latency-age children are displacement (transfer of hostile feelings, e.g., from parents to teachers) and reaction formation (replacement in conscious awareness of a painful idea or feeling by its opposite, e.g., a child's hate and resentment of a new sib is repressed and the younger exhibits extreme solicitude and concern towards the new sib). Undoing often follows and reinforces a reaction formation; e.g., in the above example of the new sib, the child would follow up the reaction formation by going to additional unreasonable lengths to be kind to the sib. Isolation "may be manifested as compartmentalized thinking . . . keeping things apart, separated . . . a child may recall an emotional experience in detail, but feel no emotion about it. He talks about it as if it had happened to someone else. Often children try to solve conflicts by isolating certain spheres of their lives from one another. They may think of themselves as two people" (Kessler, 1966, p. 65).

Additional defenses are identification with the aggressor (e.g., the feared father is identified with and peers at school are beaten up); reversal of affect (e.g., sad feelings about the parents' divorce are transformed into happy feelings); sublimation (energies of instinctual drives are neutralized and channeled into conflict-free activities that promote synthesis of the personality, e.g., artistic, musical, athletic, and academic investment); repression (conscious awareness of an idea or feeling is expelled and withheld, as exemplified by infantile amnesia and the blocking of early Oedipal feelings and attachments); and intellectualization (the older pubescent or adolescent child attempts to make everything abstract, impersonal, detached, and unemotional). Intellectualization is created to bind instinctual drives via intellectual activities. "Under favorable circumstances [it] may enrich knowledge and the intelligence, but pathological distortions create typical symptoms of obsessive and paranoid thought. Not infrequently, intellectualization is used during the course of . . . treatment as a resistance against achieving emotional insight" (Moore and Fine, 1968, p. 57).

Prior to establishing any treatment plan, the therapist must understand and accept the patient's defenses against anxiety. A nonretaliatory therapeutic stance must be maintained at all times, in the face of provocativeness, withholdingness, and other negative behaviors of the child, to enable a true working alliance to develop. Through this alliance, the child is helped to give up defenses and surmount resistance. Given the tenacity of these mechanisms, supervision and consultation are critical supports for the child therapist.

Regression

There are two types of regression: libidinal regression is manifested by a retreat to an earlier phase of instinctual organization (e.g., the latency child's reversion to thumb sucking following the stress and trauma of surgery); ego regression is manifested by a reversion to an earlier stage of mental organization (e.g., the latency child with unresolved Oedipal conflicts regresses to the anal phase, becoming stubborn, unreasonable, obsessive, and tormenting.

There are numerous causes of regression. Unpleasurable feelings such as guilt and anxiety, bodily pathology and illness, drug-induced states, and mental pathology all cause some retreat to an earlier phase of libidinal and ego organization. "The concept of regression is intimately related to the hypothesis that, in the course of attaining adulthood an individual passes through a series of maturational phases (psychosexual development), each with a phase-appropriate mental organization" (Moore and Fine, 1968, p. 86). Each phase has age-appropriate norms for instinctual drive discharge, ego functioning, and manifestations of conscience and ideals. When a phase and age-appropriate organization are substantially disrupted, regression occurs.

Fixation and regression are closely connected psychoanalytic concepts. "We speak of fixation to a given component instinct, to a phase of libidinal and aggressive development, to a type of object choice, to a type of object relationship, and to a traumatic experience" (Nagera, 1964, p. 223). We can observe children's fixation points by observing their play, behavior, attitudes, fantasies, and interests. Fixation points signify some degree of arrest in drive development. By contrast, regressive phenomena indicate that the drives have reached a higher level of development, but have been forced back to earlier developmental levels as a result of conflict (Nagera, 1964). When pregenital fixation is very strong, even slight difficulties at higher developmental levels will quickly lead to regressions. Nagera emphasizes the need for a thorough developmental history to ascertain the vicissitudes of a child's drive development, especially when there has been interference with normal development. In this way, one can pinpoint the regression. Such careful assessment aids in determining the prognosis and course of therapy.

Treatment—particularly psychoanalysis and intense, insight-oriented therapy—promotes regression in the service of the ego to allow earlier conflicts to be reactivated and reexperienced in an emotionally meaningful way. "Regression during the course of treatment is not an end in itself, but only a tactical means towards the end of helping the patient achieve emotional awareness of the nature of his conflicts. There must follow a reversal of the regression, in order for the patient to reintegrate or resolve the experienced conflicts in a more mature and healthy fashion from the standpoint of the secondary process and the reality principle" (Dewald, 1964, p. 233).

Case Example: Resistance and Regression (See Chapter 8, Borderline Syndrome—Case of Donald)

Donald, a 13-year-old borderline child, was seen in biweekly therapy for twenty months.[1] Initially, he responded with great warmth and pleasure to therapy and the therapist. In the 28th session, on the heels of some recent opposition to biweekly sessions and a stated preference for coming once a week, Donald was ten minutes late and refused to speak a word. He glared, quickly turned away, picked at his sneakers, observed his watch, feigned sleep, and would say nothing. He remained totally silent and withholding for seven months while keeping all appointments. At times he was provocatively late—sauntering in, sneering, and swinging a cowboy hat. By and large, despite his monumental resistance and regression, he was very involved in therapy and intensely related to the therapist. This was evident via most attentive listening and subsequent visible affects—anger and clenched teeth, sadness and tears, humor and delight and smiles. In addition, he attended sessions and overall was prompt. Despite his mutism in the therapy hour, outside of sessions, significant improvement took place, shared by his amazed parents who were confused by the changes in the face of what they knew to be his total silence and "lack of cooperation" in treatment. (Donald would boast about not speaking a word for months.) His grades improved immeasurably, his age-appropriate involvement with peers and athletic activities was marked, and he became more reasonable, realistic, and self-disciplined at home. When he resumed communicating in therapy sessions, seemingly out of the blue, he recounted being force fed, made by father to sit in front of cold cereal, spinach, and the like, for literally hours on end. Together, child and therapist could then link therapy with the forced feedings, and Donald could laugh and reflect with wonder that he hadn't succeeded in infuriating the therapist and making her yell at him or expel him. (Early in treatment he had been threatened with school exclusion, and in fact had been expelled from religious school.)

The therapist had used the technique of reflection, offering running comments, clarifications, and, at times, humor, amid a benign approach that was marked by calm, consistency, and punctuality. Any power struggle

[1]The assessment and diagnosis of Donald are discussed in Chapter 8 (borderline syndrome).

stance was avoided; nor did the therapist wait to be spoken to or answered. The approach was that of feeding, via offering gentle questions, comments, suggestions, and interpretations, accepting the resistance and regression, and recognizing that this youngster was gripped by something powerful and beyond his control, and that despite the conscious withholding, treatment nevertheless was occurring. It was clear that there had not been any genuine "working through" and that, ideally, Donald would return for further therapy when he could autonomously and independently seek it.[2] He chose to terminate upon entering adolescence, following a substantial period of improved functioning at an age-appropriate level.

Interpretation and Working Through of Trauma

Freud offers comforting advice when he instructs the neophyte "not to try to understand everything at once, but to give a kind of unbiased attention to every point that arises and to await further developments" (1909, p. 207). In therapy, children present material through play, toys, stories, drawings, role play, and verbal productions, and the different uses of the play material are the basis for the therapist's interpretations. The child displaces onto toys and externalizes object representations, self-representations, and the interaction between them via play material. By following the child's lead in regard to choice of material and mode of play, the therapist can sense how much to reflect and interpret to the child at any given point in the treatment process.

Many children will stop playing or cease relating dreams and fantasies if interpretation is too direct and brings the child too rapidly into painful material, especially that related to sexual or aggressive content. Usually it is less threatening when the therapist remains within the metaphor suggested by the child (e.g., uses the names the child has affixed in the role play or doll play) and initially refers to the affects aroused, rather than the core conflicts or unacceptable impulses and wishes. It is easier for a youngster to accept angry and impatient feelings such as irritation towards a sib than murderous or annihilating impulses.

One often wonders about timing and missed interpretations, though practice wisdom has shown that significant activities, themes, and epi-

---

[2]The term "working through" was "originally used by Freud to describe the continuing application of analytic work to overcome resistances persisting after the initial interpretation of repressed instinctual impulses. . . . It is the goal of working through to make insight effective, i.e., to bring about significant and lasting changes in the patient. . . . Despite initial improvements, unless these traumatic events are thoroughly worked through, therapeutic changes will not be maintained and the patient will relapse" (Moore and Fine, 1968, p. 95).

sodes will reappear in a child's play if not adequately handled the first time. Selection of relevant and important aspects of the child's material is most perplexing at the beginning of therapy, prior to knowledge of the child. Often children flood therapists with material. Sandler et al. (1980) note that "it is very necessary to differentiate between the problem of phrasing an interpretation so that the unconscious and repressed material can be made conscious and acceptable to the patient, on the one hand, and the problem of choosing the right time to give the interpretation to the patient, on the other" (pp. 178–179). While therapists may quickly ascertain what is being expressed, children may not be ready to accept information, as they have not been adequately prepared for it and have not begun to digest it, even though its presence is clear in a variety of derivatives (Sandler et al., 1980). External factors and crises very much affect the timing of an interpretation. Anna Freud describes situations of current stress and deprivation whereby the "affect of the patient is wholly engaged in the present and not, as is often said, because the present stress serves as a resistance to analysis" (Sandler et al., 1980, p. 177). The patient's conscious and preconscious preoccupations direct the therapist's course. Reality needs of children need to be met before any interpretation of current or chronic emotional deprivation can be meaningfully examined in therapy.

Caution is raised regarding the therapist possibly colluding too much with the child's defenses. When the child cannot tolerate direct interpretations, aids (e.g., metaphors, stories, universalizing the dilemma) often will diminish the child's defensiveness. In general, it seems more advantageous to make interpretations empathically and slowly, step by step, rather than by confrontation or undercutting of defenses and resistances with too direct an interpretation of content. Confronting the child directly generally only causes a resurgence of more intransigent defenses.

Significant interpretations bring about a shift in the patient's behavior or material, but they sometimes take time to effect such a change. After an interpretation is made for the first time, a period of working through is usually necessary. During this period, the interpretation may have to be repeated in different forms and different contexts (Sandler et al., 1980).

Insight and introspection often are linked with working through. Sterba (1934) describes introspection as a phenomenon in which one part of the patient's ego identifies with the analyst, shares in the analyst's increased understanding, and takes part in the therapeutic effort. Similarly, Kris (1956) defines insight as a process that makes use of the ego function of self-observation in both experiential and reflective form. Anna Freud (1965) states that while introspection and insight are normal in the adult, they are not present in the child. "Children do not scrutinize their thoughts and inner events, at least not unless they are obsessional. In the latter cases, this particular split is merely one among several other tendencies to be divided in themselves, such as heightened ambivalence, the inclination to isolate, the urge to exploit self-criticism and guilt for masochistic purposes, etc.; that is to say, in these cases, introspection serves pathological rather than constructive ends" (p. 221). Thus, children are not self-observant; they turn their natural curiosity and inquisitiveness toward the outer, rather than the inner, world until puberty, when excessive introspection may appear as part of the adolescent process (Anna Freud, 1965).

More recently, Anna Freud (1978) has reaffirmed her earlier comments on the absence of true insight in the young child patient. This reality she relates to the young child's "inability and unwillingness to embark on free association, to the difference in his transference reactions; to his unreliable treatment alliance; to his diminished sincerity and frustration tolerance, to the preponderance of motor activity over verbal expression, etc." (p. 3). In essence, the child's lack of sufficient ego development, which is a prerequisite for self-awareness and self-observation, precludes insight and introspection.

Kennedy (1971, 1978) believes that the primary aim of interpretive interventions is to help children resolve conflict impeding their development, rather than to give them insight into the past. However, she acknowledges that children can acquire specific kinds of insight in analysis during different developmental stages. Preschool children reflect a limited capacity for self-observation: via treatment, they can become aware of wishes, feelings, and some of their difficulties, but they lack the necessary cognitive skills for objective insight. Latency children direct their attention to the external world and thus, despite more developed cognitive capacities, resist introspection and insight into inner conflicts. They look for environmental solutions and external changes. Adolescents are introspective, use their intellectual capacities to gain fuller self-understanding, and have the potential for object insight, but they are not interested in their past, because their current difficulties and apprehensions about the future so absorb them. Thus, the past is inadequately understood by the young child and turned away from by the latency and adolescent child, who are greatly involved with their present and immediate concerns.

No matter how successful and productive a course of treatment, child patients do not fully internalize the analyzing function of their therapist, nor do they acquire or retain a full genetic understanding of their unconscious conflicts. Any insight acquired is directed towards aiding the child in current conflictual situations. Further, this insight will not necessarily help the child deal with later conflicts, as prelatency children generally repress much of the insight gained during treatment and older children often cannot recall much about their analysis

(Kennedy, 1978). Newbauer (1980) reminds us that the lack of introspection in child analysis and child therapy is based on a "general ego attitude characteristic of childhood and adhered to by the child as an effective deterrent against mental pain" (p. 36).

Thus, without the insight and introspection of the adult, how does the child patient achieve a working through? It is a process that reflects the elaboration and extension of relevant interpretations in different contexts over a protracted period of time, and in essence is the consolidation of the treatment work. Anna Freud (Sandler et al., 1980, p. 183) offers a rich and humorous vignette about the treatment of a little girl with "a great penis envy which I interpreted busily and repeatedly." One day the girl announced that she really understood things and realized "that there was no sense in always envying boys. After all, what boys had was not so important. What she would really like to be was an elephant because they had such a wonderful trunk. So there was the whole problem once again and it made me very thoughtful at the time. The problem just took on another disguise" (p. 183).

This illustration clearly demonstrates that an interpretation itself is not magic. The child's tenacity in clinging to wishes and distorted perceptions is rarely fully accepted by a wide range of mental health workers. The repercussions are less amusing than in the above example when one considers the frequent split between a child's cognitive grasp and emotional cathexis (e.g., to significant objects) of a situation. Child welfare workers are often puzzled and frustrated by children who comprehend the abuse they endured in the home, yet nevertheless only wish for reunion with the abusing parent. Working through and resolution of both internalized and externalized conflict require considerable time and repeated encounters, with interpretations in different contexts. The thoroughness of working through is far greater in child analysis than in child psychotherapy. Sandler et al. state "that sufficient working through has taken place when the child has moved to the next level of development and established himself there" (1980, p. 184). Working through occurs simultaneously with the child's normal structural development and the two processes interact with one another.

Sandler et al. point out that often when adults recover a memory of a traumatic early experience, it is accompanied by abreaction, relief, and even permanent change. This phenomenon is not applicable to young children, in that "the interpretation is of value only if it increases the child's understanding of what is currently happenning" (1980, p. 186).

Case Example: Working Through of Trauma (See Chapter 8, Character Disorder—Case of Mike)

In 3½ years of biweekly and triweekly psychotherapy, Mike, a 10-year-old character-disordered child, ultimately came to work through his anger, feelings of displacement, and sibling rivalry caused by the rapid succession of younger sibs.[3] Most critical was his working through of the shocking loss of grandmother, the surrogate mother of his preschool years. While his memories of his happiness and closeness with her, as well as his memory of her funeral, could be shared, he could not get connected with his shock and despair at the time of her death, or following. He could recount details and fragments connected with her, but his unresolved mourning was striking. Interpretations about his current generalized fears of the unexpected were related to phenomena of his early years (sibs unexpectedly arriving, and then the sudden loss of grandmother). Mike showed no abreaction, or breakthrough of the unshed tears for grandmother. What appeared to be fruitful was his gradual recognition of his fears of floods, tornadoes, and all forms of unexpected, uncontrollable, destructive phenomena. As his fears diminished, he entered the world of latency and peers, giving up his prior isolation and preoccupations with omnipotent fantasies and drawings. It would appear that working through had little to do with his sophisticated articulations in sessions, which were rather suggestive of underlying compliance and identification. (He spoke of interest in therapy as a process, as well as ambitions to become a psychiatrist, having surrendered "babyish" plans to become a racing car driver.) The signs of genuine working through were related to Mike's ability to move from an arrested position to an age-appropriate level of development, and to function adequately and comfortably at that level, demonstrating increased mastery in handling the significant lines of development.

[3]The assessment and diagnosis of Mike are discussed in Chapter 8 (character disorder); also see Chapters 14 (verbalization and the unconscious in children's communications) and 17.

CHAPTER 16

Collateral Contacts and Collaboration

Group Homes, Hospitals, and Residential Centers

According to the Greek myth, the giant Procustes offered travelers hospitality at his inn on the condition that they slept in a certain bed. If the bed was too long for the traveler, he was stretched in order to fit it; if the bed was too short, his feet were sawed off to make him fit. In other words, the traveler had to fit the bed, rather than the bed the traveler. "This Procustian method of adaption is used in child welfare" (Mayer, et al., 1977, p. 173). Most recently, there has been a push against any and all removal of children from home. After this period of "deinstitutionalization," we have again, most recently, recognized and accepted the reality that some children must be in therapeutic residences. We must judge

> whether the negatives outweigh the positives in the family for giving a child parental care; whether the child will gain more from placement than be remaining in the troubled home; whether it is necessary that he live elsewhere so he can have treatment for some serious emotional and mental disturbance which is more handicapping than the scars of separation and the unknowns of placement; and whether there are reality factors which make it impossible for the child to be cared for in his family [Glickman, 1957, p. 22].

Kessler (1966) reminds us of the need for careful examination of these questions before taking the drastic step of removing a child from home. There are no magic cures; residential treatment is hard work that requires the collaboration of many highly trained and dedicated professional workers who have adequate financial and community support.

Effective collaboration requires that staff or team members respect, trust, and accept one another. Compton and Galaway (1979) note that there are both cooperative and competitive elements in the relationships among the helpers. Collaboration and communication are necessary to provide the child with the most effective help possible. Hooyman (1975) notes five important team processes or team dynamics: problem-solving, communication and feedback, leadership, decision making, and conflict resolution.

Despite the reality that childcare staff, cottage parents, and mental health aides are the backbone of the varied residential programs serving children in care, they are consistently viewed as less important than professional staff and are not commonly well integrated into the treatment team. Rapid turnover among these workers is common and creates breakdowns in communication, staff tensions, and defective childcare and management (Berwald, 1960). Typically, these staff members reflect their resentment of the status system of institutions by missing conferences, forgetting children's therapy sessions, ignoring therapist's advice, and not reporting incidents of significance. "As the cottage parents' morale deteriorates, they come to feel less identified with the institution's purposes, and they may be convinced that the 'powers that be' do not appreciate them. Discouraged, they tend to become less conscientious about cottage life, and some drift into a compromise with the children's methods of managing themselves" (Matsushima, 1964, p. 288).

Effective treatment is dependent on integrated efforts and meaningful collaboration between the professional and nonprofessional staff of an institution. Improved salaries, better housing, and shorter hours for paraprofessional staff are insufficient. They must feel adequately trained for and invested in their work and respected, by their coworkers, which can be accomplished via inservice training, supervision, and consultation, and an associated communication structure that facilitates effective sharing and dialogue. In addition to requiring support and education, paraprofessionals have a legitimate need for specific responsibility, power, and authority. Mayer (1960) asks, who holds the power in the institution? The larger the institution, the more difficult it is to answer this question. One can cite the administrators, the department of mental hygiene, the director, etc., but, in fact, the institutionalized child is surrounded by surrogate parent figures. "The people who take care of the child during the day, the 'care parents,' are very important figures, although the structure of the institution and often their own personality needs let them appear as weak. . . . The person in charge of the institution, the 'power parent,' plays a remote but very important role to the child. . . . The degree to which the therapist of the child becomes a parent figure depends on the pathology of the child and the particular form of therapy" (Mayer, 1960, p. 287). All in all, the integration, collaboration, and cooperation of these surrogate parent figures constitute one of the most difficult functions of the institution.

The literature repeatedly advocates the need to elevate the status of aides, mental health specialists, childcare staff, and cottage parents, but there seems to be more lip service than readiness to act (Mayer et al., 1977). Despite recent movements (i.e., community college and graduate school programs) aimed at training the "psychoeducator," the life expectancy (the exhaustion point) of those providing direct childcare is low (Mayer et al., 1977). Such childcare staff with degrees rarely go back to childcare work, but rather, become supervisors or administrators.

Children's settings have three major staff groups: (1) the managers (i.e., executives, supervisors, department heads, and consultants); (2) the practitioners (i.e., childcare workers, teachers, therapists, recreation workers, and all those whose major function is direct work with the child and family); and (3) the maintainers (i.e., maintenance personnel, clerical workers, accountants, housekeepers, and cooks) (Mayer et al., 1977). The degree of cohesive and collaborative effectiveness appears to be based on many human variables—personal rapport, trust and familiarity, length of work relationship, etc. Many institutions request a minimum time commitment to provide better continuity of staff and thus better services to the children. In addition, a decentralized, small, intimate team format facilitates genuine communication. Sufficient time for meeting and conferring also serves as an antidote to some of the perennial dilemmas of effective collaboration and teamwork.

Despite attention to salaries, supervision, status, power, and familiarity with organizational theory, role theory, etc., considerations of effective collaboration are incomplete without a focus on countertransference. Residential facilities are intense settings that universally create inordinate demands on all staff members. "The essence of the residential treatment process is that as each child projects his inner world against the macrocosm of the residence, by and large the staff will find within itself, the strength to resist stepping into the projected transference roles" (Eckstein et al., 1957, p. 186). If a child can evoke from staff the response given by his family, treatment inevitably will flounder. This is one of the major tests and trials for those experiencing prolonged exposure to very disturbed children, and the stress can create interdisciplinary conflicts, competition, undermining, and collusions. Staff members often believe that they represent the "good" parents, replacing the "bad" and destructive natural parents; they struggle with rescue fantasies, which may become entangled with struggles between the staff members and the therapist, who has come to represent the child's natural parent. When a child is taxing, enraging, destructive, and overwhelming to unit staff, the therapist is commonly blamed. Under the onslaught of profoundly destructive and primitive behaviors, staff members can lose their perspective on the child's symptomatology, as they attempt to "master feelings of repugnance, anxiety, anger and frustration" (Eckstein et al., 1957, p. 204). Winnicott (1949) refers to the anxiety and hatred of psychotic quality produced in those who work with severely ill psychiatric patients. Eckstein et al. (1957) aptly note the peripheral spread that includes people not directly involved with a given patient (i.e., those outside the psychotherapy or living unit); a staff's fear, anxiety, and frustration can enable a single child to dominate the entire structure of a residence, disturbing every aspect of the setting.

Such breakdowns of collaboration with consequent treatment disruption are attributed to the attempt "to prevent certain unconscious conflicts in the treatment staff from coming into consciousness, namely, to keep from consciousness that potential for behaving like a real mother which the child had so deftly aroused" (Eckstein et al. 1957, p. 212). In fact, Eckstein et al. (1957) suggest that staff's intense responses arise as the child becomes "less sick, gives up his autistic preoccupations and begins increasingly to intrude into relationships around him" (p. 213).

Many children with far less severe pathology are master manipulators and splitters, having suffered families lacking a parental coalition. Thus, in placement, they replay old patterns and require care by adults who have a genuine coalition and collaboration. A residential facility for children can easily be likened to a family, with its overt and covert roles and reciprocity patterns. The healthy family or institution is an open-ended, predictable, and consistent system whose members develop rules, roles, values, and patterns of behavior, communication, and coping for managing their instinctual drives and impulses.

Collaborative Techniques

Specific techniques that promote staff collaboration and coalition entail various forms of communication and mutual support. Sharing verbally and via chart or shift notes is crucial. Regular meetings involving milieu and recreation workers, teachers, therapist, and administrators—as well as informal conferences when the need arises—are essential. Of course, such formal and informal meetings are only possible with the support and cooperation of the institution. Meeting time is critical for staff members' abreaction of their counterreactions and countertransference responses to the children, as well as discussion of their feelings about organizational and administrative policies and issues.

Maintaining the limits set by staff on duty earlier, rather than "soft guy surrender," is critical to enable the children to believe in the staff and the institution. The children inevitably will test, provoke, and reach for the Achilles heel of individuals and/or groups. Administrators and supervisors cannot unilaterally undo progress and procedures set down by staff if the staff is to be respected by, and effective with, the children.

Organizational leadership is a pivotal variable in considering collaborative efforts in a multidisciplinary setting. The literature describes the effects of the regressive pressures of psychiatric institutions on their administrators. Kernberg (1979) emphasizes the pathological character structures of many administrators; i.e., the authoritarian personality, the schizoid personality, the obsessive personality, the paranoid personality, and the narcissistic personality. He also points out that crisis in organization may appear to be caused solely by the personality problems of the leader whereas, in fact, careful analysis reveals a more complex situation. "Quite frequently, a breakdown in work effectiveness stemming from various internal organizational factors and relationships between the organization and the environment induces regressive group processes first, and regression in the functioning of the leadership later" (Kernberg, 1979, p. 24).

The decline of morale in psychiatric organizations may reflect conflicts in the organizational structure, the negative impact of the leader's personality, the regressive pull directly induced by the pressure of patients' conflicts, and the vicissitudes of patient care—or a combination of all of these factors. Clarification of the dilemma often involves task definition, and examination of the administrative structure and the quality and nature of the leadership.

The leader is evaluated according to appraisal of his or her judgment, previous experience, conceptual skills, reactions under stress, strength of convictions, tolerance for criticism, and warmth and flexibility coupled with firmness and clarity. In addition, one must determine whether the administrator encourages and facilitates genuine "participatory management," an open-systems-theory approach to organizational management which, "as a general principle, is an important protection against regressive effects of the leader's personality on the administrative structure" (Kernberg, 1979, p. 28).

Finally, under the best of circumstances, there will be built-in organizational constraints, conflicts, and obstacles to 100 percent collaboration and effective communication. These relate to the "human condition" of social organizations—that is, the inherent limitations of all the individual personalities involved. "Some battles need to be fought over and over again, endlessly so" (Kernberg, 1979, p. 38). The real question is whether an institution tolerates openness and readiness to do battle and engage in creative tension, or silences staff and thereby promotes fearfulness and compliance, which mask underlying stress and opposition. Kernberg (1979) concludes that the growing psychoanalytic knowledge about the crucial importance of internal, in contrast to external, object relations, and about the mutually regressive relationships between individuals and within groups constitutes an important practical tool for the selection of leaders.

Schools

In 1969, Peller observed and commented on the "crisis" in contemporary public education; the grim picture she portrayed is even more apt today. Peller stated that historically education had fostered great conservatism while advocating great change, and that one of the most pressing contemporary problems was adherence to outmoded practices despite lip service to new slogans about "motivating children." Given the radical societal changes that had occurred, Peller believed that schools required a thorough-going analysis, in contrast to minor improvements. A major concern was that students and teachers merely "served time"; teachers were preoccupied, struggling to discipline and to create "busy work" amid rigid timetables, so that teachers and children rarely experienced gratification and mastery in their respective roles.

A 1969 report of the Joint Commission on Mental Health of Children stated,

> The schools have become the scapegoat for the problems they reflect, but do not necessarily create. The schools have become the target for angry protests from all points of the ideological compass, and from all sectors of society. . . . These attacks spring in part from the stresses engendered in social changes and the impact of these stresses on the mental health of us all. Such attacks also erode the mental health of . . . administrators and teachers [which] cannot help but have adverse effects on the youth who attend these schools [pp. 385–386].

The report also cited the fact that many teachers tended to teach in the same constricted, "lecture and drill" way they had been taught.

Unquestionably, schools are most complex institutional systems, often nearly impossible to administrate and direct. Schools provide a wide variety of services that are extremely difficult to integrate. Among the numerous significant causes of internal problems in the contemporary school are massive educational and emotional needs of the student body, as well as staff anxieties resulting from the uncertainties inherent in the educational process and staff's enormous responsibility for the welfare of the children (Mishne, 1974).

In 1970, Lustman, the former chairman of the Task Force IV, Joint Commission on Mental Health of Children recounted the dilemma of educators:

> educators are an unappreciated, beleaguered, and underpaid profession: work fatigue, insecurity, frustration, and consequent job change remain inordinately high; and the magnitude and complexity of the tasks at hand are increasing at a disconcerting pace. . . . Physical health, mental health, and a multitude of developmental responsibilities believed to be firmly lodged in the home, parents, families, and a host of other societal institutions such as the church, industry, medicine, psychoanalysis, social work, welfare, the law, and the police are now considered integral to the province of education [pp. 483–484].

After the post-World War II baby boom, the overwhelming majority of voting adults had children in school and supported public education. Shanker (1981) notes that the situation has changed; "no longer do we have districts where 70% or more of the voters have school age children. In many communities fewer than 30% do" (p. 7E). Shanker advocates that schools will have to reach out for funds and support as never before, and he recommends tapping the military and the business community, i.e., groups interested in hiring graduates with sound educational skills.

Fiscal crises and funding problems are not the only urgent pressures. Lustman (1970) suggests that the current state of affairs has been intensified and exacerbated by a misapplication of certain political, social, and economic values to education. "I speak specifically of egalitarianism, which correctly applies to many social, economic, and civil-libertarian issues, which nevertheless obfuscates individual differences in educational capability and educational need" (p. 484). Political considerations regarding funding, demographic patterns, and the desire to remove stigma have resulted in hotly debated practices of "mainstreaming" children with insufficient attention to meeting their individual needs. The recent enlargement of the schools' mandate to include character development, delinquency, drug abuse, sexual enlightenment, and numerous mental health problems has blurred boundaries further and overburdened educational institutions (Lustman, 1970).

Lustman recommends a redefinition of education, with educational activity returned to educators, who require enhanced professional status and salaries, and new career patterns or career ladders. Schools must clarify their role as a social institution. Teachers and other school personnel must counteract the tendency of communities to expect the impossible (Mishne, 1974).

Teachers and educational administrators must be the ones to re-define and delineate their own boundaries, as well as determine the kind of consultation and collaboration they prefer. The 1969 report of the Joint Commission on Mental Health of Children states that "it is imperative that teachers operate in a climate in which they could par-ticipate as full-fledged citizens with clearly defined rights and respon-sibilities" (p. 391). Educational personnel need to feel more secure and respected before they can interact effectively with children, parents, and political groups in the community.

Psychoanalysis has had a long and fruitful association with educa-tion. "It has been said that through most of the history of psycho-analysis, there have been bridges which lead from one area of psycho-analysis to the area of education" (Ekstein and Matto, 1972, p. 25). Lustman contends that "psychoanalysts have never made 'demands' on educators [and that] their collaboration is an old and fruitful one characterized by mutual benefit" (1970, p. 486). The collaboration of these two disciplines goes beyond their mutual interest in children; in fact, some of the most distinguished psychoanalysts (e.g., Erikson and Anna Freud) have been drawn from the field of education. Kris (1948) highlighted communication between the two disciplines and predicted fruitful cross-fertilization.

In the past, this cross-fertilization commonly occurred because of the presence of social workers in the public schools; their original stated function and purpose was to help students with emotional and personality difficulties that interfered with their learning. "Students' interactional behaviors with school personnel—withdrawal, testing, restlessness—have been assessed and treated as psychological phe-nomena. As a result, school social workers have tried to help minority children to adapt and adjust to the school and its representatives; in so doing, they have placed the major responsibility and burden for change upon the children" (Gitterman, 1977, p. 114). Gitterman suggests that this single approach may have exacerbated the debilitating impact of the school experience, stigmatized the children, and reinforced their negative educational self-perceptions.

Despite Street's recommendation (1967) that the school be the ob-ject of study for change, efforts to broaden the conception of school social work function and purpose to include the school and community context have met resistance (Vinter and Sarri, 1965; Bruce, 1975; Cos-tin, 1975). Gitterman recommends a dual function for school social workers, namely, (1) engaging parents in the educational system while simultaneously influencing school administrators and representatives to be responsive to parents' interests and concerns, and (2) helping children to use the school and its staff while simultaneously influencing school representatives to be responsive and receptive to children's individualized needs. It is suggested that by this dual function, the school social workers "place themselves in the midst of the school community, teacher-student encounter, representing a dynamic third force, that assumes responsibility for keeping lines of communication open, for identifying, partializing and challenging interactional obstacles and searching out common interests and concerns" (Gitterman, 1977, p. 115). Gitterman's major conclusion is that the burden of adaptation and change should no longer rest solely upon the children.

Street (1967) notes the "sibling rivalry" between social workers and educators; he suggests that the above imaginative foci must be undertaken, not by school social workers alone, given the potential for an adversarial struggle, but rather, by a collaborative team of mental health personnel and elected or appointed educators and educational administrators. Currently, education for social work embraces consideration of specific skills as adjuncts; these skills are rooted in the dynamics of human service delivery systems. Schodek (1981) enumerates the need for understanding "(1) systems theory; (2) models for analysis of organizations; (3) concepts of power and authority (both formal and informal); and (4) the governmental, patronage, civil service, union, professional, and community needs that shape human service delivery" (p. 199). Technique for system intervention include establishing linkages between the various components of these services, fostering conflict or cooperation between various sources of sanction for human service delivery, advocacy, educating the general public, etc. Education and preventative services are inherent in an outreach approach. "Special efforts must be made within each community to reach out to those for whom services are intended, in that many clients do not know about available resources, or wait until their problems reach crisis proportions and all other sources of support are exhausted" (Toseland, 1981, p. 227).

A focus beyond the individual child is advocated by Moss (1976), who recommends ongoing consultation in the inner-city school. She believes that the role of the consultant needs to be reconceptualized to clarify the psychological effects of the educational process on the child, the teacher, and the administrator. She notes the threat to teachers' self-esteem due to inappropriate and inconsistent expectations, anxiety over adequacy and competence, and questions regarding aggression, all of which culminate in the constant bombardment of the teachers' and children's egos. Moss recommends that the consultant rely on clinical knowledge and practice skills. "The two major thrusts of intervention are ego educative and ego strengthening" (1976, p. 145).

Consultation and collaboration can both provide clients with optimal professional help and maximize staff educational development (Shelmire et al., 1980). This joint endeavor is currently hampered by xenobia, and inexperience in interdisciplinary dialogue. Sarason (1963) documents some of the inherent problems. He notes that teachers have not been adequately trained to handle children's psychological problems or to communicate effectively with parents, and they are most aware of the inadequacy of their preparation. Conversely, the bulk of mental health workers are ill prepared to communicate with teachers and often give poor advice due to their relative ignorance of the inordinate demands of the classroom and the complex overt and covert authority in school systems.

Kris eloquently discusses the phenomenon of externalization onto psychiatric consultants in the public schools. "Externalization . . . occurs within the context of an object relationship and consists of the attribution of a part of the mental structures or their contents to the object" (1978, p. 643). Externalization may be conceived as overlapping the concept of projective identification and/or as a subspecies of transference. Kris gives examples of teachers' projections and externalizations, such as greeting the consultant with, "Here comes the mind reader" or "Here comes the sex maniac" (1978, p. 644). Consultants often are greeted with stereotyped, impersonal, or anxious responses; or the overwhelming helplessness and demoralization of teaching staff may be externalized onto the consultant. Kris also cites positive and enhancing externalizations whereby the consultant is viewed as an auxiliary ego who aids in problem solving and provides a conceptual framework of understanding, as well as recognizing and validating the teachers' efforts.

There is considerable literature on the consultation process (e.g., Babcock, 1949; Berlin, 1962; Caplan, 1970; Berkowitz, 1975; Vanderpool, 1976; and Hitchcock, 1977), but less on the collaborative process. Some consultants elect a collaborative approach in work with institutional settings in order to develop competent organizational diagnosis and problem solving in the client system.

Members of institutions struggle with dependence-independence in relation to a consultant. Often the real internal problems are carefully avoided and continue to fester and erode the effectiveness of the institution's work. As in a family, there are spoken and unspoken roles and rules, as well as special relationships, affected by overt and covert conflicts, which determine authority and responsibility (Mishne, 1974).

Unlike collaboration, consultation sometimes lapses into the pitfall of providing overt or disguised therapy to the client, i.e., the school and its staff. The reality is that many phenomena in a treatment relationship are manifest in the consultant-consultee arrangement. These may be grouped in three chronological phases: (1) the initial preparation, diagnosis, and establishment of trust; (2) the middle phase of problem solving, which entails listening, defining the core anxiety, assessing the dilemma, and identifying the reality; systematic exploration of alternative solutions; and avoidance of premature interpretations or impulses to take over; and (3) termination, when the school can proceed independently (Mishne, 1974). This final step may not occur when the consultant participates in ongoing case conferences, or staffings of children presenting behavior and learning problems. Nevertheless, eventually, after exposure and education, teachers should know when and how to make appropriate referrals.

Approaches in Collaborative Work with Schools

When a child is referred for treatment, the child's teacher is contacted for information on the youngster's social, academic, and behavioral adjustment.[1] The child therapist may phone the teacher directly or proceed via initial contact with the school principal, guidance personnel, and/or psychologist or social worker. Commonly, these people cannot provide as complete and detailed a picture of a child as can the classroom teacher, who has the richest observations and the greatest amount of information. Nevertheless, initial contact with such administrative personnel may constitute the needed protocol for entree into a given school system. This contact with school personnel is routinely predicated on confidentiality and parental permission, formalized with a standardized "release of information" form. Often, the child therapist seeking the teacher's observations is not at liberty to share the family dynamics in full with school personnel.

The Buckley Amendment (19) opened school records to parents and older adolescents, thereby creating greater caution about what therapists discuss or transmit in written form to schools. This form of collaboration, minus full disclosure by therapists, is similar to the confidentiality and right to privacy of the hospitalized or placed child whose therapist does not share all with the child's natural parents, surrogate parents (i.e., house parents, aides, and childcare staff), or teachers.

Within the constraints of confidentiality, it is often fruitful for teacher and therapist to have an ongoing contact that goes beyond information sharing. Teachers in schools that lack consultants often request advice and suggestions regarding the most effective ways to approach a troubled child—in regard to limit setting and discipline,

[1]See Chapters 3 and 12.

social adjustment, and academic learning. The therapist must be sensitive to and aware of the ecology of the classroom—the number of students, the emotional environment, the needs of the class as a whole, and the overall constraints and demands on the given teacher. Recommending one-to-one tutoring in an overpopulated classroom can demoralize a teacher. A therapist lacking knowledge of and sensitivity to the typical stresses of the educational sector frequently alienates teachers.

The child's therapist should never confer with the child's teacher without informing the child. Just as children must be informed about appointments between therapist and parents, so must they be made aware of teacher/therapist communication, what won't be shared, what will be discussed, etc. If a child objects to contact with the school, it is generally essential to honor the child's feelings and work them through before proceeding with the school collaboration which, one hopes, eventually will be comprehended as being in "the child's best interest."

Collaboration is not a unilateral, universal intervention. In specific instances—for example, when the child does not have problems in the school arena, or when parents can ably handle ongoing conferring with teachers—the therapist may not need to have ongoing collaborative school contacts. In some cases, parental paranoia and fear of what might be revealed preclude teacher/therapist contact until such time as the parents are more trusting and firmly established in a therapeutic alliance. In contrast to public schools, treatment settings such as therapeutic day schools, children's psychiatric hospitals, and residential treatment institutions routinely use collaboration. Team meetings are a typical means of interstaff communication involving teachers, therapists, and milieu workers. The goal of such team meetings is to share observations and determine the most effective way to provide a structured, consistent, and predictable environment.

Outcomes of collaborative work with schools are varied. Ideally, joint efforts by teacher and therapist facilitate greater understanding of the child's symptomatology and underlying problems; the teacher may be helped to become more empathic, accepting, and supportive of the child while the therapist, by seeing a fuller picture of the child, may become less overidentified, less swayed by the child's mode of relating to adults, and more cognizant of the child's overall problems. Often, the gratifying, permissive, one-to-one atmosphere of the therapy sessions brings out islands of ego strength in the child, blinding the therapist to the gestalt of the child and causing the therapist to "blame" parents and teachers for the child's environmental conflicts. Collaboration can enrich the diagnostic assessment; in some cases, environmental alterations such as tutoring or a change of schools may be recommended as adjuncts to therapy.[2] In addition, conferring and collaboration can clarify diagnostic dilemmas inherent in children who present learning disabilities.

Conversely, conferring and collaboration can flounder if and when professional competitiveness causes colleagues to malign one another and/or to fail to respond to calls and requests for contact from fellow workers. Current reimbursement policies for both individual clinicians and mental health clinics frequently do not allow for nonpatient contacts and thus constitute a genuine obstacle to ongoing productive collaboration. Staff turnover is disruptive to collaborative working relationships, and exhausting and frustrating for both therapist and teacher.

The complexities of school systems must be kept in mind by the child therapist attempting to deal with a patient's school. A school system may evaluate and place children via its own professional staff (e.g., school social workers, school psychologists, and consulting psychiatrists), whose findings may be at variance with those of the child's therapist; repeated conferring may be necessary to arrive at a program that is in the child's best interest. Street's caution (1967) about "sibling rivalry" is apt in such instances of divergent professional views. Ultimately, the best and most effective collaborative endeavors between schools and therapists are predicated on a working alliance in which trust and respect for collegiality allow for varied perspectives.

Clearly, the contemporary school system is expected to go beyond its traditional role. Day care is one of the newer services schools in some urban areas are providing. The educational system, with its new extended boundaries, is a hub that requires a network of collaborative endeavors provided by a range of professionals. In some quarters, school systems have proceeded beyond the tradition of hiring part-time consultants. Rather, they have entered into consortiums with social agencies and mental health clinics within the immediate community.

To achieve more genuine large-scale collaboration, changes may be necessary at the university level, where teachers and mental health professionals can be offered interdisciplinary training to counteract later professional rivalries. It appears that schools no longer can rely solely on educators, just as social work and psychiatric facilities serving children cannot continue to manage without trained educators. Unfortunately, such mutually respectful collegiality and interdisciplinary training of doctors, psychologists, teachers, and social workers exist in only a few child therapy programs, such as Anna Freud's Hampstead Clinic (Mishne, 1974). Cross-fertilization among the various disciplines also exists in some graduate and undergraduate programs. "Any multi-

---

[2]See Chapter 7.

disciplinary group charged with planning for generations to come, however divergent their initial focus, must inevitably converge on our schools. This is not only 'where the children are', but is an enterprise which commands the nation's largest professionally trained group of workers" (Lustman, 1970, p. 483).

CHAPTER 17

Termination

Criteria

The criteria or indications for termination of a child's treatment are many and varied, and will be considered from both an ideal and a practical standpoint. Neubauer (1968) emphasizes that the decision to terminate is not based solely on the removal of symptoms or pathology. He states that a developmental appraisal seems more appropriate. If the child's development shows noticeable progression and has gone beyond points of fixation (notwithstanding phase-appropriate conflicts or problems), and/or if the youngster demonstrates the capacity to handle problematic environmental conditions, then termination may be indicated.

As noted earlier, less regression is encouraged in psychotherapy than in analytic treatment, and the focus is more on the here-and-now, interpersonal child-therapist relationship than on early infantile conflicts.[1] The goals of psychotherapy are to aid the child to (1) increase the capacity for reality testing, (2) strengthen object relationships, and

[1] See Chapter 1.

(3) loosen fixations. The concept of age-appropriate functioning relates to development and developmental lines. "Far from being theoretical abstractions, developmental lines, in the sense here used, are historic realities, which when assembled, convey a convincing picture of an individual child's personal achievements, or, on the other hand, of his failures in personality development" (Anna Freud, 1965, p. 64).

In determining whether a child needs further treatment, Anna Freud (1965) emphasizes that the therapist should examine the child's libidinal and aggressive expression—the ego and superego sides of the child's personality—"for signs of age-adequateness, precocity or retardation" (p. 55). The primary concerns are the norms, compromise formations, and solutions that have been achieved. The child's capacity to develop progressively—or respectively, the damage to that capacity—is the most significant feature in determining a child's mental future (Anna Freud, 1962). In considering the ideal criteria for termination, one must return to the issues of assessment, as neither symptomatology or life tasks alone serve as reliable guides. Scrutiny of the observable internal and external circumstances and symptoms that may interfere with future growth is most important. Nagera's discussion (1964) of arrest in development, fixation, and regression is applicable both to the assessment process and to the timing of termination.

Apart from the child's capacity to develop progressively, practicality requires full consideration of the parents, given the young child's dependence on them. Neubauer (1972) underscores the role of the parents during treatment and termination. Sometimes, after symptom reduction in the child occurs, the relieved parents wish to discontinue the treatment. In such cases, the child may evidence other conflicts that are not disturbing to the parents; in fact, these conflicts may provide unconscious gratification. "We must also include here, the relationship of the parents to their other children. They may feel that it would be unfair to support the needs of one child financially (and timewise, per the demands of therapy) while depriving the others thereby of the rightful fulfillment of their needs" (Neubauer, 1972, p. 249).

Ross (1964) makes the distinction between interruptions and termination of treatment but notes that whenever the therapist withdraws, the child experiences it as a rejection. In addition, when the parents pull the child out of treatment, the child may blame the therapist for not succeeding in protecting, opposing, and controlling the parents. When the therapist decides to terminate, parents as well as child often feel abandoned. Sandler et al. (1980) state that relatively few analyses of children are terminated according to plan, but in fact are interrupted by a variety of external circumstances such as therapist or family moving away, change of schools, etc.

Preparation

An important technical and clinical consideration is whether an unplanned interruption that necessitates termination comes suddenly or allows enough advance notice for some working through. The issue of preparation affects all of the technical interventions, which vary with the patient's age, developmental phase, and psychopathology. Francis (1968) believes that recommendations for environmental changes are valid in the terminal phase, particularly as a preventative measure. There has been considerable controversy and debate regarding the process of termination in child analysis and therapy (i.e., should it be gradual, with a tapering off, or final?). Weiss (1968) notes that child patients often have great difficulty surrendering the therapist, clinging to the therapist as they cling to old objects, conflicts, and wishes. Kohrman (1968) notes that the analyst often has great difficulty separating from and relinquishing the child. The questions regarding the handling of termination relate closely to those regarding transference and countertransference phenomena in the treatment of children.[2]

Anna Freud (1980) distinguishes between the handling of termination for the child and the adult analysand.

> It never seemed quite logical to me that terminating a child analysis should involve the complete separation from the analyst that it usually does for adult patients. With children there is the loss of a real object as well as the loss of the transference object, and this complicates matters. To make an absolute break from a certain date onward merely sets up another separation, and an unnecessary one. If normal progress is achieved, the child will détach himself anyway, in the course of time, just as children outgrow their nursery school teachers, their school teachers and their friends at certain stages" (Freud, 1980, in Sandler et al., 1980, p. 243).

Thus, she recommends a gradual detachment, with reduction in frequency of visits and continued availability of the analyst as a benign background figure. (Of course, this continued availability depends on the nearby residence of child and therapist and would not be possible in cases involving distant moves.)

In child therapy, the focus during termination is less on transference phenomena and more on the here-and-now real relationship of clinician and child. An unfortunate response to the mobility of trainees and mental health professionals, and thus the inevitability of case transfer, has been a less-than-humane approach based on the antiquated notion of "interference with the transference" to the next therapist. It is critical to emphasize that in such cases termination and/or

[2]See Chapter 13 (transference, the real relationship, and countertransference).

transfer of the patient is occasioned not by the readiness of the patient, but by the departure of trainee therapists. Often, ongoing communication with the previous therapist can serve as a bridge, rather than an obstacle, to the attachment to the new therapist.

The Child's Response During the Terminal Phase

A number of variables affect a child's response to termination. The reasons for the decision and the length of time available to work through the termination are crucial. Any key losses in the child's past will strongly affect the child's response to the conclusion of therapy. The timing of the termination in relation to other important events in the child's life is significant. Similarly, the therapist's reservoir of feelings and responses, dependent on current or past life circumstances, influences the therapist's response to the termination process. Sandler et al. (1980) question the frequent practice of ending treatment at the start of vacations, and suggest that this common practice may easily play into a denial on the part of the therapist and the child. Rationalizing the separation as due to vacation is a way of avoiding the painful feelings of loss and mourning.

Hurn (1971) enumerates regressive patient responses during the terminal phase, which may be accompanied by an exacerbation of symptoms. While child and adult patients often articulate the wish to conclude therapy, this does not necessarily express a real wish to terminate, but rather, may relate to a fear of rejection. Both the latent and manifest material often reflect ambivalence, fear of dependency, and fear of abandonment.

First Case Example

Ann, an 11-year-old adopted child, had been in treatment for 2½ years. She was warmly related and cathected to the therapist. In times of trouble and stress at home, she phoned her therapist, and on occasions ran away from home to her therapist's office (located in the therapist's home). She sometimes complained about being in treatment and then hastily reassured herself that the decision to come or not to come simply wasn't hers—till she was a teenager—so she would have to come for many more years. Also, after complaining, she would counter, and query whether her therapist would know her always, care about her, or even remember her name when she went off to college, or later, when she was a grown-up. Her complaints and protestations were coupled with her scrupulously punctual arrival and her reluctance to end sessions.

Hurn (1971) quotes Ekstein, who suggests that the terminal phase of treatment contains something of a rehearsal for the future and demonstrates the energies available for investment in new external objects. Hurn, Kohrman, and others emphasize the counterreactions and countertransference responses of therapists as they struggle with their own feelings about surrendering the child. Neubauer (1972) states that

> at times one has to be satisfied with the fact that the child has achieved optimal adaptation to a pathological home situation, at this present stage of development, without achieving appropriate functioning. . . . Our ability to predict is severely limited by our inability to foresee the many unusual events that may occur and exercise a regressive influence on our patients. This is even more important for the younger and more vulnerable child. Thus, one should keep the door open for the child's return [p. 250].

For these reasons, it is recommended that, when possible, termination should be planned when the relationship to the child and parents is positive.

Anna Freud emphasizes the impossibility of safeguarding a child against future dangers; one must allow the child to take a chance. Further, she doubts the prophylactic effect even of child analysis, as an emotional illness leaves scars. A recovered child is no safer from the vicissitudes of life than the person who was never ill. These perspectives must be borne in mind by community agencies and child guidance clinics, which struggle to provide services to the greatest number of children; they "must avoid carrying a case beyond the point which was originally viewed as the goal, just as [they] must abstain from continuing treatment attempts when reasonable expectations no longer promise material improvement" (Anna Freud, 1957, in Haworth, 1964, p. 291). Child therapy in community agencies is largely ego supportive, and, even where there is no resolution of basic conflicts, cases may be terminated on the basis of improved, age-appropriate functioning. Later therapy or more intensive treatment is not an uncommon recommendation.

Under more optimal conditions, when cases are not burdened by premature termination (e.g., due to a therapist's or family's geographic moves) or a pathological family situation that impedes the child's progress or development, child and therapist may set a date together, based on genuine therapeutic gains. Ending treatment under optimal conditions can constitute an achievement, a "graduation" accompanied by the pain of separation as well as the good feelings of accomplishment.

Second Case Example (See Chapter 8, Narcissistic Personality Disorder—Case of Joy)

Joy began biweekly treatment at age 4½; after two years, termination was planned on the basis of the child's considerable improvement and mother's increased commitment at her job.[3] Many symptoms—specifically, Joy's en-uresis, her sleeping with her mother, and her endless temper tantrums—disappeared. Her stance with peers and adults became less bossy and om-nipotent. She became more age-appropriate in her interactions at home with mother, and at school with peers and teachers. Still present, however, were specific narcissistic modes of relating, i.e., a paucity of empathy for peers and a preoccupation with her own needs and feelings. She was bright and did well at school, though somewhat under her potential, given the stress she experienced in an overcrowded, ghetto parochial school. A successful referral was made and accepted for Joy to attend an excellent private school on scholarship.

In working out the termination, Joy constructed "a book" reviewing her experience in therapy. The following story is one of her final productions, recounting a 7-year-old's view of her treatment goals and gains.

JOY'S BOOK

Once upon a time, a little girl was almost five years old. She was not very happy. She would cry and fight with her mommy. She would not sleep alone. She would get mad a lot.

Her mommy loved her very much and did not want the fights. She did not want her child to be so sad and mad. She took her little girl to a therapist. The little girl and the therapist worked hard together. They played and talked together for two years. Slowly the little girl became happier. She did not have tantrums, and she and her mommy did not fight. They were calmer. The little girl got a little older, and was more grown up. She could sleep alone and talk about how she felt. She hardly ever yelled—even when she was angry. She learned to read and sing in a choir.

The little girl's name is Joy M. Her mother's name is Pat M. The therapist's name is Mrs. M.

Joy cried in therapy sometimes. She also had fun, sang and danced, and colored. Then they got along very good. Now they quit coming to see each other. Because everyone got along better. They were happy with each other. All is well.

Following an early summer termination, Joy expressed wishes to see the therapist again. This was handled via four appointments in the fall. Her physical growth and apparent emotional growth over that summer were striking and she had maintained the changes and improvements seen during her treatment. Her attendance in a summer camp day care program was presented by Joy and her mother as gratifying and positive, with the acquisi-tion of athletic and social skills and more friendships.

---

[3]The assessment and diagnosis of Joy are discussed in Chapter 8 (narcissistic personality disorder); the use of play therapy in her treatment is discussed in Chapter 14.

Third Case Example (See Chapter 8, Character Disorder—Case of Mike)

Mike planned his termination a year in advance, based on his progress, and his pending entry into high school which he saw, rightly, as a developmental milestone.[4] He entered adolescence with considerable stress, manifest by a short-lived decline in his superior academic achievement; he would engage the teacher in power struggles over curriculum, Black Studies content, etc., and often not do simple assignments. He was aware of his conflictual feelings regarding his own racial identity, manifested in fantasies about his actual Indian ancestors and his wish to be Indian rather than black.

In keeping with the hallmark of character-disordered individuals, he obsessed, ruminated, and was generally ambivalent about active/passive conflicts and masculine/feminine issues. He demonstrated the heightened narcissism of adolescence and was preoccupied with his short stature, his guitar playing, his own significant independent intellectual pursuits, and his astoundingly superior scores on academic achievement tests. Though not complying with all expectations (e.g., regarding assignments), he continued to excell at school in his areas of interest, and was chosen to give several science lectures. His scores enabled him to change school districts and enter a more demanding, academically oriented high school. His current withholding in school reflected the normal regression of adolescence. He did not succumb totally to regression, did not act out otherwise, and clearly had developed age-appropriate adolescent interests and activities. At termination, it was gratifying to learn of his joining his high school swim team and thereby, on a voluntary basis (not because of father's pressure), risking himself in the area he used to fear most—athletics and competition with peers.

Mike concluded his contact in his own way, insistent on the autonomy of setting a date a few weeks earlier than the therapist considered ideal. The overriding issue for Mike at termination seemed to be trying it on his own, being available for swim team practice, and "making it" in high school. Mike's wish for autonomy, in regard to his termination/graduation from therapy, was honored to respect the child, to applaud age-appropriate self-assertion, a major treatment gain, and to conclude the treatment on a positive note.

---

[4]The case of Mike is also discussed in Chapters 8 (character disorder), 14 (verbalization and the unconscious in children's communications), and 15 (interpretation and working through of trauma).

References

Ackerman, N. (1947), Foreword. In: *Psychotherapy in Child Guidance*, ed. G. Hamilton, New York: Columbia University Press.

_____ (1958), *The Psychodynamics of Family Life: Diagnosis and Treatment of Family Relationships*. New York: Basic Books.

_____ (1966), *Treating the Troubled Family*. New York: Basic Books.

Adams, P. L. (1979), Psychoneurosis. *Basic Handbook of Child Psychiatry*. II, ed. J. Noshpitz. New York: Basic Books.

Alexander, F. (1958), A Contribution to the Theory of Play. *Psychoanal. Q.*, 27: 175–193.

Allen, F. H. (1946), Combined Psychotherapy with Children and Parents. In: *Modern Trends in Child Psychiatry*, ed. N. D. C. Lewis & B. L. Pacella. New York: International Universities Press, pp. 257–263.

Alpert, A. (1957), A Special Therapeutic Technique for Certain Developmental Disorders in Pre-Latency Children. *Amer. J. Orthopsychiatry*, 27:256–270.

_____ (1959), Reversibility of Pathological Fixations Associated with Maternal Deprivation in Infancy. *The Psychoanalytic Study of the Child*, 14:169–183.

_____ et al. (1965), Children Without Families. *J. Acad. Child Psychiatry*, 4:163–278.

Alt, H. & Grossbard, H. (1949), Professional Issues in the Institutional Treatment of Delinquent Children. *Amer. J. Orthopsychiatry*, 14.

AMERICAN PSYCHIATRIC ASSOCIATION, Division of Publications and Marketing (1980), *DSM III*. Washington, D.C.: American Psychiatric Association.

ANTHONY, E. J. (1971), The History of Group Therapy. In: *Comprehensive Group Therapy*, ed. H. Kaplan & B. Sadock. Baltimore, Md.: Williams & Wilkins.

––––––– (1964), Communicating Therapeutically with the Child. *J. Child Psychiatry*, 3:106–125.

––––––– (1976), The Self and Congenital Defects: Prevention of Emotional Disabilities. Chicago: Association of Child and Adolescent Psychotherapists, Annual Meetings, October, 1976.

––––––– & McGinnis, M. (1978), Counseling Very Disturbed Parents. In: *Helping Parents Help Their Children*, ed. E. L. Arnold. New York: Brunner/Mazel, pp. 328–341.

ARLOW, J. & BRENNER, C. (1966), The Psychoanalytic Situation. In: *Psychoanalysis in America*, ed. R. E. Litman. New York: International Universities Press, pp. 22-43, 133-138.

ARNOLD, E. L. (ed.) (1978), *Helping Parents Help Their Children*. New York: Brunner/Mazel.

AXLINE, V. (1947), *Play Therapy: The Inner Dynamics of Childhood*. Boston: Houghton Mifflin.

––––––– (1964), Non-Directive Play Therapy. In: *Child Psychotherapy: Practice and Theory*. New York: Basic Books.

BABCOCK, C. (1949), Some Observations in Consultive Experience. *Soc. Serv. Rev.*, 23.

––––––– (1964), Having Chosen to Work with Children. Paper presented to the Extension Division of the Child Therapy Program, The Institute for Psychoanalysis, Chicago, Illinois, February 10, 1967.

BARNES, M. J. (1965), Casework with Children. *Smith College Studies in Social Work*, 35 (3): 173–188.

BARNES, M. E. (1972), The Concept of "Parental Force." In: *Children Away from Home*, ed. J. K. Whittaker & A. W. Trieschman. Chicago & New York: Aldine Atherton.

BARRETT, M. & McKELVEY, J. (1980), Stresses and Strains on the Child Care Worker: Typologies for Assessment. *Child Welfare*, 59(5): 277–285. Child Welfare League of America.

BELL, J. E. (1975), *Family Therapy*. New York & London: Aronson.

BELL, N. & VOGEL, E. F. (1968), *The Family*. New York: Free Press, Macmillan.

BENDER, L. (1956), Schizophrenia in Childhood: Its Recognition, Description, and Treatment. *Amer. J. Orthopsychiatry*, 26: 499–506.

BERES, D. (1956), Ego Deviations and the Concept of Schizophrenia. *The Psychoanalytic Study of the Child*, 11: 164–235.

BERGER, M. & KENNEDY, H. (1975), Pseudobackwardness in Children. *The Psychoanalytic Study of the Child*, 30: 279–306.

BERKOWITZ, I. H. & SUGAR, M. (1975), Indications and Contraindications for Adolescent Group Psychotherapy. In: *The Adolescent in Group and Family Therapy*, ed. M. Sugar. New York: Brunner/Mazel, pp. 3–26.

BERKOWITZ, M. (1975), *A Primer on School Mental Health Consultation*. Springfield, Ill.: Charles C. Thomas.

BERLIN, I. (1962), Mental Health Consultation in Schools as a Means of Communicating Mental Health Principles. *J. Amer. Acad. Child Psychiatry*, 1.

BERNARD, J. (1973), *The Children You Gave Us*. New York: Jewish Child Care Association of New York.

BERNSTEIN, I. & SAX, A. (1978), Indications and Contraindications for Child Analysis. In: *Child Analysis and Therapy*, ed. J. Glenn, New York & London: Aronson.

BERNSTEIN, B., SNIDER, D. A., & MEIZEN, W. (1975), *Foster Care Needs and Alternatives to Placement: A Projection for 1975–1985*. New York: The New York State Board of Social Welfare.

BERWALD, J. F. (1960), Cottage Parents in a Treatment Institution, *Child Welfare*, 39 (10).

BETTELHEIM, B. (1950), *Love Is Not Enough*. New York: The Free Press of Glencoe.

———— (1955), *Truants from Life*. New York: The Free Press of Glencoe.

———— (1967), *The Empty Fortress*. Chicago: The University of Chicago Press.

———— & SYLVESTER, E. (1972), A Therapeutic Milieu. In: *Children Away from Home*, ed. J. K. Whittaker & A. W. Treischman. Chicago and New York: Aldine Atherton.

BIXLER, R. H. (1949), Limits Are Therapy. *J. Consulting Psychol.*, 13:1–11.

BLANCK, G. & BLANCK, R. (1974), *Ego Psychology, I. Theory and Practice*. New York: Columbia University Press.

———— & ———— (1979), *Ego Psychology, II. Psychoanalytic Developmental Psychology*. New York: Columbia University Press.

BLOS, P. (1972), The Epigenesis of the Adult Neurosis. *The Psychoanalytic Study of the Child*, 27. New York & Chicago: Quadrangle Books.

BLUM, H. P. (ed.) (1980), *Psychoanalytic Explorations of Technique: Discourse on the Theory of Therapy*. New York: International Universities Press.

BORNSTEIN, B. (1948), Emotional Barriers in the Understanding and Treatment of Young Children. *Amer. J. Orthopsychiatry*, 18:691–697.

BOVET, L. (1951), Psychiatric Aspects of Juvenile Delinquency. World Health Organization Monograph No. 1.

BOWEN, M. (1966), The Use of Family Theory in Clinical Practice. *Comprehensive Psychiatry*, 7:345–374.

BRENNER, C. (1980), Working Alliance, Therapeutic Alliance and Transference. In: *Psychoanalytic Exploration of Technique: Discourse on the Theory of Therapy*, ed. H. Blum. New York: International Universities Press.

BRODY, S. (1961), Some Aspects of Transference and Resistance in Prepuberty. *The Psychoanalytic Study of the Child*, 16.

———— (1964), Aims and Methods in Child Psychotherapy. *J. Amer. Acad. Child Psychiatry*, 3: 385–412.

BRUCE, F. (1975), Letters. *Social Work*, 20: 258.

BUXBAUM, E. (1945), Transference and Group Formation in Children and Adolescents. *The Psychoanalytic Study of the Child*, 1: 351–365.

―――― (1954), Technique of Child Therapy: A Critical Evaluation. *The Psychoanalytic Study of the Child*, 9: 297–333.

CAMERON, N. (1963), *Personality Development and Psychopathology—A Dynamic Approach*. Boston: Houghton Mifflin.

CAPLAN, G. (1970), *The Theory and Practice of Mental Health Consultation*. New York: Basic Books.

CHESS, S., THOMAS, A., and BIRCH, H. G. (1965), *Your Child Is a Person*. New York: Viking Press.

CHETHIK, M. (1976), Work with Parents: Treatment of the Parent-Child Relationship. *J. Amer. Acad. Child Psychiatry*, 15.

―――― (1980), Betsy: The Treatment of a Preschooler via the Mother. In: *Psychotherapy and Training in Clinical Social Work*, ed. J. Mishne. New York: Gardner Press, pp. 135–149.

―――― & FAST, I. (1970), A Function of Fantasy in the Borderline Child. *Amer. J. Orthopsychiatry*, 40:756–765.

―――― & SPINDLER, E. (1971), Techniques of Treatment and Management with the Borderline Child. In: *Healing through Living*, ed. M. Mayer & A. C. C. Blum. Springfield, Ill.: Charles C. Thomas, pp. 176–189.

COLEMAN, J. (1949), Distinguishing between Psychotherapy and Casework. *J. Social Casework*, 30:219–224.

COMPTON, B. R. & GALAWAY, B. (eds.) (1979), *Social Work Processes*, rev. ed. Homewood, Ill.: The Dorsey Press.

CONN, J. (1939), The Child Reveals Himself through Play. *Mental Hygiene*, 49–69.

COOPER, S. (1973), A Look at the Effect of Racism on Clinical Work. *Social Casework*, 54:76.

COSTIN, L. (1975), School Social Work Practice: A New Model. *Social Work*, 20: 135.

CREAK, M. (1960), Families of Psychotic Children. *J. Child Psychol. & Psychiatry*, 1:156–175.

CURTIS, H. (1977), The Concept of Therapeutic Alliance: Implications for the "Widening Scope." Presented at the Annual Meeting of the American Psychoanalytic Association, Quebec, April, 1977. In: *Psychoanalytic Exploration of Technique: Discourse on the Theory of Therapy*, ed. H. Blum. New York: International Universities Press, 1980, pp. 159–192.

CUTTER, A. & HALLOWITZ, D. (1962), Different Approaches to Treatment of the Child and the Parents. *Amer. J. Orthopsychiatry*, 32:152–159.

C. W. HECHT INSTITUTE FOR STATE CHILD WELFARE PLANNING (1976), *Finding Federal Money for Children's Services* (November).

CWIS—1977 CHILD WELFARE INFORMATION SERVICES, INC. (1976), Prepared by David Fanshel and John F. Grundy.

DESPERT, J. L. (1945), Play Analysis in Research and Therapy. In: *Modern Trends in Child Psychiatry*, ed. N. Lewis & B. L. Parella. New York: International Universities Press.

—— (1955), Differential Diagnosis Between Obsessive Compulsive Neurosis and Schizophrenia in Children. In: *Psychopathology of Childhood*, ed. T. Hoch & J. Zubin. New York: Grune and Stratton.

DEUTSCH, H. (1942), Some Forms of Emotional Disturbance and their Relationship to Schizophrenia. *Psychoanal. Q.*, 11:301–321.

DEWALD, P. A. (1964), *Psychotherapy: A Dynamic Approach*. New York: Basic Books.

DICKES, R. (1975), Technical Considerations of the Therapeutic and Working Alliances. *International J. of Psychoanal. Psychother.*, 4: 1–47.

DORFMAN, E. (1951), Play Therapy. In: *Client-Centered Therapy*, ed. C. R. Rodgers. Boston: Houghton Mifflin, 1965, pp. 235–277.

EISENBERG, L. & EARLE, F. V. (1975), Poverty, Social Depreciation and Child Development. In: *American Handbook of Psychiatry, II*, 2nd ed. New York: Basic Books, pp. 275–291.

EISSLER, R., FREUD, A., KRIS, M., & SOLNIT, A. (eds.) (1977), *An Anthology of the Psychoanalytic Study of the Child—Psychoanalytic Assessment: A Diagnostic Profile*. New Haven: Yale University Press.

EKSTEIN, R. (1966), *Children of Time and Space, of Action and Impulse*. New York: Appleton-Century-Crofts.

—— & FRIEDMAN, S. W. (1957), The Function of Acting Out, Play Action and Acting Out in the Psychotherapeutic Process. *J. Amer. Psychoanal. Assn.*, 5:582–629.

—— & —— (1959), On the Meaning of Play in Childhood Psychosis. In: *Dynamic Psychopathology in Childhood*, ed. L. Jessner & E. Pavenstedt. New York & London: Grune and Stratton.

—— & MATTO, R. (1972), Issues in Collaboration: The Mental Health Worker and Educator. I. Historical and Philosophic Overview. *The Reiss Davis Clinic Bulletin*, 9 (1).

——, WALLERSTEIN, J., & MANDELBAUM, A. (1959), Countertransference in the Residential Treatment of Children: Treatment Failure in a Child with Symbiotic Psychosis. *The Psychoanalytic Study of the Child*, 14. New York: International Universities Press.

—— , CARUTH, E., COOPER, B., FRIEDMAN, S., LANDRES, P., LIEBOWITZ, J., & NELSON, T. (1978), Psychoanalytically Oriented Psychotherapy of Psychotic Children. In: *Child Analysis and Therapy*, ed. J. Glenn. New York & London: Aronson.

ERIKSON, E. H. (1940), Studies in the Interpretation of Play. I. Clinical Observation of Play Disruption in Young Children. *Genetic Psychology Monographs*, 22:557–671.

—— (1950), *Childhood and Society*. New York: Norton.

ESMAN, A. (1962), Visual Hallucinosis in Young Children. *The Psychoanalytic Study of the Child*, 17. New York: International Universities Press.

EYBERG, S. H. & JOHNSON, S. M. (1974), Multiple Assessment of Behavior Modification with Families: Effects of Contigency Constructing and Order of Treated Problems. *J. Consulting & Clin. Psychol.*, 42:594.

FANSHEL, D. (1975), Testimony: State Subcommittee on Children and Youth, and House Select Subcommittee on Education. *Hearings on Foster Care of Children.*

―――― (1975), Parental Visiting of Children in Foster Care: Key to Discharge. *Social Service*, 49(4).

―――― (1977), *Children in Foster Care: A Longitudinal Investigation.* New York: Columbia University Press.

―――― & SHINN, E. (1972), *Dollars and Sense in the Foster Care of Children.* New York: Child Welfare League of America.

FANT, R. & ROSS, A. (1979), Supervision of Child Care Staff. *Child Welfare*, 58(10):627–641. New York: Child Welfare League of America.

FAST, I. (1970), The Function of Action in the Early Development of Identity. *Internat. J. Psycho-Anal.*, 51:471–478.

―――― & CHETHIK, M. (1972), Some Aspects of Object Relations in Borderline Children. *Internat. J. Psycho-Anal.*, 53:479–484.

―――― (in press), Aspects of Depersonalization Experience in Children. *Internat. J. Psycho-Anal.*

FEIGELSON, C. (1974), Play in Child Analysis. *The Psychoanalytic Study of the Child*, 29.

FENICHEL, O. (1945), *The Psychoanalytic Theory of Neurosis.* New York: Norton, 1972.

FESTINGER, T. (1975), The New York Court Review of Children in Foster Care. *Child Welfare*, 54(4):211–245.

FITZPATRICK, J. (1971), Mental Illness or Cultural Misunderstanding? In: *Puerto Rican Americans.* Englewood Cliffs, N.J.: Prentice-Hall.

FLAPAN, D. & NEUBAUER, P. (1975), *Assessment of Early Childhood Development.* New York: Aronson.

FRAIBERG, S. (1954), Counseling for the Parents of the Very Young Child. *Social Casework*, 35: 47–57.

FRANCIS, J. (1968), participant in panel on "Problems in Termination in Child Analysis." Reported by Robert Kohrman, Annual Meeting of the American Psychoanalytic Association, Boston, May 10, 1968. *J. Amer. Psychoanal. Assn.*, 28, 1969.

FRANK, G. (1977), *Treatment Needs of Children in Foster Care*, unpublished D.S.W. thesis. New York: Columbia University School of Social Work.

FREUD, A. (1922–1970), *The Writings of Anna Freud, I–VII.* New York: International Universities Press.

―――― (1946), *The Ego and the Mechanisms of Defense.* New York: International Universities Press.

―――― (1951), *The Psychoanalytic Treatment of Children*, 3rd ed., trans. N. Proctor. London: Anglo Books.

_____ (1952), The Role of Bodily Illness in the Mental Life of Children. *The Psychoanalytic Study of the Child*, 7.

_____ (1962), Assessment of Childhood Disturbances. *The Psychoanalytic Study of the Child*, 17.

_____ (1965), *The Writings of Anna Freud, VI. Normality and Pathology in Childhood: Assessments of Development.* New York: International Universities Press.

_____ (1966), *The Writings of Anna Freud, III. Problems of Psychoanalytic Training, Diagnosis and the Technique of Therapy.* New York: International Universities Press.

_____ (1967), About Losing and Being Lost. *The Psychoanalytic Study of the Child*, 22: 9–52.

_____ (1968), Indications and Contraindications for Child Analysis. *The Psychoanalytic Study of the Child*, 23.

_____ (1969), Film review of "John, Seventeen Months: Nine Days in a Residential Nursery," by J. and J. Robertson. *The Psychoanalytic Study of the Child*, 24:138–143.

_____ (1970), *The Writings of Anna Freuds, VII. The Infantile Neurosis.* New York: International Universities Press, pp. 157–188.

_____ (1971), The Infantile Neurosis—Genetic and Dynamic Considerations. *The Psychoanalytic Study of the Child*, 26. New York: Quadrangle Books.

_____ (1972), The Child as a Person in his Own Right. *The Psychoanalytic Study of the Child*, 27. New York : Quadrangle Books.

_____ (1976), Changes in Psychoanalytic Practice and Experience. *Internat. J. Psycho-Anal.*, 57:257–260.

_____ (1977), The Symptomatology of Childhood: A Preliminary Attempt at Classification. *An Anthology of The Psychoanalytic Study of the Child—Psychoanalytic Assessment: A Diagnostic Profile*, ed. R. Eissler et al. New Haven & London: Yale University Press.

_____ (1978), The Role of Insight in Psychoanalysis and Psychotherapy. Introduction to the Anna Freud Hampstead Center Symposium held at the Michigan Psychoanalytic Society, November, 1978. In: *Psychoanalytic Explorations of Technique: Discourse on the Theory of Therapy*, ed. H. P. Blum. New York: International Universities Press, 1980.

_____, NAGERA H., & FREUD, W. E. (1965), Metapsychological Assessment of the Adult Personality: The Adult Profile. *The Psychoanalytic Study of the Child*, 20: 9–41.

FREUD, S. (1909), The Analysis of a Phobia in a 5-Year-Old Boy. *Collected Papers, III.* London: Basic Books.

_____ (1912), The Dynamics of Transference. *Standard Edition*, 12:97–108.

_____ (1914), On Narcissism: An Introduction. *Collected Papers, IV.* London: Basic Books, 1959.

_____ (1915a), Instincts and their Vicissitudes. *Collected Papers, IV.* London: Basic Books, 1959.

——— (1915b), Observations on Transference—Love. *Standard Edition,* 12:157–171.

——— (1916–17), Introductory Lectures on Psycho-Analysis. *Standard Edition,* 15–16.

——— (1920), Beyond the Pleasure Principle. *Standard Edition,* 18. London: Hogarth Press, 1955.

——— (1922), Introduction to *Group Psychology and the Analysis of the Ego,* Standard Edition, 18. New York: Liveright, 1951.

——— (1923), The Ego and the Id. *Standard Edition,* 19. London: Hogarth Press, 1955.

——— (1925), Negation. *Collected Papers,* V. London: Basic Books, 1959.

——— (1953), The Interpretation of Dreams, Standard Editions, 4 & 5. London: Hogarth Press.

FRIGLING-SCHREUDER, E. C. M. (1970), Borderline States in Children. *The Psychoanalytic Study of the Child,* 24:307–327.

FURMAN, E. (1957), Treatment of Under-Fives by Way of Parents. *The Psychoanalytic Study of the Child,* 12:250–262.

——— (1980), Transference and Externalization in Latency. *The Psychoanalytic Study of the Child,* 35.

GEDO, J. E. & GOLDBERG, A. (1973), *Models of the Mind: A Psychoanalytic Theory.* Chicago: The University of Chicago Press.

GELEERD, E. (1958), Borderline States in Childhood and Adolescence. *The Psychoanalytic Study of the Child,* 13:279–295.

GIFFIN, M. (1981), Learning Disabilities: A Unique Diagnostic Entity. In: Group Interventions with Children and their Parents—Application of Ego and Self Psychologies, ed. J. M. Mishne & E. S. Buchholz (in press).

GINOTT, H. (1959), The Theory and Practice of Therapeutic Intervention in Child Treatment. *J. Consulting Psychol.,* 23:160–166. Reprinted in: *Child Psychotherapy: Practice and Theory,* ed. M. R. Haworth. New York & London: Basic Books, 1964.

——— (1961a), Group Psychotherapy with Children. New York: McGraw-Hill.

——— (1961b), Play Therapy: The Initial Session. *Amer. J. Psychother.,* 15:73–89.

GIOVACCHINI, P. (1974), The Difficult Adolescent Patient: Countertransference Problems. *Adol. Psychiatry,* 3. New York: Basic Books.

GITTERMAN, A. (1977), Social Work in the Public School System. *Social Casework,* 58 (2).

GLASS, S. (1969), *The Practical Handbook of Group Counseling.* Baltimore: BCS Publishing Company.

GLENN, J., SABOT, L. M., & BERNSTEIN, I. (1978), The Role of the Parents in Child Analysis. In: *Child Analysis and Therapy,* ed. J. Glenn. New York & London: Aronson.

GLICKMAN, E. (1957), *Child Placement through Clinically Oriented Casework.* New York: Columbia University Press.

GOLDBERG, A. (1973), Psychotherapy of Narcissistic Injuries. *Arch. Gen. Psychiatry*, 28:722–726.

GOLDFARB, W., MINTZ, I., & STROOCK, K. W. (1969), *A Time to Heal—Corrective Socialization: A Treatment Approach to Childhood Schizophrenia*. New York: International Universities Press.

GOLDIN, H. J. (1977), The Children are Waiting—The Failure to Achieve Permanant Homes for Foster Children in New York City. A report from the New York City Comptroller's Office.

GOLDSTEIN, J. (1975), Why Foster Care—for Whom, for How Long? *The Psychoanalytic Study of the Child*, 30:647–662.

———, FREUD, A., & SOLNIT, A. (1973), *Beyond the Best Interests of the Child*. New York: The Free Press, Macmillan, pp. 17–28.

GORE, E. (1976), *Child Psychiatry Observed—A Guide for Social Workers*. Oxford, New York, Toronto, Sydney, Paris & Braunschwieg: Pergamon Press.

GREEN, R. K. & CLARK, W. P. (1972), Therapeutic Recreation for Aggressive Children in Residential Treatment. In: *Children Away From Home*, ed. J. K. Whittaker & A. W. Trieschman. Chicago & New York: Aldine Atherton, pp. 369–382.

GREENACRE, P. (1941), The Predisposition to Anxiety, I & II. *Psychoanal. Q.*, 10:66–94, 610–638.

——— (1958), The Imposter. *Psychoanal. Q.*, 27:369–382.

——— (1959), Play in Relation to Creative Imagination. *The Psychoanalytic Study of the Child*, 14:61–81.

——— (1971), Notes on the Influence and Contribution of Ego Psychology to the Practice of Psychoanalysis, In: *Separation-Individuation*, ed. J. B. McDevitt & C. F. Settlage. New York: International Universities Press, pp. 171–200.

——— (1978), Acting Out in the Transference. In: *A Developmental Approach to Problems of Acting Out*, rev. ed., ed. E. N. Rexford. New York: International Universities Press.

GREENSON, R. R. (1965), The Working Alliance and the Transference Neurosis. *Psychoanal. Q.*, 34: 155–181.

——— (1967), *The Technique and Practice of Psychoanalysis, I*. New York: International Universities Press.

——— (1970), The Exceptional Position of the Dream in Psychoanalytic Practice. *Psychoanal. Q.*, 39(4): 519–549.

GRINBERG, L. (1968), Contributions to a symposium on Acting Out. *Internat. J. Psycho-Anal.*, 49:171–178.

GRUBER, A. (1973), Foster Home Care in Massachusetts. A report by the Commonwealth of Massachusetts—Governor's Commission on Adoption and Foster Care.

HALEY, J. (1971), Family Therapy. *Internat. J. Psychiatry*, 9:233–242.

HAMBRIDGE, G. (1955), Structured Play Therapy. *Amer. J. Orthopsychiatry*, 25:601–617.

HAMILTON, G. (1947), *Psychotherapy in Child Guidance*. New York: Columbia University Press.

HARLEY, M. (1951), Analysis of a Severely Disturbed 3½-Year-Old Boy. *The Psychoanalytic Study of the Child*, 6:206–234.

——— (1962), The Role of the Dream in the Analysis of a Latency Child. *J. Amer. Psychoanal. Assn.*, 10.

——— (1968), The Current State of Transference Neurosis in Children. Annual Meeting of the American Psychoanalytic Association, Boston.

HARRISON, S. & McDERMOTT, J. F. (eds.) (1972), *Childhood Psychopathology— An Anthology of Basic Readings*. New York: International Universities Press.

HARTMAN, N. M. & HURN, P. A. (1958), Collaboration as a Therapeutic Tool. *J. Soc. Casework*, 39:459–463.

HARTMANN, H. (1955), Notes on the Theory of Sublimation. *Essays on Ego Psychology*. New York: International Universities Press, 1974.

HATRY, H. P. et al. (1976), *Program Analysis for State and Local Governments*. Washington, D.C.: The Urban Institute.

HAWORTH, M. R. (ed.) (1964), *Child Psychotherapy: Practice and Theory*. New York & London: Basic Books.

HEACOCK, D. R. (1966), Modifications of the Standard Techniques for Outpatient Group Psychotherapy with Delinquent Boys. *J. Nat. Med. Assn.*, 58:41–47.

HELLERSBERG, E. F. (1955), Child's Growth in Play Therapy. *Amer. J. Psychother.*, 9:484–502.

HENDRICK, I. (1942), Instinct and the Ego During Infancy. *Psychoanal. Q.* 11: 33–58.

——— (1943), Work and the Pleasure Principle. *Psychoanal. Q.* 12:311–329.

HINTGEN, J. N. & BRYSON, C. Q. (1969), Recent Developments in the Study of Early Childhood Psychoses, Infantile Autism, Childhood Schizophrenia and Related Disorders. In: *Annual Progress in Child Psychiatry and Child Development, IX*, ed. S. Chess & A. Thomas. New York: Brunner/Mazel, pp. 503–576.

HITCHCOCK, J. (1977), Interventions by the Psychoanalyst in the Consultant Role. *J. Philadelphia Assn. Psychoanalysts*, 4.

HOLLINGSHEAD, H. B. & REDLICH, F. C. (1958), *Social Class and Mental Illness*. New York: Wiley.

HOOYMAN, E. (1975), Team Building in the Human Services. In: *Social Work Processes*, ed. B. R. Compton & B. Galaway. Homewood, Ill.: The Dorsey Press, 1979.

HROMADKA, V. G. (1966), Child Care Workers on the Road to Professionalization. New York: The Hawthorne Center for the Study of Adolescent Behavior (mimeographed paper).

HURN, H. (1971), Towards a Paradigm of the Terminal Phase: The Current Status of the Terminal Stage. *J. Amer. Psychoanal. Assn.*, 19.

HYLTON, L. F. (1964), *The Residential Treatment Center*. New York: Child Welfare League of America.

ISAACS, S. (1929), *The Nursery Years*. London: Routledge & Kegan Paul.

JACKEL, M. (1963), Clients with Character Disorders. *J. Soc. Casework*.

JACOBSON, E. (1954), The Self and the Object World: Vicissitudes of their Infantile Cathexis and their Influences on Ideational and Affective Development. *The Psychoanalytic Study of the Child*, 9:75–127.

_____ (1964), The Self and the Object World. *J. Amer. Psychoanal. Assoc.*, Monograph Services 2.

JACOBY, S. (1977), The $73,000 Abandoned Babies. *The New York Times Magazine*, June 5, p. 55.

JAMES, D. O. (1977), *Play Therapy*. New York: Dabor Science Publications.

JENKINS, S. (1975), *Beyond Placement—Mothers View Foster Care*. New York & London: Columbia University Press.

_____ & NORMAN, E. (1972), *Filial Deprivation and Foster Care*. New York & London: Columbia University Press.

_____ & SAUBER, M. (1966), *Paths to Child Placement*. New York: The Community Council of Greater New York.

JOHNSON, A. & SZUREK, S. A. (1952), The Genesis of Antisocial Acting Out in Children and Adolescents. *Psychoanal. Q.*, 21.

JOINT COMMISSION ON MENTAL HEALTH OF CHILDREN (1969), *Crisis in Child Mental Health: Challenge for the 1970s*. New York: Harper & Row, 1970.

JOSSELYN, I. M. (1972), Prelude—Adolescent Group Therapy: Why, When, and a Caution. In: *Adolescents Grow in Groups*, ed. I. H. Berkowitz. New York: Brunner/Mazel.

KADUSHIN, A. (1974), *Child Welfare Services*. New York: Macmillan.

KAHN, A. J. (1963), *Planning Community Services for Children in Trouble*. New York & London: Columbia University Press.

_____ (1973), Agenda for Change. In: *Child Caring*, ed. D. Papenfort et al. New York: Aldine.

KAMERMAN, S. & KAHN, A. (1976), *Social Services in the United States: Policies and Programs*. Philadelphia: Temple University Press.

KANNER, L. (1941), *In Defense of Mothers*. Springfield, Ill.: Charles C Thomas.

KANNER, L. (1943), Autistic Disturbances of Affective Contact. *Nervous Child*, 2:217–250.

_____ (1944), Early Infantile Autism. *J. Pediatrics*, 25:211–217.

KAPLAN, H. & SADOCK, B. (eds.) (1971), Introduction. *Comprehensive Group Psychotherapy*. Baltimore: Williams & Wilkins.

KATAN, A. (1961), Some Thoughts About the Role of Verbalization in Early Childhood. *The Psychoanalytic Study of the Child*, 16.

KAY, P. (1978), Gifts and Gratifications and Frustrations in Child Analysis: In: *Child Analysis and Therapy*, ed. J. Glenn. New York & London: Aronson, pp. 309–354.

KEITH, C. R. (1968), The Therapeutic Alliance in Child Psychiatry. *J. Child Psychiatry*, 7:31–53.

KENNEDY, H. (1971), Problems in Reconstruction in Child Analysis. *The Psychoanalytic Study of the Child*, 26.

———— (1978), The Role of Insight in Child Analysis: A Developmental Viewpoint. In: *Psychoanalytic Exploration of Technique*, ed. H. Blum, New York: International Universities Press.

KERNBERG, O. (1966), Structural Derivatives of Object Relations. *Internat. J. Psycho-Anal.*, 47:236–253.

———— (1967), Borderline Personality Organization. *J. Amer. Psychoanal. Assn.*, 15:641–685.

———— (1968), The Treatment of Patients with Borderline Personality Organization. *Internat. J. Psycho-Anal.*, 49:600–619.

———— (1970), Factors in the Psychoanalytic Treatment of Narcissistic Personalities. *J. Amer. Psychoanal. Assn.*, 18(1):51–85.

———— (1975), *Borderline Conditions and Pathological Narcissism*. New York: Aronson.

———— (1976), *Object-Relations Theory and Clinical Psychoanalysis*. New York: Aronson.

———— (1979), Regression in Organizational Leadership. *Psychiatry*, 42(February).

KESSLER, J. (1966), *Psychopathology of Childhood*. Englewood Cliffs, N.J.: Prentice-Hall.

KLEIN, D. & OVERSTREET, H. M. F. (1972), *Foster Care of Children—Nature and Treatment*. New York & London: Columbia University Press.

KLEIN, M. (1955), The Psychoanalytic Play Technique. *Amer. J. Orthopsychiatry*, 25:223–237.

———— (1958), On the Development of Mental Functioning. *Internat. J. Psycho-Anal.*, 34.

KOHRMAN, R. (1968), Panel report on "Problems of Termination in Child Analysis," Annual Meeting of the American Psychoanalytic Association, Boston, May 10, 1968. *J. Amer. Psychoanal. Assn.*, 28 (1969).

————, FEINBERG, H., GELMAN, R., & WEISS, S. (1971), Technique of Child Analysis: Problems of Countertransference. *Internat. J. Psycho-Anal.*, 52:487.

KOHUT, H. (1966), Forms and Transformations of Narcissism. *J. Amer. Psychoanal. Assn.*, 14(2):270.

———— (1968), The Psychoanalytic Treatment of Narcissistic Personality Disorders. *The Psychoanalytic Study of the Child*, 23: 51–85.

———— (1971), The Analysis of the Self. New York: International Universities Press.

———— (1972), Thoughts on Narcissism and Narcissistic Rage. *The Psychoanalytic Study of the Child*, 27:360–400.

———— (1977), *The Restoration of the Self*. New York: International Universities Press.

KRAMER, C. H. (1970), Psychoanalytically Oriented Family Therapy: Ten-Year Evolution in a Private Child Psychiatry Practice. Family Institute of Chicago Publication, 1: 1–42.

KRIS, E. (1948), On Psychoanalysis and Education. *Amer. J. Orthopsychiatry*, 18: 622–635.

_____ (1956), On Some Vicissitudes of Insight in Psychoanalysis. *Internat. J. Psycho-Anal.*, 37:445–455.

KRIS, K. (1978), The School Consultant as an Object for Externalization. *The Psychoanalytic Study of the Child*, 33.

KRONA, D. (1980), Parents as Treatment Partners in Residential Care. *Child Welfare*, 59(2):91–96.

KRUG, O. & STUART, B. L. (1956), Collaborative Treatment of Mother and Boy with Fecal Retention, Soiling and School Phobia. In: *Case Studies of Childhood Emotional Disabilities*, II, ed. G. Gardner. New York: American Orthopsychiatric Association, pp. 1–29.

LANE, B. (1980), Some Vicissitudes of the Therapeutic Alliance in Child Psychotherapy. In: *Psychotherapy and Training in Clinical Social Work*, ed. J. Mishne. New York: Gardner Press, pp. 119–134.

LASH, T. & SEGAL, H. (1976), *State of the Child*. New York: Foundation for Child Development.

LEADER, A. L. (1973), Family Therapy for Divorced Fathers and Others Out of Home. *J. Soc. Casework*.

LEVY, C. (1976), *Social Work Ethics*. New York: Human Sciences Press.

LEVY, D. (1937), Attitude Therapy. *Amer. J. Orthopsychiatry*, 7:103–113.

_____ (1939), Trends in Therapy. III. Release Therapy. *Amer. J. Orthopsychiatry*, 9:713–736.

LITTNER, N. (1956), *The Strains and Stresses on the Child Welfare Worker*. New York: Child Welfare League of America.

_____ (1969), The Caseworker's Self Observations and the Child's Interpersonal Defenses. *Smith College Studies in Social Work*, 39(2):95–117.

LOOMIS, E. A. (1957), The Use of Checkers in Handling Certain Resistances in Child Therapy and Child Analysis. *J. Amer. Psychoanal. Assn.*, 5:130–135.

LOWENFELD, M. (1935), *Play in Childhood*. London: Victor Gollancz.

LUSTMAN, S. (1970), Cultural Deprivation—A Clinical Dimension of Education. *The Psychoanalytic Study of the Child*, 25.

MAENCHEN, A. (1953), Note on Early Ego Disturbances. *The Psychoanalytic Study of the Child*, 8:262–270.

MAHLER, M. (1948), Clinical Studies in the Benign and Malignant Cases of Childhood Psychosis. *Amer. J. Orthopsychiatry*, 19:295–305.

_____ (1952), On Childhood Psychosis and Schizophrenia: Autistic and Symbiotic Infantile Psychosis. *The Psychoanalytic Study of the Child*, 7:286–385.

_____ (1968), *On Human Symbiosis and the Vicissitudes of Individuation. I. Infantile Psychosis*. New York: International Universities Press.

———, PINE, F., & BERGMAN, A. (1975), The Psychological Birth of the Human Infant: Symbiosis and Individuation. New York: Basic Books.

MAIER, H. (1963), Child Care as a Method of Social Work. Training of Child Care Workers. New York: Child Welfare League of America, pp. 62–81.

——— (1972), The Social Group Work Method and Residential Treatment. In: Children Away From Home, ed. J. K. Whittaker & A. E. Trieschman. Chicago & New York: Aldine Atherton.

——— (1972), The Child Care Worker. In: Children Away From Home, ed. J. K. Whittaker & A. E. Trieschman. Chicago & New York: Aldine Atherton.

MALONE, C. A. & BANDLER, L. S. (1967), The Drifters. Boston: Little, Brown.

MANDELBAUM, A. (1972), Parent-Child Separation: Its Significance to Parents. In: Children Away From Home, ed. J. K. Whittaker & A. E. Trieschman. Chicago & New York: Aldine Atherton, pp. 383–394.

MARCUS, I. (1980), Countertransference and the Psychoanalytic Process in Children and Adolescents. The Psychoanalytic Study of the Child, 35.

MASTERSON, J. F. (1972), Treatment of the Borderline Adolescent—A Developmental Approach. New York: Wiley Interscience.

MATSUSHIMA, J. (1964), Communication in Cottage Parent Supervision in a Residential Treatment Center. Child Welfare, 43(10). In: Children Away From Home, ed. J. K. Whittaker & A. E. Trieschman. Chicago & New York: Aldine Atherton, 1972.

MAYER, M. F. (1960), The Parental Figures in Residential Treatment. Soc. Serv. Rev., 34(4). In: Children Away from Home, ed. J. K. Whittaker & A. E. Trieschman. Chicago & New York: Aldine Atherton, 1972.

——— (1977) (Project Director), Group Care in North America. Residential Care for Dependent, Neglected, and Emotionally Disturbed Children in the U.S.

——— (1972), The Parental Figures in Residential Treatment. In: Children Away From Home, ed. J. K. Whittaker & A. E. Trieschman. Chicago & New York: Aldine Atherton, pp. 273–287.

———, RICHMAN, L. H., & BALCRZAK, E. (1977), Group Care of Children: Crossroads and Transitions. New York: Child Welfare League of America.

McDONALD, M. (1965), The Psychiatric Evaluation of Children. J. Amer. Acad. Child Psychiatry, 4:569–612.

MEEKS, J. E. (1970), Children Who Cheat at Games. J. Amer. Acad. Child Psychiatry, 9:13–18.

——— (1979), Behavioral and Antisocial Disorders. In: Basic Handbook of Child Psychiatry, II, ed. J. Noshpitz. New York: Basic Books.

MEERS, D. (1970), Contributions of a Ghetto Culture to Symptom Formation: Psychoanalytic Studies of Ego Anomalies in Childhood. The Psychoanalytic Study of the Child, 25:209–230.

MEYER, C. (1976), Preface. Social Work Practice, 2nd ed. New York: The Free Press.

MINUCHIN, S. (1974), Families and Family Therapy. Cambridge, Mass.: Harvard University Press.

MISHLER, E. G. & WAXLER, N. E. (eds.) (1968), *Family Process and Schizophrenia*. New York: Science House.

MISHNE, J. M. (1974), The Consultant Role of Social Workers in Public Schools. *J. School Soc. Work*, 1 (4). Reprinted in: *Psychotherapy and Training in Clinical Social Work*, ed. J. M. Mishne. New York: Gardner Press, 1980.

——— (1979), Parental Abandonment: A Unique Form of Loss and Narcissistic Injury. *Clin. Soc. Work J.*, 7(1):15–33.

——— (1980) Applications of Self Psychology and Ego Psychology: A Psychotherapy Case Illustration. Unpublished manuscript.

——— & BUCHHOLZ, E. S. (eds.) (1983), *Ego and Self Psychology*. New York: Jason Aronson.

MOORE, B. & FINE, B. (1968), *A Glossary of Psychoanalytic Terms and Concepts*. The American Psychoanalytic Association.

MOSS, A. F. (1976), Consultation in the Inner-City School. *Social Work*, pp. 142–46.

MOUSTAKAS, C. (1959), *Psychotherapy with Children—The Living Relationship*. New York: Harper Brothers.

NAGERA, H. (1964), On Arrest in Development, Fixating and Regression. *The Psychoanalytic Study of the Child*, 19.

——— (1966), Early Childhood Disturbances, The Infantile Neurosis and The Adulthood Disturbances. *Monograph Series of the Psychoanalytic Study of the Child*, 2.

NASW NEWS (1980), 25(4), April.

NEIL, A. P. (1953), Certain Severe Disturbances of Ego Development in Children. *The Psychoanalytic Study of the Child*, 8:271–287.

——— (1956), Some Evidence of Deviational Development in Infancy and Childhood. *The Psychoanalytic Study of the Child*, 11:292–299.

NEUBAUER, P. M. D. (1968), participant in panel on "Problems of Termination in Child Analysis." Reported by Robert Kohrman, Annual Meeting of the American Psychoanalytic Association, Boston, May 10, 1968. *J. Amer. Psychoanal. Assn.*, 28 (1969).

——— (1972), Psychoanalysis of the Preschool Child. In: *Handbook of Child Psychoanalysis—Research, Theory and Practice*, ed. B. Wolman. New York: Van Nostrand Reinhold.

——— (1980), The Role of Insight in Psychoanalysis. In: *Psychoanalytic Exploration of Technique—Discourse on the Theory of Therapy*, ed. H. Blum. New York: International Universities Press.

NIEDERLAND, W. (1965), Narcissistic Ego Impairment in Patients with Early Physical Malformations. *The Psychoanalytic Study of the Child*, 20.

NUNBERG, H. (1931), The Synthetic Function of the Ego. *Practice and Theory of Psychoanalysis*. New York: International Universities Press, 1955.

OFFER, D. & VANDERSTOEP, E. (1975), Indications and Contraindications for Family Therapy. In: *The Adolescent in Group and Family Therapy*, ed. M. Sugar. New York: Brunner/Mazel.

OLCH ,G. (1971), Panel Report: Technical Problems in the Analyses of the Pre-oedipal and Preschool Child. *J. Amer. Psychoanal. Assn.*, 19:543–551.

OLDEN, C. (1953), On Adult Empathy with Children. *The Psychoanalytic Study of the Child*, 8:111–126.

ORNITZ, E. M. (1974), The Modulation of Sensory Input and Motor Output in Autistic Children. *J. Autism & Child. Schizophrenia*, 4:197–215.

—— & RITVO, E. (1968), Perceptual Inconstancy in Early Infantile Autism. *Arch. Gen. Psychiatry*, 18:76–98.

—— & —— (1976), The Syndrome of Autism: A Critical Review. *Amer. J. Psychiatry*, 133:609–621.

PATTERSON, G. R. (1974), Interventions for Boys with Conduct Problems: Multiple Settings, Treatment and Criteria. *J. Consulting & Clin. Psychol.*, 42:471.

PAVENSTEDT, E. (1965), A Comparison of the Child Rearing Environment of Upper-Lower and Very Low-Lower Class Families. *Amer. J. Orthopsychiatry*, 35:89–98.

PEARSON, G. (1949), *Emotional Disorders of Children*. New York: Norton.

—— (1968), *A Handbook of Child Psychoanalysis—A Guide to the Psychoanalytic Treatment of Children and Adolescents*. New York: Basic Books.

PELLER, L. E. (1955), Libidinal Development as Reflected in Play. *Psychoanalysis*, 3(3):3–11. Reprinted in: *Child Psychotherapy: Practice and Theory*, ed. M. R. Haworth. New York: Basic Books, 1964, pp. 176–184.

—— (1969), Psychoanalysis and Public Education. In: *From Learning for Love to Love of Learning*, ed. R. Ekstein and R. Matto. New York: Brunner/Mazel.

PINE, F. (1974), On the Concept "Borderline" in Children: A Clinical Essay. *The Psychoanalytic Study of the Child*, 29:341–347.

POLATIN, P. & HOCH, T. (1947), Diagnostic Evaluation of Early Schizophrenia. *J. Nerv. Mental Disease*, 105:221–230.

POLSKY, H. (1962), *Cottage Six*. New York: Russell Sage Foundation.

PROCTOR, J. (1958), Hysteria in Childhood. *Amer. J. Orthopsychiatry*, 28:397.

—— (1959), Countertransference Phenomena in the Treatment of Severe Character Disorders in Children and Adolescents. In: *Dynamic Psychopathology in Childhood*, ed. L. Jessner & E. Pavenstedt. New York: Grune and Stratton.

PROVENCE, S. & LIPTON, M. (1962), *Infants in Institutions*. New York: International Universities Press.

RANK, B. (1949), Aggression. *The Psychoanalytic Study of the Child*, 3/4:43–48.

—— (1955), Intensive Study and Treatment of Preschool Children Who Show Marked Personality Deviations or "Atypical Development" and Their Parents. In: *Emotional Problems of Early Childhood*, ed. G. Caplan. New York: Basic Books.

REDL, F. (1959), Strategy and Techniques of the Life-Space Interview. *Amer. J. Orthopsychiatry*, 28(1).

—— & WINEMAN, D. (1951), *Children Who Hate*. Glencoe: Ill.: The Free Press.

REICH, A. (1960), Pathologic Forms of Self-Esteem Regulation. *The Psychoanalytic Study of the Child*, 15:215–232.

REID, J. (1977), Introduction to *Group Care of Children: Crossroads and Transitions*, by M. F. Mayer, L. H. Richman, & E. A. Balcerzak. New York: Child Welfare League of America.

REIN, M., NEUT, T. S., & WEIS, H. (1973), Foster Family Care: Myth and Reality. In: *Children Adrift in Foster Care*, ed. A. Schorr. New York: Child Welfare League of America.

REXFORD, E. (ed.) (1978), *A Developmental Approach to Problems of Acting Out*, rev. ed. New York: International Universities Press.

RITVO, S. (1974), Current Status of the Concept of Infantile Neurosis. *The Psychoanalytic Study of the Child*, 29:159–182.

ROBINSON, J. F. (1950), Arranging Resident Psychiatric Treatment with Foster Children. *Q. J. Child Behavior*, 2:176–184.

ROCHLIN, G. (1953), Loss and Restitution. *The Psychoanalytic Study of the Child*, 8:288–309.

ROGERS, K. (1973), Notes on Organizational Consulting to Mental Hospitals. *Bull. Menninger Clin.*, 37(3).

ROSENFELD, S. & SPRINCE, M. (1963), An Attempt to Formulate the Meaning of the Concept "Borderline." *The Psychoanalytic Study of the Child*, 18.

—— (1965), Some Thoughts on the Technical Handling of Borderline Children. *The Psychoanalytic Study of the Child*, 20:495–517.

ROSENTHAL, L. (1956), Child Guidance. In: *The Fields of Group Psychotherapy*, ed. S. R. Slavson. New York: International Universities Press, pp. 215–232.

ROSS, A. O. (1964), Interruption and Termination of Treatment. In: *Child Psychotherapy*, ed. M. R. Haworth. New York & London: Basic Books.

ROTHSTEIN, A. (1979), An Exploration of the Diagnostic Form "Narcissistic Personality Disorder." *J. Amer. Psychoanal. Assn.*, 27(4):893–911.

RUTTER, M. (1969), Concepts of Autism: A Review of Research. In: *Annual Progress in Child Psychiatry and Child Development*, IX, ed. S. Chess & A. Thomas. New York: Brunner/Mazel, pp. 379–411.

—— (1972), Childhood Schizophrenia Reconsidered. *J. Autism & Child. Schizophrenia*, 2:315–337.

—— (1975), *Helping Troubled Children*. New York & London: Plenum Press.

SANDLER, J., KENNEDY, H., & TYSON, R. L. (1975), Discussions on Transference. *The Psychoanalytic Study of the Child*, 30. New Haven: Yale University Press.

——, ——, & —— (1980), *The Technique of Child Psychoanalysis—Discussions with Anna Freud*. Cambridge, Mass.: Harvard University Press.

SARASON, S. (1963), Teacher Training and the Mental Health Professionals. In: *Modern Perspectives in Child Development*, ed. A. Solnit and S. Provence. New York: International Universities Press.

SCHERTZ, F. (1970), Theory and Practice of Family Therapy. In: *Theories of Social Casework*, ed. R. Roberts & R. Nee. Chicago & London: University of Chicago Press.

SCHIFFER, M. (1952), Permissiveness Versus Sanction in Activity Group Therapy. *Internat. J. Group Psychotherapy*, 2:255–261.

SCHODEK, K. (1981), Adjuncts to Social Casework in the 1980s. *Social Casework*, 62(4).

SCHWARTZ, H. (1950), The Mother in the Consulting Room—Notes on the Psychoanalytic Treatment of Two Young Children. *The Psychoanalytic Study of the Child*, 5:343–357.

———— (1968), Contributions to a Symposium on Acting Out. *Internat. J. Psycho-Anal.*, 49:179–181.

SCHWARTZ, W. (1968), The Practice of Child Care in Residential Treatment. Cleveland: Bellefaire Symposium (mimeographed paper).

———— & ZABA, S. (1971), *The Practice of Group Work*. New York: Columbia University Press.

SELF PSYCHOLOGY AND TRADITIONAL ANALYTIC THEORY: AGENDA OF THE SELF PSYCHOLOGY CONFERENCE (1980), Sponsored by the Boston Psychoanalytic Institute, November.

SHANKER, A. (1981), Where We Stand—A New Partnership: Schools and Business. *The New York Times*, Sunday, July 12.

SHAPIRO, D. (1976), Agency Investment: A Study. *Social Work*, 17(4):20–28.

SHAPIRO, R. L. (1967), The Origin of Adolescent Disturbances in the Family: Some Considerations in Therapy and Implications for Therapy. In: *Family Therapy and Disturbed Families*, ed. G. H. Zuk & I. Boszormenyi-Nagy. Palo Alto: Science and Behavior Books.

SHAW, C. (1966), *The Psychiatric Disorders of Childhood*. New York: Appleton-Century-Crofts.

SHELMIRE et al. (1980), The Use of a Consultant Psychiatrist in a Family Service Agency. *Social Casework*, 61(9).

SILVER, L. (1979), The Minimal Brain Dysfunction Syndrome. In: *Basic Handbook of Child Psychiatry, II*, ed. J. Noshpitz. New York: Basic Books.

SIMON, J. (1975), The Effects of Foster Care Payment Levels on the Number of Foster Children Given Homes. *Soc. Serv. Rev.*, 49(3):405–411.

SLAVSON, S. R. (1943), *An Introduction to Group Therapy*. New York: Commonwealth Fund.

———— (1952), *Child Psychotherapy*. New York: Columbia University Press.

———— (1958), *Child-Centered Group Guidance of Parents*. New York: International Universities Press.

———— & SCHIFFER, M. (1975), *Group Psychotherapies for Children*. New York: International Universities Press.

SMALLY, R. (1970), The Functional Approach to Casework Practice. In: *Theories of Social Casework*, ed. R. Roberts & R. Nee. Chicago & London: University of Chicago Press, pp. 79–128.

SOLOMON, J. C. (1935), Active Play Therapy. *Amer. J. Orthopsychiatry*, 8:479–497.

———— (1940), Active Play Therapy: Further Experiences. *Amer. J. Orthopsychiatry*, 10:763-781.

_____ (1948), Play Technique. *Amer. J. Orthopsychiatry,* 18:402–413.

_____ (1955), Play Technique and the Integrative Process. *Amer. J. Orthopsychiatry,* 25:592–600.

SOURS, J. A. (1978a), An Analytically Oriented Approach to the Diagnostic Evaluation. In: *Child Analysis and Therapy,* ed. J. Glenn. New York & London: Aronson.

_____ (1978b), The Application of Child Analytic Principles to Forms of Child Psychotherapy. In: *Child Analysis and Therapy,* ed. J. Glenn. New York & London: Aronson.

SPITZ, R. (1965), *The First Year of Life.* New York: International Universities Press.

SPURLOCK, J. & COHEN, R. S. (1969), Should the Poor Get None? *J. Amer. Acad. Child Psychiatry,* 8:16–35.

STEPHENSON, P. (1973), Working with Nine-to-Twelve-Year-Olds. *Child Welfare,* 52:375–382.

STERBA, R. (1934), The Fate of the Ego in Analytic Therapy. *Internat. J. Psycho-Anal.,* 15:117–126.

STEVENSON, O. (1965). *Someone Else's Child.* London: Routledge & Kegan Paul & Lanan, 1965.

STOLOROW, R. D. & LACHMAN, F. M. (1980), *Psychoanalysis of Developmental Arrests—Theory and Treatment.* New York: International Universities Press.

STONE, A. A. (1979), Legal and Ethical Developments. In: *Disorders of the Schizophrenic Syndrome,* ed. L. Belok. New York: Basic Books.

STREET, D. (1967), Educators and Social Workers: Sibling Rivalry in the Inner City. *Soc. Serv. Rev.,* 41:163.

STUART, R. (1968), Supportive Casework with Borderline Patients. In: *Differential Diagnosis and Treatment in Social Work,* ed. F. J. Turner. New York & London: Free Press, Macmillan.

SUGAR, M. (ed.) (1975), *The Adolescent in Group and Family Therapy.* New York: Brunner/Mazel.

SYLVESTER, E. & COOPER, S. (1966), Truisms and Slogans in the Practice and Teaching of Child Psychotherapy. *J. Amer. Acad. Child Psychiatry,* 5:617–629.

SZUREK, S. et al. (1942), Collaborative Psychiatric Therapy of Parent-Child Problems. *Amer. J. Orthopsychiatry,* 12:511–520.

TARJAN, G. (1972), Mental Retardation: A Brief Review. *Bull. N.Y. State District Branch Amer. Psychiatr. Assn.,* 15(4):7.

THOMAS, A., CHESS, S., & BIRCH, H. G. (1968), *Temperament and Behavior Disorders in Children.* New York: New York University Press.

THURSTON, H. W. (1930), *The Dependent Child.* New York: Columbia University Press.

TOLPIN, M. (1970), The Infantile Neurosis. *The Psychoanalytic Study of the Child,* 25.

_____ (1971), On the Beginnings of a Cohesive Self. *The Psychoanalytic Study of the Child*, 26:316–352.

_____ (1978), Self Objects and Oedipal Objects. *The Psychoanalytic Study of the Child*, 33.

TOSELAND, R. (1981), Increasing Access: Outreach Methods in Social Work Practice. *Social Casework*, 62(4).

TOWLE, C. (1945), Introduction. *Common Human Needs*. New York: American Association of Social Workers.

TYSON, P. (1978), Transference and Developmental Issues in the Analysis of a Prelatency Child. *The Psychoanalytic Study of the Child*, 33.

_____ (1980), The Gender of the Analyst—In Relation to Transference and Countertransference Manifestations in Prelatency Children. *The Psychoanalytic Study of the Child*, 35.

VAN DAM, H. (1966), Problems of Transference in Child Analysis. A Panel Report. *J. Amer. Psychoanal. Assn.*, 14.

VANDERPOOL, H. (1976), Mental Health Consultation in Schools. In: *The Changing Mental Health Scene*, ed. R. R. Heirschowitz & B. Levy. New York: Halsted Press.

VAN DER WAALS, H. G. (1965), Problems of Narcissism. *Bull. Menninger Clin.*, 29:283–311.

VINTER, R. & SARRI, R. C. (1965), Malperformance in the Public School: A Group Work Approach. *Social Work*, 10:13.

VON BERTALANFFY, L. (1968), *General Systems Theory*. New York: George Braziller.

WALDER, R. (1933), The Psychoanalytic Theory of Play. *Psychoanal. Q.*, 2:208–224.

WAXLER, N. E. & MISHLER, E. G. (1972), Parental Interaction with Schizophrenic Children and Well Siblings: An Experiential Test of Some Etiological Theories. In: *Annual Progress in Child Psychiatry and Child Development*, ed. S. Chess & A. Thomas. New York: Brunner/Mazel, pp. 568–589.

WEISBERGER, E. (1980), Concepts in Ego Psychology as Applied to Work with Parents. In: *Psychotherapy and Training in Clinical Social Work*, ed. J. M. Mishne. New York: Gardner Press.

WEISS, S. (1964), Parameters in Child Analysis. *J. Amer. Psychoanal. Assn.*, 12:587–599.

_____ (1968), participant in panel on "Problems of Termination in Child Analysis." Reported by Robert Kohrman, Annual Meeting of the American Psychoanalytic Association, Boston, May 10, 1968. *J. Amer. Psychoanal. Assn.*, 28 (1969).

WEISS, S. et al. (1968), Technique of Child Analysis. *J. Amer. Acad. Child Psychiatry*, 7.

WHITE, R. W. (1963), Ego and Reality in Psychoanalytic Theory. *Psychological Issues*, 3(3), Monograph 11. New York: International Universities Press.

WHITTAKER, J. K. (1976), Causes of Childhood Disorders: New Findings. *Social Work*, 21(2):91-96.

_____ (1978), The Changing Character of Residential Child Care: An Ecological Perspective. Soc. Serv. Rev., 52(1).

_____ & TRIESCHMAN, A. E. (eds.) (1972), Children Away From Home. Chicago & New York: Aldine Atherton.

WINEMAN, D. (1972), Group Therapy and Casework with Ego-Disturbed Children. In: Children Away From Home, ed. J. K. Whittaker & A. E. Trieschman. Chicago & New York: Aldine Atherton.

WINNICOTT, D. W. (1949), Hate in the Counter-transference. Internat. J. Psycho-Anal., 30.

_____ (1971), Playing and Reality. London: Tavistock.

WOLF, A. & SCHWARTZ, E. (1971), Psychoanalysis in Groups. In: Comprehensive Group Psychotherapy, ed. H. Kaplan & B. Sadock. Baltimore: Williams & Wilkins.

WOLINS, M. (1963), Selection of Foster Parents—The Ideal and the Reality. New York: Columbia University Press.

WORK, H. H. (1979), Mental Retardation. In: Basic Handbook of Child Psychiatry, II, ed. J. Noshpitz. New York: Basic Books.

WYNNE, L. C. (1965), Some Indications and Contraindications for Exploratory Family Therapy. In: Intensive Family Therapy: Theoretical and Practical Aspects, ed. I. Boszormenyi-Nagy & J. L. Framo. New York: Harper & Row, pp. 298–322.

YALOM, I. D. (1970), The Theory and Practice of Group Psychotherapy. New York: Basic Books.

YORKE, C. (1971), Some Suggestions for a Critique of Kleinian Psychology. The Psychoanalytic Study of the Child, 26.

ZETZEL, E. R. (1956), Current Concepts of Transference. Internat. J. Psycho-Anal., 37:369–378.

Index

practice. Proficiency in child psychotherapy is a clinical skill only slowly acquired, and is the result of continuing experience, training, and supervision. Nevertheless, early in their training, social work and psychology graduate students and medical residents are expected to treat children. Indeed, some settings demand instant expertise in direct work with children and their parents. Enhancement of clinical proficiency, via translation of psychoanalytic principles into psychotherapy practice, is the goal of this text.

Babcock (1964) notes the special intrapsychic stresses of clinicians who work with children: they are often seen as responsible for their patients' disturbed and neurotic behavior, and are thus maligned by fellow students, clients, patients and their parents, and even by colleagues and friends. Children rarely, if ever, are voluntary patients; they are "captive clients" brought by their parents or referred by the child welfare agency, pediatrician, school, or court. With the exception of highly organized, often well-functioning and well-parented neurotic children, such as those in analysis, treatment of a child can rarely proceed without some ongoing work with the parents; in addition, collaborative contacts between the child therapist and the school, camp, childcare worker, child welfare agency, etc., are often necessary. Given these added dimensions, work with children often is seen as more taxing than work with self-referred adult patients. In Dewald's view (1964), these problems and stresses on the beginning therapist result in a number of common responses. The therapist may lose interest, develop a defeatist attitude bordering on therapeutic nihilism, respond to the patient on the basis of "intuition" or "common sense," or attempt to implement other vague and unstructured concepts of treatment.

The extensive case material presented in this book is intended to lessen some of this therapeutic nihilism and bias, to kindle or rekindle enthusiasm for work with children, and to provide a comprehensive view of diagnosis and treatment planning for children and their parents. This author wishes to convey the spirit of the diagnostic and treatment process, and to focus on the problems and issues specific to child therapy and general childcare services. The hope is to avoid a cookbook of recipes and instead to present a survey of the literature that deliberately omits some of the highly abstract and controversial aspects of theory. In addition, this book may prove useful to professional staff and supervisors in the public and private child welfare agencies. In the opinion of the National Association of Social Work (NASW), "Some 1.8 million children now receive social services through state child welfare systems . . . [and these] services have declined in quality and have had limited relevance to the needs of children and their families" (NASW News, April 1980, pp. 1, 17). Public and private agency services have declined in quantity and quality due to funding cutbacks and staff shortages have resulted in a dearth of individualized assessment and planning, and frequent assignment of cases to unilateral forms of intervention.

We have witnessed a spiraling of dehumanized services for children in need. Lack of financial reimbursement to agencies has caused the surrender of traditional work in the realm of prevention, early detection, and school consultation; even more alarming is the dismissal by some agencies of work with parents of child patients. All services for children currently are plagued with profound disorganization and fragmentation of services; the various polarizations along policy, practice, political, and funding lines gravely affect services to all children, particularly urban minority children. Spurlock and Cohen (1969) caution us not to ascribe to the myth that individual treatment is invalid for deprived populations. They believe that we dehumanize such populations by regarding each of them as a homogeneous corps with a stereotypic intrapsychic structure. Meers (1970) suggests that the Hollingshead and Redlich (1958) findings that lower-class populations do not perceive deviant behavior as mental illness "may reflect the ghetto parent's defensive rationalization or denial; that is to say, families are unprepared to acknowledge the reality of mental illness in the absence of therapeutic help" (p. 211).

Our societal priorities and pressures create "money-saving" treatment procedures that actually result in greater emotional and financial loss, as additional expenses are incurred for treating children who have become more disturbed since entering inpatient care (Frank, 1977). The effects of separation and loss are well understood; the literature of all the helping professions abounds with research and case studies documenting the psychological impact of placement on children and their parents. Given the response to this separation, it is almost amazing how such a momentous decision is made. For example, despite the myth that placements into foster care are the result of carefully considered decisions in which trained social workers consult with troubled families, for the majority of these children and their families, such placement is an emergency measure, an unplanned traumatic experience. In fact, often the reasons behind a placement cannot be found in the child's entry records (Jenkins and Norman, 1972). Untrained, frequently inadequately supervised workers, who are burdened with massive caseloads, are overwhelmed and propelled into often ill-thought-out actions. In addition, foster-care law and its administration have produced damaging effects on children. Goldstein (1975) notes that the law and its implementation fail to foster continuity of relationship between children and their biological parents; furthermore, while temporary separations in foster care often become permanent, lasting rela-

Printed in the United States
26386LVS00001BA/253-261

9 780743 211857